BATTLEFIELD AND

Richard Henry Pratt in the uniform of major of the First Cavalry, 1898.

BATTLEFIELD AND CLASSROOM

Four Decades with the American Indian, 1867–1904

BY RICHARD HENRY PRATT

Brigadier General, U. S. Army, Retired

EDITED AND WITH AN INTRODUCTION BY ROBERT M. UTLEY

FOREWORD BY DAVID WALLACE ADAMS

UNIVERSITY OF OKLAHOMA PRESS
NORMAN

Library of Congress Cataloging-in-Publication Data

Pratt, Richard Henry, 1840–1924
    Battlefield and classroom : four decades with the American Indian, 1867–1904 / by
Richard Henry Pratt ; edited and with an introduction by Robert M. Utley ; foreword by
David Wallace Adams.
        p.   cm.
    Originally published: New Haven : Yale University Press, 1964.
    Includes bibliographical references and index.
    ISBN 0-8061-3603-0 (pbk. : alk. paper)
        1. United States Indian School (Carlisle, Pa.)   2. Indians of North America—Wars—
1866–1895. 3. Pratt, Richard Henry, 1840–1924. 4. United States. Army—Military
life. I. Utley, Robert Marshall, 1929– II. Title.

E97.6.C2P89 2004
973.8—dc22
[B]

                                                                                2004041232

The paper in this book meets the guidelines for permanence and durability of the
Committee on Production Guidelines for Book Longevity of the Council on Library
Resources, Inc.

1   2   3   4   5   6   7   8   9   10

Contents

Maps and Illustrations

Some of the illustrations used in the chapter openings are from crayon drawings made by General Pratt's Indian prisoners in Florida. Others were drawn by Dale R. Roylance, in the primitive style of the Indian drawings.

BATTLEFIELD AND CLASSROOM

Foreword to the Paperback Edition

The republication of Richard Henry Pratt's *Battlefield and Classroom*, so thoughtfully edited and introduced by Robert M. Utley and long out of print, is a welcome event for students of Indian-white history. When Pratt's memoirs appeared in 1964, standard treatments of late nineteenth-century Indian policy readily acknowledged that Pratt, the founder of the Carlisle Indian School in Carlisle, Pennsylvania, had played a significant role in policymakers' efforts to solve the so-called "Indian problem." But this acknowledgment was almost always accompanied by only the briefest mention of Carlisle or the role that boarding schools—most particularly off-reservation boarding schools—played in governmental efforts to aggressively incorporate American Indians into the society engulfing them. Utley immediately saw the significance of Pratt's manuscript and rendered historians a genuine service by skillfully editing and preparing Pratt's recollections for publication. Published some forty years ago, this important volume became increasingly inaccessible. Happily, the University of Oklahoma Press's decision to reissue *Battlefield and Classroom* makes this vital document once again available to students and scholars.

Given Robert Utley's description of Pratt's background and ideas, little attention is needed on these fronts. Pratt's core beliefs on Indian policy reform began with the proposition that Indians as a race were genetically the equal of whites, but owing to historical circumstances, were culturally "savages," several steps below whites on the scale of "civilization." Because the onslaught of white civilization—whether in the form of smoking locomotives, surveyor markers, frontier capitalism, or the seemingly endless stream of homesteaders—was unrelenting, the Indians' old cultural ways were all but irrelevant. Indeed, Pratt believed, the Indians' only hope for survival was rapid cultural transformation along the lines of their conquerors. Hence, Pratt's dictum: "Kill the Indian, save the man." But how best to accomplish this task? Pratt's answer was boldly simple: remove Indian youth from their tribal communities and place them in off-reservation boarding schools where they would be simultaneously stripped of their tribal heritage and tutored in the knowledge, skills, and beliefs of white society. For Pratt, environment was all. Just as environment had created savages, so a different environment would cause them to discard their tribal ways and lead them toward the promised land of Christian civilization.[1]

Measuring Pratt's influence on federal Indian policy is not easy. A strong case can be made that it was enormous. The opening of Carlisle Indian School in 1879 came just at the time policy makers were desperately searching for a means of absorbing Indians into the larger society. Indeed, whether this could even be achieved and on what terms were still largely unresolved questions. Pratt's Indian school offered a resounding answer to these questions. Enthusiastic supporters of Pratt's ideas soon were arguing that the Carlisle model, if faithfully duplicated on a larger scale, was the perfect institutional mechanism for transforming the offspring of savage warriors into fully civilized citizens. Pratt's influence can be seen in the dramatic investment in Indian education. Between 1879 and 1900 the Bureau of Indian Affairs created twenty-four off-reservation schools roughly modeled after the Carlisle prototype. By 1900 the Indian school system had taken on the shape of an institutional hierarchy. When the system functioned according to plan, students progressed from reservation day schools to reservation boarding schools, finally moving on to Carlisle-type off-reservation schools. By 1900 three quarters of all Indian children were enrolled in boarding school, with approximately a third of this number in off-reservation schools. When one considers that many of those attending reservation boarding schools would eventually move on to off-reservation institutions, Pratt's role in shaping Indian education policy seems unquestionable.[2]

At the same time, Pratt's influence can be overestimated. For one thing, Pratt envisioned off-reservation schools located mainly in the East, where the civilizing influences would be felt most. But this was not to be. Partly under pressure from western communities that saw a new federal installation as an economic windfall for local contractors, and partly because of the prohibitive cost of transporting large numbers of students over long distances, Congress

1. Recent studies of off-reservation boarding schools include David Wallace Adams, *Education for Extinction: American Indians and the Boarding School Experience, 1875–1928* (Lawrence, 1995); Genevieve Bell, "Telling Stories Out of School: Remembering the Carlisle Indian Industrial School, 1879–1918" (Ph.D. diss., Stanford University, 1998); Brenda J. Child, *Boarding School Seasons: American Indian Families, 1900–1940* (Lincoln, 1999); Sally Hyer, *One House, One Voice, One Heart: Native American Education at the Santa Fe Indian School* (Santa Fe, 1990); Donal Lindsay, *Indians at Hampton Institute, 1877–1923* (Urbana, 1995); K. Tsianina Lomawaima, *They Called it Prairie Light: The Story of Chilocco Indian School* (Lincoln, 1994); Scott Riney, *The Rapid City Indian School, 1898–1933* (Norman, 1999); and Robert A. Trennert, *The Phoenix Indian School: Forced Assimilation in Arizona, 1891–1935* (Norman, 1988). For Pratt's views, in addition to the studies by Adams and Bell, see Jacqueline Fear-Segal, "Nineteenth-Century Indian Education: Universalism Versus Evolutionism," *Journal of American Studies* 33 (August 1999): 323–41; and Frederick J. Stefon, "Richard Henry Pratt and His Indians," *Journal of Ethnic Studies* 15 (Summer 1987): 89–112.

2. Adams, *Education for Extinction*, 60–70. All quotations, unless otherwise indicated, are from this source.

established most subsequent schools in frontier communities such as Carson City, Nevada, and Phoenix, Arizona. Nowhere was the difference made clearer than in the efforts to transplant a key element of the Carlisle program to western schools—the so-called "outing" program. Under the outing program Pratt sent students into the Pennsylvania countryside to live and work alongside middle-class farm families, a real-life setting for students to learn the day-to-day aspects of civilized living. The problem, it was soon discovered, was that many "patrons" in the West were more apt to view the outing students as a cheap labor force to be exploited rather than as deserving recipients of cultural benevolence. Thus, in 1892, Daniel Dorchester, superintendent of Indian schools, offered this appraisal of outing programs in the Far West: "With too many the common idea is that the Indian is a creature to be cheated, debauched, and kicked out of decent society. Young Indians from the schools can not be safely located among such people." Despite Dorchester's judgment, the Indian Bureau continued to build schools in frontier communities and the outing plan followed them.[3]

An even deeper problem faced by Pratt after 1900 was convincing policy makers that the off-reservation school was the best approach to Indian education. The growing opposition sprang from several considerations. Some questioned the ethical justification for removing Indian youth so far from their families and communities. Others questioned the practicality of educating youth in vocational trades, only to send them home to the primitive conditions of reservation life where their training was of limited usefulness. An even bleaker objection was the gnawing sentiment in some circles that Indians were simply incapable of traversing the cultural gap between savagism and civilization in a single generation. As S. M. McCowan, superintendent of one of the larger off-reservation schools, remarked to a gathering of educators in 1902, Indians "cannot understand our civilization in a minute, or a generation; and not understanding it they cannot appreciate it, and will not follow it." Such views were anathema to Pratt. But even before his removal from Carlisle in 1904, the emerging policy of "gradualism" was gathering momentum. Meanwhile, the old warrior watched from the sidelines as the aim of federal Indian policy shifted from assimilation to that of preparing Indians for life on the margins of frontier society.[4]

How did students respond to a Carlisle-like education? In the forty years since publication of *Battlefield and Classroom,* historians have paid increasing attention to this question. Not surprisingly, this literature shows that students at Carlisle and similar institutions responded in different ways. At one end of

3. Ibid., 156–63; and Trennert, "From Carlisle to Phoenix: The Rise and Fall of the Indian Outing System, 1878–1930," *Pacific Historical Review* 52 (August 1983): 267–91.
4. See Frederick E. Hoxie, *A Final Promise: The Campaign to Assimilate the Indians 1880–1920* (Lincoln, 1984), chaps. 3–4, 6; and Adams, *Education for Extinction*, chap. 10.

                   Foreword to the Paperback Edition

the response spectrum were several strategies of resistance: desertion, arson, and passive noncompliance. Whether such acts of defiance constituted full-fledged cultural rejection of the schools' aims or merely a protest against an isolated aspect of school life is often difficult to tell. What is clear is that some students, after receiving a heavy dose of the Carlisle regime, set their minds against it. The tone of defiance is clearly evident in the resolution of one Apache student: "We'd lost our hair and we'd lost our clothes; with the two we'd lost our identity as Indians. Greater punishment could hardly have been devised." At the other end of the response spectrum was complete coopera-tion. In extreme versions of this response, students completely internalized the concept of the savagism-civilization dichotomy and all that it implied. "We can take two roads, one where we only pile up decayed things, and the other which is like piling up gold and silver," one student wrote home to his parents. Another reminded his mother that he would not be seeing her next summer for he was at Carlisle "to learn [sic] still better way of the civilized people."

Somewhere in between complete compliance and determined resistance were those students who operated in a sort of middle ground. This response manifested itself in a general willingness to reach some sort of accommoda-tion with the institution and its aims. For some students this came in the form of embracing selected aspects of the white man's civilization and rejecting others, a posture frequently born in the recognition that learning some ways of the white man was necessary for survival. The middle ground also might mean rejecting more overt forms of resistance for more covert ones, such as tagging a hated school employee with a derisive nickname, stealing from the school commissary, or simply going through the motions of compliance—all of which were less risky than running away or setting the school on fire. Students of the middle ground were more likely to be intermittent in their feelings toward the school, one day angered by an embarrassing moment in the classroom, the next day exhilarated by the football team's victory on the gridiron. The middle ground was about negotiating new identities in a constantly shifting cultural landscape, searching for solid ground in a sea of change.[5]

For several reasons Pratt may have encountered less resistance than sister schools farther west. First, there was Pratt's charismatic personality. One former student recalls that Pratt "made a fine appearance, especially when we passed in review before him during parades. He was over six feet tall, had broad

---

5. For student response see Adams, *Education for Extinction*, chaps. 7–8; Michael Coleman, *American Indian Children at School, 1850–1930* (Jackson, 1993) chaps, 4, 8–9; Coleman, "The Sym-biotic Embrace: American Indians, White Educators, and the School, 1820s–1920s," *History of Education* 25 (1996): 1–18; Sally J. McBeth, *Ethnic Identity and the Boarding School Experience of West Central Oklahoma* (Washington D.C., 1983), chaps. 6–8; and Lomawaima, *They Called it Prairie Light*, 123–25. The concept of the middle ground is taken from Richard White, *The Middle Ground: Indians, Empires, and Republics in the Great Lakes Region, 1650–1815* (Cambridge, 1991).

shoulders, and stood erect. We greatly admired his military bearing." Another factor was Pratt's unflinching belief in the innate capacity of his students to compete on equal terms with whites. Third, the school's location in Pennsylvania meant that students, whether on outing or walking the streets of Carlisle, were likely to encounter much less prejudice than in frontier towns like Phoenix or Santa Fe. Fourth, the vast majority of Carlisle's students came with the permission of their parents. As one father reminded his daughter in a letter (no doubt written through the agent): "When Captain Pratt was here he came to my house, and asked me to let you go to school. I want you to be a good girl and study. . . . If you could read and write, I should be very happy." Finally, because Pratt's efforts were much publicized, the institution was the beneficiary of numerous donations that lifted the material life of the school to a higher level than at most other schools. In short, Carlisle, while a prototype for other off-reservation schools, was actually quite unique.

The question of student response is related to the question of Carlisle's long-term impact on students' lives. While this question is of great interest to historians today, it was also at the center of policy makers' concerns only a decade after Carlisle's founding. The so-called "returned student problem" in the 1890s grew out of the increasing number of charges that many former students, once back on the reservation, were slipping back to the same "savage" ways from which they had emerged. Pratt was at something of a disadvantage in the debate because his vision of assimilation called for Indians to melt into the general population. His remarks to a group of returning students in 1890 are characteristic: "I advise you to flee the reservation. . . . Go out into the business of life of the country where personal rights and the light of civilization will constantly invite and help you on to higher, nobler, better things. Flee away from that which drags you down. Go where you will be free, where you will not be bound hand and foot to your past, but where you can rise and become individuals."

Vision or no vision, a substantial number of students chose to return to their reservation homes, a trend that forced Pratt and other superintendents to answer their critics. The debate quickly translated into a swirl of record-keeping and reports. Returned students' varied responses to the conflicting pressures of reservation life were forced into tabulated categories like excellent, good, fair, poor, and bad. In 1898, Pratt produced figures indicating that out of 1,021 returned students, only 171, or 17 percent, fell in the last two categories. Most former students, it was held, were living industrious, Christian lives and were leading their people to a higher plane of existence.

What former students took from Carlisle and how they remembered their experience is as complicated a subject as how they responded to it while there. Some students looked back on their Carlisle years in mostly positive terms. Consider the note that Peter Gaddy, a Delaware living in Shawnee, Oklahoma, scribbled (in less than perfect English) to his alma mater in 1911. Gaddy had attended Carlisle between 1903 and 1908, and was making his living as a blacksmith: "I am getting along fine since I left Carlisle. I can never regret going to Carlisle. The period of time I spented [sic] at Carlisle has enabled me to start out in the world and I making the best of it I can. I am interested in the school, because it is not only civilizing the redmen, but is developing him physically as well moral and ennabled [sic] him to become a true citizen of America." Those who remembered their school years in mostly bitter terms, of course, were much less apt to put their feelings down on paper. Hence, it is much easier for historians to find letters like Gaddy's than those of students who looked back on their boarding school years mainly with regret. But even Luther Standing Bear, one of Pratt's star students, would one day question whether Carlisle's singular direction of cultural exchange was in the best interests of Indians:

> So we went to school to copy, to imitate not to exchange languages and ideas, and not to develop the best traits that had come out of uncountable experiences of hundreds and thousands of years living upon this continent. Our annals, all happenings of human import, were stored in our song and dance rituals, our history differing in that it was not stored in books, but in the living memory. So, while the white people had much to teach us, we had much to teach them, and what a school could have been established on that idea![6]

One cannot begin to understand the array of these responses without understanding the tragic and perplexing circumstances in which Indians found themselves in late nineteenth-century America. Reduced to the desperate conditions of reservation life, tribal leaders were forced to contemplate the agonizing question of how to prepare the next generation for survival in a world where the old cultural standards of what it meant to be Cheyenne, Arapaho, or Crow were of limited relevance. In an era when many were predicting the complete disappearance of the race, Richard Henry Pratt and his Indian school offered a path into the future. To be sure, the choice Pratt offered Indians was a terribly problematic one: assimilation or extinction. Most modern readers of *Battlefield and Classroom* will find Pratt's solution to the "Indian problem" terribly problematic as well. Still, one cannot fully comprehend this crucial period in federal Indian policy without engaging this important work.

David Wallace Adams

6. Quotations are from David Wallace Adams, "More Than a Game: The Carlisle Indians Take to the Gridiron, 1893–1917," *Western Historical Quarterly* 32 (Spring 2001), 50; and Ruth Spack, *America's Second Tongue: American Indian Education and the Ownership of English, 1860–1900* (Lincoln, 2002), 107.

Introduction

Richard Henry Pratt had passed his eighty-second birthday when in 1923 he dictated to his daughter the final chapter of these memoirs. Still active and clear-minded, he had focused a sharp memory, buttressed by voluminous personal records, on nearly half a century of dedicated public service. The resulting manuscript summed up the history he had lived and helped to make in eight years of frontier army service and a quarter of a century as founder and builder of the Carlisle Indian School. More important, the memoirs exposed the mind and heart of a man whose life work influenced the attitudes of a whole generation of his countrymen toward the aboriginal peoples in their midst. Pratt's memory for precise detail sometimes failed him, but the memoirs left no doubt of the convictions that guided him with undeviating consistency for four decades. The unfolding history of the American Indians in the critical years after their final conquest by the white man cannot be understood without reference to the large role of Richard Henry Pratt, and the 600 typewritten pages of reminiscences that formed part of his collection of personal papers at his death in 1924 go far toward explaining this role. They are here published for the first time.

Nothing in the first thirty years of his life forecast the influential career and nationwide prominence that the future held for Pratt. Born on December 6, 1840, at Rushford, New York, Richard was the oldest of three sons. The father and mother, Richard and Mary Pratt, succumbed with many of their contemporaries to the lure of the West, and in 1846 they settled on the banks of the Wabash River at Logansport, Indiana. Still the West exerted its attraction, and the gold fever of 1849 swept the elder Richard across the continent to seek a fortune in California. A fortune he won, but it brought tragedy to him and his family when, returning home, he was robbed and murdered by a fellow prospector. Young Richard left school in 1853 at the age of thirteen to earn a livelihood for his widowed mother and her three sons. For five years he worked as a printer's devil, supplementing the meager pay of a dollar and a half a week by splitting rails. At eighteen he engaged himself as apprentice to a tinsmith in nearby Delphi and by the end of three years had mastered the craft well enough to teach it to others twenty years later.[1]

The bombardment of Fort Sumter in April 1861 lifted the young man from the tinner's bench and launched his army career. He enlisted eight days later and for four years fought bravely on the battlefields of Kentucky, Tennessee, and Georgia. Back in Indiana on a recruiting detail in the winter of 1863–64, Sergeant Pratt met Anna Laura Mason, a New York girl visiting relatives in Delphi, and the two were married on April 12, 1864. Eight days later the groom was commissioned first lieutenant in the Eleventh Indiana Cavalry. Another year in the South, and on May 29, 1865, he was mustered out of the volunteer service of the United States.[2]

The twenty-five-year-old veteran went home to Logansport and opened a hardware store. But business was bad and military life was still in his blood. He applied for a commission in the regular army, and on March 7, 1867, he was appointed second lieutenant in the Tenth United States Cavalry, a newly organized regiment composed of Negro enlisted men with white officers. He also received brevet ranks of first lieutenant and captain for gallant and meritorious service during the war. Promotion to first lieutenant followed quickly, on July 31, 1867, but it was by virtue of his brevet rank that he was addressed as captain throughout the years of frontier duty. With his arrival at Fort Arbuckle, Indian Territory, in the spring of 1867, Captain Pratt began a lifetime association with the American Indian, first on the battlefield and then in the classroom, and here, too, he begins his memoirs.

Until his death Pratt considered himself preeminently a soldier, and in fact his four years of Civil War service and eight years of frontier experience fully justified this view of his career. He wore the uniform of the United States Army for a total of forty-one years, and in his twenty years of retirement he proudly bore the rank of brigadier general.[3] Even so, it is not as a soldier that history remembers him. After 1875 he was on detached service for

1. John Bakeless, "Richard Henry Pratt," *Dictionary of American Biography, 15*, 175–76. Elaine Goodale Eastman, *Pratt, the Red Man's Moses* (Norman, 1935), chap. 1. The latter, the standard biography of Pratt, is a curious work. Mrs. Eastman was herself a pioneer worker in Indian education, but in educational philosophy she differed fundamentally with Pratt. The book is more an expression of her own views on Indian education than a biography, but much about Pratt, oddly uncritical in view of her identification with policies that he detested, may be gleaned from the book by the patient reader.

2. Bakeless, p. 175. Eastman, chap. 2.

3. Pratt retained his commission in the Tenth Cavalry throughout most of his career—a fact resented by some officers of the regiment who viewed his billet at Carlisle as a refuge from the rigors of frontier duty. He was promoted to captain Tenth Cavalry on Feb. 17, 1883; to major First Cavalry on July 1, 1898; transferred back to the Tenth on Aug. 2, 1899; promoted to lieutenant colonel Fourteenth Cavalry on Feb. 2, 1901; transferred to the Fifteenth Cavalry on March 7, 1901; promoted to colonel Thirteenth Cavalry on Jan. 24, 1903; and retired on Feb. 17, 1903. He was advanced to brigadier general on the retired list by act of Congress on April 23, 1904. F. B. Heitman, *Historical Register and Dictionary of the United States Army* (2 vols. Washington, 1903), *1*, 805.

three years as jailor of Indian prisoners at Fort Marion, Florida, and thereafter until his retirement from the army in 1903 on continuous detail to the
Bureau of Indian Affairs for the great work of his life—Indian education. Yet
his career as a field soldier should not be obscured. The eight years that he
served in Indian Territory and Texas spanned momentous events in the history of the Indian frontier and culminated in the final collapse of the southern Plains tribes. That these years loomed large in his memory is evident, for
he assigned one-third of his memoirs to them. They form a significant contribution to the history of the conquest of the Kiowas, Comanches, Cheyennes, and Arapahos.

Pratt's frontier years brought him into intimate and sustained association
with the two principal minority races of the United States. As an officer of
the Tenth Cavalry he commanded Negro units composed largely of recently
freed slaves. And he and his superiors quickly discovered that he possessed an
aptitude for organizing and leading the units of Indian scouts—Cherokee,
Choctaw, Osage, Tonkawa—that were occasionally mustered for operations
against the hostiles. These assignments stimulated the young officer to reflect
on the condition of minority races in a social and political order that he regarded with passionate conviction as otherwise the most perfect ever to en-
dow a people. He probed deeply the moral issues that were to disturb the nation for generations to come, and he swiftly matured a personal philosophy
that endured rocklike and unassailable to the day of his death.

The seeds took root during his first scout from Fort Arbuckle in 1867. He
and a fellow officer engaged in a discussion of the proposed Fourteenth
Amendment to the Constitution and concluded that it made illegal the continued segregation of Negros in the regular army and the continued segregation of Indians on tribal reservations.

> This first discussion and experience in my regular army service [he re-
> called] aroused an interest in my mind for the two races which became
> more absorbingly intense as the years enlarged my knowledge of them.
> Now, after more than fifty-four years of widest experience with them, I
> cannot see otherwise than that all the gross injustices to both races
> which have followed and become indurated policies are primarily the
> result of national neglect to give the opportunities and enforce the safe-
> guards of our Declaration and Constitution.
>
> [pp. 7–8, below]

"The rights of citizenship included fraternity and equal privilege for development," Pratt wrote. Subsequent years of service reinforced his conviction
that this was all that the Negro and the Indian needed to compete on equal
terms with the white man and assume their rightful place in American so-

ciety. Equal opportunity for the Indian was to become the great crusade of his life.

His chance to test the conclusion formed on the frontier came in 1875, at the close of the Red River War. The southern Plains tribes had been conquered, and the Government decided to remove the worst offenders among them to a place of confinement remote from the scene of their recent adventures. Captain Pratt drew the assignment of conducting seventy-two Kiowas, Comanches, and Cheyennes to the old Spanish fort at St. Augustine, Florida, and remaining there as jailor. Here was a laboratory for showing that wild Indians could be transformed into peaceful, enlightened citizens. In the brief three years before the prisoners were liberated, he accomplished enough to erase any doubts that may have lingered in his own mind and at the same time to convince others that the experiment should be enlarged and transferred to an environment more favorable than a prison afforded.

The idea of Indian education was not new. It dated back almost to the inception of the "Indian problem"—that perennial source of disturbance that flowed from the Indian's insistence on keeping what he had always owned and leading the life he had always lived. And the Indian problem dated from the time the first European landed on the shores of America with conflicting aims. Nearly as old as the Indian problem was the most insistently urged remedy, "civilization" of the Indian—i.e. culturally transforming him into a copy of his European neighbor. And theorists early recognized that formal classroom education must be a major feature of any civilization program. Since colonial times, in fact, missionary groups had made scattered and sporadic efforts to educate and civilize native Americans, but never on a scale large enough to win much public recognition or support.

Not until the United States Government began to lend moral and financial encouragement in 1819 did the idea really take root. Within the next half-century, through small annual appropriations and provisions inserted in treaties between the Government and the tribes, education became an established if somewhat insecure feature of United States Indian policy. The insecurity arose because there were always legislators and policy makers who questioned the Indian's ability to throw off the trappings of savagery and absorb the teachings of the white man. That the Indian was indeed capable given equal opportunity with the white man was a fundamental tenet of Pratt's philosophy, one that he and many observers regarded as dramatically demonstrated by his accomplishments in the Florida prison.[4]

4. For the origins of Indian education, see Francis Paul Prucha, *American Indian Policy in the Formative Years: The Indian Trade and Intercourse Acts, 1790–1834* (Cambridge, 1962), pp. 219–24; George D. Harmon, *Sixty Years of Indian Affairs* (Chapel Hill, 1941), pp. 157–66, 351–60; and Alice C. Fletcher, *Indian Education and Civilization: A Report Prepared in Answer to Senate Resolution of February 23, 1885*, Senate Executive Documents, 48th Cong., 2d sess., No. 95 (Washington, 1888), chaps. 1–6.

Others, including many congressmen, remained unconvinced or uninterested. But the Florida experiment had ended at an auspicious time. One after another the great western tribes were falling before the onslaught of railroads, buffalo hunters, settlers, and the U. S. Army. The attention of the nation was shifting from the problem of conquering the Indians to the question of what to do with them after the conquest. During the 1870s eastern humanitarian and philanthropic groups increasingly concerned themselves with the Indian, and by the close of the decade the spirit of Indian reform had produced several powerful organizations dedicated to securing justice and civilization for the Indians. Justice they had always desired, but civilization, including education, had never appealed to any great number. Now, confined to a reservation, dependent upon the Government for the necessities of life, the Indian had lost his ability to resist the programs his Great White Father conceived as best for him. For the first time, conditions favored a massive program aimed at civilizing him.

In 1878, although the opportunities inherent in the changing complexion of the Indian problem had not fully dawned on policy makers, the climate of national opinion clearly favored the further experimentation that Pratt desired. And in Carl Schurz, President Hayes' able and progressive Secretary of the Interior, the captain found a man with the imagination and drive to launch the experiment. The association of these two men gave birth to the Carlisle Indian School.[5]

Installed in the old cavalry barracks at Carlisle, Pennsylvania, Captain Pratt's school enrolled in the first academic year, 1879–80, more than 200 pupils representing about a dozen tribes. The enrollment in his last year as superintendent, 1903, had risen to more than 1,200. During his twenty-four-year tenure the school educated, in all, 4,903 Indian boys and girls from seventy-seven tribes.

From the first the curriculum emphasized both academic and manual (or industrial) education. In the classroom Pratt sought above all to equip the children with an ability to speak, read, and write the English language, for this was the most vital prerequisite to a satisfactory adjustment to the white man's world. Beyond this, he gave them instruction in the usual elementary and high school subjects of arithmetic, geography, and history. In the shops and fields the boys learned a trade—blacksmithing, wagon making, carpentry, tailoring, farming, and many others. In the kitchen and sewing room the girls were taught the domestic skills of the homemaker. Supplementing this program and gradually coming to dominate it was the Carlisle Outing, which placed children in white farm families during the summer months for practical experience in civilization. The Outing was probably the most

5. In addition to Pratt's own account see Louis Morton, "How the Indians Came to Carlisle," *Pennsylvania History*, 29 (1962), 53–73.

successful and certainly the most famous feature of the Carlisle curriculum, and it won nearly universal acclaim from experts on the Indian question. Even those who opposed the off-reservation educational concept conceded the triumph of the Outing. One of Pratt's bitterest foes, Francis E. Leupp, Commissioner of Indian Affairs in 1904 when the Carlisle head clashed for the last time with his superiors, called the Outing "an inspiration" and "the great monument of his life work."[6]

More than any other factor, Carlisle and its widely publicized accomplishments marshaled public opinion behind Indian education and led, during the 1880s, to ever increasing preoccupation with it. From $150,000 in 1880, appropriations for Indian education soared to more than a million dollars in 1887. From 1.8 per cent of Indian disbursements in 1875, expenditures for education rose to 17.1 per cent in 1887. Day schools and boarding schools multiplied on the reservations, and off-reservation schools patterned after Carlisle sprang up in Indian Territory, Kansas, Nebraska, and Oregon.[7]

Through Carlisle, Captain Pratt attempted to gain adoption and implementation of the personal philosophy he had evolved in his frontier years. Negros and Indians were no less human beings for the color of their skin. Negros, recently freed from slavery, were now by constitutional fiat the equal of their white brothers. Their segregation into separate regiments of the regular army was to be deprecated, but otherwise, Pratt believed, they were being absorbed into American life. Immigrants, too, were welcomed into the American system and swiftly lost their national identity. But not the Indian, the original American, who was locked up on a reservation and denied opportunities accorded the Negro and the immigrant.

In Pratt's mind the Negro furnished the example. Slavery transplanted him from his native habitat and tribal affiliation into a new cultural environment, where he had to adopt a new language, new dress, and new customs. As a result, in a span of several generations he had been shorn of his primitivism and elevated to American citizenship. Pratt believed profoundly that as the Negro had been civilized, so could the Indian be civilized. The ideal, in short, was no less than the complete eradication of aboriginal culture and the complete assimilation of the Indian by the American people.

In this goal Pratt reflected the conventional theories that evolved in the

6. Leupp, *The Indian and His Problem* (New York, 1910), pp. 121–22. Leupp regarded reservation schools as the best educational approach. See also his *In Red Man's Land: A Study of the American Indian* (New York, 1914).

7. Loring B. Priest, *Uncle Sam's Stepchildren: The Reformation of United States Indian Policy, 1865–1887* (New Brunswick, 1942), pp. 132–54.

1880s, for most legislators, administrators, and reformers were also dedicated to making over the Indian in the white image. Through the reservation system, with the nearly unlimited control and coercion it afforded, they sought to carry out a rigorous program of civilization that would prepare the Indians for the duties and responsibilities of citizenship. To Pratt this means to the common end was folly. To him the reservation was anathema: it preserved the old way of life by barring the Indian from free circulation in the outside world. The Bureau of Indian Affairs was anathema: its entrenched bureaucracy was dedicated mainly to self-perpetuation and thus to the status quo. The Bureau of American Ethnology of the Smithsonian Institution was anathema: its anthropologists glorified aboriginal values and ridiculed the possibility of swift culture change. And even the educational system, including his own Carlisle School, was misdirected effort: it insulated the pupils from American life and kept them from the public schools where they properly belonged.

"In Indian civilization I am a Baptist," Pratt told a Baptist convention in 1883, "because I believe in immersing the Indians in our civilization and when we get them under holding them there until they are thoroughly soaked" (below p. 335). The soaking process could not be accomplished on a reservation. In Pratt's mind Carlisle was a first step only. He would establish enough Carlisles away from the reservation and its influences to accommodate all the Indian children of the United States, and from these prep schools in civilization feed them into the public schools and thus into the mainstream of American life.

Although winning powerful support, such a sweeping doctrine also inevitably aroused powerful opposition—from policy makers and reformers who regarded the reservation as the best place for the civilization effort, from westerners still clinging to the notion of once a savage always a savage, from legislators dedicated to economy or to pork barrel spending on the reservations, and not least from Indian parents who objected to surrendering their children to a program that not only broke up the family but also aimed at demolishing all that the Indian held sacred. As a feature of Indian policy Carlisle itself enjoyed a comfortable security for a quarter of a century, but the grand design of its founder never offered serious competition to the reservation schools that most theorists looked to as the best hope of educational progress.

"Pratt was a crusader," wrote his biographer, who knew him well, "an idealist, a man of compelling personality whose whole thought and purpose . . . was so deeply fused with his work for the first Americans as to bring upon him from certain quarters the reproach of visionary and fanatic. Yet he was at the same time intensely practical, and a forceful executive."[8] For a quarter of a century he brought his powerful character to bear in a never-ending battle with the opposition. "I know I am at this time 'fighting' a greater number of 'the enemies of civilization' than the whole of my regiment put together," he wrote in 1880, "and I know further that I am fighting them with a thousand times more hopes of success" (p. 251). Undisturbed by self-doubt, he assailed any institution or individual standing in the way. His granite faith in his program and resolute determination to sweep aside all obstacles may be glimpsed in the action of a first lieutenant of cavalry, denied by General Sherman the detail of a second officer at Carlisle, writing directly and confidentially to the President of the United States: "Knowing as I do that I am supremely right, it would be wicked to falter, even though pressure to that end came in threats from the General of the Army" (p. 251).

As the means of attaining the goal he had set, the Carlisle idea may well have been supremely right. As an answer to the Indian problem, however, it achieved only qualified success. Pratt was the first to recognize and admit this. He stated in his first annual report and repeated ever after that "no educational work for the Indians will be successful in any considerable degree until the numbers educated shall form a majority of the whole." Although he regarded all educational programs as of some benefit, he likewise regarded the small fraction benefited by authorized programs, together with their return to tribal life, as a denial of his whole concept.

The great majority of students turned out by Carlisle were well equipped to make their way in the white man's world. Instead they were returned to the reservation. Here, although the agent and his staff embraced white values and rewarded Indian adherence to them, the dominant values of society were aboriginal. Moreover, with the spoils system ascendant, the few government jobs available rarely went to Indians, and few Carlisle graduates found any occupation to utilize their newly learned talents. The result was that they either existed in a shadow world neither Indian nor white, with acceptance denied by both worlds, or they cast off the veneer of Carlisle and again became Indians. The well-known case of the Sioux youth Plenty Horses, who murdered Lt. Edward W. Casey during the Ghost Dance troubles at Pine Ridge in 1891, is an extreme illustration of what happened in some degree to many graduates. Plenty Horses explained at his trial that he committed the act to wipe out the stain of Carlisle and win a place among his people.[9]

8. Eastman, p. 7.

9. Robert M. Utley, *The Last Days of the Sioux Nation* (New Haven and London, 1963), pp. 256–58, 265–67. The impact of the educational program on the Sioux is discussed in Chapter 3 of this work.

So determined, sustained, and public was Pratt's attack on all who opposed his program that he finally, in 1904, brought about his own downfall. It was a deliberate move, as he tells us himself: "It seemed best to force the issue and compel action that would change the system or end my relations with it" (p. 335). Having made this decision, he embarked on a campaign of deliberate provocation of the Indian officials that grew so vocal that they were left no choice but to get rid of him. Editorialized the *Catholic Watchman:* "Pratt, the irrepressible, has been suppressed at last. He is an honest lunatic."[10]

General Pratt had not been suppressed, for he continued, even after the Bureau closed Carlisle in 1918, to champion his cause. And he was much more than an "honest lunatic." His true significance in history lies not in his fight for a goal that was questionable at best. Modern social anthropologists would quickly point out many flaws in his philosophy and devastating cultural implications for the Indian in his program. His views were matured within the intellectual framework of his generation. A later generation would hold that the eradication of a culture entails a cost in human suffering wholly inconsistent with the ethical concepts springing from the Declaration of Independence and the Constitution, and that, moreover, this particular culture was contributing something distinctive, vital, and enriching to American life.

Pratt's true significance lies rather in his role as a determined, courageous, selfless worker in behalf of justice to a people suffering from four centuries of oppression by the dominant culture. He saw in the Indian another human being, and in his long crusade he made countless of his countrymen see the Indian through the same lenses. He convinced them that different skin color and different cultural background did not automatically produce an inferior being. He dramatized the plight of the red men as few others did, and he mobilized public opinion behind attempts, no matter how misguided by the standards of another age, to sweep aside the odious wreckage of more than a century of Federal mismanagement of the Indians. "General Pratt," wrote Hebert Welsh, energetic secretary of the Indian Rights Association, "was, in my opinion, the greatest moral force effecting the great change that has taken place in the minds of our citizens touching the Indian."[11]

For this service, paradoxical as it may seem in view of his dedication to the extinction of Indian culture, Richard Henry Pratt is due the gratitude of all American Indians. He fully deserves the inscription on the modest granite memorial standing over his grave in Arlington National Cemetery: "Erected in Loving Memory by his Students and Other Indians."

10. Quoted in Eastman, p. 262.
11. Quoted ibid., p. 7.

His forced retirement from Carlisle in 1904 did not end Pratt's great crusade. From his home in Rochester, New York, he continued for the next two
decades to champion his views in speeches and in letters to a succession of
Presidents, Senators, and officials of the Interior Department and Indian Bureau. At the age of eighty-three he was urging his policies on President Coo-
lidge, and a year later, virtually on his death bed, he could still muster
strength to war on the Indian Bureau. Throughout the years of retirement,
too, he gave thought to his memoirs, and he had written parts of them as early
as 1909. Not until 1923, however, with time clearly running out, did he see
the project through to completion.

The old general and his wife also derived much pleasure from traveling
about the country renewing old acquaintances and visiting former students.
Especially did the annual pilgrimage to Carlisle afford gratification. The
school paper recorded his last before the institution was closed in 1918:

> All departments were ordered closed at 3:30 so that everybody could take
> part in the welcome. The boys' battalion headed by the school band
> marched to the station, where the companies lined up in dress parade
> and stood at attention. . . . As the train pulled in, the band played his old
> favorite march. As he stepped off the train, his old Carlisle friends
> crowded around him, to shake the hand of the man who has done so
> much to enrich the community.[12]

On April 23, 1924, in his eighty-fourth year, General Richard Henry Pratt
died at the army hospital in San Francisco. The goal for which he had bat-
tled so fervently was to be wholly rejected a decade later, but underlying the
new deal for the Indian inaugurated in 1933 was the same deep sense of justice and humanity that had guided his actions for half a century. Although he
would hardly have approved of the new policies, he had done much to create
the climate of opinion that made them possible. For this his memory should
be cherished by every American Indian.

Pratt's memoirs and other papers were preserved for many years by his
daughter, Mrs. Nana Pratt Hawkins. After her death the Pratt heirs, anxious
to have the papers professionally cared for and made available to scholars, de-
posited them in the Yale University Library. The collection consists of the
manuscript memoirs, letters received and copies of letters sent from 1872 to
1924, a Civil War diary, scrap books, speeches, pamphlets, a file of the Carlisle
school paper, *The Red Man and Helper*, photographs, and a set of drawings
by the Indian Etadleuh depicting scenes of the prison years in St. Augustine.

12. Quoted ibid., p. 265.

The memoirs are here published for the first time. Demands of clarity led the editor to make occasional minor changes in spelling, punctuation, capitalization, and paragraphing, but in no instance has the true meaning or spirit been compromised. Also, a few cumbersomely titled chapters have been retitled. In its original condition the manuscript was deemed excessively long for publication and at times needlessly repetitious. Some of the longer quotations which seemed to add little and detract much from the continuity of the narrative have therefore been deleted. In each instance where this has been done, the omitted portions are clearly identified by ellipses and the content briefly explained in a footnote. All unexplained omissions from quotations, also marked by ellipses, are those of Pratt. The editor's contributions to clarification and explanation occasionally appear within brackets inserted in the text as well as in the footnotes.

The editor wishes to acknowledge the generous aid of the following people who contributed in one way or another to the preparation of this book: Franklin G. Smith, National Park Service, Santa Fe, an esteemed colleague; Archibald Hanna, curator of the Western Americana Collection at Yale University Library; Maurice Frink, former director of the Colorado State Historical Society; Miss Muriel H. Wright, editor of *The Chronicles of Oklahoma;* Donald Danker, archivist of the Nebraska State Historical Society; L. H. Nohl, Jr., American River Junior College; James S. Hutchins, Department of the Army, Washington, D.C.; Harry H. Anderson, county historian and executive director of the Milwaukee County Historical Society; Gillett Griswold and James Marler, U. S. Army Artillery and Missile Center Museum, Fort Sill; Louis Morton, Dartmouth College; Maj. Frederick P. Schmidt, Jr., Public Information Officer, U. S. Army War College, Carlisle Barracks, Pennsylvania; Superintendent B. C. Roberts and Historian Albert Manucy, Castillo de San Marcos National Monument.

R. M. U.

Santa Fe, New Mexico
July 1964

1. Indian Territory, 1867

"Pratt, General Davidson[1] directs that you take command of the twenty-five Indian scouts at this post and twenty men and a sergeant of Troop D, and escort him from Gibson to Arbuckle. The scouts will be ready and turned over to you by me in the morning at four o'clock. Captain Walsh has been instructed to detail the men from his troop and have them armed, equipped and ready at four. You will proceed to the ferry over the Arkansas River at the mouth of the Neosho, reaching there about five o'clock in the morning. You will find two ferry boats waiting for you manned by Indians. There will be two army wagons loaded with baggage, forage and supplies for the expedi-

1. When Pratt came under his command, John W. "Black Jack" Davidson, who figures prominently in the first ten chapters, was a veteran of twenty-five years service. An 1845 graduate of West Point, he put in fifteen years of frontier duty in the West before the Civil War. Perhaps the best known of his Indian combats was the action at Cieneguilla, New Mexico, March 30, 1854, in which Jicarilla Apaches ambushed his company of the First Dragoons. Davidson withdrew with twenty-two dead and thirty-six wounded out of a total command of sixty-two men. His Civil War service was active and distinguished, and he emerged with a brevet of major general. Although assigned as lieutenant colonel of the regular army Tenth Cavalry in 1866, he was serving, when Pratt first met him, as a district commander in his brevet grade of major general. Davidson was promoted to colonel of the Second Cavalry in 1879 and died in 1881. Unless otherwise cited, biographical data on military officers is from F. B. Heitman, *Historical Register and Dictionary of the U. S. Army* (2 vols. Washington, 1903). For Davidson, see also sketch in T. F. Rodenbough, comp., *From Everglade to Cañon with the Second Dragoons* (New York, 1875), pp. 443–44.

tion, and the post spring wagon. The General with his staff will be at the river at seven o'clock and expects your command and the wagons to be across and ready to proceed on the march." This order was given by the Post Adjutant about 6 P.M.

I had been commissioned in the regular army in March and had joined at that post only two days previously. My Captain—Walsh[2]—and the 103 men, former slaves enlisted by him at Little Rock, Arkansas, had arrived at Fort Gibson a few days before me.[3] The men, horses, and cavalry equipments, together with clothing and other army stores, had come forward by steamboat up the Arkansas.[4] We had been busy fitting the men with uniforms, organizing the troop, picking the noncommissioned officers, and starting the company records; but no bridles, saddles, or arms had been issued or horses allotted. Upon receipt of this order I went with the Captain, who from the roll detailed the number indicated, and saddles, blankets, bridles, lariats, nose

2. Capt. James W. Walsh was Pratt's troop commander in the Tenth Cavalry. An Irish immigrant, he enlisted in the Regiment of Mounted Riflemen in 1850 and in the ensuing decade rose from private to first sergeant. In the Civil War he won a volunteer commission in the Third Pennsylvania Cavalry and came out of the conflict a lieutenant colonel with a brevet of colonel. In 1866 he received a regular army commission of captain in the Tenth Cavalry and served in this capacity until his death in 1873.

3. Forts Gibson and Arbuckle, with which Pratt's opening years of western duty were associated, were prewar installations recently reactivated. Established in 1824 by Gen. Matthew Arbuckle on the Neosho (or Grand) River, Fort Gibson was for two decades the most important post on the southwestern frontier. Its purpose was to protect the migrating "civilized tribes" of the East from the wild Plains tribes. After the Civil War, with the advance of the frontier, Fort Gibson lost its prewar importance but continued to serve as a quartermaster depot; supplies were shipped by river steamer from New Orleans for dispatch by wagon to forts farther west. It was abandoned in 1889. A reconstructed stockade, part of an Oklahoma state park, now stands on the edge of the town of Fort Gibson in Muskogee County. Capt. Randolph B. Marcy built Fort Arbuckle in 1851 to enforce peace among the Plains tribes, to protect the resident Chickasaws from the wild Indians, and to afford protection to immigrants using the southern route to California. It was located on the slopes of the Arbuckle Mountains four miles west of the Washita River, in present Murray County, Oklahoma. At the outbreak of the Civil War U. S. troops withdrew, and the post was garrisoned first by Texans and then by the Confederate Chickasaw Indian battalion. Reactivated after the war, it was again abandoned in 1869 after the founding of Fort Sill. See W. B. Morrison, *Military Posts and Camps in Oklahoma* (Oklahoma City, 1936), pp. 28–47, 93–103; Morrison, "Fort Arbuckle," *Chronicles of Oklahoma, 6* (1928), 26–34; and Grant Foreman, "The Centennial of Fort Gibson," ibid., 2 (1924), 119–28. The episode here related marked Pratt's first experience with Indian scouts. In the next four decades organized units of Indian scouts, commanded by white officers detached for the purpose, were recruited from many of the western tribes as the need arose and discharged when the need ended. These were Cherokees.

4. Under the army reorganization act of July 28, 1866, six Negro regiments with white officers were authorized: the 9th and 10th Cavalry and the 38th, 39th, 40th, and 41st Infantry. In the army reduction of 1869 the four infantry regiments were consolidated into two new ones, the 24th and 25th. The 9th and 10th Cavalry and the 24th and 25th Infantry performed a highly creditable, and by historians largely overlooked, role in the Indian warfare of 1866–90. Pratt's regiment, the 10th Cavalry, wrote an outstanding record fighting Apaches in Texas and Arizona in the 1870s and 1880s.

bags, carbines, sabers, pistols, and accessories were issued, and their horses assigned. They were then under my command and ordered to be up, breakfasted, and ready for the march at four o'clock. I returned to my quarters and arranged my personal effects, slept briefly, and at three o'clock found my men getting ready. Not being able to locate the Indians, I went to the adjutant and found him asleep. I felt it important that I should see that the Indians were getting ready, and so ventured to awaken him. The adjutant was wroth at this and tartly told me the Indians had their orders and would be on hand at the time appointed. Four o'clock came, the cavalrymen were in line and their baggage in their wagon, but I could not find the Indians. Waiting a brief period, I again went to the adjutant and found him still abed, told him it was past the hour he had instructed me to start, that the cavalry part of the command was ready, but there were no Indians. The adjutant then dressed quickly and went out. It was well after five o'clock when the Indians and the other wagon and the post spring wagon appeared.

Guided by the Indian sergeant the command moved down to the ferry. Across the wide river was one of the ferry boats fastened to the shore and a house on the bank above. The sergeant of the Indian scouts said the ferryman and his family lived in that house and that the other ferry boat was more than a mile up the river on the other side. I had the sergeant call, and after some delay the ferryman came to the opposite bank. He acknowledged he had received orders to be across the river with his boat, but said he had not breakfasted. He did not know anything about the other boat. I asked the Indian sergeant if some of his men could not manage the boats. He replied: "All of them can."

There was no cable rope and the boat had to be pushed over with poles. The sergeant told the ferryman to bring his boat over immediately and he could then go back and get his breakfast and the scouts would ferry the command across while he was eating. The boat was brought over and three of the Indians were sent across with their ponies as part of the first load, with orders to hurry up the river, two of them to get the other boat and the third to lead their horses back. This first boat was back and being loaded again, and the second boat was coming down the river, when General Davidson and his staff arrived. The General demanded the reason the command was not across and ready to march as he had ordered. I explained the delay at the post and the conditions at the river when he arrived.

General Davidson had just taken command of the newly organized "District of the Indian Territory"—all of which is now Oklahoma—and we had arrived at Fort Gibson on the same steamer. The district then contained only two occupied posts, Forts Gibson and Arbuckle, with two companies of the Nineteenth Infantry at each post, and these were to have in addition two troops of cavalry from the new Tenth, a colored regiment. This regiment was then being organized, with headquarters at Leavenworth, Kansas.

There had been heavy and continuous rain and portions of the country between Leavenworth and Fort Gibson were flooded, and as the cross-country travel was by stage, that route had been abandoned.

The General and I had left Fort Leavenworth at the same time, compelled to go to Fort Gibson via rail to St. Louis, down the Mississippi by boat to Memphis, thence by boat up White River, then by short railroad to the Arkansas at Little Rock, and from Little Rock to Fort Gibson by light draft steamer.

The General and his staff, consisting of adjutant general, chief quartermaster, chief surgeon, and an aide-de-camp, went across on the first boat after their arrival, and taking two Indians to guide, proceeded on the march, ordering me to follow with the escort and wagons as soon as we had completed crossing.

The cavalrymen were entirely new to cavalry service, but quite a number had been in the infantry during the war, and several of the Indians had war service in addition to several months in scout service.[5] As the command moved forward throughout the day, I gave instructions to the cavalry how to sit on their horses, to move by twos, where the route was suitable to change from twos to fours, and to execute other movements. At stops I instructed them how to dismount and mount, and how to take care of their carbines and sabers while doing this. It was late in the afternoon before we found the commanding officer, who had turned aside where grazing was good and chosen a place for camping.

The two army wagons were placed far enough apart and a picket line of doubled lariat ropes was stretched between them. And after grazing and feeding, the new cavalry horses were tied thereto for the night, and the new cavalrymen slept in the open on the ground back of their horses. The Indians bivouacked near their horses, which were hobbled out by rawhide thongs which tied their forefeet close enough together to prevent them from any attempt at rapid movement but did not interfere with their grazing throughout the night. Grass was their only food.

I talked more with the Indian sergeant and his men of the scouts and found that most of them had received English education in their home schools conducted by their Cherokee tribal government. They had manly bearing and

5. All the Five Civilized Tribes of Indian Territory (Cherokee, Choctaw, Creek, Chickasaw, and Seminole) took sides in the Civil War, and large numbers rendered creditable service to the Union and Confederate causes. The Cherokees were slaveholders, and the largest share of them went with the South. See Annie H. Abel, *The American Indian as a Participant in the Civil War* (Cleveland, 1919).

fine physiques. Their intelligence, civilization, and common sense was a revelation, because I had concluded that as an army officer I was there to deal with atrocious aborigines. The night passed without adventure, except that both men and horses were terribly pestered with innumerable mosquitos, from which there was no refuge. The next day was excessively hot, and numerous deer flies joined the mosquitos to persecute men and horses. We passed Indians surrounded by their herds of cattle and horses in groves of trees where the tops were low and heavy leaved, and where they kept smudge fires over large areas to protect themselves and their stock against these voracious pests. It was told that the persecution was so great as to drive the animals into swamps, where they mired and perished. I continued my instructions to the Negro soldiers as they marched and again rode with the Indians and talked with them and their sergeant.

When we camped late that day, the commanding officer asked if I had ever seen a stampede of cavalry horses. It so happened that during the Civil War I had witnessed a stampede of the horses of a regiment of cavalry which had been placed out to graze, and their frantic and rapid movement en mass was somewhat alarming, but through the use of the bugles sounding feed call, they were rounded up and finally brought to their picket lines. I told of this one experience and he said that a stampede on the prairie was a far different thing; that the horses rushed through the camp, knocked down the tents, trampled men to death, and created havoc generally, and cautioned me to be careful to see that my horses were well tethered, but directed that I should lariat them out far enough from each other to prevent their becoming entangled, that they might graze throughout the night. I told him that picket pins had been neglected in the issuing of equipment, but I could make pins of wood. He said do that, and I instructed the men, and picket pins were made and I went about and witnessed, as I thought, that they were substantial and well driven and the lariats well tied. The Indian horses were hobbled as before, and the men of the two races slept near each other. Guards were placed well out for camp protection, but when the camp was quiet, the cavalry horses were frightened and every one of them seemed to have been able to get loose from his picket pin. They dashed through and over the men and one of the horses jumped over me dragging his lariat rope across my bed. I was up immediately and had the Indian bugler sound feed call and keep it up while the Indian sergeant rushed his men out to their horses, unhobbled and mounted them bareback and galloped away in the darkness after the fleeing horses. After some time they came back bringing all the runaways, and I used greater care to see that they were better fastened and then detailed one cavalryman to look after each four horses and arranged the guard to be changed at two-hour intervals during the night.

The horses were soon busy eating the excellent prairie grass, the Indian ponies were again hobbled, and I went farther away from my men and selected a bush for my place to lie down, putting my head up under the bush and letting my feet extend from the horses so if there was another attempt at a stampede in my direction, they might possibly shy the bush. I had just fallen asleep when a snake crawled across my neck, waking me instantly, and as I jumped up it lopped over my shoulder and as I jerked it off with my hands gave a yell, which awakened my command, and the Indian sergeant came quickly to find out what had happened. I told him about the snake and he quieted my nerves by telling a number of thrilling snake experiences, mostly relating to the deadly rattler. I finally lay down again, concluding that I had disturbed the resting place of the only snake there, which was probably more frightened than I, and after I had gone to sleep and was apparently going to make a permanent location in his bailiwick, he had concluded to evacuate in my favor. The Indian sergeant sat by and talked with me quite a while, and I was further impressed with the fact that he was both a manly and perfectly normal member of the human family. After he went back to his command, I lay awake.

Rain was coming. The fierce lightning became more portentous and the dark clouds came closer to the ground than I had ever known. Finally it began to rain, and as the staff officers had a tent fly under which they were sleeping, I ventured to go over and ask for shelter, carrying my blankets, leaving my saddle, bridle, and equipment at the bush covered by my rubber poncho. The officers kindly permitted me to crowd in amongst them, and as the rain and thunder grew worse the General, who was sleeping in the ambulance, vacated his bed also and crowded in with the rest of us. The storm soon passed, and I returned to my bush and reoccupied my bed and its bush protection.

Between my new command of the untrained Negro cavalrymen, the Indian scouts, the stampede of the horses, the snake, and the thunder and lightning, as my initiation into the regular army, I slept no more, and count that night's experience as having given me about as many sensations in as short a time as ever came into my long life.

The rain had modified the heat, so that we started off in the morning in better shape, with all nature more gracious. The General had trouble with his head because of a previous sunstroke and rode in the ambulance.[6] When we stopped for noon lunch that day, [Brevet] Major [Van Buren] Hubbard, the staff surgeon, concluded that the General was not in condition to go forward and finish the 225 miles between Gibson and Arbuckle, and that he

6. Correspondence in the Benjamin H. Grierson Papers at the Illinois State Historical Society Library reveals that some members of the regiment doubted Davidson's sanity and attributed his erratic behavior to a previous sunstroke.

must return to Gibson. The General accepted the decision, returned with his staff, taking part of the scouts, and sent his chief quartermaster, [Brevet] Major [Amos S.] Kimball, to make the inspection of Arbuckle he intended. The remaining scouts, with the cavalry detachment as escort for the Major, and two wagons, went forward under my command to Fort Arbuckle. The Major proved to be a jolly traveling companion, and as we rode the remaining days we discussed the Civil War, in which we both had participated, from the beginning to the end, and then the portent of our new life, in the regular service against hostile Indians. We became well acquainted with the Indian sergeant and his Indians and our confidence in them was greatly increased. Our Negro troopers grew in our estimate by their ready obedience and faithful performance of duty.

One thing the Major and I discussed freely. Being sworn as army officers "to support and defend the Constitution of the United States against all enemies foreign and domestic," we gave consideration to our immediate duties. The fourteenth and fifteenth amendments to the Constitution then pending before the states provided that "All persons born or naturalized in the United States, and subject to its jurisdiction, are citizens thereof." We talked of these high purposes and the Declaration of Independence, which affirmed that "all men are created equal with certain inalienable rights," etc., and then contrasted these declarations and the proposed amendment with the fact that the Indian scouts, who were enlisted to perform the very highest functions of citizens, even giving their lives if need be to enforce these American purposes, were imprisoned on reservations throughout the country and were thus barred from these guaranteed opportunities which they only needed in order to develop, become equal, and able to compete as citizens in all the opportunities of our American life. In considering the case of the Negro, we were agreed that when the fourteenth amendment became a part of the Constitution, the Negro would be entitled to be treated in every way as other citizens, and we were unable to reconcile that two regiments of cavalry and two of infantry then being inducted into the army of the United States, the enlisted men of which were to be Negros and the officers white, would accord with the amendment which provided that there must be no distinction. It seemed plain that under this amendment the Negro could not be relegated in army service to the Negro units of enlisted men solely, and the Indian could not be continued imprisoned on separate tribal reservations. The rights of citizenship included fraternity and equal privilege for development. None of our people were held under as severe "jurisdiction" by the United States as our Indians.

This first discussion and experience in my regular army service aroused an interest in my mind for the two races which became more absorbingly intense as the years enlarged my knowledge of them. Now, after more than fifty-four years of widest experience with them, I cannot see otherwise than that all the gross injustices to both races which have followed and become indurated policies are primarily the result of national neglect to give the opportunities and enforce the safeguards of our Declaration and Constitution.

We were seven days in covering the distance between the two military posts. Fort Gibson was within the bounds of the so-called Cherokee Nation, and as we traveled we passed through the country of the Creek and Choctaw Indian Nations into that of the Chickasaw Nation, each area being sections of our common country reserved to them for their exclusive tribal occupancy.[7]

Major Kimball made the inspection of Fort Arbuckle and then, with the Cherokee scouts but without wagon transportation, returned to Fort Gibson, and as my Troop D was to take station at Arbuckle, I remained there with its detachment. It interested me that Major Kimball was returning without wagons, and in providing his personal commissary supplies had prepared a considerable number of hard-boiled eggs which he could carry on his horse, saying eggs were the best food to sustain endurance. Game was abundant—deer, turkey, prairie chickens, and quails—and in our campaigning, so far as meat was concerned, we lived off the best in the land.

7. Between 1825 and 1842 the Five Civilized Tribes were moved from their homes east of the Mississippi River to lands beyond the western borders of Arkansas and Missouri. The Indian removal program was designed to free the states of Indian holdings and place the tribes beyond a "permanent Indian frontier," where, occupying territory ("The Great American Desert") that the white man would never covet, they would be forever free of corruptive white influences. In Pratt's time the Five Civilized Tribes inhabited the eastern half of Indian Territory (roughly modern Oklahoma), while the wild Plains tribes (Kiowa, Comanche, Cheyenne, Arapaho, and Kiowa-Apache) roamed the western portion. See Grant Foreman, *Indian Removal: The Emigration of the Five Civilized Tribes of Indians* (Norman, 1932); Foreman, *The Last Trek of the Indians* (Chicago, 1946); and Muriel H. Wright, *Guide to the Indian Tribes of Oklahoma* (Norman, 1951).

2. Fort Arbuckle and the Nomads

The two companies of the Nineteenth Infantry at Arbuckle were to be replaced by two companies of the Sixth Infantry, then en route from South Carolina, and the companies of the Nineteenth were preparing for removal. As Troop D was to take post at Arbuckle and I was to remain, the commanding officer detailed me as post adjutant, the duties of which I was to perform in addition to those with my company when it arrived. This also placed me in command of Indian scouts again. The twenty-five Arbuckle scouts were Caddoes and Wichitas from along the Washita River, northwest of Arbuckle.[1] Very few could speak any English, but there was an interpreter, Horace P. Jones,[2] speaking Comanche, employed by the Government to enable inter-

1. Natives of Louisiana, the Caddos had been pushed westward into Texas after ceding their land to the United States by treaty in 1835. Harassed and finally expelled by the Texans, they moved to the Washita River in 1859. As Unionists, they took temporary refuge in Kansas during the Civil War but returned to the Washita after the war. Like the Caddos, to whom they were related, the Wichitas were a semisedentary people who lived by agriculture as well as by the chase. They occupied the upper Red River country when first contacted by the white man, but after the conclusion of a treaty with the United States in 1835 they drifted eastward. With the Caddos, the Wichitas went to Kansas when the Civil War broke out but returned to the neighborhood of Fort Arbuckle when it was reactivated in 1867. See F. W. Hodge, ed., *Handbook of American Indians North of Mexico* (2 vols. Washington, 1912), *1*, 179–83; *2*, 947–49; and Wright, pp. 47–52, 255–60.

2. Jones had lived with the Comanches for many years and had married into the tribe. He was a prominent fixture at Arbuckle and, later, at Fort Sill, where he played a conspicuous part in the Kiowa-Comanche troubles of the seventies. He died in 1901. See W. S. Nye, *Carbine and Lance: The Story of Old Fort Sill* (Norman, 1943); R. G. Carter, *On the Border with Mackenzie* (2d ed. New York, 1961), pp. 153, 264–67; and J. B. Thoburn, "Horace P. Jones, Scout and Interpreter," *Chronicles of Oklahoma*, 2 (1924), 383–85.

course between the military and the Kiowas, Comanches, Cheyennes, Arapahoes, Apaches, and affiliated bands of Caddoes, Wichitas, Keechies, and others. There were individuals in all these tribes who could speak Comanche, that having become the court language of our southwest Indians. I was again commanding soldiers serving the Government under the same law as other soldiers and for the same purposes, but made up of men held together racially, and by that barred from material opportunity to become coequal with our other people. This held the Indians to the inadequate citizenizing opportunities race segregation inevitably imposes, and fully explains their slow progress into competent citizenship.

Cholera had invaded the country and the Sixth Infantry was coming from South Carolina, where it was prevalent. It had spread rapidly across the country and reached Fort Gibson. Captain Walsh, with Troop D, left Fort Gibson and started for Fort Arbuckle. When he was near Fort Arbuckle, one of the men became very ill. Having no surgeon the captain put grass in an empty six-mule army wagon as a bed for the man, sent an escort, and ordered the teamster to drive rapidly and without stop to Fort Arbuckle. The wagon came to the adjutant's office, and the escort reported they had a very sick man of the company. I went out and, uncovering him, found he was dead. The doctor pronounced it cholera. We buried him and the next day Troop D came in with several sick and within a few days several others died. There were no remedies for cholera in the medical supplies.

I had arranged that Mrs. Pratt with our baby boy should leave our home at Logansport, Indiana, come by rail to Memphis, and by boat up the Arkansas River to Fort Smith, where I would meet her at a date in July. Captain Walsh had left his family at Little Rock, and it had been arranged that we go for our families at the same time. In company with Jack Evans,[3] the post trader, we left Fort Arbuckle before the Sixth Infantry arrived, and found the two companies about fifteen miles out from Arbuckle. They were in camp by the roadside, where cholera had attacked them, and in the course of a few days 26 had died out of about 140 men. They were camped in a beautiful grove of trees, the tents of the camp on one side of the road, the sick in hospital tents on the other side. The new-made graves were close to the hospital and in full sight of the camp. We stopped with the officer in command, and while we were talking with him a sergeant knocked on the tent and be-

3. Formerly post trader at Fort Gibson, John S. Evans later, in 1869, won the tradership at newly established Fort Sill. He traded there until 1876, when he lost his license as a result of the scandal over the sale of post traderships that precipitated the impeachment of Secretary of War William W. Belknap. Evans had been paying tribute to Belknap for seven years. Nye, pp. 100–01, 292. Robert C. Prickett, "The Malfeasance of William Worth Belknap, Secretary of War, October 13, 1869, to March 2, 1876," *North Dakota History, 17* (1950), 5–51, 97–134.

ing told to enter, came in, saluted, and said: "Private ——— of Company E has just died."

The commanding officer told the sergeant to notify the quartermaster to have a grave dug and ordered the funeral immediately. There was great depression among the men and officers. The surgeon in charge said he had no medicines with which to treat cholera.

I recalled that a mile back we had passed a fine large spring and had stopped to drink its excellent water and had remarked that it was ideal for a camp. After seeing the sad conditions, Captain Walsh and I went outside and, talking over the situation, remembered the spring and the fine camping ground. We were satisfied that the depressing influences of the camp there accentuated the epidemic. We went back into the tent where the commanding officer was conferring with the surgeon and a second lieutenant named [John] Carland. Captain Walsh told the commanding officer of the spring and the fine camping ground and urged that he move his command there and get away from the sight of the graves. The commanding officer said that there were not enough well men in the command to move.

Lieutenant Carland spoke up and said: "If you will give me the order to move this camp, I will carry it out, immediately, and have the whole command over there by night." The commanding officer said: "You are authorized to move the camp." On our return we learned the camp was moved and there were no more deaths or new cases.

We mounted our horses, rode quite a number of miles, stopped by the roadside, grazed our horses, ate part of the lunch we were carrying in our saddle bags, and lay down to sleep. The influences of that day were sadly upon us, more especially as we were going to bring out our families. During the night I had peculiar sensations and finally began to think I had contracted cholera. I got up, moved about, exercised and breathed deeply, rubbed myself freely and after a bit felt better, laid down and slept, with no return of physical disturbance.

We reached Fort Gibson in due time and found cholera among the troops and Indians and many deaths. The commanding officer gave me the post spring wagon to bring my wife and child to Fort Gibson. My wife reached Fort Smith several days before I did. We drove back to Fort Gibson, and as we came into the fort a stalwart Indian man was lying by the roadside dying, his wife holding his head on her lap.

We were guests of Captain and Mrs. [George T.] Robinson of my regiment, and he, on orders of the commanding officer, gave me ten men and a sergeant as escort to Fort Arbuckle. The commanding officer sent the post spring wagon for my wife and child and an army wagon for our baggage, supplies, and tentage. The good post surgeon, Major Hubbard, provided medicines with careful instructions in case of cholera, for adults, and doses for the child, and we marched away to our destination.

During the later part of the day the boy had cholera; we gave the medicines as directed, went into camp and sat by the case during the night, in the morning continued our march, and by noon he was out of danger. No other cases occurred.

We passed Indian homes of the so-called civilized tribes. Some of these were comfortable, and even pretentious, and we found the people generally speaking the English language. We bought from them milk, butter, and eggs, and passed through one town where there was a store kept by an Indian, whose gentlemanly young clerk waited upon us with great alacrity and satisfaction. He was entertaining and carried the bundles out to the wagon, helped Mrs. Pratt into the wagon, and chatted for quite a while. I met him many times years later when he had become a man of distinction, and for nearly twenty years represented his tribe as their delegate in Washington.[4]

When I left Arbuckle to go after Mrs. Pratt, the wife of the new commander, Captain [Joseph B.] Rife, was the only officer's wife at the post. She sent kindly messages to my wife, full of desire that they should meet. Before we reached Arbuckle, we met the commander and husband on his way home alone on a leave of absence. Shortly after we left Arbuckle both he and his wife had cholera and she had died. The most important civil employee and his wife had also died. These losses from our small community were most depressing. The affiliated bands of Indians along the Washita west of us were attacked and about seventy died.

When we reached the Washita River, there had been heavy rain above and the river was rising and much higher than when I had crossed it. It seemed dangerous and I sent a soldier across on a horse before venturing with Mrs. Pratt in the spring wagon. It seemed practicable for us to ford, but water would run into the bed of the wagon, so we fixed our things up on the seats and started across, I with several men riding by the sides of the wagon. The driver deviated a little from the route that the horseman had taken. When we were about half way across, both the mules and the wagon lost the bottom and were floated a little way, but luckily found the bottom again and came out. It was a narrow escape, for just below the ford the river entered a gorge between perpendicular walls of rock and our drifting there would have been fatal.

4. Miss Muriel H. Wright, editor of the *Chronicles of Oklahoma,* surmises that the village was North Fork Town on the Canadian River near present Eufaula; that the store was owned by Judge George Washington Stidham, a prominent leader of the Creek Nation; and that the "gentlemanly young clerk" was George Washington Grayson, recently a captain in the Confederate Creek regiment and for many years high in the councils of his people.

When we reached Fort Arbuckle the post had come under the command of Lieutenant [Stephen] Baker of the Sixth Infantry and our first night introduced us to the excitements of frontier army life. An English Lord with special permit from our government and having a retinue of twelve or fifteen persons had been in the southwest hunting "big game," and returning east he concluded he would pass through the Indian Territory. He was camped a quarter of a mile back of the quarters of the company to which I belonged, on a little creek, in army wall tents. I had selected as quarters a house near our company. Late in the night we were aroused by the firing of guns at the Englishman's camp. I hurried to our company quarters, turned out the men, armed, sent a sergeant and three men to the rear of my quarters as a protection, and sent a messenger to bring the Indian scouts. An infantry company was sent out by the post commander to the Englishman's camp. The Indian scouts came and searched the woods, and a detachment of infantry was placed at the Englishman's camp for the night. The Englishman reported that Indians had attacked them and fired into their tents, which bullet holes proved. No evidence of the presence of Indians was found, the night passed, and the next morning the English party hastened away.

Investigation for several days finally revealed that the firing was by a Negro sergeant and four men of Troop D. They confessed and claimed provocation. It seemed that the day before, the Englishman had secured an order from Lieutenant Baker directing Troop D's blacksmith to shoe the Englishman's horses. The blacksmith had been trained by the captain to obey orders for his services only when given by his company officers. When the Englishman presented the order, it not coming from the company commander, the blacksmith refused to obey it. The Englishman, having the post commander's orders, was sure they were from better authority than the company commander, argued with the colored blacksmith, and indiscreetly become wroth, using excessively strong and profane language. A sergeant of the company, with several men, happened to hear the dispute and concluded to give the Englishman and his party a good scare, so they went out with their guns and fired into the upper part of the Englishman's tents, then hurried back and answered to roll call. They were tried by court martial and duly punished. No doubt on their return home the Englishman and those with him, in giving their repertoire of adventures in America, added a thrilling story of a night attack by Indians while they were encamped within the precincts of a frontier military post.

I returned to my duties as adjutant and commander of the Indian scouts, in addition to service with my troop, and the race question as applied to both our dependent peoples was again before me. The homes of the twenty-five Indian scouts were scattered along the Washita, northwest of us. They were as tractable and reliable in the execution of orders as the men of our own and other races, white and black, constituting our command. Their duties were to guide and scout, keeping us advised where the large camps of the Comanche, Kiowa, Cheyenne, Arapaho, and Apache Indians were. These tribes furnished many turbulent marauders in that portion of the southwest. At that time, and for eight years thereafter, men of these tribes were constantly raiding the frontier of northwestern Texas, southern and western Kansas, New Mexico, and Arizona, and even over into old Mexico.[5]

Captain Walsh, as senior officer, became post commander. We soon found that the nomad Indians were divided within their tribal organizations. Most of their leaders counseled obedience to the Government and deprecated the forays of the younger men of the tribes, and some even gave us information about the lawless of their own tribes and their achievements.

The official correspondence since the post had been reestablished after the war fell into my care, and I read it with great interest. The system as applied to Indians had been in some respects despicable. One case was then pending which involved the recovery of a white boy who had been captured from his home in Texas and carried away by the Kiowa Indians. The previous commanding officer of the post had recommended that a bonus of a mule and goods, amounting in all to about $300, be paid to the Indians for returning the boy.[6] Having only a small command of infantry, the commanding officer had no enforcing power. I called the attention of Captain Walsh to this and that buying his release was government encouragement for this kind of lawlessness, clearly saying to the Indians: "Do it again. The Government approves and will pay you for it." The Captain instructed me to write a post

5. For at least a century, with an occasional interruption of several years duration, the Kiowas and Comanches regularly raided along the Texas frontier and deep into the northern provinces of Mexico for stock, captives, and other plunder. The raiding pattern had become deeply imbedded in the culture of these tribes and could not be surrendered lightly. It was easily the most fruitful cause of difficulty between them and the United States Government. During the decade of the Republic of Texas, the Indians had concluded that Texans and Americans were different peoples, and they continued until their final conquest to regard their raids in Texas and Mexico as no concern of the United States. Although roaming the Pecos River country of eastern New Mexico, the Kiowas and Comanches rarely penetrated the settlements; and when they did it was usually to strike at their enemies the Utes and Navajos, not the New Mexican settlers. The raiding complex is illuminated from the Indian viewpoint in W. S. Nye, *Bad Medicine and Good: Tales of the Kiowas* (Norman, 1962). See also Nye, *Carbine and Lance;* R. N. Richardson, *The Comanche Barrier to South Plains Settlement* (Glendale, 1933); and Ernest Wallace and E. Adamson Hoebel, *The Comanches: Lords of the South Plains* (Norman, 1952). The Kiowas and Comanches, with the affiliated Kiowa-Apaches, were usually to be found south of the Arkansas River, the Cheyennes and Arapahos north of the river. The latter rarely raided in Texas but instead harassed the Kansas and Colorado frontier settlements.

6. The boy was Theodore A. Babb, captured in Texas a year earlier by the Comanches. The friendly Comanche chief Asa-Havey acted as intermediary in ransoming him. Although Pratt does not mention it, the price was $210 plus $20 worth of army uniforms. Nye, *Carbine and Lance,* p. 43.

letter he would sign to General Sherman, then in command of the army,[7] giving these views. I did so, and as soon as the mails could carry, we received that letter back with endorsement in General Sherman's own handwriting:

> Headquarters Mil. Div. of the Missouri,
> Fort Leavenworth, Kansas,
> June 25th, 1867.

This paper happens to meet me here. It is now about as good a time as any for us to come to an understanding, and rather than submit to this practice of paying for stolen children it is better the Indian race be obliterated.

I now have power to call out the volunteer forces of the frontier, and the Commanding Officer of Fort Arbuckle may, in his own way, convey notice to the tribe that this boy must be surrendered or else war to the death will be ordered. There will be no ransom paid.

> W. T. SHERMAN
> Lieut. General

The Indian scouts were sent to the chiefs of the Kiowas, Comanches, Cheyennes, Arapahoes, and Apaches, asking them to meet us in council on a creek emptying into the Washita at the lower end of Eureka Valley. Our two cavalry troops and Indian scouts formed the command, and we marched seventy miles to the point indicated. We reached the council grounds early in the day designated and before the Indians had arrived. A commanding position on a hill was selected, where in case of need our horses could be protected in the narrow valley along the creek, back of the camp, and we be in good fighting position.

Soon after we had established our camp the Indians appeared coming down the valley in great masses, each tribe separately. As from our elevated position we could see them miles away, it was a wonderful sight. There were several thousand men, women, and children riding horses and ponies, and driving many other horses and ponies dragging travois, carrying their tepees and domestic equipment and the little children too young to ride horseback. Each tribe had large herds of horses and ponies aggregating several thousand.

They went into camp along the river bottom where grass was luxuriant, and it was not long before there were large towns of tepees, the animals out grazing.

The chiefs from each tribe came up to see the commanding officer and arrange for the conference the next morning. Their disposition was most friendly, they having no knowledge of the message we were to give. The night

7. General Sherman, as the endorsement quoted by Pratt shows, commanded the Military Division of the Missouri, not the entire army.

was quiet and the next morning, at the time appointed, the leading Indians came dressed in their best, and without any weapons of war.

The conference opened with a speech from the Captain, the substance of which was the desire of the Great Father that we should live at peace with one another, and that the Indians must begin to recognize the fact that we were to become one people and together develop and make use of this great country in the way the white men had found best to advance the prosperity, comfort, and happiness of both the Indians and whites; that the Government was anxious to have the Indians adopt our ways of living and unite with us to use and develop the land of our great and good country which was big and rich enough to give all its people wealth and happiness; that there was no good reason why we should not live peacefully together. Leading chiefs of the several tribes accepted these sentiments, claiming it was their desire to become like the whites; that they had heard of the white man's ways of getting his living out of the ground and some of them had seen something of the white man's homes, though none of them had then been very far into the white man's settlements, and that they were ready and willing to be taught.

The Captain then spoke again and gave the message that the Great Chief of the armies of the United States had sent. At this there was quite a little disturbance and much earnest talk among themselves. The Kiowas, who had been the greatest offenders, were most demonstrative, claiming they had been driven from their former hunting grounds; that the buffalo, which gave them their food, their clothing and their houses, were being destroyed by our people; that the white man had moved in and driven them from the country, once all theirs, and had been the first aggressors. White men made war on them, not sparing their women and children; that they were only returning the treatment the white men gave to them; that the white man in raiding their homes did not stop to make prisoners, but shot and killed their women and children indiscriminately, and that they were not as bad as the white man, because they saved the lives of some who fell into their power and took them back to their camps and treated them kindly, whereas the white man killed all. Chiefs of the same tribes deprecated the acts of their raiders. Little Raven of the Arapahoes was especially conciliatory.[8] He reasoned that war was all a mistake, and ought not to be allowed.

What Little Raven and some of the other leaders said led the Indians to

8. A Southern Arapaho chief, Little Raven had signed the Fort Wise Treaty in 1861 but had subsequently led his people in the Plains wars of the middle 60s. After signing the Medicine Lodge Treaty of 1867 (see note 11, below), he exerted all his influence for peace and for the next twenty years served as spokesman for the progressive element of the tribe. That most of the Arapahos remained at peace during the Red River War of 1874–75 was largely the result of his leadership. Hodge, *Handbook, I*, 770–71. Also present at the council were Black Kettle of the Southern Cheyennes and Tosawi of the Comanches.

confer with one another right there in the open council. They carried on a conversation among themselves for quite a while and finally it was announced that they would give up the boy without reward and also any other prisoners they had captured. The council broke up in apparent harmony and intention on the part of the Indians to conform to the wishes of the commanding general of the army, and we returned to Arbuckle. The captives were with bands not at the council and were later restored to their people.[9]

Soon after our return Toshawa, chief of the Peneteticas, who were the most friendly band of the Comanches, visited Arbuckle with his people, camping near the post several days.[10] They were fed and entertained as guests. It being my duty to look after Indian relations at the post, I thought it best, though facilities were meager, to show attention to Toshawa, and accordingly invited him and his wife to dinner.

Consulting Mr. Jones, the interpreter, he advised me to provide plenty of beef, and have potatoes, bread and coffee. Buffalo beef was their staple, and the other food would be luxuries they were most fond of.

Toshawa's wife was a jolly little woman. The interpreter was not present, so we were unable to talk freely to our guests, but by motions, smiles and laughs, got along pretty well. Mr. Jones had told me they were good eaters, and it was hospitable to urge them. I accordingly kept filling their plates and finally Toshawa stopped eating; closing the last three fingers of his right hand and pointing with the index finger toward his left, with the thumb upwards, placing his hand a little below the neck, he lifted it and said "Wano." The sign indicated that he was full, and "Wano" was good. Mrs. Toshawa, however, continued accepting helpings. As she kept on Toshawa seemed to think

9. Louella Babb, sister of Theodore Babb, was released by the Comanches after this conference, but not, as Pratt implies, without ransom. Her freedom cost $333. Nye, *Carbine and Lance*, pp. 43–44. In an address to the Colorado Commandery of the Loyal Legion on April 4, 1905, Pratt said this regarding the conference: "Captain Walsh, who had served in the old army before the war, and was an experienced plainsman, and familiar with Indian character, gave them General Sherman's message, with full explanation of what it meant. Some of the chiefs were ugly in their talk, and indicated that they courted a scrap and did not intend to be abridged in their roaming over Texas and Kansas, which they claimed had always been their country. Other leaders, old men, particularly Little Raven of the Arapahoes, Toshawa of the Comanches, and Black Kettle of the Cheyennes, were more conciliatory. We secured the return of the girl and some other prisoners, without cost to the government. As the Indian warriors outnumbered our command three to one, we realized that under all the circumstances we had undertaken a somewhat perilous mission. However, it all ended satisfactorily, and I had learned something of the value of positive methods with Indians." Pratt, "Some Indian Experiences," *Journal of the U. S. Cavalry Association, 16* (1905), 205.

10. The Penatekas or Honey-Eaters composed the most populous Comanche band. They had preceded the main southward migration of the Comanches and, living in northwestern Texas, had developed closer ties with the Wichitas, Caddos, and white people than with their wilder kinsmen to the north and west. In the 1860s and 70s the Penatekas rarely gave the whites any trouble and, indeed, often helped them against the recalcitrant Comanche bands. Tosawi and Asa-Havey were the principal Penateka leaders in Pratt's time. Wallace and Hoebel, *The Comanches*, p. 25.

it was necessary to apologize for her eating, and then held up two fingers and by signs said that she was eating for two.

Toshawa enjoyed his visit, and when he came again he told us that on the way back to their camps, about eighty miles west of the post on Cache Creek, when near their destination, a boy arrived; that when the baby was coming he and his wife stopped by the creek, she had her child, and that he brought water and she took care of the child herself, and after getting it wrapped and in proper condition she took it in her arms, mounted her horse, and rode home.

Toshawa and his party were greatly interested in our cavalry and infantry drills and the commanding officer thought best to give an exhibition of what our large guns would do. A short time before, four 64-pounders with ammunition had been sent out for Arbuckle equipment by the War Department. They were from the superabundance of guns left from the war. We had no artillery organization at the post, so these guns were parked and the ammunition stored.

A very considerable number of the Sixth Infantrymen at that time had been in the army before and through the war, and it was not uncommon for men to serve enlistment terms in each of the different branches of cavalry, artillery, and infantry. Three men were found who had served in the artillery and knew how to manage the guns. We moved one out behind the men's quarters on a rise of ground overlooking a valley and high hills back of the post not far away. When the shells for the 64-pounder came, a number of the Indians lifted them, and the interpreter explained that powder was enclosed in the shells and that there was a fuse leading to the powder which could be cut at certain places, and the fuse, becoming ignited when the gun was fired, would explode the shell within the seconds indicated by the opening made in the fuse.

We indicated here and there where we would have the shells explode, over in the woods below us or up on the side of the mountain about a mile and a half away. The men arranged the shell, loaded the gun and all stood back, and when everything was ready the soldier pulled the lanyard. The loud explosion, the hiss of the ball, which we could follow and almost see as it went through the air, and then the cloud and noise as it exploded in the place indicated, impressed them greatly. It was explained that we could have the shell expode in the air over any place within reach and the pieces would fall and perhaps kill those underneath. Then we showed that we could have it explode farther away in the woods, that as the shell was so heavy it would go through trees. This was all a very proper lesson for them to have.

The next day the man who supplied milk to the post came in and reported we had killed one of his cows, demanding that we pay for it and claiming seven dollars as the price, and it was paid.

Toshawa became a friend from that time and often sent messages from his camp by my scouts.

On leaving home I promised the editor of the *Journal,* for whom, when a boy of twelve to fourteen, I had worked as a form-inker and a distributor of his paper, that I would write an occasional letter for the paper. I here add one:

Ft. Arbuckle, Ind. Terr.
Dec. 6, 1867.

Editor Journal:

When my last was written to you in July, the cholera was raging at the post; its stay in our immediate vicinity was only about ten days and the deaths at the post eleven, but for some weeks after we lived in continual anxiety because of its destruction among our friendly Caddoes and two companies of the Sixth Infantry, the first about twenty miles distant and the latter fifteen. The Caddoes numbered about four hundred, and upwards of seventy were swept away during the month of July, their principal chief—a great promoter of harmony and peace between the wild tribes and those on the reserve and the whites—included. Of the Sixth Infantry, numbering about 140 men, 26 died during the short week which the cholera stayed with them. Its appearance in this section of the country, without warning, found our medical department very poorly supplied with medicines to stay its course, or alleviate the suffering it caused.

The wild Indians of the Plains have made us a visit and quietly removed thirteen horses, belonging to the scouts, so effectually that no trace of them is yet found. Should they be found the treaty at Medicine Lodge Creek will compel the nimble (they came afoot) legged, to return them.[11]

11. Although Pratt thus briefly disposes of the Medicine Lodge treaties, they occupy a prominent place in the history that he chronicles in the first few chapters of his memoirs. At Fort Laramie in the north and Medicine Lodge in the south, the Peace Commission of 1867–68 concluded treaties that formed important parts of the foundation on which President Grant in 1869 erected his famous "Peace Policy." The commissioners negotiated the Medicine Lodge treaties at a site on Medicine Lodge Creek seventy miles south of Fort Larned, Kansas, in October 1867. Most of the principal chiefs of the Kiowas, Comanches, Cheyennes, Arapahos, and Kiowa-Apaches signed the treaties and bound their people to confine themselves to reservations in the western part of Indian Territory, to refrain from warfare, and to become farmers. Instead of bringing peace to the Plains, the Medicine Lodge treaties helped to lay the groundwork for the Plains wars of 1868–69 and 1874–75. The three treaties are printed in Charles J. Kappler, comp., *Indian Affairs: Laws and Treaties* (2 vols. Washington, 1904), 2, 977–89.

We are having the most beautiful weather I ever knew at this time of the year. I am writing at five in the morning and en-deshabille, without a fire; we have had three or four good frosts but not a particle of snow this fall. A more suitable location for the reservation of the Indians it seems to me could not be found in the limits of our vast Union. Here the soil is fertile, farms are ready cleared yet adjacent to timber, stock lives the winter through without provision or labor on the part of the owner, and every disposition of climate and country seems calculated to favor their primitive mode of life and for gradually bringing them to civilization. Fruit grows abundant with imperfect culture. Apples and peaches are all I have yet seen; of these we have the most perfect specimens. Some apples we have now, purchased from a Creek Indian, who hauled them 120 miles and sold them for four dollars per bushel, I do not think can be surpassed for luciousness. Speaking of Creek Indians reminds me that our fellow townsman and former Mayor, J. P. Dunn, Esq., is agent for that nation and that his administration is, contrary to custom, highly spoken of by those for whom he acts.

If we do pay from four to six dollars per bushel for apples, we have other luxuries at a more reasonable price. Mrs. Dickory [Mrs. Pratt] bought three hams of venison yesterday which in the aggregate weighed thirty-six pounds, for a dollar and a half. Turkeys—wild—sell at two to four "bits" and prairie chickens we have many given to us. We are now promised a treat in the shape of a ham of bear meat. The Caddoes on a recent scout found where two large ones of the cinnamon class made their home and Jones, our indefatigable scout and interpreter, with Dr. C. (also indefatigable), eight Caddoes and dogs not counted have gone to give battle. They return tomorrow. Everybody wanted to go, as fine sport was anticipated, the dogs having been in training for a bona fide specimen of the same class as those the party have gone for, belonging to Mr. Gray, an Indian trader near the post, which had got loose, but as there are only four officers with the four companies containing nearly as many men, Captain W. would not permit.

Riding out with the ladies in a carriage a short time since, I took a shotgun to defend us from any turkey that might happen to cross our way. Having arrived near the turning point of the ride I got out to hunt in a neck of the woods, and let the carriage drive on. I had scarcely left the road when a fine large buck bounded into it, paused, and stood looking at the carriage scarcely fifty yards from me. Filled with admiration by his fine proportions and elated with the opportunity—my first at a deer—I fired to wound and perhaps eventually cause the death of the noble fellow, but with no advantage to me, as the gun was loaded with turkey shot. He jumped high enough to have cleared any fence in Indiana and bounded off across the valley, still an object of admiration, and then of regret.

Dr. R. has a famous collection of the natural curiosities of the territory, among which are a cinnamon bear, a wild cat, flying squirrel and numbers of bugs and worms, tarantulas, centipedes, scorpions, etc. I must not neglect two horned toads who have lived in a cigar box since last May and have not had a particle of any visible sustenance, air being their entire food. I will not attempt a description in this letter, but will in some future, or send you an actual specimen.

Yours,
Dickory.

3. Life at Fort Arbuckle

Whenever the scouts returned from their trips west to find where the camps of the roving Indians were, their ponies were loaded with fat venison and turkeys. At first, twenty-five cents was the price of a venison ham or a turkey without reference to the size, and one time I bought at that price a turkey which weighed twenty-four pounds. In recent years I have paid more than twice twenty-five cents per pound for a turkey.

Mails for the post came in once a week and were brought on horseback from Fort Smith, Arkansas, by a contractor. The Indian Territory, now Oklahoma, at that time was frequented by white renegades from justice, and theft and murder were common. Horse stealing was their regular business. Horses were stolen in Texas and the Territory and sold in Kansas and Missouri. The sparse settlements enabled these rascals to organize and operate along the frontiers and to cross and recross the territory in some safety, usually traveling at night, having rendezvous or stations en route. Twice within my knowledge they stole large herds of cattle on the frontier of Texas and got away with their quarry by driving them through the buffalo range, where their trail was obliterated by the thousands of buffalo.

Restraining these lawless products of our America was the duty of the frontier civil authorities, aided by the widely separated army posts. In the Indian Territory, at that time, the only civil authorities were the Indian agents and the governments of the five civilized tribes—Cherokee, Choctaw, Chickasaw, Creek, and Seminole. These each had brave Indian police forces to take care of their tribal areas, who fearlessly performed their duties throughout their jurisdictions. It came to my knowledge that the Indian chief of police of the Creek Nation in performing his duties in arresting these white freebooters had killed six of them and that he had as a recognition of this public service been named "Six Killer," and that became his family name. The freebooters organized against him and finally killed him in his own town, leaving his wife a widow with a large family of children. Years after, one of his sons came under my care, and I shall speak of him later in this narrative. It is worthy of attention and serious thought that in our boasted America its army was principally engaged in restraining dangerous red Indian depredators and at the same time the Indians were compelled to defend and protect themselves against lawless white American depredators. This condition continued throughout my eight years army service in that region.

Our mail carrier was murdered and the mail rifled. It took some time to get a new man, but one was found brave enough to undertake the service. Soon he, too, was ambushed and killed and all the mail again stolen.

We then arranged that Arbuckle mail should come by way of Fort Gibson and the Indian scouts from the two posts should carry the mail between in relays of twos. Three stations equidistant were established to cover the 225 miles, with four Indians at each.

The Indians knew what had transpired and the duty was a new test of their courage and fidelity. We then got mails twice a week until one day we started the mail from Arbuckle with two Indians, one a very small fellow with a rugged pony. No mail came for nearly two weeks and finally the one little Indian with the rugged pony came back alone, bringing the mail from Fort Gibson, having traveled over 400 miles to and from Fort Gibson most of the way by himself. Reaching the first station the two Indians found that the scouts had left their post and gone to their camps. The larger Indian refused to go farther, and the small one went on alone. Finding the other posts deserted, the strong-hearted little man performed the whole service, and we had further proof that among Indians as other people there are both resolute and irresolute characters.

Bootleggers made big revenue through venturing into the Indian country with whisky on pack horses. Several of the Indian scouts somehow got whisky, and it seemed impossible to catch the introducer, whom the government laws would punish. I asked the commanding officer to let me end the traffic by punishing the Indians for using it.

One of the scouts had been reckless with his pistol during an orgy. Though no harm was done, it was evident that disaster might come. The commanding officer authorized me to treat it in any way I saw fit. I put the reckless scout in the guardhouse and when he sobered up got a stick of cord wood weighing about twenty-five pounds and had him carry it, walking to and fro in front of the sentinel at the guardhouse in plain sight of the Indian camp. He was kept at it for twenty-four hours, then taken to the camp and in the presence of the scouts restored to duty and told that his punishment had atoned for his bad conduct, but that should he offend again, he would have to carry a heavier stick and for a longer period, and if after that he again offended, there would be increase of punishment until he quit drinking. From that time forward, there was no trouble from whisky among the scouts, and they became zealous in helping us to end the career of bootleggers in our baili-wick.

Several years afterward a like experience with another band of Indians was even more effective, as will be told later.

One day in the late summer of 1867 when out riding with the post quarter-master and several miles from the post, a wild turkey flew from her nest in a clump of bushes, leaving six eggs. Tying the corners of my handkerchief to-gether, I carried the eggs home. Mrs. Pratt having a hen anxious to set, I gave her the eggs and in three days the hen had them all hatched out, which gave her great prestige for quick work. Mrs. Pratt carefully fed and cared for that family. The turkeys grew rapidly, and, when they were large enough to fol-low their turkey instincts, they abandoned roosting in the hencoop with the hen mother and spent their nights in the lower branches of a tree in the yard, and as they grew went higher.

We were interested and much amused at the anxiety of the hen to keep them on her level and get them back into the coop. Failing in this she aban-doned the attempt, but as they were fed with the mother, she retained a motherly instinct and pride until they were well grown. They developed handsomely and, so far as we could see, were in all respects just as amenable as the best domesticated members of the turkey tribe. Although it was only 150 yards back of our quarters to the woods and wooded mountains were near, they never indicated a desire to leave us and were always on hand when it came time to be fed, so that we had turkey from the wild of our own raising for Thanksgiving and Christmas.

There was a lesson in this to the man who was pondering much over the race question. He saw that even wild turkeys only need the environment and kind treatment of domestic civilized life to become a very part of it.

The post trader had two bears well grown which he had bought from the

Indians when they were small. They added distinction to the post and his store. The trader had two substantial log posts about fifteen feet long well set in the ground and on the top a secure platform and a hole through the platform so that the bears could each climb up and lie on their platforms, sun themselves, and look out over the world. They were tethered to their posts by long light chains which gave them ample room for exercise. There was a large and rather deep pool of water just below the post formed by the waste from a cold spring which gave our post its water supply.

It was the habit of the trader for his own amusement and the amusement of the people and Indians when at the post to unchain the bears and, using light ropes, lead them down to this pool and turn them loose in the water. They were always eager to go and enjoyed the bath and were most interesting, when playing with each other, in trying to throw each other down and in chasing and ducking each other to the amusement of themselves as well as the onlookers. He had trained them so that they would do things he directed. When the show was over he called them to the shore, attached the ropes, and led them back. They each had a big box in which to sleep.

Afterward this trader was removed and a new trader was appointed. Having established quite a business not only with the nearby affiliated bands but with the outer and more nomadic Indians, and with the civilized Chickasaws, who had farms east of us, he put up a store off the military reservation east of the post. This store became our objective on many an evening ride.

A party of us went out one evening and found a herd of cattle feeding on the prairie about a half-mile away. One of the bears was lying on top of its post, but the male, on the ground, was pulling his chain toward the cattle, standing up or walking to and fro and sometimes giving a growl. A large bull was quite away from the herd on our side and now and then would stop eating and look at the bear, so we suggested to the trader that he turn the bear loose and see what would happen. He accordingly unloosed the bear, and immediately the bear found himself free he began to wander toward the cattle herd. As he went out he would stop, hold up his head and look, then go forward a little way and do it again. Then he got up on his hind feet and stood looking at the herd, the bull watching the bear. When the bear had gone nearly half way to the bull from his post, the bull lifted his head and gave a bellow and started for him. The bear turned back at once and put on "high speed" for his refuge, the bull gaining on him all the time. The bear reached his post well ahead of the bull and climbed to his perch with great alacrity, where he stood looking down at his challenger, while the bull bellowed and pawed the ground daring him to come down. Finally the bear lay down and looking over the edge apparently said "It's all off," and then the bull went back to his charges.

My recreation from military duties was largely fishing and hunting. In a

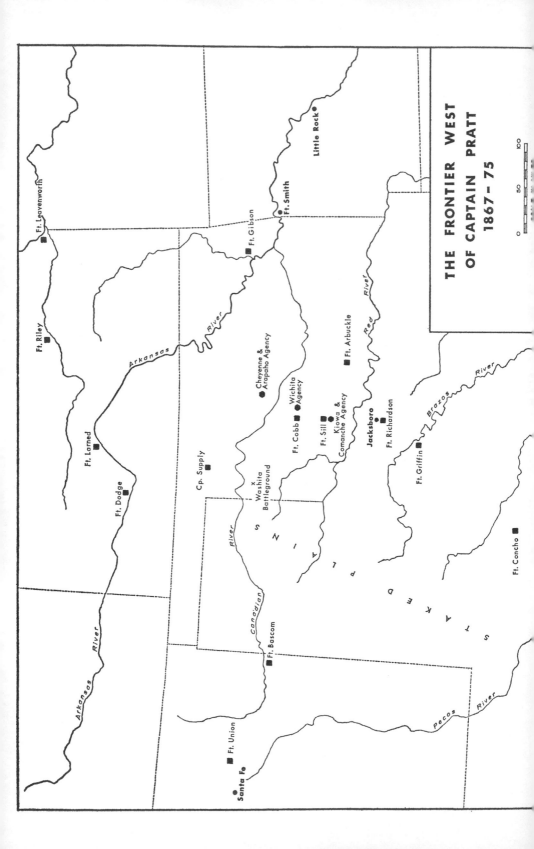

THE FRONTIER WEST
OF CAPTAIN PRATT
1867 – 75

0   50   100

spring branch back of the post I found fine minnows for bait and then fished in the Washita, which was four miles away, and in the Wild Horse Creek, which was nearby.

One day I found an especially large pool in the Wild Horse and caught so many fish I was able to send a contribution to several of the officers. This attracted the attention of the commanding officer, Major [James P.] Roy, a Virginian who had remained true to the stars and stripes throughout the war and had come forward in the regular course of promotion to be major of his regiment [the Sixth Infantry]. He expressed a desire to go fishing with me, and it was arranged that I catch the bait and we take a soldier along to carry it and bring home the fish.

The soldier reported mounted on the tallest mule from the quartermaster department, so tall that he was quite a little above us on our horses. The bait was in a keg and the Major had the soldier take it up in front of him on the pommel of the saddle, and we rode about three miles to the fishing ground.

We had great luck. The catch was divided between a gamey white fish, which was particularly nice and which I had never seen in other waters and weighed up to a pound and a half, and a good-flavored long blue catfish, weighing up to two and a half pounds.

When our bait gave out, we had many more fish than we could put into our keg. The Major put the white fish in the keg and reserved the catfish. Then he made two strings of these. The soldier mounted his tall mule, we gave him the keg to carry before him on the pommel of the saddle as before, and then at the Major's suggestion tied one string of the catfish on each side of the soldier's saddle to the rings just behind the cantel. The mule was perfectly quiet, and when the loading was completed the Major told the man he could go on ahead and we waited to see what would happen.

The route led through open woods. Soon after starting, the strings of catfish began to swing against the mule's sides, and, after brief jumping at the punishment their prongs gave, the mule ran away and the soldier was compelled to drop his keg, and soon after the strings broke and the catfish fell. After this happened the soldier was able to control the mule and bring him back. The Major greatly enjoyed the comical feature of what had happened, but praised the soldier for sticking to his seat and for his prompt return. We gathered up the spilled fish and gave the soldier the keg to carry and, getting a stiff limb of sufficient length, tied the strings of catfish one at each end to carry well out, and this I put across the front of my saddle and held balanced while we rode quietly home.

As the Major had arranged the trip and enjoyed relating it, I had a suspicion that the selection of the tallest mule, and the finale of the event, were not altogether accidental.

As adjutant it was my duty to have an extra man detailed for the guard each day and to select the cleanest and best drilled soldier as orderly for the commanding officer. The then commanding officer was a captain of the Sixth Infantry, and one private in his company was an exceptionally fine looking soldier who captured the position of orderly oftenest. As two of the troops at the post were Tenth Cavalry, and the colored men were new to the service, the orderly position did not reach them for some time. My captain [Walsh] had been in the "Queen's Own" of the English Army and before the Civil War had come to this country and served in the cavalry of our army against the Indians in the West. In the Civil War he became captain in the Third Pennsylvania Cavalry, was advanced through the grades until he became colonel of his regiment, and with his regiment was at General Meade's head-quarters. After the war he was commissioned captain in the Tenth Cavalry. He was an exceptional horseman, a fine soldier, and it was good fortune that I was assigned to his company.

There were careful drills, both mounted and dismounted, and most scru-pulous cleanliness in quarters, through daily inspection and unusual atten-tion to the horses by a captain who knew by service on the plains what was needed and what men and horses could be made to do if well prepared. The inspection of the company included knowing that the men were in clean underwear as frequently as was needed.

Guard mount was in the morning and usually witnessed by the officers and their families, because it was the spectacular event of the day. One morning the favorite private of the post commander was in the guard mount, and as I passed down the lines and looked over all the men with more care, it seemed to me that there was no difference in the quality and cleanliness of the clothing and equipment of a private from the colored troops and the fa-vorite soldier of the post commander. I therefore brought the two men to the front of the guard and put them through the manual of arms. Their preci-sion in executing the commands gave no grounds for determination. I then put them through the facings, had them march to the front, to the right, to the rear, to the left, and still found no grounds for deciding. I then ordered the sergeant to march the guard to the guardhouse, telling him that I would go there and select the orderly. I went to the guardhouse, took the white and the colored soldier into a side room, and told them to pull off their shoes. The colored man had on perfectly clean socks and clean drawers, while the white man's socks and drawers were not clean. I told them to put on their shoes and the colored man to report to the commanding officer for orderly, and went to my quarters for breakfast. When I went over to my duties at the adjutant's office, the commanding officer said:

"Mr. Pratt, was not Private —— of my company on guard this morning?"

I said, "Yes, sir."

"Why is he not detailed as my orderly?"

"Because he was not the cleanest man, sir."

He said, "Hereafter whenever he is on guard, I want him detailed as my orderly."

I said, "That is your order notwithstanding the rules?"

He said, "It is."

But I was not to execute that order for that night the white soldier deserted. He could not face the ridicule of his comrades at being beaten by a Negro.

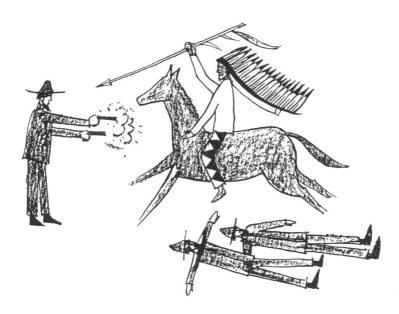

4. The Washita Campaign of 1868

Notwithstanding their treaties and the promises of the Indians at the conference in Eureka Valley, we soon had information of further Indian raids along the frontier, generally for horses of the stockmen and ranchers of western Texas and southern Kansas. These forays seldom became known to us of that part of the army on the Indian reservations until the Indians were safe back in their reservation "Cities of Refuge," where, unless invoked by the Indian management, the army was without jurisdiction.

The small forces of the army were widely scattered, and it was seldom possible to locate the raiders after they had escaped and returned to their camps. Bureau request for army help meant war and the assembling of military commands large enough to successfully combat the forces the Indians could assemble. Prior to, during, and immediately after the Civil War there was no strongly established agency control over the turbulent nomads, nor had the Civil War advanced peaceful relations between red men and white.

Lieutenant General Sheridan, with headquarters in Chicago, commanded the forces in all the Indian country east of the Rocky Mountains from the Canadian line to the Gulf of Mexico. In the fall of 1868, under President

Grant's authority, he organized an expedition under General Custer, consisting of the Seventh Cavalry, and later added a volunteer cavalry regiment, the Nineteenth Kansas, under Colonel Robinson, a former governor of the state.[1]

The dual system of civil and military control over the Indians was full of vexatious complications and lack of harmony. The army was witness that the government through its Indian Bureau was sadly lacking in keeping its treaty obligations, which goaded the Indians to rebel against being reservated. These reservations and the destruction of their game resources further aggravated them, plainly portending disaster to them, for the white man's advantage. Why should not they enforce some retaliation? The white man did not keep his promises. Why should they keep theirs?[2]

Beginning in the fall of 1868, General Custer's expedition campaigned throughout the middle and western part of the Indian Territory, which was then the winter resort of millions of buffalo, the best friend of the nomad Indians, by furnishing skins for their tepee homes, their clothing, and their bedding, and gave the meat which was their principal food. A general superintendent for the nomadic Indians of the then Indian Territory, now Oklahoma, was appointed by President Grant in the person of General W. B. Hazen, of the regular army, a distinguished Civil War commander with

1. Pratt's chain of command here is premature. Grant did not become President until March 4, 1869, on which day Sherman was elevated to full general and command of the army and Sheridan to lieutenant general and command of the Division of the Missouri. In the autumn of 1868 Major General Sheridan, as commander of the Department of the Missouri, organized the winter campaign against the southern Plains tribes that Pratt describes. Bvt. Maj. Gen. George Armstrong Custer, serving in his regular army rank of lieutenant colonel of the Seventh Cavalry, led the striking column that surprised the villages on the Washita River in November. The Nineteenth Kansas Volunteer Cavalry, which took the field but saw little action, was commanded by Col. Samuel J. Crawford, governor of Kansas, not by a Colonel Robinson.

2. The Medicine Lodge treaties had interrupted the raiding habits of the Plains tribes only briefly. If the Indians were to settle at an agency, they would have to be fed on government dole; but rations were not forthcoming at the Eureka Valley agency, and the Indians adopted the only alternative—to follow the herds. Beyond this, however, the raiding pattern was so deeply rooted that abundant rations could hardly have destroyed it all at once. As Col. Nye observes (*Carbine and Lance,* p. 47), the United States was dealing "with a people who responded only to their own desires, a race who did exactly as they chose except when compelled by superior force to do otherwise." Throughout the spring, summer, and autumn of 1868, they chose to raid the frontier settlements of Kansas, Colorado, and Texas. General Sheridan's campaign of 1868–69 was designed to apply the superior force required to compel them to cease. It was planned for the winter months in order to catch the tribes off guard in their winter camps. For further reading see George A. Custer, *My Life on the Plains* (New York, 1874); Carl C. Rister, *Border Command: General Phil Sheridan in the West* (Norman, 1944); De B. Randolph Keim, *Sheridan's Troopers on the Border: A Winter Campaign on the Plains* (Philadelphia, 1891); Charles J. Brill, *Conquest of the Southern Plains* (Oklahoma City, 1938); D. L. Spotts and E. A. Brininstool, *Campaigning with Custer and the Nineteenth Kansas Volunteer Cavalry* (Los Angeles, 1928); George B. Grinnell, *The Fighting Cheyennes* (2d ed. Norman, 1956); and Donald J. Berthrong, *The Southern Cheyennes* (Norman, 1963).

whom I had served.[3] The nomad Indians, who had by treaty accepted reservations in the Territory, were required to assemble at Fort Cobb,[4] north of the eastern end of the Wichita Mountains near what soon afterwards became Fort Sill. Four companies of the Tenth Cavalry, the two companies at Fort Arbuckle and the two companies from Fort Gibson, under command of Major [Meredith H.] Kidd, were constituted a separate command and directed to establish a camp and fortify at a point on Cobb Creek, a branch of the Washita. During the Civil War this had been the location by the Southern Confederacy of a temporary Indian agency for these tribes, but no improvements were made. I was made adjutant of this command, and my Arbuckle scouts became a part of it. We proceeded to the point indicated and on the bank of the creek built a stockade fort large enough to accommodate our men and horses as protection against any sudden attack the assembled hostiles might make.[5]

3. As part of the peace effort of 1867–68 that included the Fort Laramie and Medicine Lodge treaties, the Government established two large reservations: the northern one, encompassing present South Dakota west of the Missouri River, and the southern one, Indian Territory, for the concentration of the Plains Indians. Both were placed under military superintendents, retired Brig. Gen. William S. Harney in the north and Bvt. Maj. Gen. William B. Hazen, colonel of the 38th Infantry, in the south. As this arrangement was devised before the election of 1868, Hazen was not, as Pratt states, appointed by President Grant. *The Nation, 9* (Aug. 5, 1869), 101–02.

4. Maj. William H. Emory established Fort Cobb on the upper Washita River in 1859 to afford protection to the newly founded Wichita Agency, erected for the Wichitas and the tribes recently expelled from Texas—Caddo, Tonkawa, Anadarko, and Waco. Confederate troops garrisoned the post and maintained the agency early in the Civil War. In October 1862, however, the local Caddos, joined by Osages, Shawnees, and Delawares from Kansas, massacred a large number of Tonkawas (who were accused of cannibalism), drove out the Confederates, and burned the fort. General Hazen used Fort Cobb briefly during the winter campaign of 1868–69 as the assembly point for the friendly portion of the tribes against which Sheridan was making war, but it was permanently abandoned in March 1869 after the establishment of Fort Sill. Morrison, *Military Posts and Camps in Oklahoma*, pp. 109–18. Muriel H. Wright, "A History of Fort Cobb," *Chronicles of Oklahoma, 34* (1946), 53–71.

5. This was Hazen's temporary agency. All Indians who wished to be regarded as friendly were directed to assemble here; those who did not would be considered hostile. Of the Kiowas and Comanches who began drifting in early in November, the Penateka Comanches of Tosawi and Asa-Havey were cooperative, but the Kiowas and other Comanches gave Hazen such a bad time that he asked for more troops, and Major Kidd's squadron was sent in response. Nye, *Carbine and Lance*, pp. 56–57.

In 1905 Pratt related an interesting incident that occurred while he was at Fort Cobb: "We found wolves numerous, especially the small coyotes. I desired to get a nice wolf robe to send to a friend east, and talked with an old Comanche named Esatoyet, who could speak a little English. He suggested I get a beef and some poison. . . . We drove the steer over the hills to a secluded place. Esatoyet shot him, and he and his wife took off the hide and the best parts of the meat, leaving the carcass, on which he sprinkled poison. We had cut small sticks, about a foot long, and sharpened them at both ends. He then cut the liver and heart into chunks and put a piece on each stick and sprinkled poison on them. While doing this he explained that the liver and heart were 'sugar! wolf heap like him.' The next morning we rode over and found twenty-seven coyotes and two large gray wolves dead. Esatoyet and his wife skinned the wolves and his wife tanned the hides handsomely and made two beautiful robes, leaving the tails as ornaments." "Some Indian Experiences," p. 206.

On the 27th of November, 1868, sixty miles west of us, General Custer fought the Battle of the Washita. General Custer's full exposé of this affair and of his remarkable campaign is given in his book, *My Life on the Plains*. As one of the most notable illustrations of the kind of warfare our army was compelled to make against our Indian wards, I am permitted by Mrs. Custer to introduce General Custer's own account of the battle.

Mrs. Custer's eminent personality has been a continuing reminder of the nation's sorrow for that other great tragedy in Indian subjugation which, eight years later, now forty-six years ago, in 1876, on the Little Big Horn in Montana, annihilated five troops of the Seventh Cavalry and ended the brilliant career of her fearless soldier husband.[6] In the affair on the Little Big Horn, the northern branch of the Cheyenne tribe took a leading part.

It must be remembered that army forces had to take most reckless chances when invading the vast regions of nomad Indians, made desperate by the enforcing of our obnoxious prison reservation policies. It was perfectly human for the Indians to attempt to maintain their freedom and to hold on to their primitive life and resources when that was the only other door of escape available. How different the story had they been accepted and led to participate in the advantages of our American family.

In the same way, Indians when retaliating by invading our ever advancing frontier settlements accepted the same reckless chances. The righteousness of methods, multitude of acts, and their quantum of annihilation by either side were not materially different. General Sherman's "War is Hell" applies.

Army commands in pursuit of hostiles, by becoming remote from their supports and safety, often found it inevitable that sudden destruction of the enemy must be, else their own annihilation would follow. The responsibility for what happened was therefore not on the aggressive and resisting units but in the quality of government supervision which precipitated the conflicts.[7]

. . . .

I am compelled to resist the temptation to give much more of General Custer's graphic story, but must go on with my own. General Custer's strategy

6. Elizabeth Bacon Custer, widowed by the Battle of the Little Bighorn, survived her husband by fifty-seven years, passing away in 1933. Her writings did much to draw attention to the army's activities on the Indian frontier, and in the early 1920s, when Pratt wrote, she was indeed a widely known personality.

7. Omitted here is Pratt's lengthy quotation of Custer's Battle of the Washita, from the General's book, *My Life on the Plains* (New York, 1874, and subsequent editions). Custer surprised Black Kettle's band of Cheyennes in the Washita Valley near present Cheyenne, Oklahoma, at dawn on Nov. 27, 1868, and dealt a shattering blow. As Pratt notes below, however, Black Kettle's was but one of several villages along the Washita, and Custer, after destroying the Cheyenne camp and property, hastily withdrew with many Cheyenne prisoners. In addition to the authorities cited in note 2 above, see Edward S. Godfrey, "Some Reminiscences of the Washita Battle," *Cavalry Journal*, 37 (1928), 481–500. That the soldiers could and would make war in the winter, when food and

and quick escape with his command was a miracle. He had only destroyed an outlying camp. Lieutenant Godfrey[8] with twenty men of his company in pursuit of a small escaping party reached the summit of the hills and saw vast camps which proved to be the main forces of the Kiowas, Comanches, Cheyennes, and Arapahoes, scattered along the Washita for many miles. Godfrey reported to Custer what he saw. During the day the hosts of warriors were assembling, and a portion harassed Custer's command during their work of destruction and caring for their wounded. The Indians did not complete their combinations that day. Toward evening General Custer placed the captured prisoners—their women and children mounted on their ponies—just behind his strong advance and moved toward these camps as though for attack. When darkness came, he reversed his course and kept up his march toward Camp Supply until two o'clock next morning and thus saved his command.

Seven years later I had charge of Indian prisoners, part of them Cheyennes —Manimic, war chief of that tribe, among them.[9] With his aid I evolved the following as a fair showing of their side. Moke-Tavato (Black Kettle) was the noted principal chief of the Southern Cheyenne Indians. He was foremost in friendship for the government, but through most unfortunate and fortuitous circumstances he was unable to curb his young men in their desire to revenge the Sand Creek, Colorado, massacre of the Cheyenne women and children by a Colorado militia regiment two years before,[10] and other violences between the whites and detached parties of his people. These had all occurred within the limits of their former nomadic ancestral homes. He had led the Southern

---

forage were scarce, came as a shock to all the tribes. At Sheridan's orders, Custer made two more expeditions that underscored this truth. Except for a few bands of Kiowas and Comanches who remained in the Staked Plains area west of Indian Territory, the tribes had by spring 1869 attached themselves to their agencies.

8. Edward S. Godfrey, an 1867 graduate of West Point, later fought in the Battle of the Little Bighorn in 1876, the Nez Percé conflict of 1877, and the Battle of Wounded Knee in 1890. His writings on the Indian warfare in which he participated, especially the Little Bighorn, have long been regarded as basic sources. He retired a brigadier general in 1907 and died in 1932.

9. Minimic, or Eagle's Head, figures prominently in subsequent chapters of Pratt's narrative.

10. The Battle of Sand Creek occurred on Nov. 29, 1864, when a Colorado volunteer regiment commanded by Col. John M. Chivington, in a dawn attack similar to that at the Washita, surprised Black Kettle's camp in the valley of Sand Creek, Colorado. Although many of his people fell, Black Kettle himself survived, only to be shot down at the Washita four years later. It has become customary to attribute the warfare that spread over the Plains in the next four years to the bloody excesses of Chivington's troopers, but this is an oversimplification. Black Kettle had entered into arrangements with local military authorities that made the attack a breach of faith, but the Colorado soldiers were in fact overzealous in their Indian-killing crusade, but Sand Creek can only be understood against the background of the dangerous predicament into which Indian hostility had thrust the Colorado settlers and the state of mind this had induced. The most balanced treatment is Stan Hoig, *The Sand Creek Massacre* (Norman, 1961). Chivington is defended in Reginald S. Craig, *The Fighting Parson: The Biography of Colonel John M. Chivington* (Los Angeles, 1959).

Cheyennes in the treaty between them and the United States, entered into under the supervision of General Sherman, who in 1867 was chairman of the largest commission ever created to formulate better relations between the hostile Indians and the Government. The treaty with the Cheyennes shows Moke-Tavato's name at the head of the Cheyenne signatures.[11] That treaty fixed the limits of their reservation, which bordered the Washita on the south and Kansas on the north, within which they were to be safe, and outside of which they were to be treated as hostiles at war and attacked wherever found. Moke-Tavato, because unable to control the revengeful portion of the tribe, had taken his own immediate following and gone to what he believed to be and was the remote southwest corner of his reservation, on which the treaty guaranteed his people safety, and where, as he thought, he was farthest away from all danger, and in a little valley within his refuge was waiting for the storm to blow over. Here it was he met his sad fate.[12]

A fortnight after the battle, General Custer and his command came to our camp at Fort Cobb, and soon afterward General Sheridan arrived. Food and forage was sadly needed by the exhausted command, and the nearest supply was at Fort Arbuckle, 100 odometered miles east. General Sheridan ordered General Custer to send his wagon train to Arbuckle and directed Major Kidd to send two officers to hurry to Arbuckle and hasten forward such supplies as the wagons at that post could carry. Lieutenant [Charles F.] Nordstrom and I were selected because of our good horses. We were expected to make the hundred miles in two days. When we started, we agreed with each other to put our horses to the test of making it in one day, and we did. Resting an hour at the mail station half way, two cavalrymen curried and rubbed each horse during the rest, and we again galloped on and reached Arbuckle at midnight, having been in the saddle fifteen and a half hours. We had our stable guards rub our horses for an hour, then blanket and feed them, and the next day they showed up well. We loaded up the Arbuckle train and started it off the next day, rested the second day, started back the third day, passed General Custer's train going to Arbuckle and our train en route to Fort Cobb, rode to the half-way mail station, stopped over night, and arrived at Fort

11. See above, p. 19, note 11, for the Medicine Lodge treaties. Bull Bear signed first for the Cheyennes, then Black Kettle.

12. As a matter of fact, the Cheyennes were nearly 100 miles southwest of the Cimarron River, which was the southern boundary of the land set aside for them by the Medicine Lodge Treaty. Even had they been on the reservation, however, the Indians had been notified, as a preliminary to Sheridan's campaign, to gather at Fort Cobb or be treated as hostiles. Although Black Kettle appears to have wanted permanent peace with the whites, he had been unable to prevent his young warriors from ravaging the Kansas frontier, and there were white captives in his village at the time Custer attacked. It is true that the Cheyennes regarded themselves as at peace, but only because it was winter, when all Indians desired, in George Hyde's phrase, to put the war back in the bag until spring came.

Cobb the next day, covering the return in two days, to the great praise of our horses.

General Custer's command, through its energy and boldness in searching for the marauders in midwinter, finally compelled the hostiles to seek safety by obeying the orders to move in near our camp, which had been changed to the junction of Medicine Bluff Creek and Cache Creek. This location had been selected by the then commander of the District of the Indian Territory, General Grierson, colonel of the Tenth Cavalry, as the place for a new post to be called Fort Sill in memory of a gallant general of the Union Army killed in the Battle of Stone River, Tennessee.[13]

General Hazen had also established his Indian agency headquarters for the Kiowas and Comanches at that point, intending to divide the tribes into bands, locate them separately, and start agricultural activities. His plan was to build a house for each band chief at some favorable point along a creek or river, and break up, fence and plant corn and other products on a considerable acreage, put a farmer in charge of each band to show them how to raise crops to live on, and thus encourage them to quit their roving habits, but it was a long process, too remote from the necessary resources and unworkable in meeting their immediate needs. The Indian Bureau, through its Washington headquarters, took charge, General Hazen was relieved, and a civilian agent was appointed for the turbulent Kiowas, Comanches, and Apaches, with agency at Fort Sill. Another was appointed for the friendly affiliated tribes with agency on the Washita, and a third for the discontented Cheyennes and Arapahoes with agency on the North Fork [of the Canadian River].[14]

13. Bvt. Maj. Gen. Benjamin H. Grierson, colonel of the Tenth Cavalry from 1866 to 1890, had assumed command of the district from Lt. Col. John W. Davidson (see above, p. 1, note 1), who then reverted to command of the Tenth Cavalry. As a volunteer officer in the Civil War, Grierson had won fame and high rank by leading the widely publicized "Grierson's Raid" through Mississippi and Alabama in 1864. In 1890 he was promoted to brigadier general and retired; he died in 1911.

Named for Gen. Joshua Sill, a West Point classmate of General Sheridan, Fort Sill played a highly significant role in Plains history as base of operations against hostile Indians and as the Kiowa-Comanche agency from 1870 to 1878. Located on the edge of Lawton, Oklahoma, it is still an active installation and serves as the U. S. Army Artillery and Missile Center. Nye's *Carbine and Lance* is a first-rate history of the post. See also Gillett Griswold, "Old Fort Sill: The First Seven Years," *Chronicles of Oklahoma, 36* (1958), 2–14.

14. These events marked the inauguration of President Grant's Peace Policy, which aimed to conquer the Indians by kindness. The conquest was entrusted to agents nominated by church groups, and the pacifistic Quakers fell heir to the Kiowa-Comanche agency at Fort Sill, the Cheyenne-Arapaho agency at Darlington, and the Wichita agency at Anadarko. The Indians construed Quaker pacifism as governmental weakness and also as license to do as they pleased. Nye, *Carbine and Lance,* chaps. 6 and 7, gives an excellent treatment of the result. For the Quaker viewpoint, which gravitated toward realism under the impact of hard experience, see Agent Lawrie Tatum's *Our Red Brothers* (Philadelphia, 1899); and schoolteacher Thomas C. Battey's *The Life and Adventures of a Quaker among the Indians* (Boston, 1891).

Under General Hazen the Indians had reluctantly accepted the situation and disintegrated into the smaller bands as directed. The food and other supplies promised under treaty agreements came forward in meager quantity and poor quality. The corn planted did not ripen quickly; and if it had, the one farmer for so large a number of people, ignorant of agriculture, was inadequate to produce the quantity needed for their immediate necessities, and it was soon evident that the only recourse was to return to their former game resources. Buffalo was plentiful, but on account of the new presence of the army in that section which so recently had been abundant in buffalo, and the large mass of Indians gathered at one place, the buffalo gave that vicinity a wide berth and it was necessary for the Indians to go many miles west after the meat needed in order to live. Thus governmental failure to meet treaty obligations compelled the failure of General Hazen's plans. In permitting them to go after buffalo they got away from our observation, and it was plain that governmental default gave the Indians additional reason for distrust and even encouragement to resume their reprisals along the border.

During this period our wives were often disturbed by the visits of the Indian women and children. Suddenly the window of our huts, or door of tent, darkened with the forms of Indian women. They would gaze at the white woman and her family, no doubt interested in style of dress or quality of housekeeping. If invited in and given food, more callers followed.

An experience Mrs. Pratt gives with a sorrowing mother indicates the delicate perception of the Indian woman, and the strong mother love in all races.

"One bright spring morning I had clad our Fort Arbuckle girl-baby in her first short dress, then carefully placing her upon the bed, was standing back, mother-like, to admire. The outer door was wide open and I saw what seemed a most miserable and repulsive squaw, approaching the doorway. Her hair was cut short and hung over her forehead; her eyes, her face, neck and breast were painted in narrow stripes of many colors. About her waist was fastened a short skirt made of a part of a buffalo robe. She saw the baby and before her intentions were known she had her in her arms. I sprang forward, saying, 'You horrid, dirty thing!' and took the baby from her arms. The poor miserable woman looked at me in the most pitiful manner, then gathering up the corner of her blanket she held it as one would hold a sick infant, at the same time crooning a mournful cry, she made a sign that her baby had died, and to tell how great her grief, she showed she had cut off her little finger at the second joint, which was one of the extreme mourning customs of the Kiowas. She also pointed to the deep gashes on her breast and arms, not yet healed. Tears ran down her cheeks and my sympathies were so moved that almost unconsciously I replaced our baby in her arms. Tenderly and carefully the bereaved Indian mother handled her as she passed her hands over the plump little limbs. After some moments she handed her back with a grateful look and with a hearty handshake she departed. In a week she came back and brought with her a peck of wild plums that ripen there in the spring. The plums had been freshly washed and were carried in a new piece of pink calico. Again she held the baby and this time with signs asked permission and was permitted to kiss the child, for this sorrowing Indian mother was no longer repulsive. When departing she gave signs of great gratitude. In another week she came again, this time bringing two buffalo tongues. She would take no gift in return. All she wanted was the pleasure of holding baby. This was her third visit and her last. She came and went alone."

5. Fort Sill and Camp Supply, 1870–72

Most of the southern Cheyennes and Arapahoes, together with the Kiowas, Comanches, and Indian Territory Apaches [i.e. Kiowa-Apaches], were encamped near us along the Cache and Medicine Bluff Creeks, waiting to be located.[1] We officers had built for our families log and mud-daubed huts, having mud roofs and only the ground for floors. They were in a long line facing our companies on the other side of the parade ground. Some of us were pleased to have noted chiefs as guests at our tables, especially if they were well known to be friendly to the government. Little Raven, the leading chief of the Arapahoes, was one of this kind. We soon found he rather enjoyed accepting a second dinner, and four of us laid a plan to test his gastronomical capacity. Captain ——— up the line was to have him first, then Lieutenant ——— in the next house was to invite him, then Captain ——— to lure him. I was to be ready and inveigle him into eating a fourth dinner. Raven was a big hearty man with large dining capacity. All went well until he came out from his third dinner. Raven and I were good friends but he firmly declined, assuring me he had room for no more, and as the officers and ladies who had taken part gathered around he realized our joke, joined in our

1. The troops—part of Pratt's regiment, Custer's Seventh Cavalry, and the Nineteenth Kansas Volunteers—were bivouacked in "Camp Wichita" at the junction of the two creeks. Work commenced here early in 1870 on the permanent stone post that in the previous August had been officially named Fort Sill. Under the superintendency of General Hazen, A. G. Boone served as agent for the Indians. In July 1869, however, the Peace Policy was inaugurated with the arrival of Quaker Lawrie Tatum as Kiowa-Comanche agent. Enoch Hoag, also a Quaker, relieved Hazen as head of the Central Superintendency and established headquarters at Lawrence, Kansas. Tatum erected the agency buildings of his headquarters on Cache Creek just south of Fort Sill.

laugh, and waddled off to his camp. Until he died, Raven was among my staunchest Indian friends and ten years later, in 1879, sent his children in the first party coming to Carlisle from his tribe.

In the summer of 1870 a very large portion of the Kiowas were off their reservations, west of the Wichita Mountains.[2] The western line of their reservation was along the Sweetwater, a creek with a constant supply of good water. General Grierson took a portion of the Fort Sill cavalry and went after them. We had crossed the Sweetwater and were among the buffalo looking for the Indians. General Grierson had taken a company and gone to one side, and the command was moving under Colonel Carpenter, captain of one of the companies.[3] We saw Indians in large numbers on a rise of ground in front and, forming line of battle, continued our advance. The Indians were massed, and as we came nearer we discovered, with our glasses, that they had on their war bonnets and were evidently inviting a contest. All the conditions warranted a fight. They were off their reservation in violation of their treaty and plainly defiant. Why not charge at once and punish them for their insolence? We continued to move toward them at a walk until they were only a half-mile away, when one of their number came toward us carrying a white flag. Colonel Carpenter sent me with the interpreter to meet him. He told us that the Indians did not want to fight and that Chief Kicking Bird would like to talk to the commanding officer.[4] I took him to Colonel Carpen-

2. The effects of the campaign of 1868–69 quickly wore off. The Cheyennes and Arapahos, who had borne the brunt of Sheridan's offensive, for the most part remained quiet, but a few Kiowa and Comanche raiding parties were on the Texas frontier in the summer of 1869. By the summer of 1870 these Indians had perceived that the Peace Policy represented a radical shift from the war policy of General Sheridan, and throughout the season parties of Kiowas and Comanches ravaged the Texas settlements. One group even stole the mule herd from the Fort Sill quartermaster corral. Troops from the Texas forts spent the summer chasing the marauders while Grierson's regiment patrolled Red River, the southern boundary of the reservation, in a vain attempt to keep them at home. That the Peace Policy forbade the soldiers to attack them on the reservation did not escape the Indians; while in Texas they had to avoid the troops, but once north of Red River they and their plunder and captives were safe.

3. Capt. Louis H. Carpenter, from 1866 to 1883 a distinguished troop commander of the Tenth Cavalry, held a brevet of colonel for gallantry in action against Indians in Kansas two years earlier. He rose to brigadier general and died in 1916.

4. A chief of commanding influence among the Kiowas, Kicking Bird (Tay-nay-Angopte) had for nearly a decade inclined toward a policy of peace with the whites. His stature had suffered as a result, and to restore it he led a raid into Texas in July 1870, probably shortly before the incident Pratt narrates here. In Jack County he collided with a troop of the Sixth Cavalry under Capt. C. B. McClellan and sent it flying back to Fort Richardson. This was Kicking Bird's last raid. Thereafter he spoke for the peace element of the tribe in opposition to Lone Wolf and the war faction. To his influence was attributed the refusal of two-thirds of the Kiowas to join the hostiles in the Red River War of 1874–75. Kicking Bird's death in 1875 was probably induced by poison administered by some of his own people who resented his opposition to war. Hodge, *Handbook, 1,* 686. Nye, *Carbine and Lance,* p. 113. James Mooney, *Calendar History of the Kiowa Indians,* 17th Annual Report of the Bureau of American Ethnology, 1895–96 (Washington, 1896), Pt. 1, pp. 216–18. For other details see Nye, *Bad Medicine and Good.*

ter and he gave his message to the colonel. General Grierson came back just then and sent the Indian to tell Kicking Bird to come out and meet him, and taking the interpreter and a small party we rode toward the Indians. Kicking Bird came forward with an equal number of his men and he and the General had a long conference. Then Kicking Bird sent a messenger to his men and they disappeared.

As evening was near, it was decided to camp on the Sweetwater, and Kicking Bird agreed to show a good place. As we were going toward camp, we came upon quite a herd of buffalo. General Grierson asked Kicking Bird, through an interpreter, if the Indians could actually kill the buffalo with bow and arrow, and Kicking Bird assured him that it was easily done, and if he wanted, he would show us how, and the General was pleased. Kicking Bird got off his horse, stripped himself and horse, leaving only the lariat, one end around the neck of the horse and looped over the horse's nose. Kicking Bird, then practically nude, bounded onto his horse with his bow and arrows in one hand and we rode toward the buffalo. When we were near enough Kicking Bird dashed into the herd, selected a big fat buffalo, and compelled it to leave the herd by heading it off, we following at a gallop. He soon succeeded by running ahead of the buffalo and dodging it as it charged at him this way and that until it stopped and simply kept facing him as he rode around and around it. When we were near enough to see the operation, Kicking Bird, handling his horse deftly, started the buffalo to run away, came up on its flank, and we saw him shoot the arrow into the buffalo as it ran. The buffalo soon stopped and stood still. Kicking Bird motioned and we came forward and found the buffalo bleeding at the mouth profusely. In a little while it tottered, fell, and died. We found the arrow had entered the buffalo well up on the side just back of the shoulder, and had gone through its vitals and the point was sticking out lower down on the other side.

Before we reached our camping place, we discovered that the camp of the Indians had been beyond the Sweetwater and off their reservation, and that the Indians had maneuvered in front of us simply to hinder us long enough for the women and those in camp to take down their tepees and move over the creek onto their reservation, where they were safe from attack.

During the years 1870 to 1874, raiding into Texas and Kansas, committing depradations, killing settlers, and stealing horses again grew to considerable proportions. Usually these incursions took place during the light of the moon.

A large army post was built at Fort Sill and ten companies of the Tenth Cavalry assembled there, which made it one of the largest posts in the country. The posts along the border of northwestern and western Texas, down to the Rio Grande, were enlarged and strengthened and a military telegraph line established by which, when Indians were discovered to be off their reservations on a raid, information was at once telegraphed to all posts near their possible route. Frequent scouting by cavalry commands all along the border and especially throughout western Texas and that part of the Indian Territory outside their reservations, was adopted as the only means the army had to intimidate and compel the Indians to remain under the direction of their agents. This did not avail and as they were not punished and had wide range, it was easy for small parties of their young men to leave their camps when out buffalo hunting, raid different parts of the vast frontier, win fame among their people, and enrich themselves by robbing the settlers and cattle raisers of their horses.

During this period the agencies were not provided with the quantity and quality of supplies needed to encourage contentment, and the raiding parties grew larger and more frequent. One of the largest and most boldly aggressive placed the general commanding the army twice under greatest danger. In 1871, General Sherman made a tour of inspection of the frontier. Beginning on the lower Rio Grande, he came north along the line of posts to Fort Griffin and then to Fort Richardson, which was the next fort south of Fort Sill. On his way between Fort Griffin and Fort Richardson, and when within about fifteen miles of Fort Richardson, he passed a contractor's train of eleven empty wagons on their return trip to the railroad from having hauled army supplies to Fort Griffin. He had a small cavalry escort. Not many minutes after passing this train a party of Kiowa Indians, about 150, under the two old and famous leaders, Satanta and Satank, and a younger leader named Big Tree, came upon the train from the rear. The man driving the lead team saw them in time to unhitch a lively leading mule, jump on its back without removing its harness, and overtake General Sherman. The Indians gave chase, but failed to catch him, and when they came in sight of the General's escort they turned back.[5]

5. Although the Texas settlers cried loudly for help, many government officials, blinded by the easy philosophy of the Peace Policy, refused to listen, contending that Texans exaggerated frontier conditions in order to secure the removal of Federal troops from Reconstruction duties. Accompanied by Inspector General Randolph B. Marcy, General Sherman, himself inclined to doubt the Texan representations, had set forth to see for himself. On May 18, 1871, a large Kiowa war party watched him and his small escort cross Salt Creek prairie on the road from Fort Griffin to Fort Richardson. Some of the warriors wanted to attack, but the medicine man Mamanti (or Dohate), the organizer and leader of the expedition, restrained them with the prediction that richer prey would soon appear. Several hours later a train of ten wagons owned by Henry Warren, destined for Fort Griffin with a load of corn, crossed the prairie from the east. The Indians swept down on the train, killed seven teamsters, and plundered the wagons. Five men escaped, one of whom took word of the disaster to Fort Richardson. Sherman's doubts about frontier conditions vanished. The best account, drawn from both white and Indian sources, is in Nye, *Carbine and Lance*, pp. 124–32. See also Rister, *Border Command*, pp. 174–75; Richardson, *Comanche Barrier*, pp. 341–42; Robert G. Athearn, *William Tecumseh Sherman and the Settlement of the West* (Norman, 1956), pp. 290–91; and Carter, *On the Border with Mackenzie*, pp. 80–84.

Although Mamanti led the war party, Satanta, Satank, and Big Tree were all prominent in the at-

General Sherman hastened to Fort Richardson and started General Mackenzie and the Fourth Cavalry out after the Indians.[6] It was afterwards established that the Indians were pursuing the General and party.[7]

As the Indians had a long start and it was not far to the borders of their reservations, they got safely across Red River into their reservation "City of Refuge" ahead of the cavalry, and the pursuers had to turn back. The ten teamsters remaining had all been killed and scalped and some of them horribly mutilated. The animals belonging to the wagons were taken by the Indians, together with such plunder as they desired out of the wagons. General Sherman then with a stronger escort came quickly to Fort Sill, and immediately there were preparations for some action. While these were under consideration the marauders in their war toggery, elated with their adventure, came from their camps to the trader's store, which was in a large detached building some distance from the new post.

Sometime before, the Indian Bureau had decreased the Indians' already inadequate allowance of food. This had incited their discontent and was part of their justification for raiding. While a small portion remained at the trader's store, the main body went down to the Indian agency, passing near the post, to demand a restoration of the former quantity of their food issue. General Sherman and General Grierson arranged to get the leaders to come up to the post and see General Sherman. Knowing the demand the Indians were making on their agent, they sent Mr. Jones, the interpreter, down to tell the Indian agent to say to the Indians that as he had no authority to increase their rations, and was only obeying the Government order to decrease them given by the authorities in Washington, he could do nothing, but that the commander of the army was at the post and if the General ordered the

---

tack on the train, and Satanta took chief credit for the result. Satank (Set-an-gia, Sitting Bear), in 1871 about sixty years old, had for three decades been a commanding figure in the Kiowa tribe and had risen to first rank among Kiowa chiefs. Satanta (Set-tainte, White Bear), twenty years Satank's junior, held second rank and was well known for his oratorical genius, warrior skill, courage, egotism, and duplicity. Together with Lone Wolf, he had been held hostage by Custer for two months during the campaign of 1868–69 for fulfillment of the military demands on his people; and upon his release he had promised to remain at peace forever. Big Tree (Addo-eette), although only about twenty-five, had already won a large reputation as a warrior and raider. After the wars ended, he was reconstructed and became an elder in the Baptist Church. He died in 1927. Hodge, *Handbook, 1,* 15; 2, 469, 513–14. Nye, *Bad Medicine and Good,* pp. 276, 280–81.

6. A brilliant and somewhat erratic Civil War cavalryman, Bvt. Maj. Gen. Ranald S. Mackenzie was colonel of the Fourth Cavalry from 1870 to 1882, when he was promoted to brigadier general. His energetic campaigns against the Kiowas and Comanches in 1870–75 and against the Sioux in 1876–77 earned him fame as an Indian fighter. While serving as commander of the Department of Texas in 1884, he went insane and died in 1889. See Edward S. Wallace, "Border Warrior," *American Heritage, 9* (June 1958), 22–25, 101–05. Sherman authorized Mackenzie to pursue the warriors who destroyed the Warren wagon train on to the reservation, but incessant heavy rains caused the command to bog down in mud.

7. The Indians were not pursuing Sherman but actually let him pass in safety. See above, note 5.

agent to reestablish the ration, he would have to do it, and the better way was for the leaders to appeal to the commanding general. The Indians quickly fell into this trap.[8]

About twenty, including Satanta and Satank, went with this party to General Grierson's quarters. Big Tree and some of the younger men were still enriching themselves at the trader's store. Practically all of the Indians who had gone to the agency rode up to the post, and more than a hundred congregated at one corner of the parade ground close to the officers' homes, where they could look across the parade and see the party at the commanding officer's quarters. The cavalry companies had saddled and were on their horses in their stables, ready for any emergency, concealed by the high stone wall. Each stable was large enough to accommodate the horses of the company on the two sides with open space between sufficient to mount and get the men in line. Each company was instructed to send ten men to report to Lieutenant [Louis H.] Orleman when the signal to move was given.

The position to which each troop would hasten when the bugle sounded was designated. One company, dismounted, was to go back of the stables, get behind the bank of Cache Creek to the rear of the commanding officer's quarters and leaving a platoon there to prevent any escape in that direction, while the other platoon was to form a line around the front, taking in everything on the porch. The captain of D Troop being absent, it came under my command and was assigned a position mounted in line to the left in front of the commanding officer's quarters, while Colonel Carpenter, with his company, formed on the right, leaving a large open space between us, making it necessary for the Indians to pass between these two companies in case they attempted to escape in our direction.

Just as these formations were completed and positions were occupied, old Lone Wolf,[9] a dominant chief, who was with the party down at the store, galloped up on his pony, and rode through this open space to the commanding officer's quarters, having in one hand a carbine and a bow and some arrows.

8. Sherman arrived at Fort Sill on May 23, and the Kiowas, including those guilty of the wagon train massacre, came in for rations on May 27. At Agent Tatum's summons, the chiefs gathered for a council, during which Satanta loudly boasted of leading the party in the assault on Warren's wagon train, at the same time implicating Satank, Big Tree, and others. Satanta then demanded arms and ammunition, and Tatum replied that he could make such an issue only if the big soldier chief at the fort authorized it. This was a play for time and a stratagem to get the chiefs to go see Sherman. Tatum had become disenchanted with the Peace Policy and had determined that punishment was necessary. He promptly penned a request to Sherman to arrest Satanta, Satank, and Big Tree. Nye, *Carbine and Lance*, pp. 132–47. Mooney, *Kiowa Calendar*, pp. 328–33. Athearn, *William Tecumseh Sherman*, pp. 293–95.

9. A militant Kiowa chief, Lone Wolf became leader of the hostile element of the tribe, in opposition to Kicking Bird and the peace party, after the removal of Satanta and Satank. He led the hostile Kiowas in the Red River War of 1874–75. Confined in Florida in 1875, he died shortly after his release in 1878. Hodge, *Handbook*, *1*, 773–74.

He jumped off his pony, passed quickly through the dismounted soldiers, who were in single line in front of the porch, facing the porch, and as he stepped on to the porch he handed the bow and arrows to one of the other Indians, brandished the carbine, and began to talk vehemently. General Grierson at once took hold of the carbine and remonstrated through Mr. Jones, the interpreter, telling the Indians they could see they were entirely unable to succeed in any violence. The other Indians did not respond to Lone Wolf and when he saw the futility of his action became quiet.[10]

It only needed the firing of a shot at that moment to have brought on a disaster in which probably the general of the army with General Grierson and their staffs, as well as the Indians, would have perished.

Lieutenant Orleman with his large detachment got in rear of the considerable body of observing Indians that were in the far corner of the post, 300 yards away, and the Indians, on discovering him, at once opened fire on the soldiers and galloped away. Three of the soldiers were wounded. One Indian was killed and several others wounded, but the Indians managed to carry all of them off.

General Sherman told the chiefs and leading men that they would have to surrender the leaders of the raid then and there, and Satanta and Satank, who were on the porch, were accordingly taken to the guardhouse.

The adjutant, [Brevet] Major [Samuel L.] Woodward, who was on the porch, came and said that the General wanted me to take Troop D and go with him to arrest Big Tree. We hurried down to the store. Major Woodward dismounted, took a detail of my men, dismounted them, and entered the store to make the arrest, and I placed men in front and on the sides of the store and watched the rear to prevent escape. Big Tree was behind the counter giving out goods. The store was built on a slope, the front end near the ground and the rear four or five feet above. When ordered by Major Woodward to surrender, Big Tree ran down behind the counter to the rear of the store and jumped through a window, breaking the sash and glass in the operation. Behind the store was a considerable field, which the trader

10. The group on the porch of the commanding officer's quarters included Sherman and Grierson with several officers and Satanta, Satank, Lone Wolf, Kicking Bird, Stumbling Bear, and others. Again Satanta boasted of his deed. Sherman informed the Indians that Satanta, Satank, and Big Tree would have to go to Texas and stand trial in the state courts for murder. At this Satanta threw back his blanket and grasped his pistol butt. Sherman gave a command and the window shutters flew open to reveal a squad of cavalrymen with carbines trained on the Indians. Satanta subsided, but later in the conference Stumbling Bear and Lone Wolf attempted to kill Sherman, the former with a bow and arrow, the latter with a carbine. A soldier deflected Stumbling Bear's aim and the arrow missed its mark. Grierson grabbed Lone Wolf's carbine and the two went sprawling on the floor. The cavalrymen held their fire, and the second crisis passed. See sources cited in note 5 above. General Marcy's journal covers this episode, too. See extracts in J. W. Wilbarger, *Indian Depredations in Texas* (Austin, 1889), pp. 557–60.

was using for a truck patch. He started across this field on a run. I ordered
men on both sides to gallop along the fence outside the field to head him off,
but not to fire unless I ordered, and as I rode down one side of the fence with
the leading men kept calling on him to stop and surrender. Big Tree soon
saw that his escape was impossible, stopped, stood a little while, and then surrendered. He was taken to the guard house and placed with the other two
and all three were at once handcuffed and shackled. General Sherman told
the other Indians that there would be severe action taken by the Government
as punishment for their conduct, both while in Texas and in raiding their
agent and store and for their general misbehavior, and then dismissed them
to their camps.

All the officers' families had moved into their new quarters on the hill except mine and the family of [Brevet] Captain [A. S. B.] Keyes, which were
still in our log and mud-daubed huts 600 yards farther away from the new
post than the trader's store. They saw that something unusual was happening,
but knew nothing of it until all was over. General Sherman and his aide
General Marcy called on Mrs. Pratt the next day and chatted pleasantly
about the country, and General Marcy told of his visit to that region in 1852
with troops and his son-in-law General McClellan.[11] This was only a month
before our second daughter came, but there were no complaints made of discomfort of quarters, or danger. General Sherman, seeing the need, gave orders to hurry the completion of the new quarters for Captains Keyes and
Pratt. Eight years later, Mrs. Pratt and I called on the General at the War
Department, and were reminded of his visit, but this story comes in a later
chapter.

The governor of Texas made a demand on the Government for the leaders in this raid, that they might be brought before the state courts for their
murders in Texas. This was conceded by the Government, and about that
time General Mackenzie, who had been out with his regiment in the western
part of the territory, came into Fort Sill on his way back to his post at Fort
Richardson. The prisoners were turned over to him. He designated Captain
Thompson of his command to receive them, and it so happened that I was

11. A veteran of four decades of army service, Randolph B. Marcy had conducted extensive ex-
plorations of Indian Territory and Texas in the 1850s and won a wide reputation as an authority
on the American West. Pratt refers to his expedition of 1852 to the sources of the Red River, in
which Capt. George B. McClellan participated as a subordinate. As Pratt notes, McClellan married
Marcy's daughter. In 1871 Marcy was not Sherman's aide but colonel and Inspector General of the
Army with a brevet of major general for Civil War service. He was promoted to brigadier general
in 1878, retired in 1881, and died in 1887. See Marcy's *Thirty Years of Army Life on the Border*
(New York, 1866); and W. Eugene Hollon, *Beyond the Cross Timbers: The Travels of Randolph
B. Marcy, 1812–1887* (Norman, 1955).

officer of the day when they were turned over.[12] Under the orders of General Grierson, the prisoners had been carefully searched by the guard every morning to see if by any means they had got hold of any destructive implements.

They were kept in an above-ground cellar under one end of one of the men's quarters under strong guard. As they were brought out to be turned over, General Grierson and his adjutant, Major Woodward, and General Mackenzie, Captain Thompson, and myself and the interpreter were present. There were two wagons with hay in the bottom of the beds. When the Indians realized that they were to be taken away, Satanta broke down and appealed for sympathy. He knew a little English, and putting his fettered hands on General Grierson's shoulders said, "My friend! my friend! my friend!" very piteously.

Through the interpreter they were ordered to get into the wagons, and Big Tree and Satanta obeyed, but Satank was stolid and would not move. Captain Thompson ordered the wagon with the two willing Indians to drive on a little and brought up the other wagon. Then he directed four soldiers to take Satank by the hands and feet and swing him until they got him above the wagon and then let him go over and drop on the hay.

As the wagons drove off, Satank began to sing in a loud firm voice most dolefully. Mr. Jones, the interpreter, said: "He is singing his death song, and means to die, and if he has a chance will do anything possible to bring about his death, or he may kill himself." Captain Thompson said: "We will take care of him."

Our party walked over to the adjutant's office and the wagons disappeared over the hill to the flat below. Just as the departing officers were ready to mount, quite a number of shots were fired down where the wagons had gone. Satank had concealed his hands under his blanket and forced the handcuffs off, tearing the skin and flesh from the backs of his hands, and had stabbed a corporal and a private who were in the wagon with him, with a small penknife that, concealed in his breech-clout, had escaped the morning search. Both corporal and private jumped out of the wagon, the private not much harmed, but the corporal had been stabbed several times. While Satank was doing this stabbing, the mounted guard riding on either side of the wagon shot and killed him.[13]

12. 1st Lt. William A. Thompson, Fourth Cavalry. Mackenzie arrived at Fort Sill on June 4, ending the unsuccessful pursuit of the Kiowa raiders ordered by Sherman at Fort Richardson. Sherman had already departed. The transfer of Satanta, Satank, and Big Tree to Mackenzie occurred on June 8, 1871.

13. Satank's wagon was in the lead. The fatal shot was fired not by a mounted guard but by Cpl. John B. Charlton, a guard in the wagon containing Satanta and Big Tree. See Charlton's account in Carter, *On the Border with Mackenzie*, pp. 92–94. See also sources cited in note 5 above.

Satanta and Big Tree were tried in Texas and sentenced to imprisonment for life in the state penitentiary.[14] This proceeding had only a temporary effect on the Indians. After a couple of years the agent, a member of the Society of Friends, using the strong backing of his organization, always the most humanely interested in the Indian race of any of our people, appealed to the governor to release Satanta and Big Tree. It was argued that after their hard experience their release would have a salutary influence on their people. The governor finally decided to release them on parole, which provided that they would quit raiding, live at peace with the whites, and persuade their people to do the same, but they were to be returned to prison if they violated their parole.[15] The "good influences on their people" proved after a time to be a false hope. The obligations of the Government under its treaties to care for and help them forward into civilized living were not energetically carried out, and the Indians were again permitted to resort to the buffalo to escape hunger.

When the second war against these same Indians came on, beginning in the summer of 1874 and ending in the spring of 1875, Satanta and Big Tree violated their parole, went with the hostiles, and when captured were returned to prison life. Not long after their second imprisonment, Satanta being allowed to exercise on an inside porch of the third floor of the prison, threw himself over the railing to the ground and was killed.

Big Tree was afterwards released, returned to his people, and, as their civilization progressed, came under the influence of Baptist missionaries, joined the church, became an official of it, and was several times taken throughout the East, dressed in a Prince Albert suit, to illustrate the work of the church and to help raise money.

In the earlier days of this period a party of these raiding Indians had gone into Texas, killed a frontier farmer, made his wife and three children cap-

14. Satanta and Big Tree were sentenced by the state court in Jacksboro to hang, but the Quakers induced the Reconstruction governor of Texas, Edmund J. Davis, to commute the sentence to life imprisonment. The trial marked a stiffening of the Peace Policy, but, although the Kiowas reduced their raiding activities somewhat, another war was required to solve the problem for all time. See C. C. Rister, "The Significance of the Jacksboro Indian Affair of 1871," *Southwestern Historical Quarterly*, 29 (1926), 181–200.

15. In the summer of 1872 the Indian Bureau decided to send a delegation of Kiowas and Comanches to Washington to be impressed with the might of the white man. Ten Bears of the Comanches and Lone Wolf and Stumbling Bear of the Kiowas, with a number of lesser chiefs, made the trip. Conferring with the chiefs, the Commissioner of Indian Affairs promised that, if the Kiowas and Comanches behaved, Satanta and Big Tree would be released on March 1, 1873. The Commissioner had no authority to make such a promise, for the two prisoners were held by the state of Texas, not the United States Government. The combined pressures of the Government and the Quakers, however, overcame Governor Davis' reluctance, and after several delays he finally paroled the two chiefs, who were restored to their people in October 1873. Nye, *Carbine and Lance*, pp. 158–60, 168–75.

tives, and also captured two other children, and brought them to their camp. In negotiations between the Indian agent and the Indians, the Indians demanded a ransom for each captive, amounting to a hundred dollars apiece, which government officials agreed to give, and the captives were brought in, paid for, and returned to their people. The renewal of this vacillating policy was continuing to say to the Indians, "Do it again. It pays."[16]

Early in 1872, Captain Walsh's company, to which I was attached, and one other of the Tenth Cavalry were transferred to Camp Supply, which was on the Canadian River near the northwestern boundary and within the Cheyenne and Arapahoe reservation.[17] They had one of the ablest and most judicious and fearless agents ever in the Indian Service, John D. Miles, an orthodox Friend.[18]

Camp Supply being on the Indian reservation, our army duties were to protect the reservations from invasion and the debasing border influences, and we had no active campaign against the Indians during our service there. One of the most desperate experiences of my military service was in February 1873. "Northers" are one of the persecutions of that region, when the temperature drops well below zero and continues days at a time with such intensity that the great problem is how to keep warm. We had heard that whisky was being introduced among the Indians, although by whom we did not know; the Indians seldom came to our post.[19] The thermometer had fallen to fourteen degrees below zero, when Agent Miles came to the post and was closeted with General Davidson, the commanding officer. The com-

16. This happened in the summer of 1870. White Horse, one of the most noted Kiowa raiders, murdered Gottleib Koozer and brought back Mrs. Koozer and her six children as captives. On August 7, 1870, in a stormy conference with Agent Tatum and Colonel Grierson (both yet to lose faith in the Peace Policy), the Kiowa chiefs demanded to exchange the Koozers and the mules stolen from the Fort Sill corral (note 2, above) for arms and ammunition. Tatum promptly shut off ration issues in an effort to compel the surrender of the captives and mules. The war of nerves lasted nearly two weeks and ended in compromise. The Indians gave up the mules, received $100 each for the Koozers, and had their rations restored. Ibid., pp. 112, 115–17.

17. Camp Supply had been established as a temporary post in 1868 to serve as base of operations for Custer's column in the Washita campaign. During the early 70s most of the Cheyennes and Arapahos continued to reside in the western reaches of the reservation rather than near their agency at Darlington, and the army maintained a garrison at Camp Supply to keep watch on them. In the Red River War of 1874–75 the post was the supply depot for the column of Col. Nelson A. Miles. See Morrison, *Military Posts and Camps in Oklahoma,* pp. 137–42.

18. John D. Miles became Cheyenne and Arapaho agent in May 1872 upon the death of Brinton Darlington and served until 1884. His long and successful tenure justifies Pratt's evaluation of him. See Flora Warren Seymour, *Indian Agents of the Old Frontier* (New York and London, 1941), chap. 13.

19. The influx of whisky peddlers from Kansas and later from New Mexico was a chronic and serious problem. The Indians traded buffalo robes, their principal medium of exchange, for whisky and were thus kept in a nearly continuous state of poverty and debauchery. Some of these traders were apprehended, but the volume of trade was not materially reduced and was an important cause of Cheyenne hostility in the Red River War of 1874–75. Berthrong, *Southern Cheyennes,* pp. 372–75.

manding officer then sent for me and directed that I take a detail of twenty
men of my company and execute the agent's orders. The agent informed me
that there were five whisky ranches south of the Kansas line along the northern border of the reservation, established by white men, and that he desired
to have them broken up, the men connected with them arrested, their property taken in charge, and all brought in to Camp Supply. That he would send
one of his employees and Indian guides to take me to the several ranches and
the employee would in each case, as provided by the regulations, direct me
to take possession of all property and arrest the whisky dealers. He had selected a Norther as the best time to carry out this purpose because his quarry
would most likely be at home. We had two wagons to carry our forage and
camp equipment and haul the stuff captured, and an ambulance for any dis-
abling emergencies. The agent's employee was an elderly man of the Friends'
Society [J. J. Hoag]. Putting my men from Troop D, Tenth Cavalry (Negroes), in double underwear and buffalo-lined overshoes and giving them
the best protection possible, and myself increasing my underwear by a cham-
ois skin suit over my underwear, and the best protector outer garment I had,
buffalo overshoes, beaver cap with ear flaps, and longwristed beaver gloves,
we left the post riding in the face of a Norther.

The first day we reached Cimarron River, thirty-two miles away, and made
that our camp from which to radiate. The wind was so strong and the cold
so intense that it was a close shave to get our tents erected to withstand the
storm. We had camp stoves and wood in our wagons. During the night the
top joint of the stove pipe from the tent in which the agency official and I
slept blew off and was carried away in the darkness by the wind. Noting the
loss, I went out in the dark in search of it for some distance but failed to find
it, and had great difficulty in getting back to my tent. The next three days
were spent in going to the several dugout whisky ranches, capturing and
bringing in their proprietors and their plunder, taking a wagon along in each
case. There was little abatement of the cold during the whole five days we
were out.

We captured fifteen white men and their stocks-in-trade, consisting of barrels, kegs and bottles of whisky, guns, pistols, ammunition, canned food,
sugar, coffee, etc. These they exchanged with the Indians for horses, mules,
ponies, and buffalo robes. Of animals they had quite a number and their
buffalo robes and stocks of goods overloaded the wagons.

When we were ready to return to Camp Supply, the wind had turned and
was coming back from the south, but was scarcely less cold than before. The
drifting of the snow was also changed to come in our faces. Where there were
gulleys, they were filled up to the level. Several of the soldiers were frozen
and needed special care. The prisoners were better off than the men, for they

had been kept in a hut behind the embankment of the abandoned earthworks fort, which was protection from the wind and more stable than our tents. It was perilous to have the whisky under care; and as it was necessary to get rid of some of the plunder to relieve the overloaded wagons, with the approval of Agent Miles' representative the whisky was emptied on the ground and the containers destroyed. The morning of the fifth day, when we started to return to Camp Supply, I realized that we were in greatest danger unless the whole party could reach Camp Supply that night. When the mules warmed up and were anxious to go home the teamsters grew confident that they could make the thirty-two miles over the open plains without stopping.

Among the arms which the whisky dealers had to sell to the Indians were large self-acting Colt revolvers, the first I had seen, and a quantity of ammunition. I had placed two of these loaded in my holsters and strung one on my belt. I placed the captured animals in front, directed the fifteen prisoners to drive them and keep the road, which some of them knew well, and go straight for Camp Supply. I selected one of the best men still able for that duty, a corporal, to go with me and drive that part of the outfit and directed the sergeant to take the other men still able for duty, lead the horses of the disabled men, stay with the wagons, and be sure to bring all in to Camp Supply that night. Our road was over a treeless and comparatively level plain. Camp Supply was on the south side of the North Fork of the Canadian River not far from the crossing. We drove the prisoners in front of us and, without stopping for any purpose, reached Camp Supply after dark, turned the prisoners over to the post guard and the animals into the quartermaster corral, and I reported to the commanding officer. An hour afterwards, the wagons arrived, but thirteen of the twenty men had to go into the hospital on account of being frozen.

Mrs. Pratt had heard of my arrival and had a good fire in the fireplace and the lounge drawn up in front of it. My hands and feet were numb and were vigorously rubbed and hot brandy toddies administered by her until there was reaction and relief.

Among the prisoners was a notorious bad man of the frontier, guilty of several murders in shooting scrapes in the gambling and whisky dens then common in every frontier town. He was then under indictment for murder before the courts of Kansas. He had the best mount and General Davidson was kind enough to arrange that I become owner of that remarkable horse. His gun was taken by Agent Miles and kept by him many years as a souvenir.

The finale of these arrests was that weeks later these prisoners were sent to Topeka, Kansas, for trial before the United States court. In company with another officer and a representative of Agent Miles we gathered up a party of Indians to go along and testify. Lieutenant ——— with a detail of men from

Troop D had charge of the prisoners. He was the son of a well-known Navy officer, and one of the prisoners was the son of another Navy officer. Another of the prisoners was a brother of a then United States senator. During the night we camped on the Cimarron, the navy prisoner and the prisoner whose horse was given to me escaped safely, though the guard fired at close range.

There were three army ambulances full of the witnesses, chiefs, and leading Indians, several having their wives who were also witnesses. The ambulances had seats along the sides. I rode in one with eight Indians, including my old friends Powder Face and his wife of the Arapahoes. Power Face was a big finely built man and his wife a small, handsome, industrious happy woman, very proud of her husband. On the long ride to the railroad I had good chance through their sign language to enlarge my knowledge of the Indian as he is. Powder Face was humming some Indian ditty and I urged him to sing up loud as he had a fine voice, but he declined. I continued to urge, and finally he replied that if I would sing first he would follow. I agreed and sang an old song of my early days. Powder Face then said he could not sing well without their tomtom or other accompaniment, but if I would wait until we got to Topeka and provide piano accompaniment and an audience of white people he would keep his promise, and there it rested.

We took the Indians to the foremost hotel in Topeka and they had rooms on the top floor. The legislature was in session and many members and their wives were stopping there, among them the Speaker and Mrs. Speaker, an accomplished musician. Seeing her entertaining a party of ladies with a recital in the ladies' parlor, I went in and told them of my experience with Powder Face on the way, and suggested I would bring him down and if Mrs. Speaker would undertake the accompaniment we might get a good Indian song, which was agreed to. I found Powder Face and his wife in a large room with two beds and another couple, "Wacht," the wife, sitting on the floor making moccasins for her children. Thinking to play a joke, I caught Powder Face's eye and, without letting Wacht see, signaled to him to come out after me, and went out. He soon followed clad in a handsome buffalo robe, with beaded leggings and moccasins all of Wacht's make. He agreed to carry out his promise, went to the parlor, shook hands with the ladies with dignity, and was just seated and Mrs. Speaker beginning to thrum the piano when in came Wacht. She ran to him, pulled him to his feet, and talking earnestly pushed him to and out of the door, Powder Face laughing. The ladies wanted to know why that little Indian invaded our company and behaved that way and I told them that the little Indian was his wife, and like those of her sex of our own race was sometimes afflicted with jealousy. My mistake was in trying to play a joke on Wacht.

The next evening I took Powder Face and Wacht and made a call on a boyhood friend and Civil War comrade, Captain J. Lee Knight, then living in Topeka, whose wife and daughter were good musicians. The promised song was given and Powder Face and wife, being treated as worthy and even distinguished members of the human family, were greatly pleased with the white man's home and hospitality and concluded that if they had a chance they would have a home like that and become neighborly.

Seven years after, Powder Face and Wacht sent two of their children in the first party from their agency to the Carlisle School. Fifteen years after that I found one of these, the oldest son, then a man of family, owning and operating a threshing machine at his home in Oklahoma, having learned the money-making trick among the farmers of Bucks County, Pennsylvania, under the Carlisle Outing.

After the preliminary trial of the whisky dealers, they were bound over and held in jail for trial at the regular term of court. Several months later, after the command I belonged to had been transferred to the frontier of Texas, I was recalled to Topeka for their trial. The result was that each of the law violators received the minor punishment the law provided—ten-dollar fines and imprisonment for one month.

Frontier ethics gave the Indians whisky, and their behavior under its influence was then published broadcast as indicating their alleged savage qualities. The fact that the same whisky worked the same ruin on the white man, and that, when under its influence, the white man was constantly demonstrating no less savage qualities, did not alleviate the indictment against the Indian. At this same period in many frontier towns there was daily proof that the white man's depravities and criminality were a greater menace to civilization than the Indians they maligned.

I was one of four officers en route from Camp Supply to department headquarters at Fort Leavenworth. When we arrived at the railroad terminal, we were the guests of the leading merchant of the town and the hotel keeper at a dinner. Looking out of the window, we saw the new graveyard on a nearby hill, and many new graves, and were told by our host that there were "84 graves and 83 died with their boots on." Our hosts explained that they had been killed in gambling and drunken brawls. Such was the example of the white man's civilization then foremost in meeting and influencing our Indian wards. Two days later our party in Fort Leavenworth was shocked to read in the daily news that our hosts had quarreled and one had killed the other, making the tally of deaths by violence in that small town eighty-four.

6. Fort Griffin and the Texas Frontier, 1873–74

In the spring of 1873 our two companies were ordered from Camp Supply, Indian Territory, to Fort Griffin, Texas,[1] which was near the routes of the Kiowa, Comanche, Cheyenne, and Arapaho Indians in their raiding into that state and returning north from the border settlements south of that post. It was common routine for detachments of our cavalry and Indian scouts to be ordered out, especially at night, on reports of frontiersmen that Indians had raided the settlements south of us, stolen horses, and were making their way back to their reservations. The informers had usually followed the trail and

1. Fort Griffin was founded on the Clear Fork of the Brazos River in 1867 as a unit in the line of posts that guarded the northern frontier of Texas. For nearly a decade its garrison was chiefly occupied with the effort to catch Kiowa and Comanche raiders from the reservations north of Red River. The conquest of these tribes in 1874–75 ended the menace, and the post was abandoned in 1881. The town of Fort Griffin, in the valley below the plateau on which the post stood, grew into a wild frontier settlement. In the middle 70s professional buffalo hunters used the town as a base of operations, and it became one of the most important entrepôts of the hide trade. The ruins of the town and the fort are now contained in a Texas state park located twenty miles north of Albany. Carl C. Rister, *Fort Griffin on the Texas Frontier* (Norman, 1956).

turned aside to get help. These raids were almost as regular as the full of the moon and there was as little intermission between parties of cavalry and Indian scouts in pursuit.

On arrival at Fort Griffin, I was placed in command of the twenty-five Indian scouts and in charge of their small band of Tonkawa Indians. The Tonkawas had long been staunch friends of the white man, under a chief named Sam Houston. Before and during the Civil War they lived on the Washita River as part of the friendly affiliated tribes. In 1862 they gave information about the raiding depredations of the hostile Indians, which led those Indians to massacre more than half of the tribe. The hostiles came upon them at midnight and the 200 who got away in the darkness fled south to Fort Griffin and attached themselves to the Confederate forces then controlling the Texas frontier, and when peace came they remained. They received army rations from the military stores and furnished the post twenty-five scouts and guides. They lived close to the garrison for safety from their Indian enemies, did a little at agriculture and killed game. Their women tanned buffalo and deer hides and made beaded moccasins and curios for sale, but all suffered from poverty and a demoralizing life.[2]

Bootleggers added ruin by selling them whisky, notwithstanding the United States laws, and drunken Tonkawas were common. The commanding officer desired me to end the whisky drinking, advising that the greatest offender was the chief. He said that I might use my own methods, but if I intended to be severe, he would rather I would counsel with him first. I told him I could control the situation best by punishing the drinking Indians.

The system had been to put the drunken Indian in the guardhouse, and when he sobered up the sergeant of the guard brought the Indian to the officer in charge, who gave the drunkard a lecture and sent him to camp.

It was soon reported that the chief was drunk and in the guardhouse. I said to the sergeant: "Follow the usual course and when sober bring him to me."

Practically all the Tonkawas spoke English, having lived so many years near the fort. When the chief was brought by the guard, I said to him: "The commanding officer has ordered me to end whisky drinking among your peo-

2. Originally inhabiting central Texas, the Tonkawas were settled in 1855 on the Brazos River reservation with the Caddos, Wacos, and other small tribes. With them, they moved to the Washita River of Indian Territory when Texan hostility compelled the abandonment of the Texas reservations in 1859. The massacre of 137 of the 300 Tonkawas by Shawnees, Delawares, and Caddos on Oct. 25, 1862, was perpetrated on the pretext that the Tonkawas had allied themselves with the Confederacy, but the real cause was resentment of their cannibalistic tendencies. The survivors of the massacre gathered around Fort Griffin and, fearing to stray far from the sheltering presence of soldiers, served faithfully as army scouts until the abandonment of Fort Griffin in 1881. In 1884 the remnant of the tribe—ninety-two people—was assigned to an agency in Indian Territory. Hodge, *Handbook*, 2, 778–83. Wright, *Guide to Indian Tribes of Oklahoma*, pp. 249–51.

ple so I have made a road for you who drink and am going to make you walk in it."

The Indian replied: "That is all right, Captain, that is all right, whisky no good; me no like whisky, whisky heap bad."

I said: "Your judgment is right and this is the road. The next time you are drunk and have become sober, you will not be released from the guardhouse, but will remain there for seven days. Each day you will do what that soldier prisoner is doing out there. You will have a wheelbarrow and go around gathering up the rubbish and cleaning the parade and about the quarters as he is doing, and a soldier will be with you with loaded gun and a fixed bayonet, just as there is with that soldier, and if you do not do your work right, he will make you do it. After seven days you will be released and go back to your camp. If you get drunk again you will be in the guardhouse fourteen days and do the same thing, and after that if you get drunk again, you will be in the guardhouse twenty-eight days doing the same thing, and each time you get drunk the punishment will be doubled until you will be in the guardhouse all the time and then I know you will not get drunk. That is all, you can go back to your camp."

It was two weeks before the chief was drunk again. I was on my horse going down off the mesa on which the fort was built, passing along the road through a little woods near their camp, when I heard voices, and riding in that direction I found the chief sitting on the ground so drunk he was not able to get up, and another Indian, also drunk, was standing over him with a big rock and was swearing and threatening to kill him. Neither of them had seen me.

I slipped off my horse and, coming up behind, shoved the rock to one side and took that Indian to the guardhouse. He was also one of the principal men of the tribe.

On the way up the hill I saw the top of a bottle sticking out from under his blanket, reached down and pulled out a quart bottle half full of whisky and threw it on a rock. He stopped, looked at the spilled whisky and then at me, and I had to repeat, "Go on to the guardhouse." Taking the sergeant of the guard with a couple of men and a cart, we then hauled the chief up to the guardhouse.

The next day they had sobered up and were brought to me. I directed the sergeant to put the chief at work with a wheelbarrow and keep him at it every day for seven days and then bring him to me. I then gave the other Indian the same talk I had given the chief and dismissed him to camp. Soon after, all the old men of the tribe came to my quarters and were very indignant because their chief was being made to do such work. I told them the chief told me he wanted to do that work for seven days and I intended to oblige him; that I had told the chief if he got drunk again that was what he would have to do, and he got drunk again, which said to me that he wanted to do that kind of work, so neither they nor the chief could complain and their duty was to let him alone, go back to camp and not get drunk themselves. I said: "I shall have to treat all of you the same way. The commanding officer says your whisky drinking must end and I must obey orders."

The old men went off reluctantly and after a while quite a crowd of old women came wailing loud enough to be heard all over the post, and their spokeswoman demanded the release of their chief, and said it was wrong to make him work that way. I told them what I had said to the men and that they must stop their noise or I should have to do something about that—"this is an orderly community and we cannot have drunken people or disturbing noises around."

I told them what I had seen when I found the two Indians in the woods and that probably if I had not been there one Indian might have killed the other by dropping the big rock on him, as he threatened to do. I had been put in charge of them and ordered to end that condition among them and I should have to obey and they must also obey. I finally got rid of them, and then the chief's son, who was a sergeant of the scouts, came over and tendered thirty dollars if I would release his father. I told him that his release would only come when he finished the sentence. The sentence was finally concluded and the chief brought to me as ordered.

I then said to him: "You are the chief over these people. I am put in charge of you by the commanding officer to help you in every way I can. I cannot help you unless you Indians help yourselves. When the bootleggers come into your camp at midnight or two o'clock in the morning, if you will quietly come up and tell me they are there I will arrest them and we will ask the Government to punish them as the law provides. These bootleggers can be imprisoned for bringing whisky among you. They get your money and keep you poor and degrade you, which takes away your health and manhood. You help and we will break up the bad business." He acknowledged that I was right and promised he would help, and he did.

Not long afterwards he came to my quarters late at night and told me two white men were in his camp selling whisky to his people. I got a squad of men, went to the camp and captured the men and their stock, made the Indians give me what they had bought and threw all the bottles on the rocks, put the men in the guardhouse and reported the case to the nearest United States commissioner. The men were tried and imprisoned, as the law provided.

Thereafter I had no trouble with the Tonkawas about whisky. The chief and I worked together and became the best of friends.

The Tonkawas had no reservation allotted to them and by their hostility to the other tribes and small number were compelled to live close to the military post in constant fear of another massacre.

They were fine trailers, as we cavalrymen soon found, and in pursuit of the hostiles raiding the frontier they could take up a trail and follow it at a gallop. When the trail was dim they went in open order and formed an extended line covering the front and flanks of the command well out. If the trail was lost by one, it was caught up by another, who signaled to all. The hostile raiding parties, when returning to their reservations, usually detoured northwest so as to get into the buffalo range as quickly as possible and there their trails were obliterated by the buffalo tracks, and lost, and we were compelled to turn back.

Seldom were any of the raiding parties caught, and if they were caught it was usually the result of coming upon them accidentally. Only twice during the 1873 and 1874 service at Fort Griffin did any of our command succeed in punishing these raiders.

The commanding officer of the post went on a scout with the two troops of cavalry and half of my Tonkawa scouts. While out in the vicinity of Double Mountains, the scouts discovered a party of raiding Kiowas. They had been running away from the cavalry of a post far south of us. The cavalry had turned back, and they knew this, for they always kept watchers well in the rear. Feeling secure from pursuit, they had secluded themselves in a little valley to rest, and the Tonkawas coming upon the brink of the valley discovered their horses out grazing. The Tonkawas, unobserved, found their number and sent one back to inform the commanding officer. A charge was so quickly carried out that only one Indian and an Indian woman succeeded in getting to their horses, mounting bareback and getting away. All the others, eleven men and two women, were killed in the charge. In such a case men and women were scarcely distinguishable from each other, as all wore long hair and similar clothing. None of the charging troops were injured. They had, in addition to their own horses, about forty others they had captured. These were all brought back to Fort Griffin, and we soon learned that this party had succeeded in capturing the horses belonging to a company of Texas frontier militia in pursuit of them.

When we finally had the facts of this raid, it appeared that a party of twenty-five young Indian men and four women under the leadership of young Lone Wolf, a Kiowa, had gone well into Texas south of Fort Concho, and had captured nothing, when a command of troops from the Fourth Cavalry had surprised and killed half of them. The other half, fleeing toward their reservation, managed to throw their pursuers off their trail, and not wanting to return to camp without booty had turned east, into the settlements southeast of Fort Griffin.

When a long way southeast of Fort Griffin they were discovered by the Texas frontier guard, and Lieutenant Orleman of the Tenth Cavalry, in command of his company, being in the vicinity, was notified and joined the Texas company in pursuit. As the troops had no wagon transportation, the only food for the animals was the rich buffalo grass of that region, and this the horses must gather by grazing at night. The cavalry horses were lariated out under a guard, but the Texas company hobbled their horses and placed no guard and their horses wandered away from camp. After three days' hot chase these companies bivouacked on a creek, and during the night the Indians came back, crept around and unhobbled all the Texas horses and drove them off. The next morning the camp of the Indians was found to be only a mile above on the same creek. The cavalry followed for some distance without avail and then returned to help their Texas comrades back to their rendezvous by carrying on their horses the saddles and other impedimenta of the militia and alternating with them in riding the cavalry horses.

Young Lone Wolf was among those who were killed. His father, old Lone Wolf, one of the most noted men of the Kiowas at that time, was afterwards a prisoner of war under my care, taken from Fort Sill to St. Augustine, Florida, and held for three years.[3]

The other strike of raiding horse thieves our Fort Griffin forces made during our service there was quite a different affair. There were on the trails at times some evidence that not all the raiders were Indians. Our Tonkawa scouts would say, "Maybe so white men," and show paper cigarette stubs, tracks, etc., for their suspicions. During this period large numbers of cattle were lost as well as horses.

The sheriff of a nearby county came to the post with a small posse and asked for an officer and twenty men to help him execute his office against horse and cattle thieves he had trailed to their rendezvous well out in the buffalo region. A lieutenant and twenty men of our Troop D were sent. When the party returned, it reported finding two corrals, four miles apart, on a creek well out in the buffalo range, five white men at one and four at the other and nearly a thousand cattle, and about forty horses between them. It

3. Very soon after the restoration of Satanta and Big Tree to their people in October 1873, a Kiowa war party crossed Texas and raided into Mexico. Returning, it was camped near Kickapoo Springs, Texas, on December 9 when surprised by a troop of the Fourth Cavalry under Lt. Charles L. Hudson. Tau-ankia and Gui-tain, son and nephew respectively of the Kiowa chief Lone Wolf, and seven other warriors were slain. Lieutenant Hudson himself shot Tau-ankia with his pistol. The fight Pratt describes was the action at Double Mountain, Texas, on Feb. 5, 1874, in which Lt. Col. George P. Buell and a command from Fort Griffin intercepted the returning party and inflicted losses equalling those suffered in the engagement with Hudson. The grieving Lone Wolf went to Texas to bury his son and revenge his death. Lone Wolf later explained his hostile role in the Red River War as the result of bitterness over the death of Tau-ankia. Nye, *Carbine and Lance*, pp. 182–84. Mooney, *Kiowa Calendar*, pp. 337–38. Richardson, *Comanche Barrier*, p. 371.

was part of an organized gang regularly in the business of stealing stock and moving it north through the buffalo range to one of the Kansas railways and shipping east to market. The sheriff and his party had followed a raiding party and located their corrals without being observed. They then came back to Griffin for help and were able to capture both outfits without firing a gun, and on return reported that during the night the prisoners had tried to get away and all were shot to death. The stolen stock was driven back and restored to the owners. It developed that the sheriff's position was that stock stealing along the border was so common that it was impossible to get a clean jury against it and the best way to end it was to end the thieves when caught.

A route for the Texas and Pacific Railroad was being surveyed, and it became necessary for our post to furnish a guard for the surveyors. A captain of infantry with his company had been absent from the post some time on this duty, and, his presence at the post being needed, I was sent with a party of the Indian scouts to find him. My route was laid out so as to cover a wide circuit and going nearly a hundred miles west of the post. I had made the detour required without finding the trail of the party and, being on return to the post, concluded to take back a supply of the abundant venison and choice parts of the buffalo we could kill, the Indians being anxious for skins of both animals to tan for buckskins and robes. Having started with a wagon to haul our necessary supplies, the load was getting well lightened. We were in an exceptionally good section for deer, and during one day we killed twelve, of which I killed six.

Constantly using my field glass to survey the country, I saw a lone buck lying on the ground quite out from our line of march, near a bunch of mesquite bushes. I directed the command to halt, and taking one of the scouts made a detour so as to get near on the side from which I would be facing the wind so that the buck could not get scent of my approach. Dismounting and using small mesquite bushes to conceal my approach, I came within long range when the buck discovered me, rose, looked my way a little while, shook his horns threateningly, and then as he stood perfectly still facing me I gave him a shot, firing at his head, and he dropped instantly. Reloading, I ran to him fearing he might get up and run away, and when close to him discovered seven or eight does behind some bushes near him. From behind the bushes I dropped two of these when my Indians came galloping down upon them, and the deer seeing them and being fired at from a different direction, they ran away. The Indians had killed two more. From the behavior of the herd, had the Indians kept away, I think I might have killed all of them.

That night we went into camp in a beautiful little basin, well below the general level of the country, carpeted with rich buffalo grass, and having evergreen trees. When we first moved in, there were thousands of blue birds evidently making it their winter home, or possibly come together in some great convention. They were so numerous that when they flew from tree to tree they changed the color from green to blue. As we had some difficulty in making our way down to the bottom of this delightful spot, I concluded that it must be the beginning of broken country in front which might be an impediment to our travel. Thinking I might still find the trail of the surveyors, before unsaddling I took two Indians and went forward several miles to explore and look further for the trail we were seeking. Returning, and when not far from camp, we started a large doe and two nearly grown young ones. They kept moving ahead of us. Several times I got off my horse to shoot but they would immediately run out of range, so I mounted and followed. When they reached the edge of the basin they went down into it, but discovering our camp they went off at a right angle, stopped on the side hill near the top, and looked back at us and at the camp. I dismounted and concluded to venture a long shot at the doe. She dropped where she stood. The two young ones remained. I fired again and missed but the second shot killed one of these. The other one then mounted to the skyline just above the place where the other two lay and stood still to look back. I fired a shot and missed, but the deer remained. A second shot killed that one also, making six in one day. This was my greatest experience in killing deer. As this was in December and the nights cold and sometimes frosty, we hung all the venison hams they could carry to the bows of the wagon and fixed all the other meat where it would absorb the cold at night, removing the wagon cover to give free access to the air, replacing the cover during the day. The result of this trip was a wagon load of choice parts of the meat of buffalo, including the tongues, and much venison; so that on returning to the garrison all of the officers' families and the attachés received substantial supplies to their larders, and the Tonkawas had a prolonged feast.

On returning from a long chase after a party of raiding Indians, having pursued them north to near the Red River, across which they were in their "City of Refuge," I came upon the Clear Fork, a branch of the north fork of the Brazos River, which joined the main stream just above our post. There was no running water in the branch at this time but instead frequent and deep lakelets, some of them quite large. The water was unusually clear and in some places great leaves of water plants floated on the surface. As we rode by these, I saw beautiful large bass that were not at all disturbed, but rather showed curiosity by our passing. We camped beside one of these lakelets and, taking the quart cup which I carried tied to my saddle and which I used to make tea, and a minnow hook and line of thread and the bass line I always carried on these expeditions, and taking some of our wild meat for bait, walked downstream to a small lakelet where there were no bass but beautiful silver minnows with red fins. I soon had as many minnows as the cup could take care of, using my handkerchief for a cover. On the way, returning to the lakelet where we were camped, I found a crooked stiff limb about five feet long that had come down with the flood, tied my bass line to that, and from the bank about four feet above the water I threw out my line with a minnow on it. Immediately a large bass seized it and I flopped him over on the bank. I continued this process until I had captured nine, some of them weighing up to five pounds. This gave my twenty colored soldiers and dozen Indian scouts a much-relished fish dinner.

When I reached Fort Griffin and told the officers about this experience, there was immediate desire to make up a fishing party. Taking Captain [Philip L.] Lee's noted colored cook and a spring wagon to carry our camping impedimenta, six of us went the twenty-five miles to where I had caught the bass. This time I had taken my rod and reel and was ready for finer sport. As we went up the stream I noted a large lakelet and concluded I would go back to that for my evening's fishing. Having then a minnow bucket, I caught a nice lot and then went to this place. On one side there was a low bank but a little above the water. On the other side there was a rock cliff twenty-five or thirty feet high extending almost the full length of the water, and at the upper end there were blackberry bushes between the rock wall and water, and the deep water was next to the wall. Not being able to cast over to the deep water near the rock wall, I went around to get near the water through the blackberry bushes. Taking my minnow bucket and pole, I forced my way through the prickly bushes, but found it difficult carrying both pole and bucket, so left the bucket hanging on a bush, first putting a few minnows in my coat pocket. I got well scratched but broke my way through to near the water. Just in front of me my pole's length and about two feet under water, a large bass was facing me. All but one of my minnows had escaped while I was getting through and freeing myself from the thorns of the blackberry bushes. I put on the minnow and dropped it carefully just in front of him. As it sank near him, he moved forward and took it. I was interested in watching the operation and waited for him to turn and run away, but after working his gills he spewed out the empty hook. He stayed right there looking at me and appeared willing to have another. I said, "Confound you," and hesitated about going way back for more bait. I then thought possibly I might hook him, so I very carefully and slowly let my hook down, and when it was directly in front of him he opened his mouth and took it. I jerked it immediately, hooked him good, and after a long fight in which he ran far and tried my pole and slender line, I finally captured him. When I had him in hand, I looked him in the face and said, "What do you think of yourself now? You fooled me, I admit, but I have fooled you to more purpose." I went back for my bucket, and caught others, the rest of the party also having fine sport. When we returned to camp for supper, it was found that the illustrious cook of Captain Lee had brought along everything necessary to his profession except the utensils to cook with—no frying pan, no coffee pot, no camp kettle. We looked around and found a thin flat stone of proper dimensions, and fixing this up so as to build a fire beneath, heated it hot enough to cook our fish, and used my minnow bucket for making coffee.

The fish had never been disturbed, and apparently were just as curious as the deer to see this new creature, man, just beginning to invade their solitude. These interesting experiences were some of the recompense coming to our frontier army for its isolation. The abundance of buffalo and other game had made it unnecessary for the Indians to include fish in their diet, and the vast area and comparatively small number of nomads left many game regions unfrequented.

Back in 1869, and previous, the vast herds of buffalo numbered millions. In February of that year I was conducting recruits from Fort Leavenworth to Fort Dodge and Camp Supply, marching up the Arkansas River, and on a plateau high above the water we came to a long and wide valley, thirty to forty feet below, extending eight or ten miles on both sides of the river. In this valley were vast herds of buffalo. As we stopped to look at the wonderful sight, we made an estimate of the number we could see, and the consensus was that at least 75,000 were in sight.

About that time General John Pope came to command the Department of the Missouri, and Fort Dodge, in his command, was out among the buffalo and commanded by Colonel Dodge, a former chum at West Point.[4] General Pope wrote Colonel Dodge to send him twelve dozen buffalo tongues. Colonel Dodge detailed a sergeant and a squad of good shots, gave them a wagon, and in three days they came back with more than ordered.

Several years after this the general destruction of the buffalo was ordered as a military measure because it was plain that the Indians could not be controlled on their reservations as long as their greatest resource, the buffalo, were so plentiful.[5] Cross-continent railroads were completed, and eastern in-

4. Best known for his spectacular defeat at the Second Battle of Bull Run in 1862, Maj. Gen. John Pope became commander of the Department of the Missouri in 1870 and held the post until his retirement in 1886. Bvt. Col. Richard I. Dodge, major of the Third Infantry, was later aide-de-camp to General Sherman and author of *Our Wild Indians* and *The Plains of the Great West*.

5. Although no order is known to have been issued for the destruction of the buffalo, none was necessary. The demand for hides in the East, the advent of high-power long-range rifles, and the advance of the railroads into the buffalo country brought about the result more effectively than any military order. Nevertheless, many policy makers regarded the extinction of the buffalo as the key to the Indian problem. Thus General Sheridan: "These men [buffalo hunters] have done more in the last two years . . . to settle the vexed Indian question than the entire regular army has done in the last thirty years. They are destroying the Indian's commissary." Quoted in Mari Sandoz, *The Buffalo*

terests sought the meat, hides, hair, and bones for commerce. Scores of frontier settlers went out and made great gain from the slaughter of this greatest and then most plentiful of our American beasts. This the Indians resented and fatal collisions between them and the white buffalo hunters occurred. In a few years the buffalo were gone and the Indians driven onto the reservations they had accepted through treaty agreements.

Hunters (New York, 1954), p. 173. For another example, see statement of Secretary of the Interior Columbus Delano in his annual report for 1872, p. 7. See also Carl C. Rister, "The Significance of the Destruction of the Buffalo in the Southwest," *Southwestern Historical Quarterly, 33* (1929), 34–50.

7. The Red River War, 1874

In the summer of 1874, Indian raiding into Texas had grown so much worse and the civil control of the Indians had become so ineffectual that strong army measures to cure the situation were again imperative. General Sheridan, who had command of the troops in the Indian country east of the Rocky Mountains, asked President Grant to permit him to end these conditions, and was directed to proceed.

All the tribes committing hostilities were notified that individual Indians friendly to the United States must come in close to their agencies and the warriors answer to a daily roll call by an army officer. These, except for the roll calls, were to be under the agent's control. If on investigation any of these were found to have recently engaged in marauding and murder, they were to be arrested and imprisoned under military care and held for trial. Indians whether on or off their reservations who failed to comply with this requirement by a certain date would be considered hostile to the United States and be taken care of by the military.[1] About half of each tribe of the Kiowas, Co-

1. Angered by the death of about thirty warriors in the Texas raids of the winter of 1873–74 and further incensed by the rapid destruction of the buffalo and the scanty rations issued at the Fort Sill

manches, Cheyennes, and Arapahoes remained hostile. Six columns of troops, each of sufficient strength to combat any hostile tribal groups the Indians could assemble, were kept constantly moving during the fall, winter, and spring of 1874–75 throughout the vast plains region in western Texas and the Indian Territory—now Oklahoma—in which these hostiles sought refuge.[2] These commands were directed to pursue, attack, and compel their surrender, when they were to be deprived of their horses and arms and held by the army as prisoners of war until their cases were determined. Investigation by the army was then to be taken up, and every Indian who had participated in any of the outrages along the frontier during a number of years previous was to be placed in irons in close confinement. Charges based on testimony, either Indian or white, or both, were to be filed, with the purpose that when order was restored the major offenders would be tried by military commission.

To become a part of one of the organizations to carry out these purposes, the two companies of the Tenth Cavalry at Fort Griffin were ordered to Fort Sill, but the Tonkawa scouts were left at Fort Griffin to become part of another command in the same field service. When we reached Fort Sill after several days' marching and were going into camp near the fort in the late afternoon, we discovered the large force of Fort Sill cavalry coming south from the Washita, where it had gone to quell Kiowa Indians who had raided

---

agency, the Kiowas and Comanches were in a black mood when spring opened. The Comanche medicine man Isa-tai inflamed the tribes with war talk and promises of supernatural aid. Inspired by his preaching, a large force of Kiowa and Comanche warriors, joined by disaffected Cheyennes and Arapahos, about 250 in all, attacked the camp of a party of professional buffalo hunters at Adobe Walls, in the Texas Panhandle, on June 27, 1874. The young mixed-blood Comanche chief Quanah Parker took the most prominent part in the fight, but Mow-way, Isa-tai, and Wild Horse of the Comanches and Satanta, Lone Wolf, and White Horse of the Kiowas were there, too. The buffalo hunters drove off their assailants, and Isa-tai's influence collapsed. Then in July a war party went to Texas to revenge the death of Lone Wolf's son, and at Lost Valley near the site of the Warren wagon train massacre of 1871 they fought a battle with Texas Rangers. Depredations also occurred in the neighborhood of Fort Sill. With the backing of President Grant, Generals Sherman and Sheridan won a modification of the Peace Policy. Over Quaker objections, the Interior Department granted the War Department permission to attack hostile Indians on the reservation. On July 26 the order described by Pratt turning Indian management over to the Army arrived at Fort Sill, and action was promptly taken to separate the friendly from the hostile Indians. Nye, *Carbine and Lance*, pp. 187–206. Richardson, *Comanche Barrier*, pp. 371–88.

2. Sheridan's strategy was to pierce the area of operations with military columns converging from several directions. This was intended to keep the Indians so busy avoiding soldiers that they would have no time to hunt game and so exhausted and insecure that surrender would soon become preferable to fugitive life. Five independent columns were to converge on the Staked Plains—Col. Ranald S. Mackenzie, based on Fort Concho, from the south; Lt. Col. George P. Buell, based on Fort Griffin, from the southeast; Lt. Col. John W. Davidson, based on Fort Sill, from the east; Col. Nelson A. Miles, based on Camp Supply, from the north; and Maj. William R. Price, based on Fort Bascom, from the west. Because of the summer drouth, which had parched the grass necessary for forage, the columns did not converge until September, when the rains set in. Nye, *Carbine and Lance*, chaps. 10–12, gives the most reliable and complete account of the war.

the friendly tribes and their agency and killed several white employees. Caught in these acts, they were charged by the cavalry and sent scurrying west to their camps, but without material loss.[3]

The commanding officer of our two companies mounted his horse and galloped over to report our arrival. Soon after, he came galloping back and said: "Pratt, General Davidson wants you at once." I had unsaddled, but immediately resaddled and reported as the head of the column was marching into Fort Sill. The General said: "I have authority to enlist twenty-five friendly Indians as scouts and guides for the campaign. Captain —— of the infantry has been trying to get them, but as the Indians do not know him and he does not know the Indians, he has failed. I want you to relieve him and enlist that number as quickly as possible."

Next day I went forty miles to the affiliated bands along the Washita, among whom were my former Arbuckle and Fort Sill scouts of four to seven years previous, and then to the friendly portion of the Kiowas, Comanches, and Apaches at Fort Sill. In three days the number desired was enlisted, and the proportions from each tribe were about equally divided between the affiliated bands and the Kiowas, Comanches, and Apaches. Those from the latter tribes had friends among the hostiles.

Ten white frontiersmen, several of whom were noted as scouts, had been employed and became part of my command. Having secured a wagon and loaded it with forage, rations, tents, etc., we became part of the command which moved at once northwest to the Washita.[4] The duties of the scouts were to be the eyes of the command by covering our front, each flank, and also to watch the rear. Any trails of Indians or evidence of their whereabouts were to be reported quickly.

Phil McCusker, the interpreter, who was a most capable Comanche linguist, the court language of the southwest tribes, who was also proficient in the sign language then in common use among these Indians intertribally, became my faithful and ever-present intermediary.

When we were well west of the Wichita Mountains, we found a branch of

3. This was the Anadarko affair, Aug. 22 and 23, 1874. Colonel Davidson with four troops of the Tenth Cavalry had been called to the Wichita agency by the commander of the infantry company that guarded it. Red Food's Noconee Comanches and Lone Wolf's Kiowas were there behaving in a threatening manner. Davidson's appearance triggered an inconclusive and mostly long-range skirmish that lasted two days. Casualties were one Indian and five civilians killed and two soldiers wounded; much Indian impedimenta was also destroyed. The action had one important effect. Lone Wolf's Kiowas, including Satanta and Big Tree, who had managed to get themselves enrolled as friendlies, appeared in their true colors and thereafter were arrayed with the hostiles where they properly belonged.

4. Davidson's Fort Sill column consisted of six troops of the Tenth Cavalry, three companies of the Eleventh Infantry, two howitzers, and Pratt's scouts—more than 400 men. The command marched out of Fort Sill on Sept. 10, 1874.

the Washita leading to the northwest, which was not noted on the maps. The commanding officer took the main branch and directed that the scouts proceed for a day's march up the unmapped branch to look for hostiles and also to make an itinerary of its direction and any feeder streams, then to turn southwest and rejoin the command.

Keeping lookouts well to the front and on the flanks, we proceeded up this branch, camping that night in a deep narrow valley along the stream, posting Indian pickets along the edge of the high ground on both sides of the valley. The next day, having gone as far as instructed, we turned south by west to rejoin the command, and soon were among thousands of fine fat buffalo which was an opportunity for fresh meat the scouts asked to utilize. The command was halted, several of the best buffalo killed, and the Indians loaded their ponies.

We had not proceeded far on our way after this, the interpreter and I riding at the head, when the whole mass of Indians started pell-mell to the rear. Not knowing what the matter was, I followed with the interpreter and found our scouts surrounding a small Indian mounted on a weary pony. The scouts were threatening with their guns, talking loud, disputing and discussing, and when quiet was restored the interpreter found that the little Indian was a hostile Cheyenne and the dispute among the scouts was to determine which of two scouts from different tribes had the honor of touching him first. Touching the prisoner with gun, bow or arrow, or any other way, constituted him the prisoner of that person, who had all rights to kill and scalp or do otherwise as he pleased. Quieting them, the interpreter was instructed to tell them that the commander of the party ought to have the prisoner, at least for a time; that it was important that we get information from him if possible, and that we must turn him over to the commanding officer. The commanding officer, however, would be told about these two men disputing as to who had captured him and that either the commanding officer or the whole body of scouts would themselves settle that matter. The other Indians all said that was right and the two contestants desisted.

I ordered the prisoner to ride between McCusker and me. He was about as badly scared as could be and anxiously urged by signs that he be allowed to ride behind one of us. He was very reticent at first, but later answered my questions as we marched along.

Late in the day we found the command. The prisoner was turned over to the commanding officer, and leading men of the scouts were permitted to remain near while the commanding officer, through the interpreter, gained information from him. The Indian then talked freely and quite as proficiently in the sign language as the interpreter. The story he gave was that he was with a party of his tribe who had made a raid up north into Kansas. They came upon a family traveling west, killed the father and mother and a grown son, and took three girls prisoners. Returning to their own camps, which had been changed, they had sent out several of the party to find them. The prisoner was one of those, and finding the tracks of the ponies of the scouts, he had concluded that he was on the trail of his own people. When he found where we had killed buffalo, his conclusions were apparently verified, so that he rode rapidly and was near the rear of the command before he discovered his mistake and then tried to escape, but his pony was worn out and the scouts easily caught him.

It turned out that the family killed was named Germaine. Through Indian emissaries we carried on negotiations with the Indians to recover the three girls. General Miles, commanding another column, also engaged in this, and it was through his Cheyenne scouts that the three girls were finally recovered.[5]

Not finding this Cheyenne camp or other hostiles after six weeks, we turned toward Fort Sill to get new supplies, and the commanding officer ordered a two-week rest. The scouts from the Washita concluded that in the capture of the little Cheyenne they had been successful and wanted to have a dance in their camps. General J. H. O'Bierne, a volunteer officer in the Civil War, from New York, was the head of the *New York Herald's* Washington Bureau. He had been sent out by the *Herald* to keep the public informed of the progress of the Indian campaign and was with the headquarters of our command. When he heard that the Indians were going to have a dance at their camps, he wanted to see it. The commanding officer authorized the Indians from along the Washita to separate from the command and go directly to their homes two days before we reached Fort Sill, and directed me to take General O'Bierne, go with them, and introduce him to the principal chief at their camp.

When we reached their camp, immediately there was preparation for a dance, many Indians coming from other camps until there was a large number. When the dance began, the children led. A pole was set up in the center, and the children danced around this to the beating of tom-toms and singing, in which all the Indians joined. The tom-tom kettle drummers kept good

5. The Germaines were moving from Missouri to Colorado when a Cheyenne raiding party intercepted them on the Smoky Hill River in Kansas. Five daughters were taken, but the eldest was subsequently slain, leaving the other four, aged fifteen, thirteen, nine, and seven, as captives. When part of Colonel Miles' command attacked the Cheyenne camp of Gray Beard on McClellan Creek in November 1874, two of the girls were liberated. The other two were later discovered to be with Stone Calf's band on the western edge of the Staked Plains. An ultimatum from Miles in January 1875 produced the freedom of the sisters and the surrender of the band. Miles himself adopted the four girls. Nelson A. Miles, *Personal Recollections* (Chicago, 1896), pp. 159–60, 174–79, and passim. Berthrong, *Southern Cheyennes*, pp. 395, 400–01.

time, and there were strong-voiced leaders of the singing. Interest and enthusiasm increased, and soon the women joined in the dancing, then some of the
younger men, until a large number were dancing. While we were looking on,
one of the sergeants of my Indian scouts, who had been missing when we arrived, recklessly galloped into camp swinging his gun. He was drunk, and
rode among the dancers and drove them from the dance ground. It was a
question with me for a moment whether I or the principal chief, Buffalo
Good, was in authority.[6] I told General O'Bierne that we had better let the
chief settle the case, as it was in his bailiwick. The General thought I ought
to take care of him, as he was one of my sergeants.

I went to him, took his horse by the bridle, and demanded his gun. He
handed it to me. I ordered him to get off his horse and he complied. The chief
then came up and said something to him, and the Indians all laughed and
the drunken Indian looked foolish. After a while I found an Indian who
could speak a little English and asked him what the chief had said, and he
said that the chief had asked him where he put away his dead [head?]. I gave
his horse and gun into the possession of the chief and told him to do what he
thought best, and he sent him to his tepee and the dance went on.

Having established General O'Bierne on good footing with the chief and
Indians and having much work to do in completing the scout enlistment papers, writing the report of our portion of the campaign and also getting ready
to start out again, I left the General in the camp and returned alone to
Fort Sill, going ten miles up the Washita to see the Quaker agent for the
affiliated and friendly tribes from whom my scouts came, and then thirty-five
more miles across country to Fort Sill. This distance was something of a ride
for one day on a tired horse at the end of a six-week campaign. However, I
had the famous horse, equal to almost anything a horse could do, given to me
by General Davidson, who had been the commanding officer at Camp Supply
when I had captured the horse and its owner in the whisky crowd eighteen
months previously.

I rode to the commanding officer's quarters to report, and General Davidson came out and said: "General Sheridan is here. He has just arrived and
we have got to start out again day after tomorrow. He wants to see you at
once." I had met General Sheridan before while serving in the Army of the
Cumberland during the Civil War in Tennessee and Georgia and again in
the Indian campaign of 1868 and 1869.

As I went in, he immediately asked, "Where are your Indians?" I said:

6. Buffalo Good was chief of the Waco band of the Wichitas. This group had originally lived in
Texas and, with the affiliated tribes, had settled on the Washita River following the abandonment
of the Texas reservations in 1859.

"The most of them are along the Washita, forty miles from here." He said: "I want them all here tomorrow night." I replied: "I have but one horse which I have been riding for six weeks and have ridden forty-five miles today." "I will fix that," he said. "You can have any horse in the command. I will dismount Davidson or any other officer. Select the horse you want and I will see that you have it, but I want those Indians here. Can't you get them here by tomorrow noon?" "I can try," I replied. He said: "You had better take one of your best white scouts and as soon as you get something to eat go back to the Indian camp tonight, and have the scouts start at once for Sill, and you may enlist fifty more, making your Indian scouts seventy-five."

I went to the white scouts, selected [Jack] Kilmartin, one of the best mounted, and as he had been out and his horse was also tired and we had hundreds of captured Indian ponies in the quartermaster's corral, we concluded to select our mounts from them, gallop to the Washita, and then trade our captured ponies for fresh ponies with Chief Buffalo Good, who had many horses, and this would give us fresh horses both ways.

We started before dark, taking a compass course across country. As night came on and the stars came out, we fixed on the north star as our guide, keeping a little to the right of it as being the direct line, and rode as rapidly as we could in the dark until about two o'clock in the morning, when we came to the Washita and a Caddo camp on the south side. We wanted to reach the principal camp, where I had left O'Bierne the morning before, which was three miles farther and on the north side of the river. I told the Caddoes the order to take the field at once and one of the scouts piloted us to a fording place, and we reached Buffalo Good about three o'clock in the morning. He gave couriers and I sent them at once to all the widely scattered camps, one of them twenty miles distant, ordering the scouts to go direct and be at Fort Sill by noon, and to tell the Indians we wanted fifty more scouts.

Buffalo Good gave us a play tepee of his children, barely wide enough for our length to lie down, and his wife brought buffalo robes for a good bed. We had a short sleep, got up at dawn, and Buffalo Good swapped horses and used his crier, who had a big voice which could be heard throughout the camp, to inform the Indians that fifty more scouts were needed, that the scouts and all who wanted to go must be at Fort Sill by noon. The Indians came out of their lodges and listened, a number at once answered they would go, and I knew my fifty more were assured.

The Indians soon began to leave for Sill in twos and threes. Mrs. Buffalo Good gave us coffee, meat, and bread, and we started, reaching the post about two o'clock. On every rise of ground we could look ahead and back and see Indians from all the camps hurrying to Sill. When those who wanted to go were rounded up and counted, there were over 200 new candidates ready to serve Uncle Sam against his enemies of their own race, for the pay and allowance given to scouts at that time.

I submitted the excess situation to General Sheridan and he said, "You may increase your total of Indian scouts to eighty-five." I told him: "These people have come a long way in answer to our summons and I shall have some trouble in quieting the disappointment."

"You explain to them," he replied, "that you can enlist only sixty new men —that I am glad they are ready to help, and sorry we cannot take them all, and that I want you to select the best mounted for the number required, and that I have ordered you to give each of those who must go back rations to take to their families and a plug of tobacco for themselves." I did as he said and the candidates themselves concluded who were best mounted and could render best service.

This involved the enlistment of sixty more scouts, the making out of enlistment papers for each individual, and the drawing of rations and forage and more camp equipage, and loading of wagons for our much larger company. The names of the sixty additional scouts were taken and rations and tobacco for the home-returning party issued to them. Rations for the larger command for another six-week campaign were drawn and loaded in wagons, but I was unable to finish all the work that night.

General Sheridan wanted the Indians to give a dance that evening. That was arranged by Interpreter McCusker, and most of the Indians went to the parade ground in front of the commanding officer's quarters, where they built a bonfire and danced for the entertainment of the commanding general and his staff and the officers, their families, and the men at the post. I continued at my writing down in camp.

The command had moved out at seven o'clock in the morning, but it was nine before I was ready. After getting the Indians in line mounted and instructed how to march by twos, they were told through the interpreter to sing an Indian song and very loudly as we marched by in front of the General. With two gourd rattles to keep time and in good voice the Indians responded. The people at the post and the General and his staff were all out and clapped hands. The General was most complimentary to the Indians about their appearance. Alas, that the Kodak was not universally known that forty-eight years ago.

We reached camp early; and when I reported, General Davidson said that the friendly Indians had violated the order requiring them to keep their herds east of Cache Creek and were holding thousands of their ponies on the west side and that among them in that neighborhood the cavalry had found mules branded "U. S." The summer previous, several companies of infantry had been ordered to change station from Camp Supply to a post in the north-west, and when moving from Camp Supply to the railroad they camped on high ground near the Cimarron River and put their mules out to graze under herders on the flats below camp. In broad day a few Indians came unob-served near the herd through an arroyo and, notwithstanding the shots of the herders, drove the entire herd away, and none of the mules had been re-covered. This left the command in camp until a new supply of mules came.

The General instructed that I send my Indians through these herds and have them bring in every mule with the United States brand and then compel the herders of Indian ponies to drive their herds over and keep them east of Cache Creek. These orders were carried out and the result was the recapture of about fifty government mules.

8. Campaigning on the Staked Plains

We proceeded to the Washita River and turned west on the south side. The General[1] wanting information, he crossed the river and went a few miles below to the Wichita agency with a small escort and his post wagon. The column marched up the south side of the river for a day, and, as there had been a rain above, the river kept rising rapidly until it was bank full.

We went into camp at the point designated, and the next day the General arrived on the opposite bank and, being unable to recross, bivouacked to wait until the flood passed. Taking a few Indians into the underbrush along the river, I cut long slender poles and, getting nails from cracker boxes and string from grain bags, made the frame of a boat. Taking the heavy canvas cover from one of the army wagons, we stretched it over the form and had a fair boat. Then, with several lariats tied together, we made a rope long enough to reach across, found the champion Indian swimmer, had him carry one end of the rope well up the river above the General's bivouac, swim the rushing current, and fasten that end to a tree on the other shore, and, with our end to a tree on our shore, we had a ferry rope. Placing the boat in the water and a short rope at the upper end to slip along over the ferry rope and with an Indian in the lower end of the boat to balance it, I stood in the bow and drew the boat across the river by pulling it along the ferry rope, hand over hand.

1. Lt. Col. John W. Davidson. See above, p. 1, note 1. The column left Fort Sill for the second time on Oct. 21, 1874. The operations in September 1874 had prompted some Indians to surrender and the others to retreat deeper into the Staked Plains. Colonel Mackenzie surprised the camps of Mamanti, Moway, Tabananica, and Wild Horse in Palo Duro Canyon on September 28 and, in a nearly bloodless battle, dealt a damaging blow to hostile logistics and morale.

The General, who was watching and pleased with our success, concluded that he would venture to go back with us, bringing his personal baggage. He sent back supplies of forage and rations and directed the escort to proceed up the river, camping opposite us until the water went down. In two days' march the escort crossed and joined the command.

We continued our march and met another command from New Mexico, which had come to take part in the campaign, as one of the several commands to be kept moving through that fall and winter in order to give the hostiles no rest.[2] The day previous to our joining this command, two of their companies were out in advance some twenty miles away, and came upon two camps of hostile Cheyennes. The Cheyennes attacked and almost surrounded them, and they escaped only by a narrow margin, leaving two men and several horses killed on the field near the Indian camp. Other men and horses were wounded, but were able to get away with their command. The Indians followed them several miles, keeping up a running fight.[3]

We had joined them late and the scout party was just in, reporting that the Indian camps were immense. During the night extra ammunition was issued in preparation for a long fight. Long before day next morning both commands moved to the attack. Before we reached the Indian camps, we heard the booming of cannon, which told us one of the other commands had found and attacked the Indians, and we hastened our march, the scouts well in advance. When we reached the Indian camps, we found that they had left in great haste and gone west. On the way we had found the dead horses and the stripped and mutilated bodies of the two men. These had been scalped and in each of their two camps we found a pole and on top of each pole the scalp of one of the soldiers. The ground around each pole for a considerable distance was worn to dust, showing that the Indians had had a big dance during the night around those scalps. Without our knowing of each other's proximity, General Miles with his command had found and attacked the Indians as they were leaving their camps.[4]

In their haste they had abandoned considerable quantities of their valued lodge poles, camp equipage, and a few tepees. Under orders of the commanding officer, my Indian scouts destroyed everything that might be of value

2. This was the Fort Bascom column—four troops of the Eighth Cavalry under Maj. William R. Price.

3. On Nov. 6, 1874, about a hundred warriors jumped a troop of the Eighth Cavalry under Lt. Henry J. Farnsworth and repulsed it.

4. The Battle of McClellan Creek, Texas, Nov. 8, 1874. Lt. Frank D. Baldwin of Miles' command charged Gray Beard's Cheyenne camp with infantry mounted in supply wagons. Two of the Germaine sisters were liberated here. Major Price, strengthened by two troops from Davidson's command, had been ordered by Miles to aid Baldwin but for some reason turned about and marched in the opposite direction. Davidson's men found the body of a private killed in Farnsworth's fight of November 6.

to them if they returned. Without seeing General Miles' command, we then took up the Indian trail and followed as rapidly as we could to the breaks of the Staked Plains. General Davidson, the commanding officer, then concluded that it was not necessary to take the whole command after them and selected the fifty best mounted men from each cavalry troop and fifty Indian scouts to continue the pursuit unimpeded by wagons.[5]

The Staked Plains is a high, level plateau of immense area covering the western parts of the Indian Territory, Texas, and eastern New Mexico. For a long distance across there is no running water, and it was only during the rainy season, when water gathered in shallow water holes, mostly buffalo wallows, that any water could be found, and this was usually exhausted because of the vast herds of buffalo that then frequented that region during the winter.

The fleeing Indians made a broad trail, abandoning more of their impedimenta in their flight. We followed rapidly and the first day came in sight of their rear guard. Their first direction after rising to the plain was north of west and then almost due southwest toward the Pecos River in New Mexico.

The Staked Plains at that place were so level that a railroad could have been laid without much grading. In the rainy season and for some time after, the surface was carpeted with the finest quality of rich buffalo grass, giving excellent pasture for vast buffalo herds.

As the country was without gullies and barren of trees, our Indian scouts were soon a long way in advance of the column, a dozen of them in line in wide open order across our front. Late in the day we saw mounted Indians, and then began a long chase. By hard riding the scouts closed up on them somewhat, but were never closer than 1,500 yards. There was some firing from both sides at this long range from our running horses which gave no results except to stimulate pursued and pursuers until almost exhausted.

When too dark to see the trail, we awaited the arrival of the command, then bivouacked and at dawn next day took up the trail, followed it vigorously and found more evidence of their hasty retreat, but did not again get near the Indians, although just on the horizon we could, with field glass, now and then make out the scattered figures of their rear guard.

Water grew scarcer, and at night we estimated that we had traveled in the two days between eighty and ninety miles, making a very considerable circle in our route. We had started with three days' oats for our horses, carried on our saddles, and three days' rations for ourselves. Our forage and ration conditions were getting us into serious danger. Winter had driven the buffalo and all game to more temperate regions. A Norther portended. The pursuit seemed impossible of successful result. The Indians were certainly on the

5. Colonel Davidson sent this force under Capt. Charles D. Viele and himself remained with the rest of the Fort Sill column.

way to the remote western side of this plains country. They had been in great danger and were demoralized by General Miles' attack, by the two commands coming upon them from opposite sides at nearly the same time, and by our hot pursuit. The commanding officer [Captain Viele] therefore concluded it best to return to the main command, so we turned back the following morning.

The commanding officer directed that two of the best Indian guides lead us straight back to where we came up on the plains. There were no landmarks of hills or any kind to guide. The Indians selected two of the older men, who at once quit our outgoing trail. From the front we could look back at any time and see by the long, straight line that the command was making a bee-line in the direction the scouts selected. We kept up a rapid return march that day and the next, and about noon of the third day we struck our own trail at a point about a mile from where we had started after rising from the low country to the high plateau of the Staked Plains. We were then a weary and hungry command.

We found our command in camp. The weather had turned very cold. The command was itself almost without forage or rations, and it became necessary that we have as quickly as possible the supplies from Fort Sill then en route. Fort Sill was 150 miles away. Lieutenant Orleman of the Tenth Cavalry was sent to find the supply train known to be on the way and guide it to us, while the command moved toward it. He had a small escort which was protected in the best way possible against the intense cold.

The day after he left us, the intensity of the cold increased greatly and many of the men were frozen and disabled. The army wagons, being emptied of forage and rations, were the only means to better care for the disabled men.

When we went into camp the second night after a short march, one of my scout wagons failed to arrive. The teamster came in with his team and reported that the wagon was hopelessly struck in a partly frozen and broken-up bog two or three miles back and that his weak mules, even with help from the rear guard, were unable to pull it out, and he was compelled to abandon it.

The wagon held the ammunition for the scouts and part of our campaigning necessities. General Davidson instructed me to remain behind in camp the next morning with my scouts and send two of the best mounted men back to destroy the wagon by burning it, so that the supplies and ammunition would not fall into the hands of the Indians.

Two of the white scouts were brothers, both well mounted. I sent one of these and my cook and orderly, who was a plucky colored soldier with a good horse, back to burn the wagon, instructing them if they had trouble to fire their guns and I would come to them.

The scouts gathered around the abandoned campfires and waited, and after a while we heard faint interval shots. Taking the white man's brother and two of the best mounted Indians, I instructed the Indian chief sergeant of scouts to hold the command, but if he heard a good deal of firing to bring the whole command as quickly as he could.

During the night a slight snow had fallen and soon we found tracks of twenty or thirty Indian ponies, evidently made by hostiles following the command. This was alarming, but as the shooting was only at considerable intervals, I concluded to go ahead. After we were well away from our camp the white man began to lag behind, urging that on account of the condition of our horses we could not possibly get away if the Indians should attack us. The two Indians kept along with me. Constantly using my field glasses, I discovered nothing and kept on.

Finally the white man held back a long way and then one of the Indians began to fall back. I waited for the Indian and white man to come up, still hearing an occasional shot. The white man, notwithstanding his brother's danger, repeated his contention that it was wrong for us to put ourselves in such peril. The Indian who had held back had enough English to say: "Heap Cheyenne, No good!" I said to the white man: "We must stand by our men, come along."

Soon there was an explosion of the small-arms ammunition and the firing ceased. We went on and met our two men galloping toward us. I asked the cause of the shots, and they said they had a dispute as to which was the best shot and thinking they were beyond hearing decided to set a mark and see who could beat while the wagon was burning. They did not leave the place until everything was well destroyed.

We returned to the main party and took up the line of march. The command made only about five miles that day, and in that distance we counted sixty-four horses and mules which had been abandoned because not able to go farther, and a number of wagons were also abandoned. The animals generally stood, backs to the wind, shivering, near the route. Others had laid down and in one case a mule, evidently a leader, had dropped in the road, and the teamster, unable to pull aside, had unhitched the mule, left him lying there, and made the other mules pull the empty wagon over him. The mule was still alive.

Conditions were so bad that we had to remain in that camp and await the arrival of supplies. Fortunately, Lieutenant Orleman soon came in with the train and a good supply of rations and forage. The cold increased, and we were compelled to remain in camp and wait for warmer weather.

The General wanted to send a courier to one of the commands he believed to be near a certain place about a hundred miles away, and suggested that a couple of my white scouts carry it, advising that I call for volunteers.

When I submitted it to the ten white men, they all hesitated on account of the severity of the weather and the weak condition of their horses. The Indians were less sensitive to cold and their horses hardier, and I told the General that I was sure two Indians would satisfactorily perform the service. He agreed, and I accordingly selected the Pawnee chief Esaue-Kedadeho (Big Spotted Horse). He was a tall fine specimen of a man who relished perilous service, and he selected one of his own men to go with him.

They went off in the storm and were back in four days with answer. I took them over to the General's tent, and he was greatly pleased with their promptness. The General said privately: "Pratt, if ever men needed a little something to warm them up, these men do. I have a very small quantity of excellent whisky. What do you say to my giving them each a drink?"

I said: "You are the commanding officer, and I think it is your province to determine." He concluded to give it, brought out his bottle, and offered Big Spotted Horse a drink. The chief refused and his man did the same, saying that they did not drink whisky.

Some years after that, the border settlements of Kansas having come near the Pawnee reservation, the Indians were permitted to have passes to leave the reservation and go to a nearby town to trade. Big Spotted Horse with his family went into the town one day and was deliberately shot and killed on the street by the town marshal, who alleged that Big Spotted Horse was drunk and had insulted a woman, which the Indians said, and as the campaign incident had indicated, could hardly have been true. Within a year of that time, a neighboring frontier town was raided by a masked party of four men, who entered and robbed the bank in broad daylight and were escaping by intimidating the townspeople with their firearms. Before they got out of town, one of the townsmen shot and killed one of the bandits. When they took off his mask, they found that he was the marshal of the neighboring town and the man who had killed Big Spotted Horse.[6]

Big Spotted Horse was throughout his service the most fearless and tireless of the scouts. It was his self-imposed task when he went into camp at the end of the day's march to come with one of his men, borrow my field glass, and go out in front and scour the country for miles. On returning, he would tell me what he had found in the way of trails or buffalo or old camps. Using his

6. Big Spotted Horse was a great warrior of the Pawnees and a skilled horse thief. He was shot and killed, under circumstances that Pratt relates, by City Marshal Henry Brown at Caldwell, Kansas, on May 14, 1883. The episode is reported at length in the Caldwell *Journal*, May 17, 1883, reproduced in *Kansas Historical Quarterly*, 26 (1960), 162–63; the account is probably biased against the Indian. As Pratt notes, Brown was killed by a mob a year later after attempting unsuccessfully to rob the Medicine Valley Bank at Medicine Lodge, Kansas. See press dispatches in ibid., pp. 166–73. See also Donald Danker, ed., *Man of the Plains: Recollections of Luther North, 1856–1882* (Lincoln: University of Nebraska Press, 1961), pp. 138, 158.

own interpreter, a mixed-blood boy about seventeen years old, he talked rapidly in his own language, giving his interpreter a few sentences and then, motioning toward me, would say, "Suke Spargo," which was "Say it." On returning from one of these adventures, he brought in two big American horses. They turned out to be the property of officers of a neighboring command. The horses of that command had stampeded and these two had separated and were lost from the others. Spotted Horse had the pleasure of returning the horses to their owners and receiving their warm thanks, but he would not accept a fee.

The eyesight of the Indians was remarkable. While on the march and well in advance of the command, I have gone to a rise of ground to scan the country in front with my field glasses. The Indians standing near would search also, and they sometimes called attention to objects at a great distance which I had failed to discover, which indeed I could barely make out with my field glass, but which they with only the eye were able to identify. They always were eager to use the wonderful field glass and with it could find things I could not make out using the same glass.

One afternoon near camping time, our advance Indians discovered a herd of five wild horses, not an uncommon find at that time on those southwestern plains. The country was level and the clear atmosphere gave a wide observation. The Indians asked if they might capture them. I submitted it to the General, who approved and said: "We will halt the command and let all the men see them do it."

They arranged four parties of three men each, mounted on their best horses. These parties stripped themselves and their horses of all surplus load, discarded their saddles and bridles and most of their clothing, and mounted their horses bareback, having only the lariat ropes to guide. One party was to get behind the horses and drive them across our front toward the second party; this served their purpose best because fortunately the wind was blowing so the drive would be with the wind.

Wild horses had keen scent and great sensitivity to danger, depending entirely upon their fleetness for escape. The three other parties rode to the front, each party concealing themselves by keeping their bodies low on the side of their mounts away from the wild horses. They took positions along the route the wild horses were to be driven and dismounted and hid behind their own horses. Seeing only the scouts' horses led the wild horses to come near. The second party took position nearly a mile from the first, the third over half a mile from that one, and the fourth still farther off. These preparations and the whole event were of great interest to the cavalrymen, sitting on their horses where they could best see this movie.

The wild horses were about a mile and a half away, the end of the drive being about the same distance at the other extremity. The driving party made a long detour, concealing themselves by lying close over their horses' backs, reached their position, and when behind the wild horses drove them as rapidly as possible toward the second party. As they passed the second party, that party mounted and took up the chase, and having fresh horses kept nearer and drove them toward the third party. When they approached the third party, it was plain that the wild horses were beginning to fag. The third party had less difficulty, but they forced them forward at the top of their speed toward the fourth party. The probable camping place had been designated and the command then moved forward to camp. The fourth party and those in the other parties who could keep up then drove the horses into camp. They were covered with foam and much exhausted. Without giving them a chance to recover, the Indians immediately lassoed them, ran around them with their lariats, drew their legs together, and threw and kept them struggling to further exhaust and so reduce them to obedience. The horses kicked and resisted in every way, but the Indians had them so thoroughly tied with lariats that they could not escape the torture. When they quit struggling, the Indians slapped their sides with their hands, making a loud noise and compelling them to struggle on until finally they ceased and paid no attention to what the Indians did.

When all struggles were abandoned, the Indians loosened their legs and fixed two lariats to their necks so that an Indian on each side could hold them, and compelled them to get up, each with an Indian on him bareback. Then there was more struggling, bucking, and trying to get rid of the load, and the Indians kept them lively until they quit and stubbornly stood still. Then the Indians used their quirts, which are short stubby whip handles with a couple of rawhide lashes on each, a foot and a half long; with these they compelled them to move forward, two or three Indians on each side, holding them by the two lariats around their necks, with Indians enough to prevent running away. There was plenty of kicking and jumping and splurging, but this did not rid them of the riders. Finally the horses came to understand that they were to obey and move as directed. Then the riders dismounted and a bridle and saddle were put on each horse. And then there was further struggle to resist that, but saddles were finally cinched and Indians mounted. Soon the horses became amenable to the riders, who then rode them about camp as they willed. The horses were then unsaddled and hobbled out to graze, and being kept in the herd by the herders soon became affiliated with the Indians' own horses.

The next morning all of the wild horses were ridden by the Indians and there was no apparent difference between them and the horses the Indians had raised. Two features of this occurrence were impressive. There was no letup in the taming and training process from the time of the start until they were fully driven into the fold of usefulness, and also "self-determination" was not permitted.

One day we came upon a camp of Comanches, who had become tired of their harassment and gladly surrendered, no shots being fired.[7] They were disarmed and all the men except the very old placed under guard. The women were continued in their camp under the charge of the wife of the chief. She was a large forceful woman entirely equal to her new duties. As I remember, over 2,000 ponies, horses, and mules were captured with them. These and the Indian camp were placed under the care of the scouts, who camped near by, and the Indian men were held prisoners at the camp of the command some distance away across a creek. Indian scouts were placed as sentinels around the Indian camp with instructions to keep those belonging to the camp within its limits and to arrest any persons coming from the outside and to call for the guard. I instructed the woman in charge of the camp that if there was any trouble at any time in the night she should notify me.

During the night two soldiers evaded the sentinels and got into the camp. The chief's wife with one of her assistants came and informed me. I arrested the men and placed them under our Indian guard and notified the commanding officer, who instructed that the Indians hold them during the night. In the morning the men were openly marched by our Indian guard over to the main camp guard and turned over as prisoners there. This procedure had a salutary effect on the men for the several days thereafter, during the movement of the command and prisoners on the march into Fort Sill.

When this party reached Fort Sill, all the effective warriors were placed in the guardhouse. The women and children and old men were camped in a little bend of Cache Creek not far below the post. All were fed the usual army rations, the components of which were not only far better in quality than the rations furnished by the Bureau to the Indians, but were larger in quantity and therefore maintained life on a more contented basis. This soon created complications. Comanches and Kiowas who had proved their intention to be friendly by camping and remaining at their agency at first had been constantly hungry and irritated because kept away from the buffalo under the care of the agency all winter and fed the inferior quality and less quantity of food provided by the Bureau. Buffalo, deer, and antelope, then plentiful and not far away, were their staple food.

The same contractor supplied the army and the Indian Department with

7. This happened on Elk Creek on Oct. 26, 1874, five days after Davidson's departure from Fort Sill and before the Staked Plains scout that Pratt has just described. The Comanches were followers of Tabananica, White Wolf, Red Food, and Little Crow. A detachment conducted them back to Fort Sill while the column pushed westward.

beef, the cattle coming from the vast herds of Texas. The army specifications were stringent as to high quality and were maintained by careful inspections. The contract with the Indian Bureau was for a lower price, and I soon detected that, while good merchantable beef came to the army, unmerchantable, scrawny, and even diseased beef was being issued to the Indians. The beef issued to the army was weighed after being cut up on the block. The beef for the Indians was issued on the hoof, the agent having divided the Indians into groups, so as to give a whole beef to a group. The issue to the army was daily while the issue to the Indians was for a week at a time, and the weight was guessed at as each beef was turned out of pen and over to the chief of the group, who with his party drove each animal off on the prairie and killed and divided it among the families. It happened that some of these beeves were so poor and diseased that the Indians rejected the meat. In that case they killed the beef, took off the hide, and sold it for a few dollars at the trader's store, leaving the carcass to rot, until the flats between the beef pen and their camp had a constantly increasing number of carcasses. These friendly suffering Indians came in numbers to the camp of the prisoners begging to share the beef and food issued to them from the army supplies.

The alleged flour issued to the Indians was only coarse shorts. It was issued in muslin sacks and was a food never used by them before. After each issue, some of the Indians emptied the shorts on the ground on the way to their camps and reserved the sacks for clothing. The sugar and other parts of the Indian ration were also of a greatly inferior quality. This inefficient Bureau handling of the friendly Indians provoked hatred and more trouble. In a few days' ride from their camps to the west they could be among the buffalo, where they could select the fattest and best and then have the hides which made their clothing, beds, and lodges, and thus resume their former industries and independence in caring for themselves. I kept the commanding officer informed of these conditions, and he instructed me to write him a letter covering the facts as I found them. This I did, and the letter was forwarded to General Sheridan, commanding the military division from Chicago. He sent his aide, Major Dunn, to Fort Sill to investigate and make fuller report. Taking the Major, General Davidson, and another officer then officially visiting at the post, and who commanded one of the military units operating against the Indians throughout the winter, we visited the Indian beef corral, saw the poor quality of the cattle, and then drove around for several miles over the flats and saw the carcasses left by the Indians, and then the piles of shorts they had dumped on the ground. The report of this investigation and like reports from other parts of the Indian field helped after a while to bring better ration quality and quantity to the Indians, and a regulation by the Government required that, at each issue of food to the Indians throughout the Indian Service, there should be an army officer to oversee the issues and confirm its contract quality, and also to see that all issues of beef were weighed and correct in quantity. This army espionage over Indian Bureau management was not accepted kindly by the Bureau, and its duality made it cumbersome, but it promoted improved care for the Indians.

A band of the Comanches under the celebrated chief Quannah Parker had throughout the campaign remained the most remote of any of the Indians throughout the war.[8] They were several hundred miles to the southwest on the opposite side of the Staked Plains in the Pecos River region. Quannah remained there until the final disposition of the prisoners and so escaped an accounting for his acts of hostility. It was to his camp that Little Crow and his family fled; the details leading to this flight are as follows.

The military rules governing the Indians who had declared themselves friendly required that the chiefs bring immediately to the officer in charge any Indians coming from the hostiles to their camps. One morning early, Horse Back,[9] the chief of a considerable band of Noconee Comanches who had separated from the other bands and camped along Cache Creek above the fort, brought a young man with his horse, saddle, bridle, and gun. Horse Back stated through the interpreter that he was his nephew and that he never knew of his having been with any parties raiding against the whites and he had remained with the hostiles only because his nearer relatives were there. I questioned him and made a memorandum of the details of his incoming, and it turned out that there were four women and five men in the party, that they had first found the camp of Little Crow, another Comanche chief, living farthest from the fort, down the creek. Horse Back's nephew gave me the names of the men and women and said the men were all armed and all had come in on good horses. When he arrived in Little Crow's camp, he found that his uncle was camped above the fort and he went immediately to his uncle's camp and knew nothing about what became of the rest of the party.

8. Although a noted warrior and a prominent leader in the fight with the buffalo hunters at Adobe Walls in June 1874, Quanah Parker did not emerge as a leading chief until the surrender. On the reservation he became the most powerful Comanche chief. As Pratt notes later in the narrative, Quanah was the son of Cynthia Ann Parker, who as a twelve-year-old girl had been taken captive by the Comanches in a raid on Parker's Fort, Texas, in 1835. She later became the wife of a chief, and to her Quanah was born about 1845. Hodge, *Handbook*, 2, 204. Quanah's people were Quohada Comanches. Of all Comanche bands, the Quohada had most persistently avoided contact with the whites—except in raids on the Texas frontier. Ranging the Staked Plains, this band had tenaciously clung to the old way of life and had never signed a treaty or attached itself to an agency.

9. Both Horse Back and Cheevers, mentioned below, were influential Comanche chiefs of the peace party. They and their people remained at Fort Sill during the Red River War and, working closely with the military and agency authorities, did all in their power to induce the hostiles to surrender and acquiesce in the demands of the Government.

On his uncle's vouching that he was innocent of raiding, I disarmed him, took his horse, and sent him to stay in the prison camp, approving Horse Back for his obedience to orders.

Later in the day, Cheevers, who was the principal chief of the Comanches and lived in the camps below the fort, came with another young man who brought no firearms or horse and said that he had come in from the hostiles afoot and alone, and had no horse or firearms. He was one of the men named by the first Indian. His manner indicated that he was not telling the truth, and after making a memorandum of what he said I put him in the guard-house.

Taking the interpreter, I rode to the prison camp, called the first young man out, took him some distance away from the hearing of the other Indians, and told him I had a story about the party coming in different from the one he had told me and, taking out my memorandum book, asked him to tell me again the facts about the party with which he came, that maybe I had made a mistake. It was a perfectly clear day and the sun shining brightly. He did not answer for a minute, looking at me most intensely. He then looked up at the sun and then down at the earth and, motioning at each, said: "You put it in your book; do you think I could tell you a lie when my father (the sun) and my mother (the earth) are looking at me? All that I told you was true and I have nothing else to tell." This seemed a perfectly good voir-dire and I let him go back to the camp, and then, with the interpreter, rode up to the guardhouse and had the guard bring out the other Indian. When he came out, Black Horse, one of the Comanche chiefs who was a prisoner in irons, asked to come out with him. This was permitted and when the door was closed, holding book and pencil ready to write, I told the young man I had a story about his coming in that did not agree with his, and maybe I had mis-understood. I said: "Tell me your story again and remember that your father the sun and your mother the earth (pointing to them) are looking at you." Black Horse then asked if he might say something to the young man. I said, "Go ahead," and the interpreter explained that Black Horse said: "You have been telling this officer what those chiefs down there in the camp told you to tell him. You can't deceive this officer. He probably knows all about you now. You had better tell him all he wants to know and tell it straight." The young man then confirmed all that the first Indian had said and told further that the chief, Little Crow, and the Indians of his camp had sent the other four women and the four men back to the hostile camps with their horses and leading others as pack animals loaded with ammunition and gifts for the hostiles and they had started back long before daylight that morning.

All this I reported to the commanding officer at once and he told me to take ten of my Indian scouts, arrest Little Crow, and bring him to his office.[10] Taking the ten scouts and the interpreter, I started for Little Crow's camp. The post interpreter, Horace P. Jones, who had been the medium of communication between the governments North and South and the Comanches for twenty years, declared that our attempt to arrest Little Crow with the Indian scouts alone would not only be a failure but would probably be a disaster, and urged that I have at least ten soldiers. I wrote a note to the commanding officer, giving Mr. Jones' judgment, and requesting that a sergeant and ten cavalrymen be sent to report to me at Little Crow's camp, which was the farthest from the post down Cache Creek, and went on to that camp.

We found that all of the men of that camp were on the opposite side of the creek a mile away on a big flat which the Indian agent[11] was having plowed to put in a fall wheat crop. Leaving a scout to bring the cavalrymen, we went to that place and found the agency farmer and an assistant with two teams giving instruction in plowing. The Indian men, about 150 in number, were in little groups at one end of the field, engaged in playing various games and talking. It was a long way around the plowed ground. The plan included instruction of the Indians in driving a team and holding a plow. An Indian was required to go with each team to hold the plow part of the round and then drive the team another part of the way and then both drive and hold the plow, doing all three during one round; thus two Indians were educated in that feature of farming each round. Without stating what I had come for, we sat on our horses and watched the process, waiting for the reinforcement. As each team came around, the Indian who had been thus instructed was released and a new one designated by the chief took his place. There was bickering and laughter with each change and no evidence of real interest in the process by the party at large. The Indian designated would get up and throw off his blanket, when he was nude except for his breech-clout and moccasins. He would go to the farmer or the farmer's assistant, who would place the lines in his hands and give him instructions how to drive, the horses going on without much driving, one walking in the furrow of the last plow. We could see that before the other end of the field was reached the farmer took the lines and showed the Indian how to hold the plow and farther on gave the Indian

10. At this time, during the first two weeks of April 1875, Colonel Mackenzie was absent on special duty at Fort Leavenworth. The commanding officer to whom Pratt reported was Lt. Col. John P. Hatch, Fourth Cavalry. Post Returns, Fort Sill, March–October 1875, extracts furnished by Mr. Gillett Griswold, Director of the Fort Sill Museum.

11. Agent James Haworth, who had replaced Lawrie Tatum in March 1873. The behavior of the Indians had seriously tested Tatum's pacifism, and his action in calling for punishment of raiding warriors had brought him into conflict with Superintendent Hoag. The impending parole of Satanta and Big Tree prompted Tatum's resignation. Haworth's belief in the philosophy of conquest by kindness never weakened, and his efforts to shield patently guilty raiders from punishment produced a constant feud with the military authorities.

the lines to drive and have sole charge. At the close of each day's instruction a beef was issued to the class and this held the class together.

After waiting some time the scouts and the sergeant, with the detail of cavalrymen, reported. I then rode over to Little Crow and told him that the commanding officer wanted him. He at once got up from the ground where he was sitting, threw off his blanket, and like the apprentice plowmen was without clothing but had a belt with holster and pistol. Taking his pistol out of the holster, he ran out into the plowed land and turned so as to be facing us and the sun. He stood there holding his pistol in one hand and talking loud and earnestly. Mr. Jones said he was praying to the Great Spirit and that he would not surrender, but would die first. I waited until he was through with his devotions, when he shouted that he would not go to the commanding officer, and turning toward his camp bounded off like a deer. I ordered the scouts and men to follow me, and with the interpreter we dashed after him, following close. I rode quite ahead of Mr. Jones, who told me afterward that Esananica, Little Crow's brother, had jumped on a pony and was following close behind me with a strung bow and arrows. It so happened that one of my scouts was a younger brother of Little Crow. He told Jones to ask me to let him lariat his brother. I told him to go ahead. Little Crow was flourishing his pistol as he ran. His brother swung his lariat rope but did not gain on Little Crow, as it was evident he might have done, and I concluded that it was a ruse to let him get away. So, calling my Indian scouts close up, I dashed after him, but just then he came to Cache Creek opposite his camp, which at that place ran between high and steep banks. He slid down into the creek, and when I came up I compelled my horse to slide down after him. The Indians and soldiers followed by various routes and we got into camp together, all the Indians from the field following as rapidly as they could.

Little Crow went into his tepee and came out shortly with a Winchester rifle. His brother, Esananica, went to his tepee, also got a Winchester, and came over and stood by his brother. I had the scouts and soldiers stop a little distance away from me and instructed them that there was to be no shooting unless I ordered it. Three other Indians came with their guns and stood by Little Crow, and other Indians went into their tepees and came outside with their guns.

I argued with Little Crow against his course in refusing to go to the commanding officer. He had been in the guardhouse not long before in irons and was held quite a time for decision regarding some of his alleged actions, but not being able to substantiate what was reported I had recommended to the commanding officer that he be allowed to go to his camp, and he had been released. I called his attention to the fact that I had been his friend in this matter and had secured his release from the guardhouse. But he steadily insisted that he would not go to he commanding officer, fearing the guardhouse again. Cheevers, the principal chief of the Comanches at that time, was in a camp not far above. Hearing of the commotion, he came down and tried to persuade Little Crow to go to the commanding officer, but without success.

The commanding officer's son, a boy of about fourteen, came into the camp mounted on his pony, the beef contractor with him. I called the boy up and told him to go back to the fort, to ride quietly over a hill out of sight from the camp, and then to ride fast and tell his father that I was having trouble in arresting Little Crow and that the situation needed a squadron of cavalry. When the boy had gone Little Crow wanted to know why I sent that boy away. I told him that he was the commanding officer's son and had no business there and that I had sent him back to the fort. The beef contractor was near me, and I told him that he also had better leave and inform the commanding officer what was going on.

I continued my argument with Little Crow, Cheevers and Esananica taking part. The conditions grew more threatening. Some of the Indian women drove their ponies into camp evidently intending to leave. Mr. Jones wanted me to give it up, but I insisted upon remaining and on endeavoring to peacefully carry out my orders. Finally Mr. Jones said we were in such danger that he must refuse to stay longer and that he would give up his appointment as interpreter. I then said: "Just a moment, Jones, and just one more thing. You tell Cheevers and Esananica that I was not sent after them, but as Cheevers is the principal chief and Esananica is Little Crow's brother, I think they had better go with us to the commanding officer and talk it over with him." I had a very powerful mount and said: "Let Esananica get up behind me and Cheevers behind you, and we will go and see the commanding officer." They agreed to that, and as a parting shot I said: "You tell Little Crow that he had agreed to be friends with the Government at Washington, but he has shown by his conduct that he is an enemy of the Government. That the Government is not disturbing any of the other Indians here. The commanding officer only wants Little Crow. He has refused to go and by his refusal he has come near bringing on a great deal of trouble, both for the Government and for his people. This shows he does not belong here and that his place is out there with the hostiles."

I then called the scouts and soldiers and we started out of the camp, but had not gone far when both Cheevers' and Esananica's wives came galloping up each with a led horse and asked me to permit their husbands to ride their own horses and to let them go along with their husbands, and, as we were outside of camp and had them in our power, I gave permission. When we were near Fort Sill I met [Brevet] Major [Clarence] Mauck of the Fourth Cavalry with two companies of cavalry. I detailed to him and his officers what had happened and met some gratuitous condemnation from the other officers because I had not shot Little Crow. I told the officers that I was responsible to the commanding officer for the course I had pursued and in my judgment the emergency did not warrant action by which innocent persons would lose their lives. I went on with the two chiefs to the commanding officer and reported in detail what had occurred. He was dissatisfied with the course I had pursued, and after talking severely to Cheevers and Esananica he ordered that they and their wives be confined in the guardhouse and word sent to the camp that they would be held as hostages until Little Crow was delivered up. As the officer in charge of Indian matters at the post, I remonstrated against this course, telling what I had last said to Little Crow, but with no effect.

I went to my quarters and did not see the commanding officer again until the following morning. It so happened that the then commanding officer was only in temporary command because the permanent commander, General Mackenzie, was absent at Fort Leavenworth, the department headquarters. The next morning the commanding officer sent for me, and when I went to his office he said that since seeing me he had talked further with his son and the beef contractor and also with Mr. Jones, and he wanted to recall his condemnatory judgment of the day before. He said that my course had averted serious consequences and that had there been trouble and bloodshed it would have reflected on him as the temporary commander.

When Major Mauck reached the camp and deployed his squadron in front of it, he found that Little Crow and his family had disappeared. They did not turn up until after the war was over and final action against the most criminal offenders had been taken by the Government.

Quannah Parker, to whose standard Little Crow with his family had fled, was the most famous character among the Comanche chiefs. He was half white. His white blood and Parker name came from his mother's side. When a girl she was captured by the Comanches in one of their raids into central Texas, grew up among the Indians, and became the wife of one of them. Quannah was her son. Mr. Jones, the interpreter, who knew the Comanches best, told me that after Quannah and other children were born and she had become inured to Indian life, her family discovered where she was and arranged that she should visit them. They tried in every way to persuade her to abandon her Indian life and stay with her family, but failed. She grew discontented, ran away, and returned to her Indian husband and children.

When the tribes finally settled down and accepted the situation, Quannah became quite a cattle baron among them and was most powerful with his people in favoring the cattle interests of the Southwest by arranging consent of the Indians for the leasing of large sections of their reservations to cattle-

men for grazing. He lived in a large frame house built for him on his allotment by the cattlemen near a creek flowing south from the Wichita Mountains. In his later years he often visited Washington on tribal business, when
he received distinguished attention. He had three wives, but on these trips
took with him his youngest, who was, like Quannah, an attractive personality. During this time the Government was trying to end the Indian custom
of plurality of wives, and the Secretary of the Interior urged Quannah to conform to the rules. Quannah asked how he was to proceed. The Secretary told
him to select the wife he wanted to keep and provide for the others as best he
could, and then tell them they were no longer his wives. Quannah said: "Mr.
Secretary, you tell them."[12]

Quannah favored education and early sent his children east to the Carlisle
school. He had three daughters and a son by his Indian wives. I was at the
Comanche agency with Mrs. Pratt, making up a party of pupils for Carlisle,
and Quannah gave me all four of his children. Having enjoyed the highest
comforts of railroad travel on his Washington trips, Quannah insisted that
his children should go in the sleeper, for which he would pay, and arranged
that Mrs. Pratt should chaperone the girls. On the way, in the mornings, Mrs.
Pratt took the Indian girls into the ladies dressing room at the same time and,
in order to hasten their dressing, arranged that the girls should stand in line
behind each other and comb and braid each other's hair, Mrs. Pratt taking
care of the last one. This arrangement pleased the girls very much, and some
time after their arrival at the school, the matron was elated in reporting that
the new Comanche girls had introduced a fine hurry-up Indian trait into the
school by getting in line, one behind the other, mornings, and combing and
braiding each other's hair.

12. For Quanah's role on the reservation, including this anecdote, see William T. Hagan,
"Quanah Parker, Indian Judge," in K. Ross Toole et al., eds., *Probing the American West: Papers
from the Santa Fe Conference* (Santa Fe, 1962), pp. 71–78.

9. Kicking Bird, Dangerous Eagle, and Big Bow

During the winter of 1874 and 1875 most of the hostiles were compelled, by the severity of the weather and the constant vigor of the campaigns, either to surrender to the troops in the field or to come into their several agencies and surrender under the terms General Sheridan had arranged, and my duties were enlarged by the following:

Headquarters, Fort Sill, I. T.,
December 14th, 1874.

CONFIDENTIAL
1st Lt. R. H. Pratt,
    10th Cavalry.

      You are detailed on Special duty at these Headquarters in connection with Indian Affairs, the nature of which duty is as follows. You are directed to make at as early a day as possible, a list of all Indians at this Agency including the Comanches at the Wichita Agency divided into three heads.

First. Those against whom there is any evidence (either by accusation of Indians or of others) of having committed murders, stolen animals, attacked or killed troops within the last two years, specifying offences with date, place and evidence.

Second. Those who have notoriously been engaged in such crimes but against whom no evidence can be had.

Third. Those against whom no crime is charged but who have been turbulent, insolent, disobedient, agitators and stirrers up of bad feeling, and otherwise troublesome.

In carrying out these instructions you will endeavor to avoid publicity of your aims in order that the ultimate object of these inquiries be not suspected.

The Cheyennes would probably furnish information against the Kiowas and Comanches, the Comanches against the Kiowas, etc.

I am, Sir,

Yr. Obt. Servant

J. W. DAVIDSON

Lt. Col., 10th Cav.,

Brvt. Maj. Gen'l.

Comdg.

Several hundred Indians had been captured or had surrendered and were held prisoners, and about fifty of the leaders and most criminal had been picked out, placed in irons at Fort Sill, and held for trial with specific allegations of crime against them.

When not campaigning, my time at the post was full in making up the personal record of each turbulent Indian at the Kiowa, Comanche, and Apache Agency on testimony of both whites and Indians. General Davidson became tired of Indians coming to his quarters and appealing to him, and gave me instructions to notify the chiefs that they must come to me and make known their reasons for wanting to see him, and that I should, so far as possible, settle each case without appealing to him. When I explained this order to Kicking Bird, the principal chief of the Kiowas [see above, p. 40, note 4], he told me that General Davidson was the big officer in command of the soldiers and that he was the chief of the friendly Kiowas and a general too, and therefore he would transact the business of his tribe with the general and not with a lieutenant. I reported this to General Davidson and he said: "There is some subchief among the Kiowas who is ambitious to have Kicking Bird's place as chief. You find out who that is, ask him to come to see you, and tell him your orders and that you have been selected to get information from the Indians about those who have been engaged in marauding along the frontier. Tell him that you have heard that he is one of the leading Indians and that you are instructed by me to ask him to help you to find the bad leaders and those who joined them in these raids. If he says that he is willing to do that, you tell him that he can get the information best by calling his leaders together and talking it over with them, and that he had better have a little feast and that you are authorized to give him the necessary beef, bread, coffee, and sugar to do that. Have him tell you how many he wants to invite and you give him a liberal allowance for that number and make an appointment for him to come a few days later and give you such information as he has been able to gather. You then leave Kicking Bird alone, except to greet him kindly as you happen to meet him."

On inquiry through Jones, I found that Dangerous Eagle was the subchief who would like to be head chief in Kicking Bird's place. He came gladly to see me and was willing and even anxious to help identify the Kiowa offenders. I gave him the rations and made the appointment. When the time came he was on hand and had quite a fund of valuable information, and, acting under the commanding officer's orders, I gave him an additional issue of rations for a further conference with his head men, and he departed. In the meantime I met and passed Kicking Bird pleasantly several times.

Not long after Dangerous Eagle's second visit, Kicking Bird with his two wives and little son, all dressed in their best, drove up to my quarters in his chariot of state, which was a light spring wagon drawn by his noted span of white mules. Kicking Bird jumped out and helped his wives to alight and he and they were cordial in smiles, greeting and shaking hands. Kicking Bird by signs indicated that he wanted to talk to me, so I sent for Interpreter Jones. When he came, we had a long conference, and Kicking Bird said he had changed his mind and was now perfectly willing to confer with me and give all the help he could in ferreting out the bad men among the Kiowas. I reported this to the commanding officer, who was pleased at the success of his scheme and directed that I give Kicking Bird supplies of rations to have a conference with his leading men. The conclusion of the matter was that from these and other sources we found out who led and who were in each of the several parties of Kiowas who had been most active in hostility along the frontier during several years past. Among these was a brother of Kicking Bird's wives, who were sisters.

One of the later tribal divisions to surrender was a band of Kiowas under the leadership of Big Bow. He was the chief of a considerable following. He and those with him had been among the foremost raiders along the frontiers of Texas and Kansas, and I had traced many acts of violence to him and his followers. Big Bow, realizing he was booked for special punishment, had been keeping on the west side of the Staked Plains, remote from the field of operation, and suffering little disturbance other than that he was alienated from the protection of the Government and the ministrations of the Indian Bureau, but the conditions were becoming more and more oppressive.

While the making up of reports and other campaign duties were still on, and we were back in Fort Sill replenishing supplies and getting ready for another campaign, Big Bow came into Fort Sill quietly and made a private agreement with the commanding officer to surrender his entire band as prisoners provided that for this service he himself was exempt from punishment. While he was yet with the commanding officer, the commanding officer sent his orderly for me to come to the office. When I went in, the General took me aside and told me that Big Bow had come to get immunity for himself and had agreed to surrender his following to secure that. His proposition was to bring in his people by a particular route and arrive at the post at a given time.

I said: "General, you know Big Bow has been among the worst of the Kiowa leaders in frontier raiding and actrocities. Of all the Kiowas he is certainly one of the most deserving of punishment." He replied: "I have accepted his proposition and given my word that if he will do that I will absolve him from all punishment, and I never break my word, especially when given to an Indian." The plan was therefore closed to the satisfaction of Big Bow, and he returned to his camp.

A few days before the time at which Big Bow was to deliver his following as prisoners of war, an order was issued directing that several troops of cavalry and the Indian scouts should take the field under the general commanding. When I went to confer about the scouts, the commanding officer said his object was to meet Big Bow and his party and have them "surrender in the open field." I suggested to the General that possibly this movement might defeat their surrender, because they had agreed to surrender at Fort Sill and that was what they would expect to do. They were under more or less fear and excitement in regard to it because many of the men with him were guilty of conduct they knew would put them in the guardhouse in irons. When they saw the large command of soldiers, they might fear we intended violence, become alarmed, and run away, and the accomplishment of their final surrender would be considerably deferred. I suggested that his desire to have them surrender in the open field could be accomplished by having a small command go and meet them and receive their surrender two or three days out. A list of all warriors and their families, lodges, horses, and arms could be sent in by courier and the full surrender be accomplished just as well by a small body of troops. He accepted my suggestion, withdrew his order, and then instructed me to take a detail of my Indian scouts and a couple of wagons with rations both for my command and the Indians and meet and accept their surrender.

I took Interpreter McCusker, the only other white man in the party, and sixteen of my Indian scouts and, at the suggestion of the commanding officer, took Kicking Bird and Napawat; the latter, as medicine chief of the Kiowas, was noted and influential.

When about forty miles west of Fort Sill in the Wichita Mountains and riding well in front of our wagons and the scouts, the interpreter and I met the advance of Big Bow's party, three young men carrying a white flag. They were a long distance in advance of the main party. Not far back from where we met these three men, we had crossed a beautiful mountain stream flowing north, where there was an open flat, an ideal place for a camp. The Indians were aiming for this as their camping place for the night.

When Big Bow and his party came up, they all showed greatest pleasure in meeting us. We returned to the stream, and when the whole party was in with their horses, mules, and travois, which were used for transporting their lodges, cooking utensils, and other baggage, also the small children, there was a busy scene. I established my camp well to one side, and soon the lodges were all up and the animals out to graze, and when all were ready, as the commanding officer's representative, I received the surrender of all their war material and enumerated the guns, pistols, bows, arrows, quivers, spears, and shields. They were all brought by the owners and piled together on the ground near one of the wagons.

One of the finest younger men of the party, after bringing up his own gun and war materials and putting them in the pile, hurried back to his tepee and returned with a beautiful little quiver made of rich fur and holding a baby bow and arrows, all artistically made, evidently for a youngster not more than four or five years of age, which he ceremoniously placed on the pile. This amused the Indians and all of us. I had the interpreter tell him he could keep that for his boy, but he said the war was now over, and he did not want any war material in his family.

I then had the men fall in line so that I could take a census, receiving the names of all the warriors, the number of women and children in each family, and the number of tepees. The totals of war implements, horses and mules, and other statistics were at once sent by courier to the commanding officer.

After that business was finished, I had Big Bow get the women together and gave them the bread, sugar, coffee, and other rations I had brought. As they had just come from the buffalo range, they had plenty of meat. The guns, pistols, and other war instruments were placed in one of the wagons under guard of the Indian scouts.

The Indians went to their camp, Kicking Bird and Napawat with them. After dusk, Kicking Bird, Napawat, and Big Bow came over and said that they had had good eats and all felt happy and wanted to know if they might have a dance. I told them to dance all they wanted to. Kicking Bird, Napawat, McCusker, and I were to be the honor guests.

The camp was in a narrow valley in the mountains. It was the dark of the moon, and in the flickering light of the stars and camp fires, with the Indians moving about among their tepees, the strange scene was weird and impressive. After a while we heard the tom-toms and the Indians singing, and then Big Bow with a delegation came and escorted us over to the dance.

Big Bow had a very large tepee, which was like all the others, made of buffalo hides, hair removed, and soft tanned by the Indian women. A fire to give light had been built in the center of this and the walls had been rolled up to about six feet from the ground. On one side of the fire sat the tom-tom beaters and song leaders, while the men, women, and children were sitting on the ground in such a compact circle that a way had to be opened to the center for our party to get in. A red blanket was spread on the ground on one side of the fire between us. On the remaining side a small open space was left for the dancers.

The tom-toms were beaten, and the Indians sang, and there was much talking in their Kiowa language which the interpreter did not understand. We could only communicate with them through those who spoke Comanche. The music made several brave starts, but no one danced. The principal chiefs, led by Big Bow, and even the friendly chiefs talked loud and earnestly and seemed angry. After each talk from the chiefs the music would begin with greater energy, but still there were no dancers. Finally, when the situation began to be quite oppressive, a powerful young Indian near the chiefs took from his belt a large butcher knife and stuck it in the ground. Then intense interest was manifested by the whole company, and all began to sing. The music started with new energy; the tom-tom beaters used more vigor, and the singers' voices rose higher and were echoed back from the mountains. Then the young Indian who had stuck the knife in the ground got up and threw off his blanket. He was almost nude and his face and body hideously painted. There was still greater energy in the music and in the singing by the men, women, and children all over the company while he danced wildly with grotesque crouching, swaying, and posturing in excellent time to the music.

When he had finished, he reached down and seized the knife as though to use it in stabbing and in the most threatening manner stepped over on to the blanket where I was and leaned over me. On the instant it seemed certain that harm was intended, as all the Indians were excited and the chiefs were urging him on. There was a struggle between this Indian and an Indian sitting just back of me. Then the dancer stepped back into the open space and held up a blanket. He thrust his knife into it several times and cut it into pieces, making it worthless, threw it on the ground, and there was general approval. Replacing the knife in its sheath on his belt, he picked up his blanket, wrapped himself up, and sat down. This inspired the whole party with extraordinary enthusiasm and without delay other young men rose and danced—two, three, four at a time, and then women and children.

After many had danced and the hour grown late, I told the interpreter to ask Big Bow and the chiefs to excuse me, saying I would like to return to my tent and retire, and to tell them that I had been highly interested and entertained and was pleased to see that they were enjoying themselves. The chiefs excused me, and the interpreter asked to be excused also, and a way was again made for us out of the crowd. When far enough away I said: "Mac, I did not like the first dancer's actions and it seemed as though the knife was intended for me." McCusker, who had long experience among the Indians, said that he had been impressed with the same idea, that he had never seen anything like it and that he thought both of us doomed. We finally concluded that we had met an issue in which our courage had been put to a test, went to bed and, though the dance was continued most of the night, slept well, guarded by our trusted Indian scouts from the same tribe.

We moved early next morning, reaching Fort Sill two days after, where a number of the men in the party known to be guilty, Big Bow excepted, were placed in prison in irons.[1]

There is a sequel to this experience, and I add it here. Some weeks after that, under orders from the Government, the worst of the offenders at Fort Sill and at the Cheyenne and Arapaho Agency, seventy miles to the north, were sent as prisoners of war in chains to Florida under my care and confined in old Fort Marion at St. Augustine and there held during the three years 1875 to 1878. The severe circumstances of their imprisonment and their being taken so far away from their homes made these Indians almost lose hope, and that, added to the change from their free western life and its fine dry air to the close confinement within the casemates and high-walled area of the old Spanish fort in the humidity and heat of that southern climate, affected their health so that a number of them sickened and died within a few months.

In my daily anxiety and care for them I frequently found them greatly depressed and morose. One day the Kiowas had gathered in a group and were talking earnestly, and I saw that they were unusually gloomy. It was my custom under such circumstances to divert them, change their thought, and try to inspire them with hope and courage. On this occasion I concluded to see what effect one of my vivid Indian experiences would have. So I had the interpreter ask them if they would like to hear one of my most dangerous adventures with Indians, and, without giving names or place, I told them the

1. Big Bow (Zepko-eette) had been an influential Kiowa warrior for at least twenty years and throughout the years from 1867 to 1875 was always to be found high in the councils of the war faction. His raids in Texas, including participation in the Warren wagon train massacre, had earned him considerable notoriety. Big Bow had been induced to come to Fort Sill in January 1875 by Kicking Bird, who believed that through him Lone Wolf and the rest of the Kiowas might be persuaded to surrender. A scout detachment with Big Bow as sergeant rode west in February and, as Kicking Bird had hoped, brought in most of the remaining hostile Kiowas.

story of receiving the surrender of some Indians in the mountains out west and of going over to their camp to witness a wild dance, and about the young man who stood over me in a threatening manner with a knife in his hand, sparing nothing of description to make it graphic.

All the prisoners had gathered around and were listening with greatest interest as the interpreter gave them the story, and when I said, "I almost felt the knife enter my body," the Kiowas laughed and one of them said, pointing to Zotom, sitting over there, "he was the man who had the knife," and Awlih, sitting by Zotom, was to have danced first because he was the best dancer, but that when the time came Awlih refused to dance and that was why the chiefs scolded. Failing to get Awlih to obey, the chiefs told Zotom to dance first and then take Awlih's blanket away from him and cut it to pieces as a punishment.

Probably many tales of Indian treachery, and of thrilling adventure, have originated from just such a misapprehended cause as this I had experienced.

One of the highest tests of the qualities of our Indian scouts came early one morning while we were striking camp and loading the wagons in preparation for the day's march. My orderly was saddling my horse and the Indians were about ready to move, when all at once without any information to me of what had happened, the Indians mounted promiscuously and with all their speed rushed across the uneven plain, which, so far as I could see, contained nothing to lead to such a spontaneous movement. I wrote a note to General Davidson that the Indians were after something, I knew not what, that I would follow and inform him as soon as I knew, then mounted my fleet, long-winded horse and made all the speed I properly could in view of a prolonged chase. I soon got ahead of most of my scouts and among the foremost, where all were doing their best to get to the front, when I saw in the distance a compact body of forty or fifty horses driven by two Indians.

Probably no people in the history of the world ever excelled Indians in ability to drive a large number of animals rapidly. Their system of herding their own ponies and driving them to and from grazing grounds had trained them to perfection in that art. They would mount bareback the best horse of the herd, using one end of a lariat rope tied about its neck and looped over its nose, as the only rein they needed, and this was held in the left hand. The remainder of that rope, thirty or forty feet long, was held in coil in the right hand or dragged on the ground in the rear. They thus rode from side to side behind a herd, kept up the stragglers, and drove the whole herd at top speed with wonderful ability. Lagging members of the herd got punishment by the Indian who let his lariat drag and with his right arm as a whip handle whipped it to the front so the end of it would whack the side of the lagging animal with a severity that the animal would avoid receiving again.

When I saw the situation and that there were only four or five of my scouts ahead of me, I stopped short and wrote another note to the General, saying: "Following a large drove of horses driven by two Indians. Advance scouts nearing the herd"; and sent an Indian back with it and again hastened forward. One of my scouts, getting within range of the fleeing Indians, began to shoot. The Indians did not return his fire but kept forcing their herd, which had evidently been on a vigorous drive and were fagging. An Indian driving a herd could cut out a fresh horse, lasso him, and without losing much speed jump from the back of the horse he was riding to the back of the new horse, at the same time removing the lariat to the new horse and turning the fagged one into the herd. Esauekadadaho (Big Spotted Horse) [see pp. 79–80] was the nearest scout to the fleeing Indians, but his horse was failing. However, he got near enough to make an effective shot and the horse of the man he shot at faltered. The rider of that horse yelled to the other Indian driving the herd who cut out a horse and took it to his comrade, who jumped from the horse he had been riding to the back of the one cut out from the herd, took his lariat from the horse he had been riding and put it on the new horse, and then abandoned the failing horse. This was accomplished so quickly and with so little delay that even the foremost pursuer did not get much nearer to the two Indians. When this change was made, they dashed after the herd with tenser energy, and then the herd and the two Indians began to get away from us because we had so extremely forced our own horses encumbered with our campaigning impedimenta.

The abandoned horse followed his herd a short distance, then stopped and fell down. When Esauekadadaho reached it, he got off his horse and was standing by it when we reached him. The horse soon died. Esauekadadaho told me by signs that it was one of his own best horses and he had recognized others from his herd, which he had left at his home on the banks of the Washita, a hundred miles east, where some of his Pawnee people were temporarily living with the Wichitas, with whom they were linguistically connected.

These two hostile Kiowas had raided the Pawnee and Wichita herds at night, captured these horses, and were driving them to their camps on the plains far west of the Wichita Mountains. When they came in sight of our camp they changed their course, and, as the sequel proved, made a successful escape, losing only one horse of their capture, and that horse because it was shot by its owner.

Our chase had taken us miles away from the line of march, and we were a much fagged lot when we reached camp at the end of the day's march by the main command.

During the winter the Indians who had declared friendliness to the

United States and were living near their agencies held a number of solemn councils in regard to their future. I was invited and participated in two of these, and with the interpreter, sitting in the council circle, I shared in the sedate ceremony of smoking the pipe preliminary to discussion, taking the smoke into my lungs and blowing it out through the nose as they did. The older men spoke first and, as these were intertribal affairs, the Comanche language was used by the speakers, and what they said was given to me in undertone by the interpreter. The burden of their talks at each council was the wonderful "white man's road," as they called his power and improvements, and how they best could get into that road. My judgment was invited and I used the opportunity to suggest to them that their only safe future was to be found in merging their interests with ours and becoming a very part of the people of the United States; that vast numbers of people coming from many countries across the ocean were continually doing this, all soon learning to speak our language and uniting with us as one people under the best system of government the world had ever known; that it would be easy for them to do the same; that the small number of Indian people as compared with our millions and their division into many different tribes speaking separate languages and having different purposes made it entirely impracticable to think of their successfully continuing as separate peoples; that their only safe course was to quit being tribal Indians, go out and live among us as individual men, adopt our language, our industries and become a part of the power that was fast making this country so great and was sure to make it vastly greater as the years rolled on. I found this view entirely acceptable to them then when we were at war with them, and in all my wide opportunities to council with many tribes since I have ever found that Indians everywhere have had the good common sense to appreciate these facts and a perfect willingness to begin to accomplish that purpose. The hindering influences came from the white man's denial of these privileges to the Indians and keeping them away from opportunities to become useful and acceptable citizens. I hope to make plain the righteousness of my long contentions and the results of my experiences along this line as this narrative progresses.

One morning two young Comanches came to my quarters and wanted to talk. I sent for the interpreter and they told that there had been a debate at the camp the night before and that they had been unable to decide the question, and had concluded to submit it to me. The question was: "If an Indian, when on a long journey across the plains, was tired and hungry and came to a place where there was plenty of tobacco and also a horse, and he could have only one, which would he take?"

Although I was addicted to smoking at that time, it was not difficult for me to indicate my judgment in favor of the horse, which was acceptable to one of them, but the other was sure I was wrong.

One night about two o'clock I was awakened by a knocking at the door of my quarters and when I responded found the orderly with a message from General Davidson saying that the Indian women down in the camp were making a great noise, and directing me to go down and find what it was about and stop it. Taking Mr. Jones, I went to the camp and found that three women were using lusty lungs in mournful wailing. I had Mr. Jones quiet them and ask what was the matter. They said that the body of one of their young men who had been missing from their camp before they were captured had been found; he had been killed by a bullet, and they, as the camp mourners, had been directed to mourn for him all night. I told them that of course that was all right, but that the commanding officer had sent me down to find out what it was about and have them quit making so much noise, because it disturbed the people at the post. I advised them to go a half-mile away beyond a hill and keep up their mourning as long as they wanted to, as at that distance it would not disturb anybody. The three women held a little council and then told the interpreter that they would not mourn any more, and went to their lodges.

During the winter, after we had established the prison camp and the prisoner Indians in them began to feel reconciled, they resumed their natural order and had their usual games and entertainments to pass the time. One of the games that aroused the most interest was played by both girls and boys, sometimes girls alone and boys alone, and sometimes the sexes as opponents. We army people were invited to witness one of these played by the most active and larger girls of the tribes. The girls were picturesquely dressed in suits of buckskin with beaded moccasins and tasselled leggings. Their long black hair was divided into two braids, one hanging on each side of the face.

The ground was level, with a soft carpet of buffalo grass. There was a central line across the field where the game began, with the two goals equidistant from the center, as in football. Two posts, about twelve feet apart, were set up at the ends, between which the ball had to be driven to secure a score. Each player had what we boys used to call a shinney club—that is, a club about as long as a golf club with a crook at the lower end. There were ten on a side. Each side protected its own goal and was to drive the ball through the goal of the opposite side. A large number of Indians had gathered from all the camps and stood well outside the lines of the field. The two leaders went to the center line with their clubs, the homemade ball was thrown out to them, and the game began. Immediately there was rushing to and fro across the field, and a skill in knocking the ball to the front, back, right or left as they ran that was intensely interesting. Like our old game of shinney on the ice, they would drive the ball back or forward toward their own goals as they rushed after it or by it, striking front or backward or sideways with a precision that was fine. Their grace and exceptional speed in getting over the field was a revelation. Like our football and baseball, the fans were divided and vociferously applauded the success of their favorites. The contest was long drawn out and there were no timekeepers or delay in the play until the goal was reached, when there was a short wait before beginning again.

The day was clear and beautiful, the Indian camp of tepees along Cache Creek, the military post above on the hill, and the Wichita Mountains just beyond, the hundreds of onlookers in their gala Indian costumes, with officers and ladies and soldiers from the post, made an intensely interesting picture. The play was continued until the players were well exhausted. The only stimulation was the glory of winning.

The young men among the Indians sometimes played this game on the ice, where, having no skates and only moccasins, there were many falls and no little amusement to the onlookers, but that was slow compared with the game on the ground or as compared with the same old skating game of shinney.

In the fall of 1874 a commodious hospital was built at Fort Sill and finished in the late winter. The officers and ladies concluded to celebrate the occurrence by having a dance in the large ward, followed by a banquet. The officers managing the affair urged me to bring secretly some of the big chiefs in their regalia to look on at the dance and participate in the banquet. I accepted this duty and arranged with the six principal chiefs that I would come to their camps and escort them. When I reached Kicking Bird's camp, the ceremonies of dressing and adornment for the occasion were not completed, and while I was witnessing the deftness of his wives in helping him to paint and feather himself, I asked whether they could paint and dress me as one of the chiefs. This pleased Kicking Bird and wives very much, and they agreed to fix me up all right. Borrowing some things, they gave me Indian garments, leggings, moccasins, beaded shirt, etc., which I put on over my underwear, and they painted my face most vividly and furnished me a fine war bonnet. Kicking Bird and his two wives were intensely gratified that they had made me look so completely Indian.

We drove up to the post at the proper time when the dance was in full swing under the orchestral leadership of the colored musicians from our regimental band. I led the Indians into the large rooms and about on the floor. The dancers stopped to look at the Indians, and as I walked about as one of them among the dancers standing in their places in the quadrille, I came near Mrs. Captain —— but was not recognized and heard her remark:

"It is real mean of Captain Pratt to bring these nasty old Indians up here to interfere with our pleasure."

Only those officers who knew I had gone to bring the Indians recognized me at first. Later, when the refreshments were passed around, and the Indians were given what to some of them at least was their first taste of ice cream, Lone Wolf asked to have his taken out and warmed.

10. Exile of the Indian Prisoners

General Sheridan kept the several columns of troops vigorously moving throughout the late summer and fall of 1874 and the following winter, covering the vast area of western Indian Territory, northwestern Texas, and western Kansas. These operations gave the hostiles no rest, and all were finally driven to their reservations except Quannah Parker and his band of Quahada Comanches, who remained on the west side of the Llano Estacado and changed their hiding places between the western branches of the Pecos River in southeastern New Mexico to over the line into old Mexico.[1]

The information gathered against the individual bad leaders and their followers was considered sufficient to warrant the trial of some of them before a military commission, as General Sheridan had recommended to President Grant before inaugurating the campaign. Major C. D. Emory, Judge Advocate of General Augur's Department of Texas, came to Fort Sill to consider further the evidence and indicate the persons to be tried.[2] Evidence of com-

1. Mackenzie sent Dr. J. J. Sturms, a veteran frontiersman, and Sgt. J. B. Charlton with a few Comanches to induce the Quohadas to give up. The mission was accomplished without mishap, and the last sizable band of hostiles, including Quanah, reached Fort Sill on June 2, 1875. Carter, *On the Border with Mackenzie*, chap. 19.

2. Fort Sill and the Kiowa-Comanche country of southern Indian Territory at this time lay in Brig. Gen. Christopher C. Augur's Department of Texas, headquarters at San Antonio. Darlington Agency, Camp Supply, and the Cheyenne-Arapaho country of northern Indian Territory lay in Brig. Gen. John Pope's Department of the Missouri, headquarters at Fort Leavenworth. Both departments were part of General Sheridan's Division of the Missouri.

mitting atrocities had been secured, largely from Indian witnesses, against about forty of the Kiowas and Comanches covering several years previous. Major Emory's orders covered our active war period only. The fact that war against them did not begin until midsummer of 1874 put great limitations on the plans of General Sheridan and indicated the escape from trial of some of the most persistent of the raiders. We found, however, that several murderers of innocent noncombatants during the short war period could, under the ruling, be brought before a military commission. There the proceedings rested while General Sheridan was awaiting final direction from the President. While in the beginning President Grant had approved General Sheridan's program, when it came to the necessary authorization of a military commission to try the culprits, President Grant thought best to submit that feature to his Attorney General, who ruled that "a state of war could not exist between a nation and its wards," and as the law required that there must be a state of war to warrant a military commission, it was therefore not possible to bring any Indians before that kind of a court. The frontier feeling against the Indians was so intense that an impartial trial was hardly to be anticipated if they were brought before a jury in civil courts. It was therefore concluded best to punish the most notorious of the recent offenders by arbitrarily sending all of them to some remote eastern fort to be held indefinitely as prisoners of war.

A party of seventy-two was therefore made up from the Kiowas, Comanches, Cheyennes, and Arapahoes. The official list of these furnished me at the time by the Adjutant General of the Department of the Missouri shows that there were thirty-three Cheyenne men and one woman, two Arapahoes, twenty-seven Kiowas, nine Comanches, and one Caddo. Naming and giving the charges against them filled fifteen pages of foolscap paper and included the longer period covered by my orders for the investigation. The official report of the Indian agent for the Kiowas and Comanches for 1876 protests the punishment of the worst ringleaders in border raids among his charges, but the facts were against him.

The Cheyenne and Arapaho leaders selected for banishment were sent to Fort Sill from their agency about seventy-five miles north. The selection of these was made under the direction of General Neill, Colonel of the Sixth Cavalry.[3]

3. The hostile Cheyennes had drifted into their agency at Darlington throughout the winter and spring of 1875 and settled near the camps of Little Robe and Whirlwind, who had remained peaceful during the war. Guided largely by Mexican informers, Lt. Col. Thomas H. Neill selected the Indians who were to be imprisoned. On April 6, 1875, one of the prisoners attempted to escape while being ironed. The guards opened fire, and their bullets, entering the Indian camps, precipitated a stampede to the sand hills across the river. The frightened Cheyennes fortified, and a desultory long-range duel developed between them and the soldiers. During the night the In-

A little prior to this, my regiment, the Tenth Cavalry, was relieved from duty in the Indian Territory and ordered to Fort Concho on the southwestern frontier of Texas, and the Fourth Cavalry, under its colonel, General R. S. Mackenzie, was sent from that post to Fort Sill.

During these preliminaries, having had General Sheridan's encouragement to write him personally, I wrote the following letter, which I insert with special reference to the last clause:

Fort Sill, I. T.,
April 26, 1875.

Dear General:

General Mackenzie has just offered me the detail of going as far as Leavenworth in charge of the criminal Indians being sent east under the arrangement you suggested in your correspondence with the Secretaries of War and Interior. As my company is just moving to Concho, I do not care to go for family reasons unless I could stay east a while, so have said I prefer to go with my company.

If, in the care of these Indians east, the government requires an officer of my rank, I want to go, because I have been on duty in the Indian Territory eight years and desire a change. I know the leading Cheyennes from a two years' duty at Camp Supply, '72 and '73. Having had charge of Indian prisoners here since December and having sought out the offenses for which those from here are sent away, I am well acquainted with the Kiowas and Comanches going, their dispositions, etc.

I am sorry to hear there is a probability that none of them will be tried. Lone Wolf, and five others of those from here, can clearly be tried and convicted on acts committed since the war began August 22nd last, and charges have been sent in against them either by Major Emory or myself. All the requisites indicated in the opinion of the Attorney General in the Modoc cases are filed in their cases.[4] White Horse should go to Texas for civil court trial as he can be convicted in both the Koozier

---

dians slipped away and took refuge in the camps of Little Robe and Whirlwind. The prisoners were promptly moved to Fort Sill. Grinnell, *Fighting Cheyennes*, pp. 325–27. Berthrong, *Southern Cheyennes*, pp. 401–03.

4. The costly Modoc War of 1873 occurred in the lava beds of northern California. During a peace conference on April 11, 1873, the Modoc leaders treacherously murdered Brig. Gen. Edward R. S. Canby and thus incurred the wrath of the nation. At the close of the war the army tried six of the Indian leaders by military commission for violating the rules of war. Convicted, four were hanged and two imprisoned. The Modoc cases thus set the precedent by which the army intended to prosecute the Plains raiders in 1875. A recent history is Keith A. Murray, *The Modocs and Their War* (Norman, 1960).

and Lee family murders.[5] Some of them ought to be tried and punished here in the presence of their people.

Most of the young men being sent away have simply been following their leaders, much as a soldier obeys his officers, and are not really so culpable. As, under the changes of administration, public opinion, etc., they will be returned to their people sooner or later, much can and should be done to reform these young men while under this banishment.

Respectfully yours,
R. H. PRATT,
Lieut. U.S.A.

When this letter was written, as a part of the regiment Mrs. Pratt and I had all our household belongings packed and loaded in the wagons to go with the regiment. At the last moment my discretion to decide whether to go with my regiment or as far as Leavenworth with the prisoners was withdrawn, and I was advised that I was to remain at Fort Sill until the prisoners went east and then accompany them as far as Leavenworth. The arrangement indicated that I would then rejoin my regiment, going by rail as near Concho as possible and then by stage on to the fort. This information led us to let our household goods and my horses go with my company under care of its captain, which in the outcome proved to be material inconvenience and loss, for my two horses had to be sold in a region where horses had little value, and it was many months before we recovered a portion only of our household goods again.

When everything was ready for the transfer of the prisoners from Fort Sill to the railroad, 165 miles to the east, the day and hour for their departure was fixed and their friends notified they could come to see them start. There were eight army wagons to carry the prisoners, in each of which one end of a long chain was securely bolted to the center front end of the bed of the wagon and reached back to the rear where a staple had been fixed so that end could be padlocked. The prisoners, when placed in the wagons, were strung on this chain by putting it between the legs above the shackle chain, and they were alternated to sit, one on each side, on the bottom of the wagon where had been placed a quantity of hay. When each wagon was loaded, a link on the

5. For the Koozer case see above, p. 49, note 16. A Kiowa raiding party under White Horse wiped out the Abel Lee family at their ranch on the Clear Fork of the Brazos River near Fort Griffin, Texas, on June 9, 1872. Lee, his wife, and one child were brutally slain and mutilated, and the three other children were made captives. The perpetrators and particulars of the atrocity were well known. Nye, *Carbine and Lance,* pp. 153–56.

end of the chain at the rear was put over the staple and padlocked so that escape was impossible.

During these preparatory operations, in the presence of their people, a strong force of troops ready for action controlled the situation. The friends of the Indians were permitted to come to them after they were in the wagons and to say their good byes. A great many Indians gathered to witness the departure. Two troops of the Fourth Cavalry commanded by [Brevet] Major [Theodore J.] Wint formed the guard. There was some evidence that their tribesmen would attempt a rescue at the start or en route. Loud wailing by the Indian women, which was not interfered with, came from their masses crowded on the hillside and about the grounds during these preparations. As we moved away, and throughout that long march, every precaution was observed by advance and rear guards and flankers well out on both sides. At night two army wagons were set far enough apart to admit of the prisoners sleeping between them, and five fifth chains were padlocked together making a continuous chain on which the prisoners were strung, half on one side and half on the other, the ends being padlocked to the wagons.

During each day there were halts during which the prisoners were let out of the wagons, and we camped by running water each night, when the prisoners, under guard, went to convenient places where they could perform such cleansing of themselves as they were able to under the limitations of their shackles.

Just before she was leaving Fort Sill, General Mackenzie informed Mrs. Pratt that it was not likely we would rejoin our company for some time, as I would probably be continued in charge of the prisoners and go east as their jailor. Two days after we started, Mrs. Pratt and the children left by the stage, went to the railroad, and to our home in Indiana to await developments.

There was no attempt at rescue, and the only special excitement that occurred during the march was at about two o'clock one morning when an outpost sentinel fired his gun at what he thought were horsemen coming toward him in the dark and who refused to halt. A section of the guard hurried to his post and on investigation found that he had fired at, but happily missed, oxen belonging to a train which had camped late not far from us and which had been turned loose to graze.

The events of this part of their trip were vividly impressed upon the Indians, and some of them, with artistic ability, drew pictures of its features and sold them to visitors throughout their imprisonment. Some of these are preserved in a book given to me by one of the artists.

When we reached the railroad a special train was ready to take the party and the guard to Fort Leavenworth, Kansas. Only one of the prisoners had ever been on a railroad train before. That was Lone Wolf of the Kiowas, who, several years before, was sent with a small party on a trip to Washington. As the train started, the prisoners were at first greatly interested, but as it increased in speed beyond anything they had ever experienced, it was plain that some of them were not a little disturbed, and these at first pulled their blankets over their heads and quit looking out.

When we reached Fort Leavenworth they were all placed in the guard-house waiting orders from Washington. I went over the cases of the Kiowas and Comanches with General Pope. As a member of an Indiana cavalry regiment early in 1862, I had been part of his command in the Battle of Iuka, Mississippi, which occurred soon after the Battle of Corinth, following the previous Battle of Shiloh, in which battles I had also participated.

General Nelson A. Miles had returned from the Indian campaign and was in the immediate command of the post of Fort Leavenworth. He was greatly interested in Gray Beard, the principal Cheyenne chief, whose two camps General Miles had attacked early one morning, as heretofore detailed.[6] General Miles interceded for the release of Gray Beard but without avail. Gray Beard attempted suicide in the prison. He cut off a strip from one side of his blanket, fastened one end of it to the iron bars of his window quite above his head, and then found something to stand on while he tied the other end of the strip around his neck as high up as he could and kicked away the support. It was in the dark of late night when all others slept but his friend and war chief, Manimic, who was near him, heard his struggles and quickly got the Indians together and untied the blanket before strangulation had occurred.

The following orders directed my destiny:

War Department,
Adjutant General's Office,
Washington, May 11, 1875.

Special Orders }
   No. 88   }

1st Lieutenant R. H. Pratt, 10th Cavalry, is detailed to take charge of and accompany the Indian prisoners to be sent from Fort Leavenworth, Kansas, for confinement in Fort Marion, St. Augustine, Florida. Lieutenant Pratt will remain in the immediate charge of these Indians until further orders and will attend to the supply of their proper wants, etc.

The guard for the prisoners will be furnished by the garrison at St. Augustine, under direction of the Department Commander, and the necessary supplies will be drawn from the post.

An accurate account will be kept of all subsistence and clothing drawn

6. The Battle of McClellan Creek, Nov. 8, 1874, where the Germaine sisters were liberated. See above, p. 75.

from Army supplies, that the cost may be reimbursed by the Indian Department.

Lieutenant Pratt will make his reports in relation to the Indian prisoners through the Department Headquarters, whence they will be forwarded *direct* to this office.

By order of the Secretary of War:

E. D. TOWNSEND,
Adjutant General.

Headquarters Army of the United States
St. Louis, Mo., May 12, 1875.

General Orders ⎫
   No. 3   ⎬

I. Pursuant to instructions of the Secretary of War, as contained in a dispatch of the 11th instant, the Indian prisoners now held at Fort Leavenworth will be sent to St. Augustine, Florida, to be confined in Fort Marion, under the immediate charge of First Lieutenant R. H. Pratt, 10th Cavalry, but subject to the supervision of the Commanding Officer of St. Augustine, who will be held responsible for their safe custody.

II. The Commanding General Department of the Missouri will cause the detail of a suitable guard under a commissioned officer, to conduct these prisoners to St. Augustine and deliver them to the Commanding Officer, after which the guard will return and rejoin their proper command.

III. The Quartermaster's Department will furnish the necessary transportation.

By Command of General Sherman:

JOSEPH C. AUDERIED,
Colonel and Aide-de-Camp.

Headquarters, Department of the Missouri,
Assistant Adjutant General's Office,
Fort Leavenworth, Kansas, May 15, 1875.

Special Orders ⎫
   No. 76   ⎬

Extract

.   .   .   .

3. In accordance with orders from the War Department, the Indian prisoners now in confinement at this place will be transferred, under charge of 1st Lieut. R. H. Pratt, 10th Cavalry, to Fort Marion, Florida. The Commanding Officer Fort Leavenworth, Kansas, will detail a com-

missioned officer and twenty (20) enlisted men as guard to the Indians to Fort Marion. As soon as the Indians are turned over to the Commanding Officer at Fort Marion, the detachment will rejoin its station.

The Cheyenne interpreter, Romeo, will accompany the Indians to Fort Marion.

The Chief Quartermaster of the Department will cause the necessary arrangements for the transportation, by rail, of the Indians, escort, etc., as above specified, to be made at as early a date as practicable, and will give timely notice to the Commanding Officer, Fort Leavenworth of the time when the transportation will be ready.

. . . .

By Command of Brigadier General Pope:
R. WILLIAMS,
Assistant Adjutant General.

A further delay was experienced while the several railroads over which the transfer to St. Augustine could be made had time to mature and put in their bids for transporting the prisoners and their guard to Florida.

Romeo, the interpreter, who had been interpreter for General Custer at the Battle of the Washita, understood only Cheyenne, and the Indians of the other tribes did not know that language, which proved a serious disadvantage. There were among all the tribes those who spoke Comanche, the intertribal language of the Southwest, so I asked General Pope to add the services of a Comanche interpreter. This was authorized and I wired George Fox, who had been long at Fort Sill with the post trader and had become a most capable Comanche interpreter. He was visiting his home in Camden, New Jersey. He accepted and would meet our train in Indianapolis, Indiana. I also arranged that Mrs. Pratt and the children should meet us there.

There was lively competition among the railroads for the business of transporting the prisoners because of the notoriety of the movement. Several prominent officials of the road which secured the business were present in Leavenworth at the starting, among them the superintendent of transportation and one of the assistant passenger agents, who accompanied us on the train. The superintendent of transportation, who was the principal in authority, had been drinking and held the train at Kansas City beyond its starting time. The assistant general passenger agent asked me to help him urge this official to let the train move. We succeeded after material delay, and he came out to the train insisting on my coming with him to the engine and we two rode in the engineer's caboose. Their talk showed that the engineer and superintendent were old friends. Soon after starting, the superintendent insisted on taking the engineer's place and running the train, which the engineer permitted, and we whizzed along at a great pace, lunging from side to side, as I thought dangerously, while the engineer stood near and watched. I suggested danger, but he said: "I will take care of him."

At the first stop, which we had reached ahead of time, the conductor came forward to remonstrate. It was no use. He could not get the superintendent to leave the engine, nor was he willing that I should do so. I then arranged with the conductor to have the interpreter find an Indian with an extra pair of moccasins and send me word that he wanted to make a present of them to the Big Chief of the railroad and come forward at the next stop and tell me. At the next stop, which we again reached still more ahead of time, the interpreter came up and told me that the Indian chief Lone Wolf wanted to give the Big Chief of the railroad a pair of moccasins. I told the superintendent this and he immediately was willing to go back and receive the present. We brought him to Lone Wolf, who made a speech, largely by signs, which the interpreter gave to the Big Railroad Chief, in which he extolled the railroad and its wonderful rate of travel and the big loads it could haul. The superintendent replied. Passengers had crowded in from the other cars. Among those who had come in and was standing near the superintendent was the train boy with a basket of oranges. The superintendent reached over and took the basket and distributed the oranges by throwing to the Indians, much to their delight. The train boy, seeing his opportunity, ran forward to his supplies, came back with a box of cigars, and stood where the superintendent could see him. These also the superintendent took and distributed, still further pleasing the Indians. In the meantime the assistant general passenger agent and the conductor had planned to incapacitate the transportation manager by getting him into the men's room of the sleeping car for further imbibing. They succeeded and kept him at it until we reached Sedalia, Missouri, when, unable to navigate, he was removed to the railroad hotel close by the track.

Mrs. Pratt and the children and Fox joined us at Indianapolis, where the great station was filled with a compact mass of people anxious to see the prisoners. The same conditions existed at all the other large stations at which we stopped—St. Louis, Louisville, Nashville, Atlanta, Jacksonville, and others.

We were due in Nashville very early in the morning. Just before arriving, one of the guards in the car next in front of ours, which contained half of the prisoners and part of the guard, ran in to the sleeper to tell me that one of the Indians was giving trouble. I hurried into the car, and as I entered it from the rear Lean Bear, one of the principal Cheyennes, and a guard were in the front end of the car, both gripping the guard's rifle, struggling for its possession. When I reached them, the Indian desisted and fell to the floor. He had occupied a seat to himself. His neck, chest, and blanket and the seat were bloody. He lay on the floor apparently dead. I sent the officer commanding the guard through the sleeping cars in the rear and he found a medical officer of the navy who felt the pulse of the Indian, turned down his eyelid, put his hand on his chest, and pronounced him dead. He had stabbed himself several times in the neck and chest with a small, short-bladed penknife and bled profusely. We straightened him out on his blanket on the floor in the open space near the stove. As there were troops in Nashville, I concluded to leave a guard with the corpse to have it buried and they were then to follow on the next train. When we reached the station, soldiers carried the Indian out on his blanket and dropped him on the platform near the omnibuses. He was a small man. Before the train started, Lean Bear got up and tried to get away. Two soldiers held him through a short struggle when he again dropped down, apparently as dead as before. The same doctor came, looked him over again, and said: "Well, he's dead now." But the guard remained with him and we went on to Florida. The guard followed on the next train, as directed, and reported that the Indian had again revived after they arrived at the military post and he had been left in the care of the hospital authorities. Several weeks after our arrival in Florida, the town bus came up to the old fort with our twice-dead Indian riding on the top, under the care of two soldier guards. He was locked in one of the old casemates by himself, made as comfortable as practicable, and kept that way for a time. He steadily refused to take any food, would not talk even to his own son, also a prisoner. Dr. Janeway, the post surgeon of St. Francis Barracks, pronounced him demented. So long as he was strong enough, he was taken out twice daily to the top of the fort, where he could walk around, look over the town, the bay, and out through its entrance to the ocean. He was accompanied by a guard and went and returned to his casemate quietly. He finally became too weak to leave his bed. Dr. Janeway then had him taken to the army hospital at St. Francis Barracks, put him in a wall tent under the care of the hospital attendants, and used every measure to induce him to take food, but he continued to refuse all nourishment and finally died.

During the trip I was quite constantly with the prisoners and, through the interpreter, endeavored to build "hope—that best comfort of our imperfect condition," which, Macaulay adds, "was not denied the Roman slave." Going through the cars with my oldest daughter, then six years of age, I stopped to talk with Gray Beard. He said he had only one child and that was a little girl just about my daughter's age. He asked me how I would like to have chains on my legs as he had and to be taken a long distance from my home, my wife, and little girl, as he was, and his voice trembled with deepest emotion. It was a hard question.

We passed through Atlanta near midnight, and we who were in the sleeper had to change cars. So dense was the crowd of people that it required considerable force from the police to help us from one sleeper to the other. Soon after arriving in Florida I received a copy of the *Atlanta Constitution,* containing the account given by one of its reporters of our arrival in the city and his alleged interviews with the prisoners, given in "Chinese English," naming several of the most noted in the party. It covered a column, all absolutely bosh. The Indians could not speak English at all, were in their darkened cars asleep with guards at each end, and no persons were permitted to enter the cars. Some weeks after that, there came an excursion to St. Augustine from Atlanta. Excursions from nearby and even somewhat remote places were a special feature during the early period of the confinement of the prisoners. One of these Atlanta excursionists asked me if I had received a copy of the *Constitution* giving an account of our passing through that city. I told him I had and there was no truth in it. He laughed heartily and said: "To be honest with you, Captain, your train was late coming and I went out with the boys and we took several drinks and before I knew it your train had come and gone. I had been detailed to write it up, so I sat down and wrote what I sent you."

As we were nearing the state line between Georgia and Florida late in the night one of the guards awoke me and said that one of the Indians had jumped out of the car window. I pulled the bell rope, and the train stopped. The conductor came back and I told him what had happened. We found the open window and Gray Beard absent from his seat, his blanket and bundle gone. The train backed and we got down on the steps of the different cars on that side and watched carefully while the train backed slowly. After quite a long time we found his blanket, stopped the train, and with the guards, trainmen, and passengers searched diligently thereabouts through the low big-leafed palmetto. The trainmen had their lanterns but it was an unclouded night and not so very dark. After long search and failure the engineer informed the conductor that we must start soon or we would not have water enough to reach the next water tank. I then detailed a sergeant and three men to remain on the ground and continue the search, giving him railroad tickets and telling him that he could signal the next train, which would be notified, and it would stop and bring him and his party on to St. Augustine, and we boarded the train and started. We had gone only a few yards when there was a shot and call from the soldiers. The sergeant reported that when the train moved Gray Beard jumped out of the palmettoes near its rear and was hopping across the track and he ordered him to halt. Gray Beard did not do it and the sergeant then shot him. The bullet passed through his chest from one side to the other. He was still living. We fixed a place and lifted him into the rear of the last car and brought Manimic, his old friend and war chief, and others of his tribe back to see him. The interpreter stood by and told me what they said. Among other things Gray Beard said he had wanted to die ever since being chained and taken from home. He told Manimic what to tell his wife and daughter and soon died.

At Jacksonville we took the steamer to Tocoi and then the Tocoi and St. Augustine Railroad to St. Augustine, where we entered the old fort. This, as it transpired, was to be the home of the prisoners for three years.

11. Prison Life at Fort Marion

Most of our states in their early history, through the hatred and greed of the early settlers, had unfortunate experiences with Indians. These usually involved the arbitrary removal of the Indians from the state or their restriction to limited reservation prisons. Although the race has never been numerous within our limits, it has, throughout all our intercourse, been treated as inimical and alien to our interests and has never been admitted to the opportunities to become the useful fellow citizens we extend to the immigrating races.

Florida, from its earliest settlement, antedating almost every other section of our domain, was from the beginning among the foremost in harshness to her natives. Not only this, but St. Augustine, its oldest settlement, was established through horrible massacre of one European settlement by another, inspired thereto by desire for conquest and by religious and race hatred.[1] Such were the examples of our alleged Christian civilization to the natives.

1. Moved by the threat of French expansion from the north and by a desire to afford additional protection to the sea lanes, Spain planted the colony of St. Augustine on the Florida coast in 1565, thus earning for the city the distinction of being the first permanent European settlement on the mainland of the United States. The violence Pratt refers to occurred immediately afterward, when the Spaniards seized the French Huguenot settlement of Fort Caroline on the Carolina coast near the mouth of St. John's River. Most of the Frenchmen were absent on an expedition against the new Spanish colony, but they were subsequently captured. Two groups, one numbering 150, the other 200, were put to the knife by the Spanish commander, Don Pedro Menéndez de Avilés. This destroyed France's pretensions in Florida.

The town of St. Augustine is on a peninsula projecting southward. The land entrance from the north was fortified against approach by a wall across it and the old Spanish fort, San Marcos (later called Fort Marion), on the ocean side, protecting the inlet to the bay and also strengthening the protection from water to water of the wall across the peninsula. The fort was strengthened by a moat retained by a wide sea wall on the ocean side and by a heavy embankment on the other sides. This, in the beginning, was arranged to be flooded and its crossing at the entrance protected by a drawbridge, which together with the entrance was further rendered impregnable by an outer fortification covering both the entrance and the drawbridge. There is still standing a portion of the original wall across the upper end of the peninsula which was on a line with the south side of the fort. An inscription above the entrance to the fort recites that these fortifications date back to the year of 1565. They constitute our greatest memento of the methods of European military defense acquired when we purchased Florida from Spain.[2]

The fort itself had been previously used as a prison for Indians by the United States Government during our wars with them in Florida and the neighboring southeastern states. It was a sturdy structure, built entirely of the shell-rock formation called coquina, which underlies large sections of that part of the state. Coquina is somewhat soft when taken from the ground, but hardens under exposure to the weather. Quite a proportion of the older houses of the town were built of the same material. San Marcos well commanded the tortuous inlet entrance from the ocean and could easily prevent any war vessels of that day from entering the harbor.

The arrival of the Indian prisoners was anticipated by the local military authorities, and the ramp from the court to the terreplein [platform behind the parapet] had been boarded up, leaving a door with lock at the lower entrance so that their living was to be in a large pen permitting no outlook except toward the sky. The court was about 100 feet square, with casemates on all sides. On one side was the entrance, facing south and toward town, and the casemates on that side were to be used for storage and kitchen purposes. The only entrance was by way of the drawbridge through a wide hall and two massive pitch-pine doors. When these were closed, there was a small door

2. Castillo de San Marcos was constructed between 1672 and 1696, more than a century after the founding of St. Augustine. Its purpose was to meet the English threat from the north and to help protect the Spanish treasure fleets en route from the Indies to Spain. The oldest masonry fort in the United States, it is a symmetrically shaped, four-sided structure built of coquina blocks, a native marine shell-rock. During the first half of the eighteenth century, when English and Spanish rivalry over southeastern North America reached its greatest intensity, Castillo de San Marcos was the objective of several English attacks. It was besieged in 1702, in 1728, and again in 1740, but each time successfully withstood the siege. After Florida passed to the United States, the Castillo, renamed Fort Marion, served as a United States Army post. It became a National Monument in 1924.

through one of them for individual passage. The roadway and the bridge across the moat permitted quick passage of commands and also of heavy war materials. There were dismantled ancient cannon within and without the fort and many large cannonballs stacked up on the floor of the court.

The casemates had no windows that could be used for looking outside, and the two inside windows in each casemate looking into the court were iron-grated. A heavy door and bolt to each casemate was arranged for padlocking. There were narrow slot openings to the outside near the top in each casemate ten feet above the floor for ventilation and through which small arms might be used in defense, but the principal fighting was to be done from the top, or terreplein, which was well protected by a thick parapet with apertures for discharging the heaviest cannon of the sixteenth century. The only outlook besides the sky the prisoners could have was by going to the terreplein under charge of the guards, which was done several times each day. Otherwise they were confined to the court below and the casemates in which they slept. Plank floors had been put into several of these to make them more sanitary. The prisoners slept on the floors.

We arrived in the beginning of hot weather. The change from the dry atmosphere of their native country to the extremely humid conditions at St. Augustine, the depressing effect of their being in irons, and their long trip had serious influence upon their health, so that, early in the first weeks of their confinement, there was considerable sickness and several deaths. The presence of a large guard and the strict orders in regard to oversight added reason for depression and hopelessness. To overcome these conditions I made appeals and after a time was allowed more liberty of judgment in methods of care.

Very soon after being allowed larger discretion, their shackles were removed. It also seemed best to get them out of the curio class by cutting their hair and having them wear the clothing of the white man. There was some objection by them to these changes, but by kindly persuasion it was gradually accomplished. This change to army clothing had an unexpected feature. Soon after the clothing was issued, a number cut off the legs of the trousers at the hip, laying aside the upper part and using the trouser legs as leggings in the Indian way. This called for immediate correction. They were formed in line and a pair of the mutilated trousers shown them. They were emphatically told that the clothing belonged to the United States Government and that it was only loaned to them so that they might dress themselves becomingly, like the people they were meeting daily, and thus rid themselves of the stare of visitors who invariably noted every difference between them and ourselves. They must not, therefore, under any circumstances mutilate the clothing but must wear it just as the white man wore it. They yielded good naturedly and soon became accustomed to the white man's toggery and wore it with satisfaction to themselves. I had the soldier guards teach them how to be neat in the care of their clothing, how to clean it and crease their trousers, keep the brass buttons on their coats and caps bright, and polish their shoes, and in a short time there was pride established in the wearing of the army uniform.

A large one-room shed was erected largely by Indian labor to cover the entire space of the terreplein on the north side. Rough board beds were made and bed ticks filled with grass, and the whole party of prisoners moved up to better air. This greater freedom of movement and observation, with work and regular army drill exercises, soon drove bad health away.

Employment was early provided for them. "Sea beans" found along the ocean shore were sold by the curio dealers.[3] The shells were so hard and of such fiber as to be susceptible of a high polish. The principal dealer in St. Augustine was a Mr. Ballard, who had accumulated 10,000 in preparation for sale to northern visitors the next winter. The dealers, when ordered, ornamented them with gold insignia or the initials of the wearer. He paid ten cents apiece for polishing and, when it was suggested, was glad to have the Indians undertake it, as it would add to the salable quality when he told purchasers the beans were polished by Indian prisoners. He offered to let the Indians polish the whole 10,000. The art was soon learned, and a system was established of giving them out unpolished, taking them back polished, and paying the money to the Indians each time for their work. Another curio dealer, from Jacksonville, brought 6,000 more which the Indians polished, and these, with the 10,000 from the St. Augustine dealer, were polished within the first months, giving the Indians a revenue of $1,600 with which they could purchase things for their personal comfort.

I visited the fort at night several times a week, usually between midnight and morning, never letting the guard know the hour. There had been an increase of the command at St. Francis Barracks through recent arrival of recruits, and these visits, aided by the noncommissioned officers on duty, found remisses on the part of members of the guard requiring disciplinary action. The behavior of some men in the guard led the Indians to be apprehensive, particularly as one of the prisoners [Gray Beard] had been shot and killed by a guard while en route. The fact that I had commanded Indian scouts during the years while serving against Indians previous to coming east had given me confidence in their good qualities, particularly when pledged to obedience. This led me, within the first six months, to request the commanding officer [at St. Francis Barracks] to allow the organization of the younger men

3. Any of the varieties of beans or beanlike seeds common in the tropics. Ocean currents deposit them on the beaches. Those found on the Florida shores are usually the chocolate-colored mackay bean and are carried there by the Gulf Stream.

into a company with sergeants and corporals, to loan some old guns, and to use the Indians to guard themselves. In making this request the doubt of the commanding officer led me to pledge my army commission for its successful results. He said, "put it in writing," which I did, and a company of nearly fifty of the youngest was organized and drilled, and for the remaining period of their three years imprisonment they guarded themselves without a material mishap.

Daily drills had been resorted to early, particularly in what in the army is called the "setting up process [gymnastic exercises]," which greatly benefited the health of those who participated, and the drill hour became the favorite period for visitors, attracting attention and favorable comment from distinguished citizens and army officers. The commander of the Department [of the East], General [Winfield Scott] Hancock, visited the fort, coming unexpectedly at the drill hour when the Indians were going through movements at double quick with laudable precision. He had watched them some time before he was recognized by a visitor, who came and told me we were under distinguished military observation. I brought the company to a halt, ordered a hand salute, and went over to the doorway where the general stood and saluted. Returning my salute but keeping his eyes on the Indians, he inquired, "What troops are these, sir?"

There was a sandy beach just north of the fort on the government reservation, washed by the tide, which gave good bathing facilities and at that time was not subject to much observation. This was regularly used and was an invaluable resource.

Visitors were welcome during most of every day except Sunday, when there were restrictions except to those who came to give instruction. I conceived it my highest duty to correct the unwarranted prejudice promoted among our people against the Indians through race hatred and the false history which tells our side and not theirs, and which has been so successfully nursed by keeping them remote and alleging that they alone have irredeemable qualities. It was just as important to remove from the Indian's mind his false notion that the greedy and vicious among our frontier outlaws fairly represented the white race. To help do this the utmost freedom between visitors and Indians was cultivated.

During the winters there were many visitors to the old fort and among them considerable numbers of people of importance in the country. There was always a desire to see and know about race peculiarities. Many of the early visitors wanted to see an Indian dance and urged their desires on the post commander, and it was concluded to let the Indians give one. Night was selected as the best time. Wood was brought for a bonfire in the court and the terreplein was crowded by the audience. Necessary paint was procured and the best dancers selected. They carried out their home methods of dress and adornment, stripping to the skin, wearing only the gee string and the breech clout which it supported, and painting their bodies most impressively. They made tom-toms, provided a chorus of singers, and gave a varied exhibition of different tribal dances. This was perhaps as picturesque and thrilling a performance as any of its kind ever produced on the continent. The Omaha dance, celebrated and used throughout the central West by all the Indians, was the most spectacular because of its very remarkable posing and posturing. There was soon great urgency for another, which was granted, but that ended such performances. They were not calculated to promote any advantage to the interracial respect. I had the consciousness, however, forever after that, that had I been so minded I could have handled the Indians more wisely and out "Buffalo Billed" Mr. Cody in his line.

Promoting English speech was among the earliest and most persistent of our efforts in order to bring the Indians into best understanding and relations with our people. Trading and talking with visitors was valuable help in forwarding this purpose. Excellent ladies, who had in their earlier years been engaged in teaching, had volunteered to give daily instruction to the prisoners in classes, and throughout their whole prison life there were from four to six classes almost constantly under instruction. All the young men were ambitious to learn and received instruction. Among the older men a number were beyond sixty. These at first begged off but later, finding it to their advantage, came into a class taught by Miss Mather, a very successful and enthusiastic educator, and she and Mrs. Pratt persuaded and taught some of the older ones. Miss Mather and a Miss Perrit were from New England and before and during the early part of the Civil War had conducted a young ladies' boarding school in St. Augustine. Miss Mather was a member of the first class to graduate from Mt. Holyoke. Two others who lived in St. Augustine and who were most faithful and enthusiastic were Mrs. Couper Gibbs and Mrs. King Gibbs, widows of two brothers in the Confederate service during the Civil War. During the winter season, when visitors were present, there were always applicants desiring to teach the Indians. Among the most successful of these each winter was a Mrs. Doctor Carruthers from Tarry-town-on-the-Hudson. To the faithfulness of these and other fine women was largely due the quick progress in intelligence the Indians made, and the rapid growth among our people of a Declaration of Independence and U.S. Constitution sentiment in the Indians' favor. Most of the young men learned to write fairly intelligent letters during the three years of their imprisonment, and the English language became the common tongue among them, thus breaking down the wall of language which separates the tribes as fully as between them and our own people.

When the health of the prisoners had become normal and they had learned the kindly feeling the mass of our people had toward them and their people, their whole attitude toward the white race underwent a great change. Within the first year, after long councils among themselves intertribally, and entirely of their own motion, they asked for a conference and desired to send a talk to Washington. Mah-Mante, a chief of the Kiowas, was spokesman.[4] The burden of their appeal was to have their women and children sent to them. My report of this forceful and united action of the prisoners and my views thereon is in my letter herewith:

Fort Marion, Florida,
June 11th, 1875.

To the
    Adjutant General,
      U. S. Army,
        Washington, D.C.
  Sir:

I have the honor to report that the Indian prisoners, confined here under my charge, have made very urgent appeals to have something done in their case. They are particularly distressed about being separated from their women and children. On the 9th inst. the Kiowas and Comanches gave a talk through the Kiowa Chief Mah-Mante which they desired to send to "Washington" and to ask "Washington" to do something for them. Mah-Mante said:

"We are termed by all the white people a very lazy class of men, not willing to do anything for our own support. This is not so. We have been taken away from our wives and children, relatives and friends, chained and sent down to this place to remain, we do not know how long. We are willing to show that we are not too lazy to support ourselves. If there is anything 'Washington' wishes us to do, tell us what it is and 'Washington' will see how willingly we will do it. We do not care what kind of work it is. We want to show 'Washington' that we are willing to do anything he wants us to do. We want to learn the ways of the white man, first we want our wives and children and then we will go any place and settle down and learn to support ourselves as the white men do. If you go with us and 'Washington' says so, we will go across the big water. We want to learn how to make corn and work the ground so we can make our living, and we want to live in a house just as a white man. Take us to any part of the country and we will go like a man that is blindfolded, knowing

---

4. Mamanti was the medicine man who led the Kiowa war party in the attack on the Warren wagon train in 1871 and was in general charge of the camps in Palo Duro Canyon, Texas, when Mackenzie and the Fourth Cavalry attacked on Sept. 28, 1874. He died at Fort Marion.

you are ahead and no harm will come to us. We do not want to go back to our country to live, that is a bad country and bad people live there. There has been dark work done there, the people are crazy and now we want to go to another where the people are not bad and crazy where we can settle down and live in peace. There are a great many Indians at Ft. Sill and in that country who have done more bad work than we have, and why should they be allowed to go free, and be happy with their families and we sent down here as prisoners to live in these dark cells. That is not right. Tell 'Washington' to give us our women and children and send us to a country where we can work and live like white men. You can tell 'Washington' how we have behaved since we left our country, how we have obeyed you and done everything you told us, we have not been afraid to come down here with you, and wherever 'Washington' wants you to take us we will go, we have thrown our mad away. I am speaking now for the Kiowas and Comanches here; and as sure as God (the sun) hears me speak, I am telling you what our hearts all say, only give us our women and children."

I believe these protestations to be the result of convictions deep and lasting and these people will now take hold of any method offered for their future self-support with a will, that will overcome the difficulties that such a change of life must bring. If managed by persons aided by experience and knowledge of their character and weaknesses who desire that result, not more than two or three years need elapse before they are self-supporting. A small few of the most hardened characters might with benefit be taken out and held in confinement for the present, but the great majority are ready and anxious to be lead in the paths of the new life which they are all convinced they must now lead. When we consider the fact of the freedom of their former lives, which the greater part of them came in and knowingly surrendered together with the loss of their horses and arms (all the wealth they had) we must concede strong intentions. The periods of their confinement, ranging from three to eight months, rests much heavier upon them than it would on most any other class of men. Mah-Mante well asserts there are men back among their people as bad as these sent here.

Very respectfully,
Your Obt. Servant,
R. H. Pratt,
1st Lt. 10th Cav.,
In charge of Indian Prisoners.

After receiving that talk I felt assured that the best and highest results would have followed a compliance with their wishes. This appeal received sympathetic attention by the military but the reverse conclusion of the Indian administration. It was false information to his superiors from a narrow-minded and unvisioned Indian agent [Haworth] that prevented the same advancement in civilization coming to the wives and children of the prisoners that the prisoners themselves attained.

At first a cook, detailed from the army, receiving extra pay for his extra duties, took charge of that need, but soon his two Indian assistants were able to perform that duty with equal satisfaction and he was returned to his army service.

Bread was at first issued from the post bakery at the other end of town. Having had experience in army service in managing post bakeries, I took brick found in and about the old fort, built an oven in one of the casemates, asked [Brevet] Colonel [John] Hamilton, commanding at St. Francis Barracks, to permit one of the Indians to go to the post bakery and learn the art of making bread, and when he became somewhat proficient Colonel Hamilton allowed one of his bakers to come to the fort for a few days to help him in his baking until it was a success. As the bakery was just at one side of the entrance, this feature was one of the attractions to all visitors, and the wholesome fine brown loaves were a source of praise from visitors to the two bakers who performed that service through the remainder of their prison life. My news from their agency, long after their release, advised that the head baker, named Star, through the selection and wise management of Agent Miles, creditably served the Government as chief of the agency police for quite a number of years.

When the heat of summer was on, Colonel Hamilton allowed the use of army tents, and we encamped on the ocean side of Anastasia Island. The remarkably solid beach which extended sixteen miles south to Matanzas Inlet was, at low tide, used for foot races and other sports. One day it was arranged between two of the long-distance runners that they should contest in a race of thirty miles to Matanzas and return. These contests were usually intertribal, which was great stimulation. A camp guard was established, more particularly with reference to keeping out of camp wild "razor-back" hogs which intruded at night.

One of the prominent young ladies of St. Augustine was a special friend to the youngest Cheyenne. While we were in camp, boating parties came over to see us. Their boats would land a little distance away from the camp in a sandy cove. This young lady, with a party of other young people, visited us one afternoon, and, on returning, the young Cheyenne was persuaded to accompany the party to the boat without first securing the required permission to leave camp. When they arrived at the boat, he was further persuaded to cross the bay with the party under promise that he would be returned at once to the other side of the island from where he could get back to camp. He was late in returning and it seemed best to administer discipline to curb both the lad and lassie. A light stick of wood was given to him to carry on his shoulder in front of the guard tent until midnight. I awakened at daylight and, looking out of the tent, saw the boy still carrying the stick of wood. Calling for the sergeant of the guard, who belonged to the same tribe, I asked why he had not relieved the young Indian at midnight. He replied that it was a very bad thing the boy had done and that my punishment was not severe enough, so he had kept him at it all night.

During this encampment on the island the Indians discovered where sea beans could be found, and a general search rewarded them with considerable numbers, which they polished and sold to visitors on their own account, receiving from twenty-five cents to a dollar each, according to size and quality, and this resource continued throughout their imprisonment.

During our first encampment on Anastasia Island, I wanted to go over to St. Augustine one afternoon and took the interpreter, Mr. Fox, and two of the most distinguished old Indians—Manimic (Eagle's Head), who had been war chief of the Cheyennes, and Lone Wolf, who had been principal chief of the Kiowas. Lone Wolf was the only Indian in the party who had previously been east. Several years before, he had been taken to Washington with a party of the leading men from his agency. Interpreter Fox was in the habit of using that experience of Lone Wolf to lead him into taking the advance in any new movement, saying: "Lone Wolf, you have been to Washington, you understand all about this." That would at once put the old man on his mettle. On this trip from the camp to St. Augustine, as we were rowing over, Fox told me that a new restaurant had been opened in one of the narrow streets where exceptionally fine oysters were served, and he suggested that we take the Indians there and have a treat of oysters on the half shell. This program was carried out and the chef placed before us, on Mr. Fox's instructions, four dishes of unusually large oysters. Fox and I put on the necessary condiments and began eating. Lone Wolf immediately took up an oyster and ate it. Manimic watched us carefully and finally, smiling, took an oyster on his fork, put it in his mouth, and immediately jumped up and ran out of the door. He soon came back laughing but would eat no more oysters, notwithstanding our urgencies and the satisfaction he saw we had.

As confidence grew and it seemed best to give wider experiences, we several times went down the inside route to encamp at Matanzas Inlet with the whole party. At that point during low tide just inside of the harbor we found an abundance of very large fine oysters. We camped near an oyster shell mound, which, from its ancient appearance, might have been the creation of the Indians prior to the advent of the white man. This shell mound was seven or eight feet high. On the opposite side of the inlet was another long mound containing several times as many shells.

On later trips to Matanzas we carried plenty of condiments for oysters and several oyster irons for opening them. We could sit in our boat, lying on the oyster beds at low tide, and eat our fill. One day we found Manimic in the boat all alone, opening and eating oysters with apparent relish.

Matanzas Inlet became something of a sanatorium for ailing prisoners, and several times, on advice of the army medical officer, small parties were sent there for a week or so of encampment to recuperate by fishing, hunting sea beans, finding material for the canes, bows and arrows which they were permitted to make and sell to visitors. Part of the equipment of the old fort was a couple of ship's yawls which had been secured by purchasing a wrecked schooner that had brought ice from Maine to St. Augustine, and when attempting to sail out to sea was thrown by the current up on the sandy beach and became a wreck. I gave the captain a force of Indians to help to get the vessel off, but each tide only sent her farther into the sand. The captain then sold her to me, which gave us the yawls. Fixing sails and having the oars, the Indians were taught to sail and row, and they soon became something of a favorite feature in the local services of that kind to visitors.

One day, having some fifteen young Indians who were on the ailing list, on the army doctor's direction I equipped them for a week's stay at Matanzas under the care of Mr. Fox, the Comanche interpreter. Fox said he did not know the channel. I told him there were plenty of colored boys who did and he could get one of them. As the party started off we were all gathered on the top of the fort to watch them sail down in front of the town. On account of the wind and tide they had to tack. When opposite the lower end of the town we saw the boat suddenly stop, then in a little while go forward and disappear around the bend of the inlet.

When the party returned Fox told us about the stopping. They had run on to an oyster bed. His colored pilot wore only a hat, shirt and pair of trousers, and Fox turned on the boy and said severely: "You rascal, I thought you knew the channel. Jump out and shove the boat off." The colored boy threw his hat in the bottom of the boat and jumped overboard and, happening to be on the deep water side, disappeared, and when he came up said: "Dis de channel, Mistah Fox." He swam around on the other side, got a footing, shoved the boat off, and climbed aboard.

There were a number of sailing yachts owned by citizens of the town; several that were engaged in the business of taking parties out sailing and fishing. Among these was a very large one, capable of accommodating our entire party. The owner, a Mr. Pacetti, often interested his patrons by taking them out on successful fishing expeditions. One feature of his program was catching sharks. Very early in the day I engaged him to take our whole party to the north beach after sharks. When we reached the fishing place, which was just inside and along the deepest place entering the harbor, a very substantial post was set deep in the sand and the shore end of his heavy shark line tied to it. A big hook, with a chain between the line and hook, was at the other end. Eight to ten pounds of fish or meat on the hook was the bait. This was placed in the stern of his rowboat and the sharp line coiled on top, and as he rowed into deep water the line passed out until he reached the end and then dropped the hook overboard. It was a favored place of the sharks in passing to and from the harbor. Sometimes the shark was the stronger in the tug of war and would successfully pull against the Indians until all the line was paid out and only the fastening at the shore end stopped him. It was great sport for the twenty or more Indians who whooped and tugged and pulled until the shark surrendered. Sometimes when they were pulling their hardest the shark would turn suddenly and dash toward shore and the crowd all fall down, and before they could get up the shark was going the other way. When finally tired out he was dragged up on the sand, flopping and squirming. Mr. Pacetti had a sharp axe and showed the Indians how to kill the shark by sinking it into his head. The Indians called the sharks "water buffalo." On one trip of this kind we captured five, one of which Mr. Pacetti estimated would weigh 1,200 pounds.

12. Prison Industries

The polishing of sea beans by the prisoners was a beginning for the meager industrial efforts that the conditions and environment permitted. They were found in the litter thrown up along the coast by the waves and tides and were staple souvenirs sold to northern visitors. Such occupations as the old Spanish town afforded were utilized. Picking and packing oranges needed brief help at the ripening each year, and the owner of one of the largest groves found the Indians increasingly satisfactory.

A dentist from the North, who sought health improvement by winter residence in the South, bought five acres of land across the bay on Anastasia Island on which to start an orange grove for the purpose of having some interest and income during his convalescing residence. He first agreed with a party of colored men to clear the ground. It was covered by a dense mass of large-leafed low palmetto. He had agreed with the colored men to clear the land for $35.00 per acre. At the end of their first week they drew their wages and then failed to continue. He then employed another set, still agreeing that he would pay the $35.00 per acre. At the end of that week he made them a payment and they did not appear Monday morning. He then came and told me his dilemma and asked if the Indians would not undertake the job and he would still pay the $35.00 per acre. Five of the sturdiest, each from a different tribe, were selected and the case laid before them, telling them the facts in regard to the two failures of the Negros and that it was their opportunity to show that they were reliable workers. They were told of the blistered hands which would come but would disappear by keeping at it; the back aches that would go away if they stuck to the job; how they would have to handle much of the soil on the entire five acres because the large roots of the palmetto embedded near the surface must all be taken out in order to get rid of the palmetto growth so as to give the oranges all the strength of the soil; how they would be in sight of the old fort and we would establish signals and have the guard watch so that if they had need they could put out the signal and the boat would be sent; and how they would have a tent to live in and must do their own cooking except on Sundays, which they could spend at the fort. Notwithstanding the hard prospect they agreed to undertake the job. The program was carried out and in about six weeks they had completed their contract and each received $35.00. On my first visit they showed their blistered hands and told of their aching backs, and later were pleased to show how their hands had become hard and in telling that their back aches were gone. Their physical improvement was very considerable and became an object lesson to the whole party.

The baggage man on the Tocoi Railroad had some difficulty in securing satisfactory help and applied for an Indian. He was permitted to arrange with one of the strongest, who, throughout the winter, when northern visitors increased the work, made regular trips to and from Tocoi and performed his service satisfactorily, which led our people to a kindlier estimate of Indians.

The sawmill in St. Augustine required men to handle lumber, taking it from the saw and stacking it in proper shape in the yard. Indians performed that service with entire satisfaction, receiving just compensation.

Lieutenant Zalinski, one of the earlier inventors experimenting with submarines and also inventing devices to increase the range of cannon, was then serving with the Fifth Artillery stationed at St. Augustine.[1] His active mind conceived that better water might be had for the town through deep-driven wells. He secured the interest of a few citizens who undertook the small expense and then asked, in the absence of machine power, the service of Indians and agreed to pay them for their labor. A party of the prisoners undertook this service and operated the block and tackle which lifted the heavy

---

1. 1st Lt. Edmund Louis Gray Zalinski, Fifth Artillery. A Prussian immigrant, he had served on Gen. Nelson A. Miles' staff during the Civil War and won a regular army commission in 1866. Between then and his retirement in 1894, he perfected a pneumatic dynamite torpedo gun, an entrenching tool, a ramrod bayonet, a telescopic sight for artillery, and a system of range and position finding for coastal artillery. He died in 1909. *Who Was Who in America, 1897–1942*, p. 1394.

driver, and a pipe was driven which finally reached good water and gave a flowing well. Other wells were driven, and this source of supply gave a valuable asset to the community.

It was desired to move the detached Sunday School building of a church several blocks to a position back of the post office nearer the center of town. It was a large building with a cupola and bell. The operation required that it should be taken most of the way over land submerged at high tide and that during this operation it be turned from facing east to facing west. One of the teachers of the Indians, Miss Mather, was active in gathering funds to cover the cost and in securing the new site, which was on government ground. She was unable to raise enough money to pay the price asked for the removal by the regular movers and urged that we use and pay such per diem as we could to the Indians. They, as well as the rest of the community, were to be benefited by having church and Sunday School services more convenient. By hiring a man who had experience in moving buildings, making our own windlass power and rollers, renting at low cost the timbers necessary, borrowing heavy ropes and blocks from a naval vessel, and renting the lifting screws from a contractor in Jacksonville, the job was undertaken and successfully carried out, only Indians doing the heavy work. The balance of funds gave what was to them acceptable pay and it was a valuable object lesson.

Other of the prisoners served in various capacities as helpers in the limited industries of the old town.

Professor Baird of the Smithsonian in Washington,[2] with whom I was in correspondence and who, in company with Senator George F. Edmunds of Vermont, visited Florida while the prisoners were there, wanted for the Smithsonian whatever of scientific value might be found in three Indian mounds not far from St. Augustine, and we undertook to carry out his wishes. Drawings of the mounds and their location were first made, the trees and their proportions growing on each mound were noted, and then all the earth was handled and all relics found were shipped to Washington. Several shipments in barrels were forwarded containing crania, bones, shell implements and ornaments, pieces of pottery, and stone axes, all duly noted and accredited to the place where found.

2. An eminent zoologist, Spencer Fullerton Baird (1823–87) was assistant secretary of the Smithsonian Institution from 1850 to 1878, when he succeeded to the secretaryship vacated by the death of Joseph Henry, and he also served after 1871 as head of the U. S. Commission of Fish and Fisheries. Among his duties at the Smithsonian, he was charged with building the museum collections of the institution. Pratt was but one of many military officers whom Baird enlisted in attaining this objective. After Pratt founded the Carlisle Indian School, he and Baird developed a close association, for Baird was a graduate of Dickinson College at Carlisle and had served on the faculty there from 1846 to 1850. *Dictionary of American Biography, 1,* 513–14.

Years afterward, when at Carlisle, I felt much indebted to the constant friendship of Professor Baird. Previous to his duties at Washington as head of the Smithsonian he had been a professor in Dickinson College in Carlisle and had relatives in the town and therefore was again, and locally, interested in what I was undertaking, and I frequently called to see him. On one of these visits I asked about our contributions from Florida and he told me they had been placed in the cases. I went among the cases to find them and after a long search finally recognized some of the stone axes and Indian implements and ornaments, but, instead of being accredited to us who worked for weeks to unearth and forward them, all were marked: "From the Indian mounds of Florida. Presented by Major J. W. Powell."[3] I protested and found that the collection had been turned over to Major Powell for cataloguing and display, and was told there would be correction, but a later visit failed to show any recognition of the real contributors.

The Minorcans supplied the town with seafood. One of them set his net offshore on the inside border of Anastasia Island just across from the old fort and caught a large sawfish, which wrecked his net, but in doing that it became entangled and so helplessly wrapped up in it as to enable the fishermen to tow him across the bay and, with the help of the Indians, lift him over the seawall. He was a fine specimen, his body sixteen feet long, and his toothed snout about five feet long. I telegraphed the catch to Professor Baird, who wired to secure it, get a taxidermist to skin and prepare it for display, and ship it to Washington. The taxidermist was found and the Indians helped in the skinning and preparation. When ready it was placed on a thick board long and wide enough to keep it in shape and shipped as directed. This promoted our education in the wonders of the ocean.

Another adventure was the capture of an immense sea turtle. The Indians had learned from the fishermen that sometimes when the sea turtle sleeps, he floats on the surface of the water, and if he is carefully approached, caught by his flippers, and quickly turned on his back and held there, he becomes helpless and can be lifted into the boat and by being kept on his back can be easily transported. One day a party of Indians out in the yawl discovered a sleeping turtle, handled him as directed, brought him in, and kept him for a few days on exhibition in the old fort. It was part of their amusement to stand on his back and be transported, somewhat slowly to be sure, but never-

---

3. John Wesley Powell (1834–1902), the famed one-armed Civil War veteran who in 1869 led the first expedition to navigate the great canyons of the Colorado River. He served as director of the Bureau of American Ethnology of the Smithsonian from 1879 until his death and also as director of the United States Geological Survey from 1880 to 1894. *Dictionary of American Biography*, *15*, 146–48.

theless they actually rode on a turtle. He afterward made excellent soup for the entire party.

One day an Indian ran down from the top of the fort to report that "a water horse" was out in the bay. I went to the terreplein and saw what looked like the face of a very large horse minus ears and just under the water could trace what seemed the back of a long body and thought it some unusual sea monster. I took one of the army guns and some cartridges, ran outside, jumped down into the moat, got in one of the angles nearest the water, peeked over, and as the supposed "water horse" came floating by saw the glint of his eyes, at which I aimed, and made a lucky shot, knocking out both. He gave one flop and turned bottom up, died instantly and, as he floated, revealed that he was no sea monster but a large alligator. Several Indians hurried off in the yawl, brought him ashore, and carried him into the fort. He measured nine feet and two inches from tip to tip. He was a new wonder and the object of much discussion by the Indians as they curiously examined his anatomy. They had seen plenty of the small ones, both alive and stuffed, as sold by curio dealers to visitors. These were not so curious to them because they were somewhat like the lizards in their country. They had not seen alligators that grew so large and, by this experience, were ready to believe that in Florida they grow to be much larger.

Quo-yo-uh, one of the Comanches, was a large, powerful man with considerable adipose. He belonged to the guard and was not enamored with that part of the military drills called the "setting up process," in which some of the movements required him to extend his arms and swing them around rapidly, and to go through movements giving exercise to the elbows, the wrists, and the fingers. After inspecting the alligator right side up, they turned him on his back to investigate his methods of locomotion. Quo-yo-uh took hold to examine the forearm, looked at the five claws, or fingers, and the rest of the paw, or hand, and said: "just like man." He then moved the wrist as he was required to do in his drill and said "just like man." Then the elbow, and said "just like man," and then the shoulder joint, and swinging the arm of the alligator around, said "Heap good soldier!" which greatly amused the guards and the whole party.

Discontent appeared in the old town because the Indian prisoners were allowed to go out from the fort. The first I knew of this was from an article in the town newspaper as follows:

> It Should be Prohibited.—Complaints are being made in regard to permitting the Indian prisoners in the fort to roam the streets at night after the sun is down. The people do not think and believe alike as to

the impossibility of an insurrection among them at some unguarded moment, and either murder the inhabitants or fire the city. While some have faith in their obedience and docility, others are ever watchful and expectant of an outbreak, causing to many an intense uneasiness. In order to pacify all, we coincide with those who protest against the Indians being without a sufficient guard at night from the Barracks, and also against any of them being allowed on the streets at night. A few nights since, in fact several nights of late, a number of them, including some of those interested in the recent restless demonstration [see below, Chap. 14], have been seen upon the streets after 10 o'clock at night, some with bayonets and cartridge boxes strapped about them. We have been prompted by the complaint of many, to make mention of the above facts through the columns of the PRESS, hoping that the same would be well weighed in the minds of those who have the control of the Indians.

My letter to the editor is relevant and is herewith inserted.

Mr. J. O. Whitney

Fort Marion,
July 20, 1876.

Editor, PRESS

Dear Sir:

I am unable to find that your article in reference to the Indians being out after 10 o'clock nights has sufficient base. You say, "a few nights since, in fact several nights of late." On Tuesday evening the 10th inst., for sufficient reasons, permission was given to a party of fourteen to go down town to trade. Two of them belonged to the guard. They were all back by nine o'clock. I do not find that any were out on any other nights and I fear you have been incautiously led into a harmful statement without good grounds, which is to be deplored for many reasons, but mostly because it will be (as it has already been) copied into other papers to our detriment as a community. Without discussing with you the righteousness of the abridging dictations of your protest, I may with propriety invite your attention to the fact that on the night of the fire you, as well as all citizens so far as I can learn, were quite willing the Indians should be out after 10 o'clock, and further to the fact, that after 14 months of unexceptional good behavior of the Indians and in the absence of direct cause your agitation of apprehension is not well timed. If any citizen or citizens had been disturbed in their persons or property by any of the Indians since their arrival here, the solicitude might be justified.

The citizens have treated the Indians with greatest kindness and I need only again refer to the night of the fire to show what their temper is in return for that treatment. Instead of disturbing the public peace they will be found foremost to fall in, if need be, in its defense, and there seems to be no reason why the relations or management should be changed. The recent calamity in the northwest[4] has no more to do with it than does the cannibalism of some of the blacks in the South Sea Islands to do with our good feelings toward those of that color in our midst.

I do not purpose ferreting out and trying to correct all the reports in regard to the Indians, that may be afloat, but it seems well in this case, although you did not ask it, to aid you in giving correct impressions to the public.

Anticipating you will be glad to rectify an error, I am,

> Yours truly,
> R. H. PRATT,
> Lt. U. S. Army.

Only a brief synopsis of this letter was published by Mr. Whitney.

The fire referred to occurred at two o'clock in the morning not far from the old fort. There were two residence buildings burned and others endangered. The old town had no fire department and was entirely dependent on water being brought in buckets. An account of it is given in full in the *Press* under the editorship of Mr. Whitney and I extract from the description all that is said in regard to the Indians' services: "Men with buckets and blankets now began to arrive and just in the nick of time came Captain Pratt and the entire number of Indians with buckets and blankets."

Then in a card of acknowledgment for having his own home saved, a Mr. Russell says this: "The undersigned takes this opportunity of returning his heartfelt gratitude to those citizens of St. Augustine for saving his premises from destruction by the recent fire, and to Captain Pratt for his promptness in marching a number of Indians from the fort and their wonderful exertions are deserving of all praise."

A grocer named Greatorex was a welcome visitor at the fort and had a number of friends among the Indians. In his early life he had traveled the country as a prestidigitator and often entertained the Indians with his art, teaching some of them samples of his ability to entertain. He came one day much perturbed to tell that a petition which was to go to Congress protesting against the Indian prisoners being allowed to go out to work was being circulated and already had many signatures. He said he had done all he could

---

4. The annihilation of Custer and part of the Seventh Cavalry at the Battle of the Little Bighorn, June 25, 1876.

to prevent such action, telling the people the Indians were a great asset to bring visitors, who were the greatest source of income the town had, but he could not stop the petition and thought I might find a way to do that. I told him to go back and sign the petition and get everybody he could to sign it; that if he could help lead Congress and the country to understand that Indians were peaceful and could and would work he would be helping the Indians to overcome part of the false reputation given them by their enemies.

The petition went forward and soon afterward press news from Washington told the country that Senator Jones of Florida had introduced the following resolution:

> The Senate, August 4th, 1876. Resolved: That the Secretary of War communicate to the Senate whether or not the hostile Indians sent to St. Augustine, Florida, to be confined in the fortress at that place are permitted to go at large unguarded; and if so by whose authority these savages have been set at liberty among the inhabitants of said town, and what, in his judgment, ought to be done with these dangerous persons if the Government should decide to restore them to permanent freedom.
> Senator Conkling of New York: "I suggest that that resolution lie over until tomorrow morning unless the Senator is tenacious about it this morning."

The record shows that while the Senator had complied with the appeal of his constituents, the petition was laid on the table and went into "innocuous desuetude," for there was no notice of it thereafter and no decree was placed against continuing the freedom and labors of the Indians.

13. Anthropological Interest in the Prisoners

Clark Mills, the sculptor who gave the country the Jackson statue in Lafayette Square in front of the White House, was sent to St. Augustine by Professor Baird, the head of the Smithsonian Institution, to make plaster cast busts of the prisoners. The subject was seated in a chair and a large muslin sheet tucked in about his neck to protect his clothing. A flexible cap, fitting close, protected the hair. A preparation of plaster which hardened quickly was built over the head, the neck, then the ears and the face. Breathing was accomplished through apertures to the nostrils. When the material hardened, it was carefully broken, removed, and piece by piece built back into form. When this was completed it became a perfect mold; a material which prevented the plaster from sticking was put over the inside and then a plaster mixture poured within this and rolled around until it was made sufficiently thick for shipment. When this hardened the mold was broken off and an exact head of each subject produced. I was the first victim. Then Lone Wolf, and when his and my heads were reproduced perfectly the Indians were entirely satisfied and the whole of them passed through the process.

Sculptor Mills pronounced Zotom, one of the younger Kiowas, as perfect a specimen of physical manhood as he had ever met, and he made a cast of his entire body. For years after, throughout Professor Baird's management, the busts occupied a conspicuous place on the show cases of the Smithsonian.

The historical value of the Mills collection with an account of the events which enabled its acquirement is told in the "Proceedings of the National Museum for 1878" and is introduced here, giving the name and tribe of each prisoner, omitting the offenses alleged.

> Catalogue of casts taken by Clark Mills, Esq., of the heads of sixty-four Indian prisoners of various western tribes, and held at Fort Marion, Saint Augustine, Fla., in charge of Capt. R. H. Pratt, U. S. A.
>
> The attention of anthropologists in later years has been directed very closely to the shape of the head, of the lineaments, and of the external form generally of mankind during life, instead of being confined to that of the cranium and the skeleton, and every opportunity of securing accurate casts, in plaster, of native races of a country is eagerly embraced. The face masks made by the brothers Schlagintweit, of Asiatic tribes, are well known standard objects in the principal ethnological collections of the world and constitute the largest single series yet brought together.
>
> It has always been difficult to obtain face casts of the North American Indians. They manifest a deeply rooted aversion to the process required, and, indeed, a superstitious fear generally of being imitated in any manner, even by the pencil or camera. The face masks from nature now in existence have, for the most part, been taken from the dead, with the consequent lack of vital expression, and the opportunity of obtaining life-like similitudes of 64 Indian prisoners of war, of at least six different tribes, was promptly embraced by the Smithsonian Institution. No difficulty was experienced in securing these cases, as the Indians had every confidence in the statements of Captain Pratt, who had them in command, that there would be nothing detrimental to either soul or body in the process, and, indeed, he himself was first subjected to it to reassure them. In fact, understanding that the casts were destined for the city of the Great Father at Washington, there to be preserved forever, one invalid whose treatment was deferred until the last could scarcely be satisfied even with the assurance that he should not be neglected.
>
> S. F. Baird

Fort Marion, St. Augustine, Fla.,
February 9, 1878.

Prof. Spencer F. Baird,
Smithsonian Institution, Washington, D.C.

Dear Sir:

In reply to yours of the 23d of January, I am authorized to forward the categorical list and offenses of the prisoners, compiled from the official reports of the officers having the matter of looking up offenders in charge at Indian agencies. I have added to that list the date and place of arrest or capture, and the date of death of those who have died. To give the other information asked, I add in general some account of our later dealings with these people. This you can abridge or rearrange to your purpose.[1]

. . . .

Personal history sufficient for your purposes will probably be found in the list, but the charges are only alleged and not proven.

It is simply just to say that since being here these men have set an example to civilization in good behavior; twenty-two of them have learned to read and write, understandingly; while in the matter of labor, at such as could be given, they have not failed or weakened in the slightest degree.

Respectfully and sincerely yours,
R H. Pratt,
U. S. Army.

List of Indians[2]

CHEYENNES

1. *Heap of Birds.* Mo-e-yau-hay-ist. Chief. Age 49. Weight 177 lbs. Ht. 6 ft. ¼ in. Arrested at Cheyenne Agency, Indian Territory, April 3, 1875. Died October 9, 1877. Ringleader.
2. *Bear Shield.* Nock-o-yo-uh. Chief. Age 45. Wt. 140 lbs. Ht. 5 ft. 7½ in. Arrested at Cheyenne Agency, Indian Territory, April 3, 1875. Killed Watkins.
3. *Eagle's Head.* Minimic. Chief. Age 50. Wt. 195 lbs. Ht. 5 ft. 11¾ in. Arrested at Cheyenne Agency, Indian Territory, April 3, 1875. Ringleader.
4. *Medicine Water.* Mi-huh-yeu-i-mup. Warrior. Age 40. Wt. 139 lbs. Ht. 5 ft. 7¼

1. The remainder of Pratt's letter, a long narrative of the history of each tribe, is omitted here.

2. In his manuscript Pratt gives only part of the statistical data on sixty-four Indians whose casts were taken by Mills, omitting the additional data on place and date of arrest and offenses alleged, as well as the names of those Mills did not study. The following list, compiled directly from the original in the *Proceedings of the United States National Museum for 1878*, pp. 204–14, has been substituted as containing more information of historical value. This list includes all the Indians who were originally deported and also sets forth certain physical characteristics of the Indians studied by Mills.

in. Arrested at Cheyenne Agency, Indian Territory, March 5, 1875. Charge 1st—Wilful and deliberate murder. Did kill or assist in killing a party of surveyors, white men, consisting of Capt. Oliver F. Short and his son, F. D. Short, James Shaw and his son, J. Allen Shaw, and J. H. Renchler, residents of Lawrence, Kans. Also, Henry C. Jones. Charge 2d—Abduction. Illegal detention. Kidnapping. Did carry off or assist in carrying off Catherine, Sophia, Julianne, and Mary Germain, aged, respectively, 18, 13, 7, and 5½ years. Held the first two as captives from September 11, 1874, until March 1, 1875.

5. *Long Back.* Cha-se-yun-nuh. Subchief. Age 53. Wt. 184 lbs. 8 ou. Ht. 6 ft. 1¾ in. Arrested at Cheyenne Agency, Indian Territory, March 18, 1875. Held and abused Germain girls.

6. *White Man.* Ow-us-sait. Warrior. Age 24. Wt. 174 lbs. Ht. 5 ft. 11¼ in. Arrested at Cheyenne Agency, Indian Territory, March 5, 1875. Accomplice in Short and Germain murders; pointed out by Medicine Water.

7. *Rising Bull.* O-to-as-tuh-hos. Warrior. Age 30. Wt. 133 lbs. Ht. 5 ft. 5 in. Arrested at Cheyenne Agency, Indian Territory, March 5, 1875. Accomplice in above murders; pointed out by Germain girls.

8. *Broken Leg.* Co-hoe. Warrior. Age 24. Wt. 131 lbs. 8 ou. Ht. 5 ft. 8¾ in. Arrested at Cheyenne Agency, Indian Territory, January 9, 1875. Accomplice in Germain murder; pointed out by Big Moccasin and Medicine Water.

9. *Bear's Heart.* Nock-ko-ist. Warrior. Age 26. Wt. 136 lbs. 8 ou. Ht. 5 ft. 9 in. Arrested at Cheyenne Agency, Indian Territory, April 3, 1875. Accomplice in Germain murder; pointed out by Big Moccasin and Medicine Water.

10. *Star.* Ho-i-toich. Warrior. Age 29. Wt. 162 lbs. Ht. 5 ft. 9¾ in. Arrested at Cheyenne Agency, Indian Territory, April 3, 1875. No offense charged.

11. *Howling Wolf.* Ho-na-nist-to. Warrior (Minimic's son). Age 27. Wt. 161 lbs. Ht. 5 ft. 9 in. Arrested at Cheyenne Agency, Indian Territory, April 3, 1875. Ringleader.

12. *Making Medicine.* O-kuh-ha-tuh. Warrior. Age 33. Wt. 145 lbs. Ht. 6 ft. ¼ in. Arrested at Cheyenne Agency, Indian Territory, April 3, 1875. Ringleader.

13. *Antelope.* Wuh-ah. Warrior. Age 39. Wt. 152 lbs. Ht. 5 ft. 10¼ in. Arrested at Cheyenne Agency, Indian Territory, April 3, 1875. Ringleader.

14. *Wolf's Marrow.* Come-uh-su-rah. Warrior. Age 49. Wt. 137 lbs. 8 ou. Ht. 5 ft. 7¾ in. Arrested at Cheyenne Agency, Indian Territory, April 3, 1875. Ringleader.

15. *Little Medicine.* Ma-ha-ih-ha-chit. Chief. Age 35. Wt. 148 lbs. Ht. 5 ft. 7¾ in. Arrested at Cheyenne Agency, Indian Territory, April 3, 1875. Ringleader.

16. *Shave Head.* O-uk-ste-uh. Warrior. Age 23. Wt. 124 lbs. 8 ou. Ht. 5 ft. 9 in. Arrested at Cheyenne Agency, Indian Territory, April 3, 1875. Ringleader.

17. *Roman Nose.* Wo-uh-hun-nih. Warrior. Age 22. Wt. 154 lbs. 8 ou. Ht. 5 ft. 9¾ in. Arrested at Cheyenne Agency, Indian Territory, April 3, 1875. Ringleader.

18. *Big Nose.* Pa-e-yis. Warrior. Age 22. Wt. 135 lbs. Ht. 5 ft. 6¾ in. Arrested at Cheyenne Agency, Indian Territory, April 3, 1875. Ringleader.

19. *Squint Eyes.* Quch-ke-i-mus. Warrior. Age 20. Wt. 134 lbs. 8 ou. Ht. 5 ft. 8½ in. Arrested at Cheyenne Agency, Indian Territory, April 3, 1875. Ringleader.

20. *Little Chief.* Ko-we-o-narre. Warrior. Age 23. Wt. 144 lbs. 8 ou. Ht. 5 ft. 10 in. Arrested at Cheyenne Agency, Indian Territory, April 3, 1875. Ringleader.

21. *Matches.* Chis-i-se-duh. Warrior. Age 21. Wt. 136 lbs. Ht. 5 ft. 8½ in. Arrested at Cheyenne Agency, Indian Territory, April 3, 1875. Ringleader.

22. *Buffalo Meat.* O-e-wo-toh. Warrior. Age 30. Wt. 152 lbs. 8 ou. Ht. 5 ft. 8 in. Arrested at Cheyenne Agency, Indian Territory, April 3, 1875. Ringleader.

23. *Buzzard.* Mo-he-wih-kio. Warrior. Age 22. Wt. 172 lbs. Ht. 6 ft. 1 in. Arrested at Cheyenne Agency, Indian Territory, April 3, 1875. Ringleader.

24. *Soaring Eagle.* O-uh-o. Warrior. Age 26. Wt. 128 lbs. 8 ou. Ht. 5 ft. 7 in. Arrested at Fort Wallace, Kansas, December 25, 1874. Brown murder near Wallace. Had Brown's pistol when captured by Lieutenant Hinkle.

25. *Bear Killer.* No-co-mis-ta. Warrior. Age 33. Wt. 148 lbs. Ht. 5 ft. 4¾ in. Arrested at Fort Wallace, Kansas, December 25, 1874. Brown murder.

26. *Left Hand.* No-mohst. Warrior. Age 32. Wt. 141 lbs. Ht. 5 ft. 10¾ in. Arrested at Fort Wallace, Kansas, December 25, 1874. Brown murder.

27. *Chief Killer.* Noh-hu-nah-wih. Warrior. Age 28. Wt. 131 lbs. Ht. 5 ft. 5½ in. Arrested at Staked Plains, Texas, September 24, 1874. Participated in the killing of the Germain parents and son and daughter, and in carrying away into captivity the four sisters.

28. *Buffalo Calf.* Mo-chi. Woman. Age 34. Wt. 138 lbs. 8 ou. Ht. 5 ft. 6¾ in. Arrested at Cheyenne Agency, Indian Territory, March 5, 1875. Put an axe in head of Germain girls' father.

29. *Gray Beard.* Chief. Arrested at Cheyenne Agency, Indian Territory, April 3, 1875. Jumped from the train en route near Houston, Fla., May 21, 1875, and was shot by the guard and died in two hours. Ringleader.

30. *Big Moccasin.* Warrior. Arrested at Cheyenne Agency, Indian Territory, December 14, 1874. Died November 4, 1875. Captured by Captain Keyes and pointed out by Medicine Water. Ringleader and murder.

31. *Lean Bear.* Chief. Arrested at Cheyenne Agency, Indian Territory, April 3, 1875. Died July 24, 1875. Ringleader.

32. *Shaving Wolf.* Warrior. Arrested at Cheyenne Agency, Indian Territory, April 3, 1875. Died December 5, 1876. Ringleader.

33. *Spotted Elk.* Warrior. Arrested at Cheyenne Agency, Indian Territory, April 3, 1875. Died January 2, 1877. Ringleader.

ARAPAHOES

34. *Packer.* Nun-ne-ti-yuh. Warrior. Age 26. Wt. 143 lbs. Ht. 5 ft. 9½ in. Arrested at Cheyenne Agency, Indian Territory, March 5, 1875. Wilful murder. Killed Leon Williams, a Mexican herder in the employment of the United States Government, at the Cheyenne and Arapaho Agency.

35. *White Bear.* Huh-noh-uh-co-ah. Warrior. Age 25. Wt. 126 lbs. 8 ou. Ht. 5 ft. 7¼ in. Arrested at Cheyenne Agency, Indian Territory, March 5, 1875. Attempt to kill. Did shoot at, with intent to kill, F. H. Williams, an employee of the United States Government, at the Cheyenne and Arapaho Agency.

CADDOS

36. *Choctaw.* Huh-nah-nee. Prominent man. Age 49. Wt. 160 lbs. 8 ou. Ht. 5 ft. 7¼ in. Arrested at Fort Sill, Indian Territory, April 7, 1875. Killed E. P. Osborne (Black Beaver's son-in-law) near the Wichita Agency, Indian Territory, August 22, 1874.

KIOWAS

37. *Woman's Heart*. Chief. Arrested at Cheyenne Agency, Indian Territory, October 3, 1874. Released by order of the Secretary of War, April 18, 1877. Participated in the assaults on Amos Chapman and party and on Major Lyman's train near the source of the Washita River, Texas, September 9 to 13, 1874. Participated in the murder of Jacob Dilsey on the North Fork of the Canadian River below Camp Supply, near Cottonwood Grove, Indian Territory, November 21, 1873.

38. *White Horse*. Isa-tah. Chief. Age 30. Wt. 197 lbs. 8 ou. Ht. 5 ft. 7¼ in. Arrested at Fort Sill, Indian Territory, December 17, 1874. Led the party killing Manuel Ortega and Lucien Muñus, near Dr. J. J. Sturms, on the Little Washita River, Indian Territory, August 22, 1874. Participated in the Howard's Wells, Texas, massacre, 1872. Led the party killing the Lee family and abducting the Lee children near Fort Griffin, Texas, 1872. Led the party killing Mr. Koozer near Henrietta, Texas, and carrying his wife and four children into captivity, 1870. Led the party attacking the mail stage, dangerously wounding the driver, robbing the stage, killing, wounding, and robbing the stage of its mules, near Johnson's Station 25 miles west of Fort Concho, Texas, July 14, 1872. Notoriously a murderer and raider.

39. *Beef*. Wo-haw. Warrior. Age 22. Wt. 133 lbs. 8 ou. Ht. 5 ft. 4½ in. Arrested at Cheyenne Agency, Indian Territory, October 3, 1874. Participated in the murder of Manuel Ortega and Lucien Muños. Was in the party killing Jacob Dilsey.

40. *Bad Eye*. Ta-na-ti. Alias Bird Chief; alias Bird Medicine. Warrior and Leader. Age 43. Wt. 153 lbs. Ht. 5 ft. 7¼ in. Arrested at Cheyenne Agency, Indian Territory, October 3, 1874. Participated in the assaults on Amos Chapman and party and Major Lyman's train near the source of the Washita River, Texas, September 9 to 13, 1874. Led the party killing Jacob Dilsey on the North Fork of the Canadian River, below Camp Supply, near Cottonwood Grove, Indian Territory, November 21, 1873. Was in the party killing J. H. Martin, Mr. Canala, and Mr. Himes near Kiowa or Medicine Lodge Creek, Barbour County, Kansas, June 16, 1874. Participated in the murder of Earnest Modest; seized Modest by the wrist and held him while another shot him, near Wichita Agency, August 22, 1874.

41. *Double Vision*. So-gau-se. Petty Chief. Age 62. Wt. 160 lbs. Ht. 5 ft. 8 in. Arrested at Cheyenne Agency, Indian Territory, October 3, 1874. Was in the party murdering Earnest Modest. Held the bridle of Romero's horse all the time the murder of Earnest Modest was being accomplished.

42. *Bear-in-the-Clouds*. Sa-a-mi-a-da. Leader. Age 48. Wt. 159 lbs. Ht. 5 ft. 9 in. Arrested at Cheyenne Agency, Indian Territory, October 3, 1874. Participated in the murder of Earnest Modest. Took care of the horses of the party while the other Indians hammered Earnest to death with their hatchets.

43. *Lone Wolf*. E-si-sim-ers. Chief. Age 55. Wt. 162 lbs. Ht. 5 ft. 9½ in. Arrested at Salt Fork, Red River, Indian Territory, February 18, 1875. Headed a party of Kiowas killing two buffalo hunters, Dudley and Wallace, on the Canadian River below Adobe Walls early in 1874; led a party of 100 Indians, more or less, in assailing a party of non-combatants, citizens of the United States, viz. E. P. Os-

borne, E. H. Barrett, Jackson Clark, and Charles Losson, and did murder, or aid in, assist, and abet the murder, with firearms, of three of the aforesaid noncombatants, viz, Osborne, Barrett, and Clark.

44. *Biter.* Zo-tom. Warrior. Age 24. Wt. 175 lbs. Ht. 5 ft. 7 in. Arrested at Salt Fork, Red River, Indian Territory, February 18, 1875. Was in party headed by Mahmante, killing two colored men on Salt Creek Prairie between Jackson and Belknap, Texas, 1870 or 1871. Participated in attack on buffalo hunters at Adobe Walls early in spring of 1874.

45. *Ankle.* On-ko-eht. Warrior (Mexican). Age 28. Wt. 131 lbs. Ht. 5 ft. 2¼ in. Arrested at Salt Fork, Red River, Indian Territory, February 18, 1875. Bad man; was with Mah-mante, killing two colored men.

46. *High Forehead.* Ohet-toint. Warrior (Mexican). Age 25. Wt. 151 lbs. 8 ou. Ht. 5 ft. 9 in. Arrested at Salt Fork, Red River, Indian Territory, February 18, 1875. Was with Mah-mante when he killed the man in the wagon; was with Lone Wolf killing two buffalo hunters.

47. *Boy.* E-tah-dle-uh. Warrior (Mexican). Age 21. Wt. 166 lbs. Ht. 5 ft. 10 in. Arrested at Salt Fork, Red River, Indian Territory, February 18, 1875. Was with Lone Wolf killing buffalo hunters (Dudley and Wallace); was in the party attacking buffalo hunters at Adobe Walls early in spring of 1874.

48. *Toothless.* Zo-pe-he. Warrior (Mexican captured at age 18). Age 45. Wt. 133 lbs. 8 ou. Ht. 5 ft. 1½ in. Arrested at Salt Fork, Red River, Indian Territory, February 18, 1875. Participated in the killing of two colored men. Went to Texas with a party of Comanches and participated in the killing of two men on the Clear Fork of the Brazos in the summer of 1873.

49. *White Goose.* Tash-dle-tah. Warrior. Age 30. Wt. 156 lbs. Ht. 5 ft. 10 in. Arrested at Salt Fork, Red River, Indian Territory, February 18, 1875. Was with Lone Wolf, killing two men, buffalo hunters, Wallace and Dudley; was prominent in the attack on troops on the Washita August 22, 1874; helped to kill the white men Modest, Osborne, and others.

50. *Teeth.* Zone-ke-uh. Warrior. Age 20. Wt. 150 lbs. Ht. 5 ft. 7 in. Arrested at Salt Fork, Red River, February 18, 1875. Was with Mah-mante killing the two colored men. Was with Lone Wolf killing two buffalo hunters, Dudley and Wallace.

51. *Old Man.* Beah-ko. Warrior (Mexican captured at age 6). Age 38. Wt. 151 lbs. 8 ou. Ht. 5 ft. 2¼ in. Arrested at Salt Fork, Red River, Indian Territory, February 18, 1875. Helped rob Shirley's store at the Wichita Agency, Indian Territory, August 22, 1874.

52. *Good Talk.* To-un-ke-uh. Warrior. Age 19. Wt. 145 lbs. Ht. 5 ft. 6 in. Arrested at Salt Fork, Red River, Indian Territory, February 18, 1875. Stealing in Salt Creek Valley, Texas, late in 1871. Was with Lone Wolf killing Dudley and Wallace, buffalo hunters.

53. *Wild Horse.* Ko-ba. Warrior. Age 29. Wt. 153 lbs. Ht. 5 ft. 7¾ in. Arrested at Salt Fork, Red River, Indian Territory, February 18, 1875. Was with Mah-mante stealing a lot of mules in the Brazos country in 1872. Participated in the attack on General Davidson's command at Wichita Agency, August 22, 1874.

54. *Flat Nose.* Mau-ko-peh. Warrior. Age 21. Wt. 149 lbs. Ht. 5 ft. 5 in. Arrested at Salt Fork, Red River, Indian Territory, February 18, 1875. Stealing horses, and was with Mah-mante stealing a lot of mules in the Brazos country in 1872.

55. *Wise.* Au-lih. Warrior. Age 28. Wt. 169 lbs. Ht. 5 ft. 10¼ in. Arrested at Salt Fork, Red River, Indian Territory, February 18, 1875. Was with Lone Wolf killing

Dudley and Wallace. Was with Mah-mante when he killed the man in the wagon. Stealing horses. Helped rob Shirley's store. Participated in the attack on General Davidson's command August 22, 1874.

56. *Kicking.* Ko-ho. Alias Club Foot. Warrior (Mexican captured at age 5). Age 27. Wt. 126 lbs. Ht. 5 ft. 3½ in. Arrested at Salt Fork, Red River, Indian Territory, February 18, 1875. Was with Lone Wolf killing Dudley and Wallace. Was with Mah-mante killing the two colored men. Helped rob Shirley's store. Participated in the attack on General Davidson's command. Stealing mules.

57. *Bull (or Buffalo) with Holes in His Ears.* To-o-sape. Warrior (Mexican captured at age 8). Age 45. Wt. 132 lbs. Ht. 5 ft. 2¼ in. Arrested at Salt Fork, Red River, Indian Territory, February 18, 1875. Was with Mah-mante killing the two colored men. Was with Lone Wolf killing Dudley and Wallace. Stealing mules.

58. *Bear Mountain.* Tsait-kope-ta. Warrior (Cheyenne father, Pawnee mother; has lived with Kiowas for fourteen years). Age 25. Wt. 166 lbs. 8 ou. Ht. 5 ft. 9¾ in. Arrested at Salt Fork, Red River, Indian Territory, February 18, 1875. Helped rob Shirley's store. Stole horses. Was with Lone Wolf killing Dudley and Wallace.

59. *Pedro.* Warrior (Mexican captured at age 5). Age 48. Wt. 136 lbs. 8 ou. Ht. 5 ft. 5 in. Arrested at Salt Fork, Red River, Indian Territory, February 18, 1875. Killed a colored man, known as Frenchy, near the Wichita Agency, Indian Territory, August 22, 1874. Was in a party killing two white men below Fort Griffin, Texas, in the winter of 1872–73. One of the men was riding a mule, and the other a horse, at the time. Was a prominent character in the party robbing Shirley's store. Stole horses and mules. Was with Mah-mante killing the man in the wagon.

60. *Straightening an Arrow.* Ih-pa-yah. Warrior. Arrested at Salt Fork, Red River, February 18, 1875. Died October 5, 1875. Stealing horses in or near the Salt Creek Valley, Texas, in the spring of 1873.

61. *Sun.* Co-a-bote-ta. Warrior. Arrested at Sulphur Courthouse, Indian Territory, October 23, 1874. Died May 24, 1875. Participated in the murder of Jacob Dilsey.

62. *Coming to the Grove.* Ah-ke-ah. Alias Pah-o-ka. Warrior. Arrested at Cheyenne Agency, Indian Territory, October 3, 1874. Released by order of the Secretary of War, April 18, 1877. Participated in the murder of Jacob Dilsey.

63. *Man-who-Walks-above-the-Ground.* Mah-mante. Alias Swan. Chief. Arrested at Salt Fork, Red River, Indian Territory, February 13, 1875. Died July 29, 1875. Led a party killing two colored men on the Salt Creek Prairie between Jacksboro and Belknap, Texas, 1870 or 1871. Killed a man on the road south of Fort Griffin, Texas, sometime in 1870. Two men were riding in a lone wagon, Mah-mante lay concealed and shot one. Led a party stealing a large lot of mules in the Brazos country in 1871. One mule was spotted. Killed a white woman and child in revenge for the loss of two of his men while on a raid in Southwestern Texas, in fall of 1874. Was with Lone Wolf, killing two buffalo hunters, Dudley and Wallace, &c.

COMANCHES

64. *Buck (or Red) Antelope.* Eck-e-nah-ats. Warrior (Mexican). Age 31. Wt. 137 lbs. Ht. 5 ft. 5½ in. Arrested at Elk Creek, Indian Territory, October 26, 1874. Was in Texas with a party and stole horses about December 1873.

65. *Dry Wood.* Wy-a-ko. Warrior (Mexican father, Comanche mother). Age 30. Wt.

140 lbs. Ht. 5 ft. 9 in. Arrested at Elk Creek, Indian Territory, October 26, 1874. Has been in Texas stealing horses; was in Texas last in winter of 1873–74.

66. *Black Horse.* Po-ka-do-ah. Chief. Age 46. Wt. 150 lbs. Ht. 5 ft. 8 in. Arrested at Fort Sill, Indian Territory, March 7, 1875. Talked defiantly in council with Governor Davis at Fort Sill, Indian Territory, 1873. Killed a white man near Fort Cobb, Indian Territory, 1867. The man went in his company on a hunt, and it was thought at the time that Black Horse procured him to go for the purpose of killing him. That the Indian Agent [Jesse] Leavenworth and an inn-keeper named Lewis had engaged him to do the job on account of some trouble they had had with the man, who was a bad character.

67. *Mad-a-with-t.* Warrior. Age 26. Wt. 145 lbs. Ht. 5 ft. 11 in. Arrested at Fort Sill, Indian Territory, March 7, 1875. Died July 21, 1877. A raider. A bad man. Always trying to persuade young men to go off to Texas, always going himself.

68. *Telling Something.* Ta-a-way-te. Alias Buffalo Scout. Warrior. Age 22. Wt. 160 lbs. Ht. 5 ft. 7½ in. Arrested at Fort Sill, Indian Territory, April 18, 1875. A raider. A bad man. Always stealing horses or on a warpath. Never brings his horses to Sill. Steals them, and takes them to the Quahada Camp on the Staked Plains.

69. *Tail Feathers (or Little Feather).* Pe-eh-chip. Warrior. Age 25. Wt. 155 lbs. Ht. 5 ft. 5½ in. Arrested at Fort Sill, Indian Territory, April 18, 1875. He is one of the five fellows that shot their father and was outlawed, and whom Captain Lee, Tenth Cavalry, was sent down to Double Mountain after in the fall of 1873. He has been on the warpath ever since.

70. *Always-Sitting-Down-in-a-Bad-Place.* Tis-cha-kah-da. Warrior. Age 31. Wt. 141 lbs. Ht. 5 ft. 5¼ in. Arrested at Fort Sill, Indian Territory, April 18, 1875. A bad man. Always off trying to steal horses, or on the warpath, &c. He is one of the desperadoes Captain Lee, Tenth Cavalary, was sent down to Double Mountain for late in 1873.

71. *Pile of Rocks.* Quoi-yo-uh. Warrior. Age 46. Wt. 186 lbs. Ht. 6 ft. Arrested at Fort Sill, Indian Territory, April 8, 1875. Bad man. Stealing horses. Stole thirty or more horses from the Chickasaws.

72. *Little Prairie Hill.* Pa-voor-ite. Warrior (Mexican). Age 42. Wt. 133 lbs. Ht. 5 ft. 4½ in. Arrested at Wichita Agency, Indian Territory, December 25, 1874. Helped steal forty-six horses from near Fort Sill belonging to Kiowa and Comanche Agency and John Madden, citizen, May 11, 1874. Threatened to kill Mr. Clark, Comanche innkeeper, on the day of the Washita disturbance, August 22, 1874. Drew pistol on Clark.

73. *Mother.* Pe-ah-in. Woman (not a prisoner). Age 31. Wt. 136 lbs. Ht. 5 ft. 3½ in.

74. *Ah-kes.* Small child (not a prisoner). Girl. Age 9. Wt. 64 lbs. Ht. 3 ft. 11½ in.

While the work of taking casts was going on, a couple of gentlemen came in and were watching. I noted that one of them wore a wig, which offered an opportunity for illustration of the white man's progress. I asked the gentleman if he would object to letting the Indians see that he had been scalped and had secured a replacement. As I was preparing the subjects for Mr. Mills, I had the man take the chair, and putting the protecting cloth around him, took up the skull cap and, as I attempted to slip it over his head, slipped his wig off, and behold, he was without a single hair on his head. The astonishment of the Indians was most interesting. Several of them ran outside the room and turned and looked back, while the gentleman himself, his friend, Mr. Mills, and I greatly enjoyed the situation; I then had him tell how, through sickness, he had lost his hair which never came back, and had worn his wig for a great many years.

Captain Williams, a retired officer of the army, visited St. Augustine.[3] It so happened that, as a lieutenant serving in New Mexico, he was in command of an escort conducting the paymaster from making payments to the troops in New Mexico back through western Kansas to the railroad. One day while marching, buffalo came in sight and Williams resolved to bag his buffalo. Being mounted, he started after the buffalo, but it was a long chase, and before he got near enough to execute his purpose, and when a long way from his party, he was discovered by a party of Cheyennes and had great difficulty in keeping ahead of their pursuit until he reached his command. They fired at him several times and one shot shattered a bone of his leg so badly that the leg had to be amputated, and he had a cork replacement. Having both seen service on the plains, we became chummy. One day we were up on the terreplein of the fort among the Indians at their work. We each had a cane and I suggested that we get into a heated argument and threaten each other and then begin to cut, thrust, and parry with our canes as we had been taught to do with our sabers, and when the Indians became thoroughly interested I would hit his wooden leg. He agreed, and when the Indians were concerned and gathered to see our conflict, I gave his leg a whack which sounded so loud I stopped instantly in apparent wonder and looked at him and he laughed heartily. I then took hold of his leg and called the Indians to come and see what it was made of, which they did and were greatly interested that such a remarkable repair to the body could be made. Williams then told them, through the interpreter, how and where he lost his leg and said, "Maybe some of you shot me." None of them acknowledged that they were in the affair, but several admitted that they had heard about it. Although Williams before that had been somewhat unfriendly to them, his subsequent visits were of more interest to him and also to the Indians.

A party of visitors were looking through the fort and I discovered that one of the gentlemen had a glass eye. I told him I was using every opportunity I could to show the Indians the wonderful things of the white man's civilization and asked him if he would take out his glass eye and show them how completely facial appearance could be restored. We gathered a party and called their attention to his face and asked if they saw anything peculiar in

3. Probably 1st Lt. Ephriam Williams, Fifth Infantry, breveted captain for coolness, gallantry, and good conduct in action with Cheyenne Indians near Pawnee Fork, Kansas, Sept. 23, 1867. He retired in 1869.

it, and they said no. The gentleman then removed his eye and showed them how different his face was without it and then replaced it, and they became further impressed with the white man's wonderful accomplishments.

A gentleman with a wooden arm and hand, on which was a glove, came to the fort and he demonstrated another feature of the civilized method of making repairs to the human body.

14. The Kiowa Escape Plot

Following the methods of my Irish Captain Walsh in the Tenth U. S. Cavalry, a daily inspection was instituted, when every Indian stood at the foot of his bed, which must be made up in regular order, and his simple belongings displayed. He was to be clean in person and the barracks room swept and everything in place. This inspection included the dining, kitchen, and bakery casemates and their appurtenances, and the general cleanliness of the whole fort. The work was divided so that individuals or parties could be held responsible for the cleanliness of that portion under their care. It was part of the daily program to catch every Indian's eye as he was looked over from head to foot standing by his bed. Conviction came that something was wrong with the Kiowas because their eyes were evasive. White Horse, who had been one of the worst of their leaders in frontier lawlessness, attracted special attention. He asked permission to go over alone to the coast to a particular sand dune in sight of the old fort to perform some religious ceremony. To disarm any suspicion that he was being observed, his request was granted.

Ah-ke-ah, one of the Kiowas who was very sick with a fever when we left Fort Sill and had to be much cared for en route had shown warm gratitude. A Mrs. Pacetti, who had a fine voice and led the singing in the Catholic cathedral, had been kind to Ah-ke-ah after his arrival and during his convalescence and several times had entertained him and Mr. Fox, the interpreter, at her home, which was not far from the fort. I told Mr. Fox my suspicions and asked him to arrange with Mrs. Pacetti and take Ah-ke-ah for an evening and on the way back to the fort to say to him, "the Captain thinks there is something wrong with the Kiowas," and then wait for his answer. Fox carried out my instructions, and after having said it they walked some distance in silence, then Ah-ke-ah stopped and said: "I can tell you what is going to happen but if they find out I told you they will kill me. If you promise not to tell anybody I will tell you." Mr. Fox said: "If it is something the Captain ought to know I must tell him." Ah-ke-ah waited a little while and then said: "All right, but you tell him to do just the same to me that he does to all the others so they will not know I told." He then told Fox that the Kiowas had a secret plan to leave the fort and try to make their way back to their old home, that they intended to start at the full of the moon, which was only three days away, that they were obligated to each other not to be taken alive, that they had prepared bows and arrows so as to kill game and protect themselves on their way, and that White Horse and Lone Wolf had planned the scheme.

The next morning I went to [Brevet Brigadier] General [Frederick T.] Dent, brother-in-law of President Grant and lieutenant colonel of the Fifth Artillery commanding the post, told him, and asked to handle the case in my own way. I assumed responsibility for any failure and guaranteed that the Kiowas would get a lesson they needed. All I wanted was the temporary restoration of the army guard of a sergeant and twelve men to be under my orders as a force to guard the fort and help work out the plan. General Dent consented to my arrangement. He selected the sergeant to take charge of the first guard and sent for him, and in the General's presence I gave him instructions to march his guard detail into the fort at precisely twelve o'clock that day with bayonets fixed and guns loaded, ready to execute commands instantly. I particularly desired old soldiers and large strong fellows.

When I went back I called Manimic, the former war chief of the Cheyennes, and Heap of Birds, his friend and lieutenant, into a closet conference. I told them what was pending and that I relied upon their control of the Cheyennes for help in case of trouble, that they should not speak about what I had told them but be sure that all the Cheyennes could get their bows and arrows quickly. All the Indians had been making bows and arrows for sale to visitors. These agreed to my wishes and said they and their men would stand by me to the death in case of trouble, that they had suspected the Kiowas were going to do something but had not been able to find out what it was.

All visitors were excluded, the massive entrance doors closed, and all the Indians marched down to dinner, the cooks and the guards included. My aids were Mr. Fox and the army hospital steward, who came to the fort daily to look after any ailments and carry out the doctor's orders. We each had hip-pocket pistols. The Kiowas realized that something was up, and Lone Wolf and White Horse were last and hesitated about going into the dining casemate. I stepped inside with Mr. Fox and told them to come in and take their places at the tables as I had something important to say. When they were all in, the hospital steward closed the door and shoved the ancient outside bolt which locked us in together. As a ruse I then told them (which was a fact) that a bottle of poison had disappeared from the doctor's medical supplies, which were in one of the casemates and open daily. They all knew what it was by the picture of skull and cross-bones on it. I said, "Whoever took it intended no good purpose and it must be returned to me at once," and then waited. The men of the several tribes then began to talk among themselves, and as I watched I felt satisfied that Lone Wolf and White Horse knew about it. After waiting quite a while I told them that if the man who had taken it gave it back it would save a great deal of trouble, that although it would be necessary to punish him it was the easiest way out.

The hospital steward admitted the sergeant and his twelve men, who marched in and formed in front of the casemate, and I gave the sergeant orders to place a guard at the entrance, admit no citizen visitors, and hold his men in line. After quite a little discussion it seemed plain, as I had anticipated, that the poison was not to be found that way, so I told them to eat their dinners and I would have the soldiers search their quarters and belongings carefully. The soldiers came back and reported that they had not found the poison. By this time the Indians were through dinner. They were then brought out by twos and each one searched carefully from head to foot by two soldiers. We began with the Cheyennes, calling Manimic and Heap of Birds first and then the remainder of that tribe, requiring them to fall into line after being searched, and when through with the Cheyennes I dismissed them to their quarters. Then the Arapahoes, Comanches, and the Caddoe, dismissing each party to quarters. When searching the Comanches one of them named Wyako made a threatening remark to Mr. Fox which Fox reported, and on being asked the reason, and unwilling to explain, he was locked in a casemate by himself. Finally came the Kiowas, and as they were searched the two leaders were put in one casemate and bolted in. Then Lone Wolf was searched and put in a cell by himself. As we opened the door to bring out White Horse he stood at the far end of the casemate, head erect, and arms folded. Evidently realizing the futility of his plans, he said to the interpreter: "Tell the captain it is all right. I understand and I want him to kill me now." I told Fox to ask him "who said anything about killing anybody," and he was silent. After searching he was put in a casemate by himself and the door bolted.

About this time [Brevet Lieutenant] Colonel [Edmund C.] Bainbridge, the senior captain with the troops at the other end of town, came in with his sword on and advised me that the entire command from St. Francis Barracks was outside, the fort entirely surrounded, and he had orders from General Dent to assist me in every way.

The marching of the guard from St. Francis Barracks to the fort had disturbed the town, and when the whole command moved through the town and surrounded the fort there was much agitation. Of this I knew nothing until later. I showed Colonel Bainbridge that everything was absolutely safe, that only the Kiowas were involved in the proposed escape, and that I was sorry the General had felt so disturbed, after he had agreed to leave it all to me, that he could see I had all the help needed and his command might just as well return to their barracks, and they marched back. The sergeant and his twelve men took up the guard duties and the guard was changed daily as at first.

In the afternoon I went down to the barracks, where they had a strong guardhouse with dark cells, and asked General Dent to receive the two ringleaders and Wyako for dark-cell confinement and requested that the post cart be sent up about eleven o'clock that night, when they could be brought down without further disturbing the people of the town. To this he agreed, and I told him that I would like to have a little ceremony in connection with the transfer to impress all the Indians, and he agreed to that. My plan was to have the post blacksmith come and replace the shackles and handcuffs on the two ringleaders and Wyako, which was attended to during the afternoon in the court where all the other Indians could see; then to have the post surgeon, Major [John H.] Janeway, come to the fort about ten o'clock that night with some preparation to render them unconscious.

At ten o'clock Dr. Janeway appeared, and with the interpreter and a guard we went first to Wyako's cell, blindfolded him, and then had two stalwart soldiers take him firmly by the arms and march him around the open court, backwards and forwards in the moonlight, until he began to weaken and the soldiers said they had to hold him up, when he was taken back to his cell and his eyes uncovered. Then Lone Wolf was given the same treatment, and in a very little while he too had to be supported back to the cell. Then White Horse was taken out in the same manner, but he, with head erect and firm step, marched throughout the prolonged treatment and went back to his cell without having shown fear. No remarks were made during these operations. We then went to Wyako's cell and Dr. Janeway, using a hypodermic syringe on his arm, produced unconsciousness. Nothing was to be said, but if the Indians spoke, the interpreter was to give exactly what they said and the reply, nothing more. After treating Wyako and Lone Wolf in silence, we went to White Horse's cell, and as he watched the doctor using the hypodermic he said something. Mr. Fox interpreted: "Captain, he wants to know what you are doing to him." I said: "Tell him that I know the Indians have strong medicine and do some wonderful things, but the white man has stronger medicine and can do more wonderful things, and I am having the doctor give him a dose of one of our strong medicines." White Horse immediately asked: "Will it make me good?" I said: "Tell him I hope so. That is the object." In a little while they were unconscious. The cart was brought in and each one, apparently dead, was carried out by four soldiers and laid in the cart, side by side, and the cart drove out of the fort down to the barracks. The other Indians were watching from their quarters on the terreplein, the bright moonlight enabling full observation.

After three days, half of the youngest men of the Kiowas were brought into my casemate office and through the interpreter told that if they had succeeded in getting away from their prison life in the old fort they could not possibly have gone far without soldiers and citizens with guns being after them from all sides and that they would soon have been recaptured or killed, that if they had only continued their good behavior sooner or later the government would have concluded they had punishment enough and might have released and restored them to their people or permitted them to have their women and children and live some place away from their tribe. Also that many of our people did not agree with my methods of kindly treatment and that my career as an army officer would probably have ended; that notwithstanding all this I would overlook their conduct and put them back into the same freedom and responsibility they had before; that I still had faith in them and believed that after this lesson there would be no more foolishness but that they would now go on as before and that in the end all would work out as I believed for the best. In a day or so after that in the same manner I released the other Kiowas who had been confined in the general casemate. After a few days the military guard was again relieved, and the Indian guard, which included the Kiowas, was restored.

The three prisoners at the barracks were reported upon daily, but I did not go to see them for three weeks and then found them glad enough to see me. After four weeks they were brought to the fort and held under care of the Indian guard. Wyako was first released and shackles removed, after being told that, as he could now see, threats would not be allowed. Several days afterward Lone Wolf was released and had the best talk I could give. A few days later White Horse was released and told that because I had believed him trustworthy and had known for several years that he was a leading man among his people and strong to control them, I had at the start made him a sergeant of the Indian company which guarded the fort and that every time he went on guard he officially represented the Government of the United States in seeing that everything at the fort was just what the Government wanted; that I had trusted him notwithstanding I knew of the bad things he had done, that I could understand how hard it was for him to endure the imprisonment and how anxious he was to bring it to an end and said: "You can't do that yourself. Every attempt you make to end it your way will react upon you. There is only one thing safe and best for you to do, and that is to accept patiently all your punishment and await the outcome, and the Government will in its own time bring to pass whatever it thinks best. Now I want you to see that I can still trust a man of your character in spite of what you had planned to do, and you will return to duty in the company and will again help guard the fort, but as a private and not as a sergeant." He and Lone Wolf said they were sorry for what they had planned to do and White Horse was especially grateful that I still trusted him. Later he was again made a sergeant and to the end of his imprisonment rendered most satisfactory service.

One of the personal letters General Sheridan had asked me to write him occasionally is explanatory and is therefore inserted.

Fort Marion,
St. Augustine, Fla.,
May 25, 1876.

Lieut. Gen. P. H. Sheridan,
General:

The Kiowas have all been returned to duty as they were before arrest, except that White Horse goes back as a private instead of Sergt. White Horse, Lone Wolf, and the Comanche Wy-a-ko were in irons about six weeks. Part of the time they were confined in the Post Guardhouse at St. Francis barracks, but the last two weeks I had them here in a casemate guarded by their fellows and treated in all respects as we do soldiers in confinement in irons. The sergeants turned them over daily to each other and examined the irons with greatest formality. I now think it impossible for any emergency to arise that I cannot meet with my Indian Guard. Had they been enlisted as I requested I should not have asked help before.

The very best of discipline prevails. The school goes ahead and in two or three months I shall have a 1st Sergt. that can call a roll and keep a roster.

I had a Cheyenne taught how to bake, whose bread will average with that baked at frontier posts. The oven I built at an expense of $11.00 and the pans I made myself. We can bake 160 rations at a time.

I have brought logs into the fort and am giving instructions in building log houses, riving shingles, etc.

The prisoners have made from $3000 to $4000 since they came, polishing sea beans, selling drawing books, bows and arrows, canes, etc. It does not come up to my idea of what they should be working at but seems to be the best that can be done here just now.

The health is excellent. Have just had a new issue of clothing and a majority of them went voluntarily and paid the barbers for a hair cut. They make fine looking soldiers.

> Very respectfully,
> Your Obedient Servant,
> R. H. Pratt.
> 1st Lieut. 10th Cav.,
> In charge of Indian Prisoners.

This recital covers what took place. There were dispatches with vivid detail published in the papers over the country giving false statements of insurrection, shooting, and death. When routine was restored, I felt all was more secure than it had been before. As it was, no violation of the duties of the guard had actually occurred.

Several years after the prisoners had been released, I visited their agencies and asked Colonel [Laban T.] Moore, a Union veteran of the Civil War from Kentucky, then agent for the Kiowas, how White Horse was behaving, and he said: "Good and bad. He takes hold and runs well in the white man's road for a long time and then comes a dance or Indian orgy and he flops, but with encouragement gets up and goes on again." This led me to say that reforming a drunkard by keeping him in a saloon would be quite as sensible as our method of trying to civilize and Americanize our Indians by keeping them separated in tribes on prison reservations excluded from all contact with our civilization and the advantages of our American life.

15. Prison Educational Programs

Miss Mather, spoken of in a previous chapter as one of the teachers of a class of Indians, was a friend of Mrs. Harriet Beecher Stowe, who had a cottage on the St. John's River between Tocòi and Jacksonville.[1] During the winters Mrs. Stowe was now and then a guest of Miss Mather in St. Augustine and when there accompanied Miss Mather when she came to teach her class. The casemate Miss Mather occupied as her schoolroom was next to the casemate in which I had my office. One day, while the classes were in session, there was quite a commotion in Miss Mather's schoolroom, and two of the Indians were outside and looking back when I went to see what was the matter. Mrs. Stowe was sitting near the blackboard by Miss Mather and both were

1. By 1877 Mrs. Stowe, author of the prewar propaganda classic *Uncle Tom's Cabin*, had become a venerated reformer and humanitarian. It is interesting to note that a number of prominent abolitionists of the prewar era turned their attention to the Indian problem once slavery had been abolished.

laughing heartily. The Indians were quiet. To keep from looking at Miss Mather, White Horse had his arm up in front of his eyes when I went in, and said to me, "Miss Mather no good." This renewed the ladies' amusement. Then Miss Mather told what had happened. She was trying to teach them to pronounce words ending in *th* and was using the word *teeth*. She had them well along in the concert pronouncing and then, wanting to show them what "teeth" are, removed and showed them her complete set. She closed her jaws, which made a remarkable change in her facial presentation. White Horse meant only that, to his way of thinking, she was defective.

These experiences created more interest in the white man's power to repair the body and led the Indians to a greater desire to know and become a part of our civilization.

For many years after their release I had letters, somewhat crude but intelligible, from some of these older members of this prisoner party, their ability to write having been obtained through this meager teaching, received after they had become men with families.

The letters following are selected from Mrs. Pratt's scrap book as indicating their estimate by America's eminent workers in our public welfare:

(*The Christian Union*, New York, April 18, 1877.)

The Indians at St. Augustine
By Mrs. Harriet Beecher Stowe

Between two and three years ago there passed by us on the St. Johns River, a party of captured Indians from our Western Frontiers. They were the men who had been the terror of our settlers, who had done many a deed of savage cruelty and blood. They were selected and sent to St. Augustine for safe-keeping simply as being the wildest, the most dangerous, the most untamable of the tribes. The conscience and Christianity of our century did not admit of their being shot down like so many captured tigers, and so they were sent to the Fort in St. Augustine merely to keep them out of mischief.

They were looked upon in their transit with the mingled fear and curiosity with which one regards dangerous wild beasts. Gloomy, scowling, dressed in wild and savage habiliments, painted in weird colors, their hair adorned, they seemed more like grim goblins than human beings. Apprehension was entertained that some day they might break loose from their confinement and carry bloodshed and murder through the country. One of the number on the transit threw himself from the cars into the palmettos, and was shot as would be a tiger escaped from a managerie.

There were two women and one child—a little girl eight years old—among them. One of these was a woman so distinguished for fiend-like fierceness and atrocity that it was not deemed safe to leave her on the frontier.[2] The other was the young wife of the chief, Black Horse.[3] She was, for an Indian, a handsome woman, who followed her husband in his captivity. When the time came to send the men prisoners to Fort Leavenworth, the wives were all commanded to leave them; but this woman threw her arms around her husband and declared that they might kill her if they chose but that she would not leave him.

"Well," said the commanding officer, "take them both. If they can separate them at Fort Leavenworth, they may; I can't." And at Fort Leavenworth, the commanding general in the same way gave in, and the woman and child went on.

Such was the party as they passed on our river about two years ago.

A day or two since we visited them at the fort in St. Augustine. We went in company with a lady, who, with other ladies of St. Augustine, regularly devotes two hours a day to the work of instruction among them.

We found now no savages. A dark complexioned orderly, with the high cheek bones and black eyes and hair of the Indian race, and dressed in the United States uniform was pacing to and fro on guard as we and the lady teacher entered. The bell soon rang for school hours, and, hurrying from all quarters came more dark men in the United States uniform, neat, compact, trim, with well-brushed boots and nicely kept clothing, and books in their hands.

As but one of the teachers had arrived on the ground, they were for a time all collected in her room and drawn up in a hollow square around the blackboards. Large spelling-cards adorned one side of the wall, containing various pictures and object-lessons adapted to the earliest stages of learning. Here they were around us—the very beings that had been the terror of our Western settlements, and what did they look like?

The Indian face is naturally a stern and hard one, but as they gathered round their teacher and returned her morning greeting the smiles on those faces made them seem even handsome. There were among these pupils seated, docile and eager, with books in hand, men who had been the foremost in battle and bloodshed. Now there was plainly to be seen among them the eager joy which comes from the use of a new set of faculties. When they read in concert, when they mastered perfectly the

2. Mo-chi, or Buffalo Calf, wife of Medicine Water, a Cheyenne.
3. Pe-ah-ni, or Mother. Black Horse was a Comanche.

pronunciation of a difficult word, when they gave the right answer to a question, they were evidently delighted. They specially prided themselves in showing how plainly they could speak the "th"—which embarrasses every foreigner in the English tongue—rendering it with an anxious and careful precision.

The lessons proceeded; reading, spelling, explaining the meaning of each word, and when a meaning was made clear that had been obscure, the bright smile on the swart faces showed the joy of a new idea. Their teacher was one of those women with a born genius for instruction—one whose very life is in teaching; and the lesson was full of animation. There was not a listless face, not a wandering eye, in the whole class.

After a little the other ladies arrived and portions of the class wheeled out into side apartments, each with its separate teachers. While the lessons were progressing we visited with Captain Pratt the barracks where the Indians are lodged. This is a structure more than a hundred feet by forty or fifty, covering the top of a portion of the old fort. The roof was entirely shingled by the Indians, and a great part of the inside work done by them, under the direction of the builder, who found them both docile and competent workmen. A double row of rough board bunks occupies each side of the building, and the blankets and mattresses were rolled up and disposed in each with perfect neatness and precision. The barracks were perfectly clean. Large stoves in the center afforded means of warming in chilly weather.

All along we saw traces of Indian skill and ingenuity in the distinctive work of the tribes. Bows and arrows skillfully made and painted, sea beans nicely polished, paper toys representing horses, warriors and buffaloes, showing a good deal of rude artistic skill and spirit in the design and coloring, were disposed here and there to attract the eye and tempt the purse of visitors. Captain Pratt said that during the time of their stay, not less than five thousand dollars had been taken in by the whole company from the sale of these curiosities to visitors. They are allowed each one the free use of the money they earn, and they do not spend it foolishly. The most of it has been sent back for the use of their wives and families. Yes, these fearful beings whom we were tempted to look on only as noxious wild beasts have the hearts of men. They have warm and constant family affection. A continual correspondence has been kept up between them and their families, and letters and gifts constantly interchanged. We saw displayed over one of the beds a hunting pouch of dressed deer skin elegantly embroidered with beads, the gift of a distant wife; and in other places elaborate moccasins which had come in the same way. One old chief who bears the surname of "Woman's Heart," is especially noted for the strength of his family affection.[4] It is said he wears the little moccasin of one of his children tied round his neck and that he has seemed at times to suffer from homesickness. Captain Pratt said that a short time before, one moonlight night, this chief asked permission to go outside the fort and take a bath, which was granted. From the top of the fort, the captain watched him returning from his bath; he kneeled down on a little elevation and raising his hands towards heaven prayed some time with great fervor. Is there not something touching in the thought of this solitary prayer of the chief to the Great Spirit?

Captain Pratt has for a long time held a weekly prayer-meeting to which the Indians have been invited, and they seem gladly to attend. We very gladly accepted an invitation to attend one which was to be held at seven o'clock the next evening. It was in a little vaulted room which was used as the old Spanish Chapel of the fort. There were traces still of the high altar and the places for holy water. It was roughly fitted up with board seats, and the whole of the Indians were there seated together. It was the last meeting in which they were to have their interpreter with them, as the government has retrenched that expense in their keeping. Mr. Fox, who has from his youth resided among the Indians and understands their language and feelings and ways of acting perfectly, is very much beloved by them, and on this account the parting meeting was somewhat exceptional in character and of such interest that our account of it cannot be condensed into one article.

(*The Christian Union*, New York, April 25, 1877)

The meeting, whose opening we described last week, was one of a series of prayer-meetings in which from the first the Indians had themselves taken part. The Indians are Theists; the Great Good Spirit in whom they believe is represented with the same attributes with which we clothe our idea of the Supreme. The services began with the hymn, "Just as I am." It was curious to see produced from the breast of each coat the little Moody and Sankey hymn-book; and each found the place himself. It may be said, in passing, that they have learned to sing many of these hymns, and that the meaning has been translated by the interpreter so that they have at least a general idea of what they sing. They keep the tune well, pronounce the words distinctly and sing with an expression of intense solemnity. The Rev. Dr. Marsh then spoke to them

4. Woman's Heart was one of the most notorious Kiowa raiders and played a conspicuous part in the attack on the Warren wagon train in 1871.

of their distant wives and children; our wishes that they might be in time restored to their families; that there should be no more fighting or contention, but that they should teach their people the good ways they had learned themselves.

An opportunity was then given, through the interpreter, for any of the Indians to speak. Immediately an old chief rose and came forward to the middle of the floor. This was Manimic, or Eagle's Head, a Cheyenne chief of great influence. He stood before us in the garments of civilization as a stalwart old man, with strong and thoughtful cast of face. Over his United States uniform he wore a long linen coat, bought with his own money, and in which, for that reason, perhaps, he seems to take special pleasure. As he stood on the floor his dark features seemed working with some strong emotion, and solemnly raising his right hand to heaven, he said, in his own tongue, "Let us pray." Immediately all the Indians knelt, bowing their heads with the most prostrate reverence.

The sound of that prayer was peculiarly mournful. Unused to the language, we could not discriminate words. It seemed a successful means of imploring wails; it was what the Bible so often speaks of in relation to prayer, a cry unto God. In it we seemed to hear all the story of the wrongs, the cruelties, the injustice which had followed these children of the forest, driving them to wrong and cruelty in return.

After the prayer, which was quite short, he addressed us, seemingly in reply to the address of Dr. Marsh. He said that they thanked the Great Spirit, that he had shown them a new road, a better way; opened their eyes to see, and their ears to hear. They wanted to go again to their own land to see their wives and children, and to teach them the better way.

"We like the white ways," he said; "we like the dress," and here he stroked his linen robe complacently. "We would like to have farms and houses, and live peaceably in a good way. "The Great Spirit," he said, "speaks in my heart he loves his dark children as he does the white, and this makes my heart glad."

There was after this a succession of four or five speakers. Almost every one commenced by the same solemn form of raising the right hand, and invoking the Great Spirit, and each time the Indian company all kneeled and bowed their heads towards the earth. The purport of all the prayers, as interpreted by Mr. Fox, was that the Great Spirit would help them in the right way, that he would bring them back to their own land, and to their wives and children, and enable them to remain true to the good that they had learned, and teach it to their people. All, in so many words, professed their desire to live hereafter a different and better life. One said, naively, "I want to live in a wood house. It will be easier to be good if I live in a wood house." Another said, "I shall try to work; if I have only a little help at first to begin, then I can go on by myself."

Now, there was deep philosophy in the speech about the wood house. A skin lodge that can be pulled up and carried anywhere on horseback, is the emblem of a wandering savage life, a wood house is a home, a settled habitation, a center of industry, for acquisition; and this is truly what every human needs to make him a good man.

The purport of all the speeches and prayers, as interpreted, left the impression of a strong, thoughtful, sensible race, not emotional, like the negro, or liable to shifting phases, but deeply constant. For good or for evil, the Indian's nature is strong, persistent and enduring.

There was the most solemn air of sincerity in all that was said and done. One of the speakers said, "The Great Spirit who sees all within us, knows that we do not lie."

Such, then, has been the result of two years' imprisonment of these Indians in the center of a Christian community, who have cared for them and treated them in the spirit of the Christian religion. For two years they have been comfortably fed and housed, have been encouraged to practice various industries and the results of their labor, or ingenuity, have been allowed to them to use for their families.

In return, they have showed themselves faithful, ingenious, trustworthy, and delighted with the acquisition of every new faculty. Indians constructed and shingled the barracks that lodged them, and very proud they were of the work. A large oven was constructed in one of the vaults of the Fort, and the Indians assisted the mason in preparing the brick and mortar, and much interested in watching the process they were. After the oven was ready, a baker was for some time hired, and two Indians were given as his assistants. In a very short time these Indians learned the trade, and now all the bread of the Fort is made by them. We saw and tasted the bread, which is white and light, and of a superior quality, to the great delight of Charley, the head baker, who said: "Me make. By and by, out there, will make bread, and get money." Already the idea of a profitable trade has opened before him.

In the vicinity of the oven, where the bread is baked, is a vault transformed into a great kitchen, where the terrific woman, who once was so formidable, now presides over a Peerless cooking stove, and made the day we were there a great caldron of savory soup, which we saw, in passing upon the dinner-table of the tribes, flanked by large dishes of boiled meat, and great white blocks of bread. We cannot but think that such an experience may suggest to her a pleasanter style of diet.

But the question now arises, what is to be the result of all this? Many seem to doubt the power of any teaching, or any experience, to reclaim an Indian, and suppose that these will at once go back to all their old lawless ways, but the last *Missionary Herald* gives a case just in point.

"There is now," says the April number (page 102), "located near the eastern line of the Dakota Territory, in the fertile valley of the Big Sioux River, a colony of Dakotas, who, fifteen years ago, were blanket Indians. They have now 500 acres under cultivation. They own eighty-three horses, and more than 150 head of cattle, and raised last season 1100 bushels of wheat, and 4000 bushels of oats and barley. They live in comfortable log houses, have a Presbyterian church of 160 members, ministered to by a native preacher, more than half of whose support is raised by the people of his charge. These men were, in 1862, engaged in the Sioux outbreak in Minnesota. For three years they were held in military power. The germs of their present life were started in their prison experience. All of them, in some sense, experienced a conversion of thought and purpose, and began a new life and agreed to abolish the old tribal arrangements and customs. But when they came back to their people they found that only by going back under the old chiefs and customs could they live and receive the appropriations of the United States Government. They must be Indians or starve. Nothing remained, then, but to seek another settlement. One of them said, 'I could not bear to have my children grow up Indians'; so they started and performed on foot a journey of 130 miles, through terrible hardships, to their present settlement. This shows the energy and persistency of the Indian character, and sheds a light of hope on what has been accomplished for these in St. Augustine."[5]

Captain Pratt recently called the whole number together before the interpreter departed, and asked them what their wishes for the future might be. The family men all desired to return and to have some assistance at first in starting a civilized settlement.

But about thirty vigorous, bright young men declared their desire to remain and go anywhere where they could get an education that would fit them to go back and teach their people the arts and trades of civilized life. These are splendid specimens of youth and physical vigor; they are the young braves of their tribes, and unmarried. They want to learn farming, blacksmithing, and other useful arts, as well as to carry on the

5. One of these Indians was Many Lightnings, who changed his name while in prison to Jacob Eastman. His son, Charles A. Eastman, won a medical degree and achieved a wide reputation as a writer on Indian topics. In 1891 he married Elaine Goodale, schoolteacher on the Pine Ridge Reservation, where Eastman was agency physician. Nearly half a century later Mrs. Eastman wrote the standard biography of Pratt. She treats with the refugee Flandreau Sioux in chap. 11 of *Pratt, the Red Man's Moses*.

study of the English language and literature, with a view of being useful to their own people.

Is not here an opening for Christian enterprise? We have tried fighting and killing the Indians, and gained little by it. We have tried feeding them as paupers in their savage state, and the result has been dishonest contractors, and invitation and provocation to war. Suppose we try education? Suppose we respond to the desire of these young men, and give them, for two or three years, teaching and training in some such institution as the Amherst State Agricultural School? The Government of Japan thought it worth while to send young men here to be educated, to learn our customs, manners and ideas, the Government paying a commissioner to superintend, and bearing their expenses. Might not the money now constantly spent on armies, forts and frontiers be better invested in educating young men who shall return and teach their people to live like civilized beings?

(The *New York Daily Tribune,* Saturday, April 1, 1876)
MERCY TO INDIANS
A Letter from Bishop Whipple[6]
The Indian Prisoners at St. Augustine
Their Education as Soldiers—
Success of the Effort to Christianize Them

To

The Editor of the Tribune.

Sir:

Many of your readers are deeply interested in the poor red men of the West. They do pity the helpless, but are powerless to help them. It is not often that they find a silver lining to the cloud. May I write you of some Indian work which will bring joy to many Christian hearts? You are aware that for some time past we have had trouble with the Kiowas, the Comanches, the Cheyennes and the Arapahoes. It is the old story of our wrongdoing, the violation of treaties, until it has ended in savage war. Indian war means a war of races and the massacre of women and children. Our troops captured a number of these hostile Indians. They selected some 70 warriors and chiefs and sent them as prisoners to Fort Marion, at St. Augustine, Fla. A portion of these were as desperate In-

---

6. Henry Benjamin Whipple (1822–1901) had been a champion of Indian rights since his appointment as Episcopal Bishop of Minnesota in 1859. By the 1880s he had become one of the nation's most effective workers in the cause of Indian reform and commanded great influence among government officials and eastern philanthropists. His autobiography, *Lights and Shadows of a Long Episcopate,* published in 1899, recounts his career as a friend of the Indian. *Dictionary of American Biography, 20,* 68–69.

dian warriors as ever carried the tomahawk and rifle. A few of the chiefs were sent as hostages for the good behavior of their people. They were placed in charge of Capt. R. H. Pratt. They were sullen, revengeful, full of hate, and had to be brought in double irons. One of their number committed suicide on the way. It was an unpromising field for Christian civilization and missionary effort. As soon as they reached St. Augustine, Capt. Pratt selected ten of the best behaved Indians, cut their hair, and dressed them in the uniform of soldiers. A few days later, he released others. In less than two weeks he was drilling all his prisoners in an organized company. They had non-commissioned officers of their own number. They guarded themselves in the fort, and discharged every duty of a well-appointed garrison. Col. Hamilton, the former, and Gen. Dent, the present commander of the post, seconded every effort made by Capt. Pratt. They learned by heart life's first lesson, "to obey." They received every kindness when they deserved it, and suffered severely for every violation of orders. There is not today a more orderly body of soldiers in the service.

Some devoted Christian women became their teachers in a school. They are beginning to read and write. They have learned the Lord's prayer. They sing very sweetly several Christian hymns. I was never more touched than when I entered this school. Here were men who had committed murder upon helpless women and children sitting like docile children at the feet of women learning to read. Their faces have changed. They have all lost that look of savage hate, and the light of a new life is dawning on their hearts. It was my privilege to preach to them every Sunday, and upon week days I told them stories from the Bible. I have never had a more attentive congregation. At times they seemed to hang upon my words as if I were a messenger of life from heaven. You could see on every face that the "old, old story" sounded to them as it does to us, as they heard of One who was the friend of every one who needed a friend. Providentially we had the best of interpreters. Mr. Fox speaks the Comanche language fluently, and he also speaks the sign language perfectly. This sign language is common to all Indians, and Mr. Fox is so much at home with it he could translate a sermon in it so that all could understand it. The day before I left St. Augustine I asked the privilege of meeting the chiefs with Capt. Pratt and the interpreter. I told them that I came to say "Good bye." I believed God sent me to them. Their home was 2000 miles away in the Southwest. My home was 2000 miles away in the Northwest. I did not know them, they did not know me, yet I had been permitted to tell the sweet story of God's love, and of Jesus their Savior. We shall never meet again on earth, but I hoped that we should both follow the good trail which led to heaven. The chief, Manimic, was silent for a moment. He then said with deep feeling: "You may wonder whether your words reached me. They did not go into my ears and then go away; they went down, down into my heart. They will always stay there. I go to church now, and when I see the white man kneel, I know that he is talking to the Great Spirit and asking for himself and his children. I too try to send one little breath of prayer to the Great Spirit that he will have pity upon poor me." He said, "It is not you alone that have pointed me to the good trail"; and then turning to Capt. Pratt, he said, "He has tried to lead me to it, his words are always good. I shall walk in that path until I die." He could not go on. He choked, then ran up to Capt. Pratt and threw his arms around his neck and kissed him, first on one cheek and then on the other. He then embraced me, kissed me on both cheeks, and laid his head on my shoulder and cried like a child. All the chiefs embraced us and kissed us and were moved to tears.

It shows that even in the most savage men there is a heart which can be reached by discipline, kindness, and Christian teaching. The older chiefs ought to be sent back to their people. They can do much to keep them from joining the Sioux in the present war. Some of them may not live this summer in prison. The effect of their death would be very deplorable upon their people. Some of the younger men are very intelligent, and they ought to be educated as teachers and craftsmen. They ought to become leaders of their people in the path of civilization. I am more convinced than ever that there is not the slightest necessity for Indian wars. They are the fruit of our wretched policy. It would make our own white race Ishmaelites to leave them without government, without personal rights of property, to be the prey of the dishonest and corrupt. Capt. Pratt's success is due to the fact that he has taught these Indians to obey; that he has encouraged them to labor; he has given to them, in its best sense, a Christian school. They are gaining manhood, and the Gospel of Jesus Christ will do for them and their people, if they have the means to learn its good news, what it has done for other heathen folk in the ages passed away. I feel that a deep debt of gratitude is due to the officers of the army at St. Augustine for having solved that vexed question, "What shall we do with hostile Indians when taken prisoners?" From my heart I can say, "God bless them!"

Yours faithfully,

H. B. Whipple

Savannah, Ga., March 24, 1876

This is a good place for the following: Manimic was often a welcome visitor in our Florida home and sometimes broke bread with us. Five years after, in 1881, he died in his tepee home, among his people. On his return from captivity he was at once foremost in urging his people to take up civilized ways of living. With the help and advice of his good Quaker agent John D. Miles, he undertook contracts to furnish 900 cords of wood for a year's supply at the Cheyenne Agency and 1,500 cords for the military post close by. Taking young men who had been his soldiers in war, he camped in the woods and directed the cutting down of the trees, their being chopped or sawed into cordwood lengths, then split, corded up for measurement, and finally hauled to delivery points. When his contracts were nearing completion he was attacked by the illness which ended his life. Letters in my files from Agent Miles during this period give the foregoing facts.

Soon after his death one of Agent Miles' helpers visited us at Carlisle and gave Mrs. Pratt details of his last days and she at once wrote the following for the monthly school paper, *Eadle Ketah Toh* (Big Morning Star), printed therein November 1881.

Minimic's Prayer

Among the Indian prisoners confined in the old fort at St. Augustine, Florida, was one whose affable manner won the admiration, if not the affection of the frequent visitors. Many times I have heard the remark: "Minimic is a native-born gentleman." Yet he was an Indian, had fought against the whites, and was a believer in the incantations of the Medicine Men. But a new light was sent into the darkened minds of the Indian prisoners. Minimic saw, believed and followed this light, even after he returned to his old home in the Indian Territory.

Last spring he was very sick, and when able to be about again, one Sunday attended a Christian service, and was asked by the missionary who conducted the meeting if he would not say a few words or pray.

Minimic arose from his seat and speaking in his own language, his expressive face and eloquent gestures made his words very effective. This is what he said: "I have been very sick; I thought I was going to die. I said to my wife, bring me the good Book which was given to me in Florida; put it under my head, now I feel better. Soon I felt that was not enough, so I said to my wife, make the fire brighter, help me up, now hold the book open before me that I may look at the words in it. The light from the fire shone on the words in that book—Jesus' book I call it —and the good words that I had been told were in this Jesus' book came into my mind, and I prayed to understand them. Then I layed down again on my bed and put the book open over my forehead and felt that I did understand what Jesus wanted."

Then bowing his head, he reverently said: "Let us pray." One petition of his prayer was that "God would make his heart larger, yes, very large," and in his earnestness he extended his arms in a circle before him, then paused, and there was perfect silence for a minute, then arose this rich plea, "and fill it full of love for Jesus. Amen."

Our genial old friend has since died, and up there, in that throng, among prophets and kings, he enjoys the promise of God.

A. L. P.

16. Opinions, Progress, Appeals

The Indian prisoners were held to confinement in Fort Marion for three years, with some privileges of encamping on Anastasia Island and at Matanzas, boating, and working outside. This history would be incomplete if I omitted and did not emphasize the views and purposes given in the following excerpts from my letter book. They are therefore made a chapter of this record. A few weeks after reaching St. Augustine, I wrote the following:

Fort Marion, Fla.,
June 29th, 1875

General E. D. Townsend, Adjt. Gen.,
   Washington, D.C.
Dear Sir:

I look upon S.O. No. 88 W.D.A.G.O. as giving me some privilege to address you personally.

The duty of the Govt. to these Indians seems to me to be the teaching of them something that will be permanently useful to them. Teaching them to work is one thing, but St. Augustine offers almost nothing in that line. They have besought me repeatedly to try to get Washington to give them an opportunity to learn. They say they want to learn to build houses, to make boots and shoes, to do blacksmith work, and to farm, etc. I have known for years that much could have been done in this direction had there been proper effort. I can take these men and push them patiently along to a knowledge of any mechanical or laboring means of gaining a livelihood and make it a success. Is it not possible to dispose of them at some of our Northeastern Penitentiaries where facilities for learning trades is offered and where they can be kept at work? I will answer that such a course will meet with gratifying results. I have said Penitentiaries because they offer the greatest diversity of facilities and Northeastern because of greater perfection of industry; guarding them is only of secondary consideration. These are the bad men. Showing what can be done with them will shame the want of success with the others.

I appeal to you and through you to the Hon. Secretary of War personally in these interests because I believe results can and should be accomplished with these men, bad as they are, that would patent the benefits of a change in Indian management.

> I have the honor to be, General
> Very respectfully,
> R. H. PRATT

> Fort Marion, Fla.,
> July 17th, 1875.

To the
  Adutant General,
    U. S. Army,
      Washington, D.C.

Sir:

Referring to the endorsement of the Lt. Gen. and action at Washington on the talk made by Indian Prisoners transmitted by my letter dated June 11th [see pp. 122–23] I have the honor to state that I hoped that that part of their appeal asking that some kind of work be given them, would attract the most attention. I still hope that it may receive notice and action.

They have exhibited the greatest willingness and industry in performing such work as I have been able to give them since arrival here and I repeat that "I believe that they will take hold of any means offered for their future self support with a will strong enough to overcome its difficulties."

They say they want to learn to do any and all kinds of work done by white men and they will learn anything Washington wants them to. They have individual preferences as to the kind of employment which it would be well to consult.

I have been in their country since 1867 and have heard many talks in which the "white man's road" was the prominent part, but I never heard the talks and anxiety for action I have heard here.

We try in our state prisons to keep our criminals employed and generally at trades that may eventuate in placing them in a position to earn a livelihood after release; why not do the same for these people when they want it? They say they have never had any one to show them how to work like the white man and they say truly.

Constant employment is a necessity and of the greatest importance and benefit. Give them individually the proceeds of their own labor and they take hold of work with avidity.

If they are to be held in close confinement it seems to me that some of our Northern Penitentiaries would be the place offering the greatest diversity of labor. This is not a good place to advance them; they are simply objects of curiosity here. There are no industries worth noting; they polish sea beans and alligator teeth as well as professionals and have earned in their two months stay over three hundred dollars, but they have glutted the market; they might learn to make palm hats and find a market for all they can do, but that will be no material benefit in comparison with what they might be taught under more favorable circumstances, and then it requires an organized effort and capital their uncertain stay does not warrant. If their women and children come and they are to be kept here, employment for them, may take this shape. I urge that they be sent to a place with more and better opportunities. If they stay here I request that I be allowed to enlist a force of not less than twenty-five, to include two Sergeants and three Corporals and use them in guarding themselves, dispensing with other troops. This is perfectly feasible and will add in every way to the success of their management. They are trustworthy and will act against each other under orders as well as soldiers.

I made repeated arrests of Indians at Fort Sill last winter with my Kiowa and Comanche scouts. While on this subject I may say that a picked fifty to sixty of these very men enlisted as scouts would form the best corps for operating in conjunction with troops on the Staked Plains, and in the country about the head waters of Red River, the Brazos, Concho, Colorado and Pecos, that could be sent there. This is also perfectly practicable and if they were stationed so as to operate from one locality, their time of service sufficiently long and their women and children allowed with them; something worth while could be done in instructing them in farming and gardening. Their women will make their own shelter anywhere in the vicinity of the buffalo, so that there would be no expense for tentage. I am informed from Fort Sill that the Kiowa chief, Big Bow, the leader of the Howard Wells Massacre, the hero of numerous other atrocities and the peer of any here in bad acts, whose offences were condoned for special services last winter, is a government enlisted scout at the cantonment on the North Fork of Red River. Many of the young Kiowas imprisoned here justly attribute their unfortunate position to his bad influences and sensibly contrast their situation with his. I do not forget they have been retaliating murderers of men, women, and children. Having been the worst, because the most active element, they will become the best of their people for the same reason if permitted and aided to it, and as they are not to be tried and some executed as their crimes deserve, it is protection to ourselves to open wide the door of civilization and even drive them to it, if we find that necessary. But we will not find it necessary. They will enter of themselves; they may lag, but under proper management will recover and push ahead.

Very respectfully,
Your Obedient servant,
R. H. PRATT

Fort Marion,
St. Augustine, Fla.,
Jan. 17th, 1876.

General P. H. Sheridan,
Chicago, Illinois.
General:

The behavior of the prisoners has been so good that I would recommend their release and return to their people at an early day. There is a difference in guilt, and it might be better that the worst cases be held longer than the less guilty. I am satisfied, however, that all have been cured.

I have used them as soldiers and have had no other guard at the Fort for three months. There has not been a single case of breach of discipline and the duty has been performed much better and with less anxiety to me than when by the recruits of the 1st Artillery, for then there were cases of drunkenness and sleeping on post. One prisoner was killed and five have died since leaving the Indian Territory; all but one very bad cases.

If they are to be held another season I would ask an opportunity in some good agricultural district to show what they can do at raising corn and other products. Quite a number of the young men have sufficient skill to become fair mechanics. If released and these opportunities could not be afforded, they can be very much advanced in agriculture by enlistment as soldiers at their agencies under special direction to this end.

Manimic wants to point out a few Cheyennes and Black Horse a few Comanches whom they think deserve a trip here under the same circumstances as they came. They say they are soldiers now and will walk right in and jerk them out for us.

Major [C. D.] Emory [aide-de-camp] showed me your correspondence with the Secretaries of War and Interior in the inception of this action to govern in selecting cases for trial last winter, which is my sanction for writing this.

I have reason to hope the results of this will be as satisfactory to you as you anticipated.

With great respect
Yours truly,
R. H. Pratt.

Fort Marion,
St. Augustine, Fla.,
March 17, 1876.

General P. H. Sheridan,
Chicago, Illinois.
General:

When these Indians were to be sent from Fort Sill, I wrote you that "much could and should be done for them while undergoing this banishment." They have been benefited (enlightened) very much more than I thought they could be in the same time, and their application and desire to learn is a source of the greatest possible encouragement. Under the system of instruction adopted, many of the young men are fast learning to read and to talk and even now would be a strong civilizing element among their people. I intend they shall advance every day.

If forty or fifty of them can speak our language on their return and all have a fair knowledge and practice of labor and its benefits, I think you will be pleased with the experiment. This seems in a fair way of accomplishment. We have the assistance of five ladies who have, for the past two months, given instruction daily to about fifty of the youngest men. This has been regular and enthusiastic so that the Indians have been thoroughly interested. Bishop Whipple of Minnesota [see p. 162, note 6], who has been here the latter part of the winter, has given much good help and is converted to Army management for the Indians.[1] I regret two things. One is that the women and children are not here to share the progress of the men, and the other that there is not good opportunity to instruct in agriculture. If they are to stay here long I would renew the application and repeat it until the women and children are sent, for these men will lose so much of what they have gained when they go back and join their wives and families who have not advanced.

Not one of these men will ever take up arms against the Government unless driven by the grossest bad treatment. Instead of joining the Sioux, they will all fight them.[2] They might now be released with perfect safety.

I will report progress, as you desire, from time to time.

Respectfully and truly yours,
R. H. PRATT.

Fort Marion,
St. Augustine, Fla.,
March 21, 1876.

Adjutant General, U. S. A.,
Washington, D.C.

General:

It is found that quite a number of the younger prisoners develop an aptness in learning, and an eagerness to learn, which ought to be taken advantage of and I would respectfully urge that six to ten of the brightest and most eager, be selected from the different tribes and sent to some agricultural or other labor school for more thorough education. The efforts here have developed those who would be best to send, and they have learned to appreciate the advantages of education and a knowledge of our ways of earning a livelihood. If this can be done, and after three or four years schooling they became able to make themselves useful as helpers about their agencies and are so returned to their people the best results must follow.

If this cannot be done by the Government I have the honor to request to be informed if private enterprise to this end would be sanctioned. This latter request is instigated by the questions of influential parties

1. In the five decades following the transfer of responsibility for Indian affairs from the War Department to the newly created Department of the Interior in 1849, there were periodic movements, stimulated by revelations of corruption and incompetence in the civilian administration, to transfer the Indian Bureau back to the War Department. The scandals of the Grant regime had revived the question, but the forces promoting transfer failed in the campaign. Loring B. Priest, *Uncle Sam's Stepchildren: The Reformation of United States Indian Policy, 1865–1887* (New Brunswick, 1942), pp.15–27.

2. The Sioux campaign of 1876 had just been organized. In fact, on the very day that Pratt wrote this letter Gen. George Crook fought the Battle of Powder River.

whose interest would no doubt bring about a charitable enterprise of this kind.

Very respectfully,
Your Obedient Servant,
R. H. PRATT.

Fort Marion, St. Augustine, Fla.,
April 17, 1876.

General W. T. Sherman,
Commanding the Army.
General:

I enclose a copy of a recent letter to the Adjutant General in reference to educating some of the younger men of the Indian prisoners under my care. This is such a promising field for the good of these people that it justifies me in asking your attention to it.

I can select nine or ten from the different tribes who are quite boys, and unmarried, who can be educated and then made use of about their agencies, as I have suggested, with greatest benefit. I can conceive of no better expenditure of effort for their people. The number I have suggested will take an education rapidly. About thirty of the others can be successfully taught. This enforced separation from their people without some determination of its duration and design, is very oppressive and a great hindrance now, and should cease. From ten to fifteen ought to be held in confinement much longer than the others, but I can certainly recommend most earnestly an exercise of clemency now for a large part. If it is considered best to hold them all here a much longer time, I hope their families may be sent as ordered by the President and countermanded last summer.

I am, sir,

With great respect,
Your Obd. Servant,
R. H. PRATT.

Fort Marion,
St. Augustine, Fla.,
May 1, 1876.

General W. T. Sherman,
Commanding the Army.
Dear General:

Bishop Whipple has sent me the letter of the Hon. Sec. of War concurring in your views in reference to a release of part of the Indians. I believe I see that my application for a thorough schooling for some of the young men will not meet with favorable action and that whatever is done in this direction for them must be done here.

I shall do the best I can on the basis of your endorsement. That they are to be returned *"in a body* to form the nucleus for the organization of their tribe."* This implies that the Government will, by some organized method, sustain them and hold them up as an example to instruct and lead their people. If, sustained in what they have attained and carried ahead by authority, their people will try to rise to them instead of their dropping back to their people, which would be the case were they merely taken back and turned loose. It seems to me that if I could confer personally with you and the Hon. Sec. a few minutes in reference to my work here, it would facilitate matters very much.

> With great respect,
> Your Obd. Servant,
> R. H. PRATT.

> Fort Marion,
> St. Augustine, Fla.,
> May 18, 1876.

General H. J. Hunt,
    Col. 5th Artillery,
        Charleston, South Carolina.
General:

.   .   .   .

The school was carried on continually for four months prior to April 1st, and before that from their arrival, somewhat irregularly. It will begin again next Monday. It was attended by an average of fifty and was in every way a success. Military drill is given sufficient to enable a handling in mass and to keep them set up. After adjournment of school they were encamped two weeks at Matanzas, and since their return to the Fort have been under instruction in building log houses.

Your attention was invited to their general appearance, to their industry in the manufacture of canes, bows and arrows, polishing of sea beans and drawings, from all of which they realized considerable money by sales to visitors. They work at anything faithfully,—the guard, the cooks, the baker, the mess room, etc.

White Horse, whom you saw on guard as a private, was formerly a Sergeant, and the leader in the recent scheme to escape and return to their people, was but a few days ago released. I organized a court of prisoners some weeks ago, and tried a Comanche for stealing a dollar and threatening one of his fellows. He was found guilty and sentenced to ten days in the dungeon, which was more than I thought necessary, but they insisted and I had it carried out.

It is to be hoped that they will soon be returned to their people and placed under instruction in the permanent business of life, or that some change of locality will enable far better chances while yet prisoners; they are anxious to learn agriculture.

Very respectfully,
Your Obedient Servant,
R. H. PRATT.

Fort Marion,
St. Augustine, Fla.,
July 19, 1876.

Lt. Gen. P. H. Sheridan,
   Chicago, Illinois.
General:

There is nothing of note to report regarding these prisoners unless that fact is of itself important. They are simply under good discipline; quiet, well-behaved, doing the work I can find for them to do, cheerfully and industriously. They have abandoned about all the appurtenances and characteristics of the aborigine and are as neat and clean in their dress and persons as the men of a disciplined company. My 1st Sergeant is about as competent as the average of those we get in colored troops. I have a two-hours school daily with an average of fifty pupils, divided into four classes, with a good teacher for each. The teachers work from the purest and best motives of Christian charity and, as a consequence, successfully, and there is no cost to the Government. I am especially helped by lady residents but during the winter any amount of assistance in the way of teaching is proffered by visitors who idle away four or five months here each year and are glad to improve part of the time. The intention of sending women and children is abandoned, which is a misfortune to these people and their tribes.

I am not convinced it would not have been better had some been tried as you first designated. Some of those we could have tried by Military Commission, are the ones, if any, who will give trouble hereafter. It will depend on the management. I try offences by a jury of their own number which works well and the few cases I have had have been awarded ample punishment.

I am, with great respect,

Your obedient servant,
R. H. PRATT.

Fort Marion,
St. Augustine, Fla.,
October 31, 1876.

General W. T. Sherman,
    Commanding the Army.
Sir:

The Army re-organization Board may take into consideration the enlistment of Indians as regular soldiers, or the continuing in some more
permanent manner than now, their use in the army. You were pleased to
comment favorably, some time since, on the results of my efforts here,
and it may not be out of place to mention the conclusions of an experience and observation of now more than nine years.

When I joined the 10th Cavalry in June, 1867, my first station was Ft.
Arbuckle, Indian Territory, where I was at once placed in charge of the
twenty-five Caddoe and Wichita scouts at the post, and commanded
them until their discharge in the first months of 1868. These were a
mixed lot of old and young enlisted for a year for the purpose of obtain-
ing information in relation to the hostiles and to guide scouting and
campaigning commands. These duties were well and ably performed,
and in addition, for several months they were entrusted with carrying
the mails from Fort Gibson to Arbuckle in conjunction with the Cherokee scouts of Fort Gibson. In these and in various other independent
positions of trust, such as pursuit of deserters and of wild Indians who
had stolen stock or committed other depredations, they were found reliable. On one occasion they pursued and attacked a party of wild Comanches, who had stolen stock near the post, killing one of the Comanches and wounding another, losing one of their own number in the
engagement.

I noted the individual career of most of these scouts since and am satisfied they were greatly benefited by their service and obedience, and their
standing in their tribes elevated. One of them was elected Chief of the
tribe soon after his discharge, by the vote of a majority of his people, and
served them very acceptably.

I served at Fort Sill during the years '69, '70, '71, and '72 and at Camp
Supply in '72 and '73, where I had many opportunities to observe the
Comanches, Kiowas, Apaches, Cheyennes and Arapahoes, who occupy
the country about those posts and also saw much of the affiliated tribes
on the Washita. I commanded the Tonkawa scouts at Fort Griffin in '73
and '74 and in the fall and winter of '74 and spring of '75 enlisted and
commanded the Indian scouts at Fort Sill, and I had charge of the Indian
prisoners at Fort Sill. I used the scouts several times to arrest their own
people and found them true to all trusts. I brought the Indian prisoners

here and have now used the young men as soldiers to guard themselves for more than a year, requiring of them all the duties that devolve upon a guard under such circumstances.

Several breaches of discipline by members of the white guard that preceeded them occurred, requiring the action of court martial. The Indians have performed the same duties so well that I have been unable to detect a single breach of discipline or instructions. White men went to sleep on post; none of the Indians have so trespassed. I have tested them nightly and at odd times and found them the most perfectly alive sentinels in my army experience. White men got drunk on duty; I have not had a single whisky case on or off duty, though always giving them the freedom of the town on the next day succeeding their day of duty.

I can see no good reason why Indians should not enter largely and permanently into army organization. All my experience fully sustains the opinion you expressed that "they would act promptly against the lawless of their own tribes and make the best police force that could be used among their own people."

I have the honor to be, General,

Respectfully,

Your most obd. servant,

R. H. Pratt.

Fort Marion,

St. Augustine, Fla.,

Feb. 20, 1877.

Adj. Gen. of the Army,

Washington, D.C.

General:

I have the honor to report that the Indian prisoners confined here have been counseling together for more than two weeks with a view of sending a talk to Washington in reference to their condition. A few evenings ago they notified me of their desire to make a talk, and all gathered in one of the casemates, when they put forward "Making Medicine" to speak for the young men first, and Manimic to follow in behalf of the old men.

Mr. Fox interpreted and I wrote down what they had to say, which is here given in their own words.

"Making Medicine" said: "I have learned to sing the Saviour's hymns and have given myself to Him. Heretofore I have led a bad life on the plains wandering around, living in a house made of skins. I have now learned something about the Great Spirit's road and want to learn more. We have lived in this old place two years. It is old and we are young. We are tired of it. We want to go away from it, anywhere. We want Washington to give us our wives and children, our fathers and mothers, and send us somewhere where we can settle down and live like white men.

"Washington has lots of good land lying around loose; give us some of it and let us learn to make things grow. We want to learn to farm the ground. We want a house and pigs and chickens and cows. We feel happy that we have learned so much, that we can teach our children. I speak for the young men. We want to work, we young men all belong to you. You have put a great deal into our hearts that was never there before. Our hearts are getting bigger every day. We are thankful for what we have learned. This is the feeling of all the young men that are here. We are willing to learn and want to work."

Manimic's talk for the old men: "It has been a long time since we came here. We came here with lying and stealing and killing in our hearts, but we have long ago thrown all that away. Today our hearts are glad, our heads are bigger and we are all glad for what we have learned. Two years have passed since we came here. We are tired of this old place, although our hearts are all glad. We want to go away from here. We want you to ask our Father at Washington to have mercy on us, and give us our wives and our children, and send us some place where we can learn to live in peace and by our own labor.

"Ask Washington to give us some land. He has a great deal of it and might give us some to raise things on. Tell Washington to let us go back and get our wives and children and send us to a new country where we can learn to work and support ourselves. We can handle the axe and shovel [even] if we are old. Ask Washington to let us go at it now and take it up right and learn at once. We want you to say a few good words and send it to Washington too. This is what all the Kiowas, Comanches and Cheyennes wanted me to say."

All indications favor that the best results will follow clemency and practical assistance to these people. Their conduct here is deserving of the highest praise, and should be rewarded with a change of condition. A few of the old men would be an element of great good sent back to their tribes. The younger men can so easily be carried forward to industrious civilization that it would seem a sin to deny them the facilities, but their women and children should be included, else much labor is lost.

> Very respectfully,
> Your obedient servant,
> R. H. PRATT.

While the military authorities to whom these letters were written were entirely sympathetic, no action was taken until the spring of 1878, when the prisoners were released and returned to their agents, to again become a very part of the reservation herds with their people, under the scant and lax methods of progress the Indian system provides.

17. Primitive Correspondence and Incidents of Prison Life

I lived much with the prisoners. My office in one of the casemates of the old fort was always open, and they were welcome. Some, especially the older men, were invited and frequently visited at my home, where we talked more freely. I found among them admirable principles of life and service and many times realized that here were men who only needed proper opportunities for development in order to easily become civilized and valuable citizens. High sense of honor was not lacking. There were statesmen, and though when our relations had become the most frank and friendly I was denied the advantage of interpreters, and bothered with their limited acquirement of English, I was still able to get more of their qualities and gain many interesting facts in regard to their personal and tribal affairs, which increased my respect for them.

One of the things of greatest interest was their method of communicating through picture writing. They received crude picture letters from home which, to them, were full of information. Mrs. J. Dorman Steel visited us in

1877 and made friends with some of the older Indians.[1] I called her attention to the picture writing and secured from Manimic a specimen which she made use of in writing about the prisoners.

(*The National Teachers' Monthly*, August 1877)
The Indian Prisoners at Fort Marion

It may not be generally known that at Fort Marion, St. Augustine, Florida, are about sixty-five representatives of the Cheyenne, Kiowa, Comanche and Arapahoe tribes, who, having been selected as among the worst specimens of the wild, cruel Indians of the far west, have, through the influence of judicious discipline and Christian kindness, become industrious, and tractable, creditably advanced in military training, able to read and to write, and, in some instances, unmistakable Christian converts. Only two years ago they came to Florida as prisoners convicted of the grossest outrages and murders. They entered St. Augustine clad only in their blankets, chained hand and foot.

Last February and March, I had the pleasure of often visiting Fort Marion, and its Indian inmates. What did I find? A military company neatly dressed in United States uniform, with hair cut and brushed, nails cleaned, manners respectful and faces more or less intelligent. In the morning there were three or four schoolrooms filled with earnest learners who watched every motion of their teacher's lips and eyes with an absorbed interest that even the presence of strangers could not interrupt, who read whole chapters from the New Testament in unison and sang in harmony many of Moody and Sankey's hymns. There were bakers whose shapely loaves were white and light, and carpenters who made their own benches and bunks. Their quarters were clean and orderly, and it was the unanimous verdict of the citizens of St. Augustine that it was always pleasant to meet the Indian prisoners from the fort.

What had wrought this wondrous change? It is not too much to say that it is entirely due to Lieutenant Pratt, in charge, aided by a few noble Christian women who have volunteered their services as teachers two or three hours daily. Lieutenant Pratt believes the American Indian to be a human being, quite as capable of civilization, and presenting quite as desirable a field for missionary labor as the far-off denizens of Borrioboola-Gha.

What if, instead of the dreaded war-whoop, and news of fearful massacre, and the sudden cutting down of the flower of our army,[2] and the

1. Esther Baker Steele, wife of Joel Dorman Steele, educator and author of numerous textbooks. *Dictionary of American Biography*, 17, 556–57.
2. Another reference to the Little Bighorn disaster the previous summer.

continual trembling of women and children on our frontiers, and a great war debt to be wrung from lank pockets in hard times, the next generation should witness peace in every tribe, Indian youth in schools, Indians in the Army thoroughly trained and worthy of trust as guardians of the peace in the west, a war debt replaced by an educational or civilization fund, and an end forever to the spilling of our bravest American blood? In a word, that we have accepted as brothers our natives whom this recent experiment has proved to be susceptible of transformation and responsive to Christian teaching. Shall we recognize them as men and women, and for the sake of humanity and our country's welfare, offer them the same opportunities which we lavish on immigrants from all lands, or shall we continue to prolong the popular cry of extermination?

The Creeks, the Cherokees and the Choctaws have proved that their civilization is not a failure. Why not give the same opportunity to the Comanches, the Kiowas, even the bloody Sioux? It is Lieutenant Pratt's firm belief, based upon his recent wonderful success, that if the Government would grant to the tribes now called hostile the same privileges and endowments which forty years ago were conferred upon their dusky brethren, the Cherokees, Choctaws and Creeks, an equal lapse of time, with judicious management of detail, would witness similar results. Let all good people pray for "a consummation so devoutly to be wished."

It is my good fortune to possess an original letter sent in June, 1876, to Manimic, a Cheyenne Chief at Fort Marion, by his wife in the Indian Territory. It affords an admirable specimen of Indian picture writing, of which so few examples are extant. The address is at the right, and includes (1) Manimic or Eagle Head, (2) Howling Wolf, his son, and (3) Making Medicine. The symbol for the last named is a wigwam with sticks placed horizontally at the apex, the cabalistic sign by which a "medicine-man's" hut is distinguished. Manimic is informed that his son, (5) Buffalo Head, desires to come to him, but is held back by his mother (4) Shooting Buffalo. The olive branch in his hand conveys assurance of his love. Manimic's daughter (6) Flying Dove and her young child Arrow, join in the greeting; also his daughter (7) Big Turtle, the belle of the tribe, an Indian beauty with "hair seventeen hands long" as the proud father informed us in his pantomimic way. Curly-Head (8) wife of Howling Wolf, has a young child, Little Turtle, named after his handsome aunt. Running Water (9) is the daughter of Manimic by another squaw, Shield (12) whom he afterwards repudiated, or in his own expressive words, "threw away." With a shade of disgust on his usually placid face, the old chief pointed to the picture of her grave and ejaculated "That squaw no good; too much talk!" Shield's daughter, White Feather (13) is buried by her side, and the frequent tracks about their grave show that Running Water—whose attitude also betokens grief—goes often there to weep, though the single track which leads to the spot shows that she goes alone. Making Medicine's two wives (10, 11) with his children go together to mourn at the grave of his dead child, exhibiting a state of harmony between his squaws which must be very gratifying to the feelings of an absent husband. Thus it will be seen that this letter conveys intelligence of three births, two of them males, as the faces are painted red; gives the names of the little ones; reports the ability to walk of Making Medicine's oldest child, as her little tracks accompany the others to her sister's grave; announces three deaths and the honors paid to the memory of the lost ones; gives assurance of the good health of the remaining parties represented; mentions particularly Buffalo Head's desire to greet his father, and every face being turned in that direction, expresses a general desire on the part of the writers to see the distant prisoners. [See illustration 18.]

Mrs. J. Dorman Steele.

Soon after the affair on the Little Big Horn in the summer of 1876, the Cheyenne prisoners received a letter from their people in the Indian Territory, now Oklahoma, forwarding a large picture letter from the Northern Cheyennes containing an account of the fight and their part in annihilating General Custer and five troops of his Seventh Cavalry and of the approach of reinforcements for General Custer, showing that in fleeing from their camps the different bands of Sioux and Northern Cheyennes separated from each other, Sitting Bull and his followers going toward Canada.

This picture letter was on a blank army muster roll probably found in the plunder taken in the fight. It was of such historical interest that I sent it with their explanation of what it told to General Sheridan, who acknowledged its receipt and value.

It was common for the Indians whom I had come in contact with most, the Kiowas, Comanches, Cheyennes, and Arapahoes of the then Indian Territory, to present something of family and even tribal history in their ornamentation of their buffalo skin lodges and robes. The industrious wife and mother in tanning robes for the family's tepee home removed the hair and made them pliable for rolling up into transportation size. These gave large field for picturing and ornamentation. When tanning a buffalo robe with the hair on until it was as soft and pliable as cloth, to be worn by the husband, self, or child, she often covered it with pictures showing something of the family history of special interest to the wearer. This was evidence, not only of the possession of fine native ability and art, but of family affection, and indicated qualities which, if transferred to civilized pursuits and properly developed, would have produced admirable accomplishments. As the buffalo were being exterminated and soon would fail to supply home, clothing, and food, transformation of art qualities should have been promoted.

Nothing stimulates the young more, nor better leads to the building of high ideals and ambitions, than having good friends with these qualities who take a personal interest in our welfare, and keep it up through correspondence when separated. Having had this advantage in my earlier years, I sought to bring about such relations between the Indian prisoners and the best among our people who visited and showed interest in them. The effort met with remarkable success. A considerable number of the Indian prisoners came to have substantial friends who took sufficient interest in them when visiting Florida to see them on every visit to the old fort, conversing with them and showing their friendship in many ways. Thereafter these friends on return to their northern homes wrote to and received letters from the Indians who had gained the ability to write, even though imperfectly.

This led to another development of value. The persons of influence who visited the old fort and took an interest began to suggest and practice various little devices for the uplift of the individual prisoners. There were notable cases.

The wife of one of the most influential lawyers of New York City, Mr. Joseph Larocque, visited St. Augustine with her family of four children. She came to the fort and at once became interested in the Indians' industries and bought liberally of their products, among other things the finest bows and arrows. She then proposed to have her children learn archery from the Indians. I selected two young men who could give the best instruction, the hours were fixed, and she brought her children for daily lessons. She had the Indians make targets as she directed and then watched them teach her children how to use the bow and arrow most effectively. A friendship grew which was continued both to the prisoners and to my efforts, and for years afterwards led to large benefactions to the Carlisle School.

J. Wells Champney, artist, noted for his pastel portraits, visited St. Augustine at this time with his wife, a gifted writer, and became interested in the Indians.[3] "Champ" was asked by *Harpers* to furnish something for *The Weekly*. Two of his pictures from that periodical illustrating Mrs. Larocque's archery scheme and the school feature of the prison life were pre-

---

3. James Wells Champney (1843–1903) was a distinguished artist and longtime illustrator for *Scribner's Monthly*. After 1878 he held the professorship of art at Smith College. *Dictionary of American Biography*, 3, 610.

sented. Genial old Manimic and "Champ" became chummy, which led to a full-length portrait in oil of the famous chief clad in some of Mrs. Pratt's collection of Indian war toggery, and a duplicate of it was given to Mrs. Pratt.

Mrs. Larocque afterwards corresponded with the two young Indians who had instructed her children and sent them helps and mementoes of her interest.

One of these Indians was my quartermaster sergeant in charge of the government property connected with the prison. It was his duty to take care of all the stores for which I was responsible to the government, to keep memorandum of issues of food and clothing, and to know that tools were properly restored to their place after being used and that nothing was left around promiscuously. He also drew these stores from the army commissary and issued to the cooks the food supplies in proper quantity daily, keeping record of the same. He and the first sergeant of the Indian company were also intermediaries next to me in command and particularly responsible when I was absent from the fort. They had freedom to come to my house with messages. I had had much to do with white, colored, and Indian soldiers, and among all these experiences there are none that showed finer manhood and fidelity to duty and ability than these two Indians, and there were others like them among their fellow prisoners. Their interest and concern for the righteous working out of what I was trying to do was constantly in evidence in their actions. Two incidents will illustrate.

One night Mrs. Pratt and I were away from home until late, visiting military friends at the lower end of town. When we returned, I found on the stand at the head of my bed this note:

Captain Pratt:
His Zotom heap sick. You come see him quick.

Etahdleuh

I hastened to the fort and found Zotom lying on his bed moaning and all the Indians anxiously gathered about. His face was livid and his eyes set in a stare. The doctor was a mile away at the lower end of town. I had had many experiences with soldiers under emergencies and at once asked what he had been eating. Etahdleuh replied, "He go down town today and buy big piece beef. He cook and eat and cook and eat just like old times with buffalo out west." This was the clue to the situation. I shook Zotom and called his name loud and louder, but he did not respond.

On our way to Florida while we were waiting in Fort Leavenworth, Kansas, I had become acquainted with one of the older surgeons of the army, whose service began during the Mexican War. In our conversations he told me of an experience at that same post of Leavenworth in the early fifties, in which a noted cavalry general of the Civil War was the central figure. This officer, then a young lieutenant in the cavalry stationed at the post, had typhoid fever. The case was critical, but he was brought through to convalescence. He was cared for in his quarters. He was in high esteem among the officers and ladies and a leader in the social affairs of the post. When he began to mend, the doctor gave strict instructions about limiting his diet, which necessarily had to be attended to by those who took care of him in his quarters. One day the doctor received a message urging haste, that the lieutenant was dying. He said he realized that no such condition could have happened so suddenly, and he was rather deliberate in getting there. When he reached the lieutenant's quarters, he found anxious ladies and officers and a platter with evidences of a somewhat liberal meal which had been brought in by a certain captain's wife. The doctor sent the ladies away, had the hospital steward bring muslin and a quantity of mustard, and made a large mustard poultice, which he placed on the stomach and bowels of the officer. He appointed four of the officers standing about to hold him by the arms and legs and waited. When it began to burn, and hurt outside worse than inside, the sick man came to his senses and, finding himself strenuously held in position, talked in rather radical language to the doctor for holding him to such punishment. But the doctor kept him on his back until just before the mustard began to blister, then removed it, and from then on there was recovery.

I at once realized that the Indian was in the same condition as the lieutenant, and sent my handy Indian Pedro to our medical supplies for a can of mustard and some muslin, made a fat plaster, placed it over the stomach and bowels of Zotom, appointed four Indians to hold him by the arms and legs, and waited the result. This worked out exactly as the doctor described on the lieutenant.

Zotom was one of the most powerful of the Indians and tested the strength of his holders greatly. He talked Kiowa with rapidity and the Kiowas laughed. When the burnt district was near blister, I removed the poultice and had the Indians let go. Zotom got on his feet at once and, holding his clothes away from the irritation, walked up and down the room, continuing to talk Kiowa and evidently abusing me. I asked if he was swearing, and they said: "No. Indians have no swear words."

Next morning at inspection Zotom's countenance was still dark; but he soon renewed our friendly relations. I told them of the young lieutenant who became a famous general, and a good lesson on gormandizing was not lost.[4]

4. Pratt thought highly of Zotom and expected much of him. In the early 1890s, however, James Mooney wrote that "Paul Zotom (Zoñtom), was regularly ordained as a deacon in the Episcopal church. He returned in the summer of 1881, but has sadly fallen from grace." *Calendar History*, p. 216.

Okahaton (Making Medicine), a Cheyenne, the first sergeant of the company, mounted the guard each morning and selected the cleanest and most soldierly Indian for my orderly. The orderly went with me during the day, and when I was in my office he was on call to show visitors about the fort and to go on errands to town, to my house, or to the commanding officer or adjutant at the lower end of town. He did not have to stand guard, so there was incentive to become orderly.

One morning as the guard was being mounted, I noted that there was considerable delay, and Okahaton came to the office and said, "Captain, two just same. Me no understand which cleanest." So I went out and looked them over, and sure enough I was also perplexed to know whether the Cheyenne or the Kiowa was the cleanest. Their clothing was brushed as clean as possible, their brass buttons were as bright as they could be, and their shoes equally well polished. As I passed front and rear, they stood equally erect in the position of a soldier. The whole body of Indians was out observing and I concluded that there was a contest as to which tribe would secure the orderly for the day. I kept on looking them over, even their ears, to see if they were clean, and their hair to see if it was nicely brushed, and noted that their shirts and stockings were clean. Finally I saw that the finger nails of one of the candidates were long and unclean, and looking at those of the other who stood beside him found them clean. The first sergeant was watching carefully. I took hold of a hand of each and held them side by side so he could see the contrast. He at once made the Indian sign with his forefinger extended, raised his hand and brought it down quickly, which meant "I understand." When the decision was made, there was applause from part of the Indian audience. Thereafter, the finger nails did not escape Sergeant Okahaton's attention, and even the older men were found cleaning their nails when getting ready for inspection or to go down town.

In the late winter of 1877–78, I again urged higher educational chances for a part of the younger and most promising prisoners. This appeal was warmly approved by General Dent and reached the Indian Bureau, which replied that it did not have enough money to educate the youth under its care and could not therefore spare any for adult prisoners under care of the War Department, but if the funds could be found the Bureau had no objection to the plan. General Dent and I then concluded it best that I go to Washington and see the President, and others in authority, and again try to secure the release of the prisoners. I was armed with letters from General Dent to President Grant[5] and the Secretary of War and two letters from President M. B. Anderson of Rochester University, New York, then visiting in St. Augustine.

5. As Grant was no longer President in 1877–78, this must have occurred in the winter of 1876–77.

One of these was to General John Eaton, United States Commissioner of Education, and the other to President [Julius H.] Seelye of Amherst College, then a member of Congress. The President referred the case to be determined by the War Department. President Seelye and General Eaton took an active interest and thereafter as long as they lived were influential friends to what I undertook in Indian education.

There was no immediate conclusion, and I returned to St. Augustine. Soon after this General Hancock, who commanded the department from his headquarters in New York, came to look over the situation. He covered the whole three years of prison life and was most interested in the case of the young men who wanted to go to school, and he saw and talked to them individually.

The ladies teaching the Indian classes had social distinction in the town, and their ability and enthusiasm in their work met with good success in the way of English speaking and educational progress. Their talk among the visitors aroused much interest. Each teacher was anxious to see the bright products of her labor given advanced opportunities and talked freely about it. It was generally conceded that Etahdleuh was quite foremost among those who were entitled to such privilege. He was the most anxious among those who wanted to go away to school and get a better education. It offered a profitable way of escape from prison life and tested governmental purposes. All of these young men were in their late teens or early twenties. The teachers joined to create a sentiment among the visitors in Etahdleuh's favor to see if they could not raise at least enough money to send him away to school. Finally, ladies in St. Augustine, largely northern visitors, decided to give an entertainment to raise the money.

They selected a "Mother Goose" program, using their own and our children, and went into a very elaborate system of training, with about twenty-five boys and girls, all aged less than eight years. When they had completed their program, they asked me to witness it, and when I expressed the great pleasure and satisfaction I had in their success, they wanted to include something by the Indians. I asked them what they would like. One proposed an Indian dance. I said, "I will arrange that." Another thought an Indian war whoop would be proper. "That is easy." Another wanted an Indian love song. "We will have one." And finally, they wanted a demonstration of the sign language. "All right, we can give that." Then they asked me to undertake the publicity and take over the business management. They furnished the name and part of each little actor, and I got out an elaborate program, naming each performer and their part, including the Indian dance by four of our best dancers, naming them, an Indian war whoop by White Horse, an Indian love song by Etahdleuh, and a talk in the Indian sign language and explanation by Tsait-Kope-Ta. We arranged with the proprietor of one of the hotels for the largest dining room in town, as there was no town hall. Removing the tables, it seated about 300 after taking out space for the platform. I fixed the price of admission at one dollar without consulting the ladies, and circulated the program. Immediately, a number of the ladies came to remonstrate and said that would never do. They had no idea of charging more than twenty-five cents, and I must change it. I said, "Ladies, I have witnessed what you are going to present, and am very sure it is worth fifty cents; and I know the Indians' part is worth fifty cents, and don't that make a dollar?" and they yielded. They used the little folks to sell tickets and quickly sold over 700 so that two performances were necessary. The hall was packed both nights, and the receipts above expenses were more than was needed for Etahdleuh.

Every feature of the performance was greatly relished by the audience. Especially was this so when Etahdleuh sang his love song. I left the preparation of their parts to the Indians themselves, had the old men designate the dancers, and they chose White Horse to give the big war whoop. I said to Etahdleuh, "This is for your benefit. Can't you sing an Indian love song to oblige the ladies?" He replied, "Yes, Captain, I will sing a love song." I said, "Very well, I want you to fix yourself up just as if you were in camp in the old days. I will depend on you and will think no more about it." He said, "All right, Captain."

When Etahdleuh came out to sing his song, he was dressed in the old way. He had saved his Indian garb and the braids of his long hair, which he fastened on each side of his face. He had a big eagle feather which projected above the back of his head and his face was painted liberally; he wore his moccasins, buckskin leggins, and beaded coat. He stood erect before the audience, folded his arms, and began to pat the floor with his left foot, and then in loud clear tones he sang: "Ho-Nan-Ke-Ah-Bo-Mo, Ho-Nan-Ke-Ah-Bo-Mo, Ho-Nan-Ke-Ah-Bo-Mo, Ho-Nan-Ke-Ah-Bo-Mo." This he repeated about a dozen times. The audience was very quiet and like myself was waiting for a change in the words and music. As none came, I said to him, "Subick," which means, "stop." Etahdleuh quit instantly and hurried behind the curtain. The audience exploded and he had to go out and repeat it. He was the hero of the occasion anyway, and his song added greatly to his notoriety.

Behind the curtains was the most interesting picture of the occasion: the mother trainers, their costumed Mother Goose performing children, and the Indians decorated for their parts, all on fraternal relations, eager to begin a small effort to lift Indians into their rightful place as real potential Americans. Such was the hearty interest and enthusiasm of all from the smallest child to the biggest "injin" that there were no failures, and that night was lit an illuminating north star that has been a guide to the way for all the forty-five years since. Every child had to talk to Etahdleuh, who was happiest of all because of his intuition and vision of his own possibilities.

The interest created by these performances led a number of people then visiting in Florida to agree individually to stand for the three years' expenses of all those who wanted to go to school. Bishop Whipple took four; Mrs. Mary H. Burnham of Syracuse, for the Diocese of Central New York, took four; Mrs. Joseph Larocque, who had taken the lead in the archery, took two; and other friends became responsible until all were provided for.

Then I began a correspondence to find where I could best locate them for industrial education. As the whole Indian population by edict of the government were consigned to agriculture for a living, I sought entrance for them in state agricultural colleges; but the several I applied to hesitated to undertake the bad Indians. Their case was pre-judged because they were prisoners of war with reputation for atrocities.

Miss Mather, one of the teachers, knew General Armstrong of the Hampton Agricultural School for Negroes,[6] and wrote him, to which he replied, showing a willingness to undertake one. I then wrote him, explained the situation, vouched for the integrity and good behavior of the young men, and guaranteed success. Under this pressure General Armstrong gave way and agreed to take several. When he found the distinction of the people who were willing to pay for this education, it influenced him to take all he could get. Mrs. Burnham wanted to oversee the education of the four she would undertake herself. Mrs. Curuthers and her husband, Dr. Curuthers, who lived at Tarrytown, wanted Tsait-Kope-Ta, a pupil in her class who had become very proficient in the use of English and was a most promising subject, save that he was threatened with tuberculosis, but the doctor thought he could handle that. It was therefore arranged that seventeen of these young men should go to Hampton Institute, Mrs. Burnham's four to Paris Hill near Utica, New York, under the care of Reverend J. B. Wicks, an Episcopal clergyman, who took them in as members of his family and himself promoted their education, and Tsait-Kope-Ta to Tarrytown into the home of Doctor Curuthers, where he remained several years as a son in the family.

6. Samuel Chapman Armstrong (1839–93) had commanded a regiment of Negro troops in the Civil War and, at its close, received a brevet of brigadier general. His conspicuous success with Negro soldiers led to his appointment in 1866 as an agent of the Freedmen's Bureau. While in charge of a freedmen's camp at Hampton, Virginia, he conceived the idea of an educational institution combining mental and manual training that would equip the newly freed slaves to assume their place in society. With the backing of the American Missionary Association, Armstrong in 1868 opened the Hampton Normal and Industrial Institute and as its superintendent built a large reputation as an educator and humanitarian. *Dictionary of American Biography, 1,* 359–60.

18. Recruiting Indians for Hampton

Early in April 1878 the War Department released the prisoners to the care of
the Indian Bureau. I explained to the Bureau the provisions that had been
made for the education of twenty-two, that seventeen were to go to Hampton,
and that it would be well if the route back west lay that way. I was then instructed to make arrangements for their transportation to that point.

The winter visiting season in Florida was over. There had been a river
excursion steamer coming from the Chesapeake Bay region every fall, and
returning north in the spring, commanded by a Captain Starke of Virginia,
who had graduated from Annapolis, served a number of years in our Navy
before the Civil War, and then became an officer in the Confederate Navy.
His winter route was on the St. Johns River, and he was about to return
north and would pass Hampton. I asked him to take the prisoners and my
family to Hampton on his return trip. This he kindly consented to do, but
having no license for ocean service it had to be without cost, providing I took
care of the food supply. He brought his steamer around from the St. Johns
by the ocean to St. Augustine and took us aboard right at the old fort. It was
a great day. Practically all St. Augustine was out to see us off.

My notion was that, being from the interior and having lived for three
years in sight of the ocean, it was a fitting climax of their experience for the

Indians to have a trip on old ocean itself and by that add to their civilization and knowledge. I explained to them the results on a great many people who travel the ocean, how the waves would roll and toss the boat, and that would disturb our stomachs, but it would be good for us, and they became even anxious to undertake the experience.

During the trip north I had long conversations with Captain Starke, and he gave many interesting experiences he had had as a United States officer on foreign service before the Civil War, and afterwards during that war when he was an officer on one of the Confederate raiders which destroyed so many of our ships in foreign trade.

The Indians and members of my family had the discomfort of ocean travel, but being prepared for it some of the Indians were amused, even to laughter, when under the experience.

We reached Hampton at midnight on the 13th of April and were warmly received by General Armstrong and his people. At Hampton I found an Indian Bureau order directing that the prisoners, except the young men for education, be taken over by General J. H. O'Bierne, who was still in charge of the Washington office of the *New York Herald,* who would conduct them to their western homes. This was a disappointment, for I had expected the advantage of traveling with them back to my regiment still on that frontier, which would enable me to take my goods and family without material expense. Being denied this, and not having had a leave of absence for a number of years, I asked for four months' leave, which was granted.[1]

I remained with the prisoners at Hampton for a few days. During that time we visited Fort Monroe at Old Point, where we went through the then-strong fortifications, and also the Norfolk Navy Yard, where we were shown through one of our largest naval war vessels. Everything impressed the white man's power upon the Indians, particularly the immense 20-inch gun in Fort Monroe then being tested at long-range firing and into the mouth of which a boy of eight years might crawl. After locating my family in New York I returned to Hampton for a time to be present at the commencement exercises, and to ensure the content of the Indians with their surroundings. General Armstrong and I talked much about the future of these young men and the need for them to become Americanized. As our Indian system contem-

1. The Cheyennes and Arapahos arrived at Darlington Agency on April 28, 1878. "The return of these people has had a good effect," reported Agent John D. Miles, "and has stimulated afresh the desire these Indians have manifested to engage in the pursuits of civilized life. The exertions of one of the returned prisoners (Howling Wolf) have resulted in more than twenty of his friends and relations adopting the dress, habits, and ways of the whites." The Kiowas and Comanches reached Fort Sill on May 1. Agent P. B. Hunt observed "a very great change in these people, not only in their appearance, but a complete and thorough reformation in every particular." Secretary of the Interior, *Annual Report* (1878), pp. 551, 555.

plated that all Indians should become farmers, I urged that during vacation they have privileges among our farmers to gain practical knowledge for managing their own farms. Deacon Hyde of Lee, Massachusetts, was one of Hampton's trustees, and I was introduced and told to explain to him what I had in mind. Mr. Hyde thought that the whole party could be cared for in the country about Lee. Soon after his return home, Mr. Hyde wrote that he had given two days among the farmers without being able to get any places, and only two seemed at all willing to consider it. General Armstrong handed me his letter and asked, "What shall we do?" I said, "Let me take Etahdleuh as a sample and go to Lee." The General said, "That's it. You had better start tonight." It was too late to take the boat to New York at Norfolk, but we could meet it when passing Old Point by going out in a row boat, as it sometimes received passengers in that way. Etahdleuh and I were hurried over to Old Point, a boatman rowed us out, and when the steamer approached we signaled with a lantern. A voice megaphoned, "What do you want?" And we said, "Two passengers for New York." The steamer slowed down and we were told to come alongside. A rope ladder was let down from the deck, probably twenty feet above us, and Etahdleuh went up first. When he got close to the top two stout sailors caught hold of his arms and helped him over on to the deck, and I followed.

We reached New York in the morning and went immediately to Lee. Deacon Hyde had been advised of my coming and said that the Congregational Church had a missionary meeting that evening and our arrival was opportune. It was arranged that Etahdleuh should repeat an address he had given at Hampton commencement and that I should follow and explain my mission. I told the Deacon that being unaccustomed to audiences of that kind, I might be confused and lose myself, and if he would help me over a danger of that kind by asking a question or two it would help me to pull through. On the way over to the church, Mrs. Hyde took my arm and was exceedingly gracious. She was a fine New England woman, daughter of a former lieutenant governor of the state.

After Etahdleuh made his speech, I began to give out the thoughts I had arranged, and soon I became confused. The pastor of the church spoke up at once and asked if the Indians were at all witty. I replied that they were quite given to wit and then gave this incident: During the winter of 1868 we were camped on the upper Washita. I was adjutant of four companies of my regiment, the Tenth Cavalry, and Major Kidd of the regiment the commanding officer. We jointly occupied two wall tents pitched together, the rear tent for sleeping, and the front for office and dining room. The cooking was over an outside fire. I got up one Sunday morning and, looking out, found that there had been a light fall of snow, and told the commanding officer. "Good," he said. "After breakfast we will go out and kill some turkeys." Taking a soldier apiece to help carry our game, we started out mounted. We soon found turkey tracks, followed and came upon a flock, killed a number, and kept killing until each of us and the two orderlies had several turkeys tied to our saddles. Concluding that we had enough, we started back to camp. On the way, in a little valley, we came upon a lone Indian tepee. There were two women outside cutting wood, and they continued talking with men inside. I recognized that they belonged to the Caddo tribe, and the Major thought he would like to see the inside of a tepee. Leaving our horses with the soldiers, we asked permission, opened the flap door, and stepped inside. Three Indians were sitting on the ground at one side of a fire in the center playing cards. I recognized one of them, named George, who was a cripple, and could speak a little English. He was dealing the cards, so I austerely said, "George, don't you know it is wrong to play cards on Sunday?" George replied at once without stopping the dealing of the cards, "That's all right, Captain. That's all right. Injun play cards, officer hunt turkey. All same."

I did not realize until I had started into the story that at a missionary meeting in a church with New England surroundings I might be hurting my cause through showing a lack of sabbatical observance. Having started, I could not well stop. On the way home, Mrs. Hyde did not take my arm, but walking by my side a little distant in manner said, "Captain Pratt, I cannot understand how you could be hunting turkeys on Sunday," and I had to confess to some retrogression and having fallen into army and frontier ways.

I told the people something about Indians and their good qualities and that they would prove themselves useful farm helps; how the government plans intended all Indians to become farmers and it would greatly advance them if they had chances to learn our American farm life by becoming a real part of it and this would lead them to adopt our ways of living. A number of farmers agreed to take pupils and others wanted to think about it for a day or two. Mr. Hyde, with his carriage, took the Indian and me about the country, which gave Etahdleuh a chance to see the farm homes and meet the kind people so he could explain to his comrades when he returned to Hampton. We soon found summer places for all the seventeen former prisoners. They went to Lee that summer, and some of them the next, with abundant benefit to themselves and satisfaction to the people who employed them.

This was the beginning of the system which I afterwards at Carlisle called "Outing." It was born through the experiences heretofore related, during which I came upon a phrase which exactly covered my idea. It was: "The contact of peoples is the best of all education."

I argued quite a little for it with General Armstrong, urging that it was the best method possible for removing prejudice between the races. The relations between peoples inevitably become amicable and established in proportion to the knowledge and value of each to the other. If as individuals the people of one race can be made to add material help to the other, they become proportionately acceptable. Creating opportunities for this is a reasonable duty of government. The Indians, by being held on reservations remote from contact with the white race, have been under almost insurmountable disadvantage. I count it among the very greatest of all the wrongs we have committed against the Indians that we have so imperiously excluded them from all possibility of demonstrating their possibilities to labor and learn. In a country like America, composed of people from all races, it has seemed to me both the highest privilege and a sacred duty devolving upon our government and people to see that the original inhabitants, from whom we were wresting so much, should be admitted to the very best opportunities to prove their worth. What brighter glory could shine from our national escutcheon than to give the native people we found here foremost privileges to become a very part of our citizenry under our benign Declaration of Independence and Constitution! History and many transactions show that the Indians are not lacking in qualities of a high order.

United States commissioners were sent to Red Jacket in western New York to treat with him for a concession of his land. During the conferences all sat on logs, Red Jacket by the side of the principal commissioner. As they talked, Red Jacket crowded the commissioner. The commissioner moved along, and as they talked on, Red Jacket again crowded the commissioner, and the commissioner again moved along, until finally the end of the log was reached. The commissioner then said, "Red Jacket, you are crowding me off the log." Red Jacket said, "That is just what you are trying to do to me and my people." Giving them opportunity and fellowship in our prosperous American civilization would not impoverish but would rather enrich us and would vastly enrich them. It would also be the best recompense we could make for what we have seized.

I told General Armstrong that with these seventeen Indians from Florida as a nucleus, it would be easy for him to add hundreds of Indian youth of both sexes, and if they were handled properly, in the course of a few months it would be difficult to distinguish the newcomers from the first party, and he would find such an undertaking a gratifying success.

Not long after going on leave, I received a personal letter from the Secretary of War, Mr. McCrary,[2] asking me to go to Leavenworth, Kansas, and with tribal and parental consent secure for Hampton fifty boys and girls

2. George W. McCrary (1835–90), Iowa congressman from 1869 to 1877 and Secretary of War in President Rutherford B. Hayes' cabinet from 1877 to 1879. *Dictionary of American Biography*, *12*, 2–3.

from the Nez Percés under Chief Joseph, who were then being held as prisoners of war at that point. After having killed settlers in and about their old
home in Idaho, they had been captured after a thousand miles of pursuit by
our army, when trying to escape from the United States into Canada.[3] The
Secretary in his letter said that if I would do this he would extend my leave
to cover the time needed for this service. I accordingly went to Leavenworth.
When I arrived I found that General Pope, the department commander, had
received the order and, not waiting for me, had undertaken to get the Indians' consent to let their children go, but they had refused because they
wanted to know first what the Government was going to do with them. I insisted, however, on having a try myself by seeing and explaining to the
Indians, and a council was held with Chief Joseph and his subchiefs. They
all persisted in refusing their children until they knew their own fate. Chief
Joseph was noted as an orator, and his long speech was full of impressive
arraignment of our government and people for mistreatment of his people.
I went to Washington, informed the Secretary of their conclusion, and returned to my leave status. Soon thereafter I received the following order:

Headquarters of the Army,
Adjutant General's Office,
Washington, September 2, 1878.

SPECIAL ORDERS   ⎫
  No. 190   ⎬
              ⎭

Extract

.   .   .   .

2. By direction of the Secretary of War, 1st Lieutenant R. H. Pratt,
10th Cavalry, now on leave at Indianapolis, Indiana, will proceed to this
city and report to the Hon. Secretary of the Interior for duty in selecting Indian children to be placed at the Hampton Normal and Agricultural Institute for a course of instruction. Lieutenant Pratt will accom-

---

3. One of the great Indians of all time, Chief Joseph led his people in a 2,000-mile dash for
Canada in 1877 after troops were sent to enforce the tribe's removal from Oregon to Idaho. In a
series of bitter engagements, he beat off his pursuers and won high praise from army officers for
his military genius and humane conduct of the war. Col. Nelson A. Miles intercepted the fugitives
at Bear Paw Mountain, Montana, fifty miles south of the Canadian border, and after a severe
fight and siege forced Joseph to surrender. Miles' promises to the chief were ignored, and the Nez
Percés, numbering 431 people, were taken to Fort Leavenworth and later to new homes in Indian
Territory. In 1883 and 1884 most of the tribe was permitted to return to Idaho, but Joseph and
150 people were sent to the Colville Reservation in Washington, where he died in 1904. Helen A.
Howard and Dan L. McGrath, *War Chief Joseph* (Caldwell, Ida., 1946). M. D. Beal, *I Will Fight
No More Forever: Chief Joseph and the Nez Percé War* (Seattle, 1963).

pany the Indian youth to the Institute and assume charge of them for such time as may be required to accustom them to their new mode of life and enable them to become interested in educational pursuits.

· · · · · · · · · · · · · ·

By command of General Sherman:
E. D. TOWNSEND,
Adjutant General.

The Interior Department instructed me to go to the Missouri River agencies, from Fort Berthold to Yankton, and secure from them an aggregate of fifty boys and girls as pupils for Hampton. In this case, on my suggestion, I carried with me the orders to those in charge of the Indians, so that I might be the first to present the subject of my mission. I went by rail to Bismarck, Dakota, having telegraphed the agent of my coming, and requested that he send a wagon to meet me there and bring me the eighty miles to Fort Berthold. The wagon was there with an Indian as driver, and we made the trip in two days, I sleeping in and he under our wagon one night.

The Fort Berthold Indians were three different tribes—Gros Ventres, Mandans, and Arikaras.[4] I was the guest of the Reverend C. L. Hall, a Congregational missionary who had been at work among them for a number of years, and who had a church and schoolhouse and was successfully promoting their Christianization and education. He at once took a hearty interest in the plan. The agent assembled the chiefs and leaders, and I explained to them what the Government intended. One of the old chiefs who wore spectacles assumed at once to answer through the interpreter for all of them with an emphatic no. I was looking the crowd over while he was talking and asked Mr. Hall, sitting by me, if there was not a younger man among them anxious for this Methuselah to pass on. He said there was and pointed him out. When the old fellow quit talking, I stated that it was only proper that the parents should conclude for their own children, and because it was a general matter everybody should be heard; perhaps there were those who differed from the head chief, and we must hear all sides. This younger man got up at once, emphatically opposed the position taken by the old chief, and said what they needed was education and here was a big chance and they must not pass it by. He was sustained by most of the others, and it was apparent that the old chief was overruled. The problem then was to get the parents' consent and the young people to go. It was suggested here in the council that we make up a

4. The Fort Berthold Reservation had been established in 1868 on the Missouri River above Bismarck, Dakota Territory, to care for the small, semisedentary river tribes on which the powerful Sioux had long preyed. E. H. Alden was agent at the time of Pratt's visit.

list of those whose parents consented and the people thought most worthy of the opportunity. As Mr. Hall had been managing their school, they deferred to his judgment and he made the selections. Ten was the number I would accept from that agency. After the list was thus made up in the council, we started out with the young chief and parents to get the childrens' consent and to examine and enroll them.

The first name on the list was that of a young man who was in the dance house getting ready for a performance the Indians had planned to give that evening. We went to the dance house and called him out. Except for breech clout he was nude and his whole body painted black with white ornamentations, particularly on the face and upper parts of his body.

That our first Indian candidate for education at the great school for black youth should be painted black on being presented for enrollment made me laugh heartily, and I gave him a silver dollar, which made him laugh too. When he learned of his selection, he readily consented and was enrolled right there. The enrollment was soon completed, so I could proceed the following morning. That night the big dance house was packed and I witnessed another of the many peculiar dances and pantomimes with which the different tribes entertained themselves. In this one, Bear and other animals appeared in their skins only, Indians old and young inside providing the locomotion, growling and imitating animal antics. I admit I had a little apprehension when an enormous bear waddled in near me with a ferocious growl, but was relieved when I saw he wore moccasins. The ventilation of the dance house was by the small door entrance and a hole in the roof for the smoke escape. As the place was packed with as many as could be jammed into the standing room with only a few of the chiefs and guests seated on the ground, the air was soon abominably foul.

One of the memories of that visit to Fort Berthold forty-four years ago is the hospitality of Mr. and Mrs. Hall and the enormous and deliciously mealy potatoes of their own raising they set before me. That region has since become most famous and valuable to the country as a prolific producer of high-quality potatoes and wheat.

The plan was to go down the river, make preliminary arrangements for the parties of pupils from each agency, and then come back, take a steamer, and gather them up.

The same Indian drove me back to Bismarck. I had wired the agent at Standing Rock, thirty miles below Bismarck, and the agency spring wagon met me. Standing Rock Agency was then in care of the Catholics under President Grant's peace policy. The newly appointed agent was a priest named Stephan, of whom I had known during the Civil War as a chaplain at Army of the Cumberland Headquarters, who had the distinction of being with General Thomas through the Battle of Nashville.[5]

He told me he was on horseback and near General Thomas when the battle was on, and the Confederates were falling back when General Thomas received the dispatch from General Grant telling him that General Logan was on the way to relieve him from command of the Army of the Cumberland. General Thomas handed him General Grant's dispatch to read. After reading it, he handed it back and said: "General, shall I answer this for you?" General Thomas said: "Let me see what you would say." He then wrote: "General Grant, City Point, Va. I am fighting. I am driving the enemy. G. H. Thomas, Major General." General Thomas read it and said 'Send it."

This former service in the same army was a good introduction. He took hearty interest in what was proposed but being new to the agency had not acquired material influence with the Indians. Securing of children was therefore left to me, assisted by the very efficient interpreter who had an Indian wife and had lived among these Indians several years and had their confidence. Going from tepee to tepee, we enrolled the number of prospective pupils in one day.

Boats were scarce, and the agent sent the agency spring wagon to take me to Cheyenne River Agency, next on my list.[6] Some of the Sioux Indians were then giving trouble, and the Northern Cheyennes, because of participating in the Battle of the Little Big Horn, had been arbitrarily moved from Montana to the Indian Territory and made a part of the Southern Cheyenne and Arapaho Agency. Their dissatisfaction at being sent south had increased, and they were just then trying to escape and return north.[7] It was therefore thought best that I have an escort from the Indian police to the Cheyenne

5. Father Joseph A. Stephan was agent from 1878 to 1880. Standing Rock, located on the west bank of the Missouri River about seventy-five miles south of Bismarck, was the agency for the Hunkpapa, Blackfeet, and Upper Yanktonai Sioux. When Pratt visited the agency, most of the Hunkpapas who fought at the Little Bighorn had surrendered and settled on the reservation, but Sitting Bull and about 200 were still in Canada. Had the chief been present, it is doubtful that Pratt would have enjoyed much success in recruiting pupils.

6. Cheyenne River Agency was built in 1868 on the west bank of the Missouri River at the mouth of the Cheyenne River. In 1880 about 3,000 Miniconjou, Blackfeet, Sans Arc, and Two Kettle Sioux were administered from this agency.

7. After their surrender in the spring of 1877, Dull Knife and his Northern Cheyennes were sent to Indian Territory to live with the Southern Cheyennes. Unacclimated and ill-fed, many sickened and died. In October 1878 they made a break for their northern homes and in an epic fighting retreat reached northwestern Nebraska before troops apprehended them. They were confined at Fort Robinson but in January 1879 tried against overwhelming odds to escape once more. Many of the people fell before army rifles, but the rest were permitted to settle with the Sioux at Pine Ridge and in 1891 were at last returned to their Montana homes. Grinnell, *Fighting Cheyennes*, chaps. 29, 30.

River Agency. I started out for a two-day trip with an Indian driver, followed by five Indian policemen on horseback. We jogged along rapidly over a dim road, mostly in the river bottom, at times on a bench considerably above the river with a second bench above that to the general level of the country.

Driving along close to the river, a large buck deer with fine antlers came up from the river just ahead of us, stopped a moment to look at us, and then attempted his escape to the upper level by passing close to us along the bluff wall. I motioned to the driver to stop, pulled out my 22/100 hip-pocket pistol, fired at him, and he dropped. I was greatly elated, jumped out of the wagon, and ran over to the deer, where the Indians had gone on their horses. I held up my pistol and indicated I was pleased with my shot. One of the Indians looked at me quizzically, got off his horse, and went and found the bullet hole reaching to the vitals of the deer; he put his finger in it and then tried to put his finger in the muzzle of my pistol to show me that the hole was too big for my pistol. He showed me his gun and said by signs that he had killed the deer. We had fired at the same time and I did not know he had fired, although I was surprised at the loudness of the explosion. I realized the situation, but concluded to joke. I insisted on my success and told him by signs that I had fired just a little ahead of him and that my bullet had gone in first and killed the deer, and that his bullet had followed right after mine and made the hole larger. The other Indians insisted I was right, to the disgust of the fellow who had actually killed the deer. Anyway, we had choice venison thereafter on the trip.

At Cheyenne River I found that Major (now General) Schwan was agent, assisted by Lieutenant Brown of his regiment, the Eleventh Infantry.[8] Six years before, we had all served together on the Texas frontier. The Cheyenne River Sioux had been for several years under the ministrations of the Episcopal Church. They had good mission and school buildings; the missionaries and teachers aided the agent and Lieutenant Brown in promoting the object of my visit, and we soon secured a fine party. My escort returned to Standing Rock, and I was sent forward to Crow Creek by Major Schwan in his agency wagon. There Captain Dougherty of the army was agent, and with Episcopal

8. Capt. (Bvt. Maj.) Theodore Schwan and 2d Lt. George LeRoy Brown. Schwan was a German immigrant who had come up from the ranks during the Civil War. He was at Cheyenne River under the authority occasionally used of detailing army officers as Indian agents. He was promoted to brigadier general and retired in 1901. According to George Hyde, Schwan imposed a Prussian discipline on the Indians that made them very unhappy. "They called him The-Man-Who-Never-Smiles. He was the first Sioux agent to recruit a force of uniformed and armed Indian police, and after that the only way in which his Sioux could have any freedom or ease was by camping many miles away from the agency and only coming there once in ten days to collect the free rations that were their due under the treaties." *A Sioux Chronicle* (Norman, University of Oklahoma Press, 1956), p. 30.

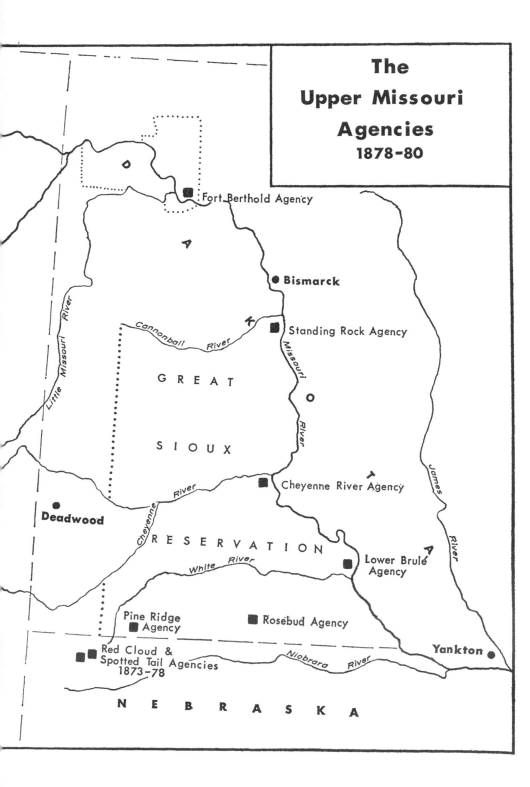

The Upper Missouri Agencies 1878-80

Fort Berthold Agency

● Bismarck

Standing Rock Agency

Cannonball River

GREAT

Little Missouri River

SIOUX

Missouri River

● Deadwood

Cheyenne River

Cheyenne River Agency

RESERVATION

White River

Lower Brule Agency

James River

Pine Ridge Agency

Rosebud Agency

Yankton ●

Red Cloud & Spotted Tail Agencies 1873-78

Niobrara River

N E B R A S K A

teachers and missionaries to help, the necessary part was quickly enrolled. Lower Brulé Agency was also under Episcopal care and soon gave a party.[9]

The next place on my list was the Spotted Tail and Red Cloud Agencies, which had a short time before been established at the abandoned Pawnee Agency on the Missouri River. The Pawnees had been removed from their ancestral homes to the Indian Territory to carry out the Black Hills treaty with the Sioux, which gave all that region to them and required them to settle on the Missouri River, where such supplies as the Government was to furnish could be easily forwarded by boat. Red Cloud and Spotted Tail, with the largest following, had become discontented and gone west and located in two different bodies, Spotted Tail and his people 100 miles from the river and Red Cloud, with his, 100 miles farther west.[10] The rebellion of these two large bands made it almost hopeless to undertake to get children from them. Nevertheless, they were on my schedule, and the Commissioner of Indian Affairs had particularly desired that I get delegations from them, saying that the children, if brought east, would become hostages for tribal good behavior.

Newspapers I found at Crow Creek told that the Northern Cheyennes had made a successful escape from their agency in Indian Territory and were on their way north. This complicated the situation very much, for they were likely to pass north, crossing my route to the Spotted Tail and Red Cloud camps. Determined to try, I secured an Indian with a spring wagon and drove rapidly for some forty miles over a roadless route and camped. The next morning we started to complete our journey and soon saw smoke sig-

9. Crow Creek and Lower Brulé Agencies were situated on opposite sides of the Missouri below the mouth of the Bad River. Crow Creek enrolled about 1,000 Lower Yanktonai Sioux and Lower Brulé about 1,000 Lower Brulé Sioux. Like Schwan, Capt. William E. Dougherty, First Infantry, was a regular army officer detailed to the Indian Bureau. He served as agent for both Crow Creek and Lower Brulé from 1878 to 1881.

10. The Whetstone Agency had been founded on the Missouri River to implement the Treaty of 1868 with the Brulé and Oglala Sioux. Although the agency remained here until 1871, few Indians attached themselves to it in practice, preferring to remain farther to the west. In 1871 the Indian Bureau, recognizing the reality of the situation, permitted the establishment of the Brulé and Oglala agencies on the North Platte River in Nebraska. In 1874 they were moved to the upper reaches of White River in northwestern Nebraska, where Spotted Tail Agency ministered to the Brulés and Red Cloud Agency to the Oglalas. Remote from civilization, the Indians did nearly as they pleased, although the erection of Fort Robinson near Red Cloud Agency in 1874 had a calming effect. As the agencies were outside the Great Sioux Reservation, the Government attempted in 1877 to move them back to the Missouri but had to compromise on sites west of the river. In 1878 Rosebud Agency was established for Spotted Tail's Brulés on the south fork of White River and Pine Ridge Agency for Red Cloud's Oglalas on a tributary of White River 100 miles farther west. Pratt arrived on the scene in the autumn of 1878, a few months after the Government had capitulated and permitted the chiefs to have their agencies where they wished. These events are interestingly chronicled in George E. Hyde, *Red Cloud's Folk: A History of the Oglala Sioux Indians* (Norman, 1937); and Hyde, *Spotted Tail's Folk: A History of the Brulé Sioux* (Norman, 1961).

nals on the distant hilltops. The Indian was much disturbed and by signs told me that there was trouble somewhere and he wanted to go back. I insisted on going forward, but soon changed my mind and concluded that it was better to return, which we did rapidly, arriving at Lower Brulé late that night. I sent a message to General Sheridan at Chicago, telling him of the smoke signals and suggesting that they probably indicated that the Cheyennes were coming that way.

I then went forward to Yankton Agency and secured the promise of a party large enough to almost complete the number authorized, omitting those I had expected to get from Spotted Tail and Red Cloud. I then telegraphed to Hampton for Mrs. Pratt to meet me at Bismarck to take care of the girls. It was a roundabout route back to Bismarck, but I arrived a little ahead of Mrs. Pratt. The agent had again sent his wagon and in two days we reached Berthold to begin collecting our party. It was getting late in the season and ice was forming in the river, and there was only one boat above to come down, which would give the only facility for collecting the party and reaching the railroad. That boat came along and our Berthold party went aboard. By keeping the agents advised ahead, the parties were ready at each landing, and when we picked up the Yankton party we lacked only three of the fifty I was to secure.

Mrs. Pratt gives this experience: "As we approached the town of Yankton, I noticed that the Indian girls were much impressed with the two-story houses near the landing. I called all the girls to me. There was one who had attended the mission school and could understand and speak English. I told her to tell the girls that in three days we would come to a place where, if they looked this way and that (pointing to the four points of the compass), they would see buildings five times as high, and more people, horses, and wagons than they could count. When I had finished I noticed that the girl did not tell as I had directed, so I said, 'Tell them what I said.' 'No,' replied the girl, 'maybe so you lie.' When our train was leaving Chicago, the girls were all intently looking out the car window, and I placed my hand on the shoulder of the girl who had doubted my word. She looked into my face, and her own became suffused with shame and she covered her head with her shawl."

This new move in Indian education had been widely noted in the papers. When the Indians took the railroad, messages had preceded us, and at every station curious crowds were gathered to see the young Indians. When we reached Chicago, the crowd was immense. We had several hours' wait, and the railroad was compelled to send our cars out into a caryard enclosed by a high fence in order to get rid of the crowd in the depot. Even there, men and boys climbed the fence to stare at and deride the Indians.

I needed a bath and, finding that not far away was a Turkish bath place, took a robust Indian boy with me to give him the sensations. He was a manly young fellow in Indian garb, with painted face and long hair. I instructed his operator to give him the same treatment I was to receive. We went through the steam, hot and cold water, soaping and spraying processes, even our heads being soaped and washed, and then on the forms had the usual massage. The Indian was in the next section, and I knew by the slapping that he was receiving full treatment, for I heard him hiss his breath through his teeth. However, as he could hear that I was going through the same operation, he held on. When we returned, the boys gathered around and he gave them a graphic description of what he had been through.

Our journey to Hampton was without material incident except the continuous and enlarging attention we received at the different stations. General Armstrong and the faculty and students and the Florida boys all received the newcomers with great cordiality. They were quickly put through cleansing and vermin-destroying processes and habilitated in our garb, and in the course of a few hours were a radically different and civilized looking crowd.[11]

11. Pratt secured a total of 40 boys and 9 girls—9 boys and 4 girls at Fort Berthold, 3 boys and 1 girl at Standing Rock, 9 boys at Cheyenne River, 5 boys and 1 girl at Crow Creek, 6 boys at Lower Brulé, and 8 boys and 3 girls at Yankton. He had enlisted a female contingent at Cheyenne River, but at the last moment they were dissuaded from going by the local educators, who, Pratt said, were prejudiced against Hampton because it was a Negro institution. Pratt encountered this attitude in varying degree, he reported, at all the agencies. Pratt to Commissioner of Indian Affairs, Nov. 22, 1878, in Secretary of the Interior, *Annual Report* (1878), pp. 669–70.

19. Mission to the Indians of Florida

In June 1879 the Commissioner of Indian Affairs asked me to go to Florida to locate, enumerate, and report on the condition of the Indians in that state with a view to extending Bureau control over them. The only information on file was that they lived in small communities in the south-central and extreme southern part of the state, most of them in the Everglades south of the Calousahatchee River.

It appeared that the Bureau had sent agents at different times to find where each band was located, how many there were, and their condition, in efforts to get them under Bureau care, but all had failed. The state of Florida wanted to get rid of its Indians. The emissary who had given the most elaborate report was a Catholic priest who made a prolonged visit but gave no definite information. The reports showed that the Indians were against accepting government control.

The alleged intention of the Department in sending me as published by dispatches from Washington to Florida papers before my arrival stated that the removal of the Indians to the Indian Territory was intended. This in itself was sufficient to prevent any attainment of the purposes of my mission. The disastrous Florida war against them in 1833–37 had been caused by our Government's attempts to remove them forcibly west of the Mississippi.[1]

Taking Tichkematse, a Cheyenne, one of the prisoner boys at Hampton, I went first to St. Francis Barracks at St. Augustine for military information, but got nothing. Lieutenant [Edward T.] Brown of the Fifth Artillery, whom I had known while there in charge of Indian prisoners, volunteered and went with us to report for the military records.

The bodies of the officers and men of two companies of the Fifth Infantry that were surprised and annihilated by Indians while moving to Fort Brown in 1835 were buried at St. Francis Barracks, under a monument reciting that fact. As Major [Francis L.] Dade commanded, it was called the Dade Massacre, notwithstanding it was a time of war and the Indians only used the same methods of surprise and destruction the troops used toward them.

We went by steamer to Jacksonville, crossed by rail to Cedar Keys, then down the coast to Fort Mead near Tampa by steamer. Chipko, reputed to be 100 years old, had a small village among the lakes near old abandoned Fort Clinch, thirty miles east of Fort Mead. His people were Creeks; all others in Florida were Seminoles. Another village, under a chief named Tuscanugga, was located some place about Fort Center, west of and near Lake Okeechobee. A larger body under the old chief Tiger Tail was reported to be scattered along the border of the big Cypress swamp near Fort Shackleford. Young Tiger Tail, recently chief of the whole body, ruled the largest number scattered in villages through the Everglades between Miami and Fort Myers. The forts named had been abandoned many years.

The plan was to secure a concert of action through conference with the leading men of all these villages, and to this end Fort Myers, near the mouth of the Calousahatchee, was appointed the place to meet and the 7th of July the date. Capt. F. A. Hendry, the largest cattle owner in the state, a worthy

1. The Seminoles were originally Creeks who took refuge in Florida during Spanish colonial times and, with liberal admixture of Negro blood from runaway slaves, had evolved into a distinct tribe by about 1775. Their attitude toward the Americans was almost continuously hostile or at best isolationist throughout the nineteenth century. Andrew Jackson conquered them in the first Seminole War in 1817–18, and in 1823 they agreed by treaty to accept a reservation. By a second treaty in 1832 tribal leaders consented to take new lands west of the Mississippi as part of the Indian Removal program, but most of the tribe refused to abide by the agreement and under Osceola engaged U. S. troops in an eight-year struggle known as the Second Seminole War. At the close of this conflict in 1842 most of the Indians were moved to Indian Territory to become one of the Five Civilized Tribes, but a remnant of several hundred remained in the virtually inaccessible Florida Everglades and another band, largely Seminole Negroes, took refuge in Mexico across the border from Eagle Pass, Texas. Hodge, *Handbook*, 2, 500–01. Edwin C. McReynolds, *The Seminoles* (Norman, 1957).

and warm friend of the Indians and one of the few whom they trusted, lived there and undertook to assemble those from Forts Center and Shackleford and the Young Tiger Tail villages.

A native Floridan who knew something of the language and lived not far from Chipko's settlement was engaged to act as guide and interpreter. Having a covered spring wagon—for it rains in Florida—we reached Chipko's camp after dark and, without negotiating permission and notwithstanding a furious rush and yap of dogs, drove right in to near a low fire where a dozen Indians and Negros were sitting in a circle, Chipko among them. After some parley we were hospitably received, and Chipko gave us his guest house to sleep in. It was a staunch roof on posts, without walls, with a floor four feet above the ground, the space under used for pigs and chickens.

I briefly told the purpose of my visit and deferred a full conference until next day. Chipko talked in an undertone to his people about the fire long after we had retired, but in a way that the interpreter did not understand. Late in the night, after his people had retired, Chipko came and called in a low tone and wanted a fuller statement of just what we had come for, and I gave him all the facts of my mission. After I was through, he silently waited a little and then went to his other house, and we had a quiet night, except for the mosquitos and fleas, with both of which the country was overstocked.

The village was on a slight elevation in the piney woods, in the vicinity of four lakes, and was composed of ten open buildings located convenient to each other, but without regard to order. Although so open and crude, they were quite ample for the climate and showed good mechanical skill in their construction. The timber for beams, rafters, posts, and floor sills were of hewn logs, while the clapboard used for floors and roofs were rived out as neat and true as any I had ever seen. A few young orange trees, boxed or fenced in, were growing here and there about the village. Chipko showed us their fields with evident pride in all that indicated thrift. The fields comprised about fifteen acres cleared out in the midst of a dense growth of trees, saplings, and vines and were reached by a winding path. The surrounding trees, underbrush, and vines were so dense as to conceal the fields from view and make approach almost impossible except by the path. The clearing away of this patch had surely been some labor. The land was rich and the crops exceptionally abundant. Each family had its separate patch of corn, rice, and sweet potatoes, and Chipko's patch had a few tobacco plants. Weeds were scarce and cultivation creditable. They had no plows, depending entirely on well-worn old time-heavy iron hoes to stir the ground.

One of the Indians, named Tom, came in from fishing after we arrived. Three hooks knit together concealed by pieces of deer tail and red flannel with a three-foot line attached to a long hardwood pole was his outfit. He had twenty-five to thirty pounds of black bass and sold us the largest for ten cents. The meat was excellent. Tom went again in the morning and took with him a small boy, with like result. On his return, when a quarter of a mile from the village, he gave the fish to the boy and himself shouldered and brought in for firewood a limb so large and heavy that I doubt if any in our party could have carried it so far.

I persuaded him to give me a chance to show him how to catch bass. I had a fine jointed rod with reel, long line and lures for trout and bass. Tom watched while I selected an open place and made my best casts, but got nothing. After witnessing my failure a little while, Tom went along the shore where large plantain leaves lay upon the water with here and there an opening. Finding I could not lure the bass with my civilized outfit, I stopped and watched the Indian. He danced his hooks in openings between the plantain leaves, and when the bass jumped for and caught his hooks he threw them well back from the water, went on, and caught another. He let me take his pole and catch one, which happened to be extra large and on my return saved my reputation.

They had a revenue from hogs, chickens, and eggs. When moving them from place to place for feeding or to market, the hogs followed like dogs. They raised many chickens, and when we asked for eggs more were produced than we wanted. They had a few lank ponies living on the scant native grasses thereabout.

The men wore calico shirts ornamented with bright ribbons and a small shawl of bright colors, folded the width of the hand and wound around the head like a turban. This, with the usual breech clout, completed their home costume. All were barefooted and barelegged, but the interpreter told us that on special occasions they wore, in addition, a light hunting frock with bright ornaments; also leggings and moccasins of buckskin, ornamented with beads. The women wore short jackets and skirts made of calico. The jackets were so short that a portion of the body between the jacket and the skirt was exposed. Beads large and small and of all colors were strung in large quantities about their necks. The hair of the old women was done up in a conical knob on the back of the head, while the young women wore theirs long and flowing behind, and banged in front.

They had a few Negros who were still held as slaves. A year before, Chipko had offered one of his for sale in Tampa at $800. One Negro woman braided her hair in long spirals, which she made stand out stiff in all directions, making her look fiercer than she really was.

They had quite a stock of deer skins, showing that considerable of their food and clothing needs were supplied from this source, but Chipko complained that game was getting scarce. I told Chipko that the Government had heard he was poor, that game was nearly gone, that his crops had failed, and that it was ready to help him and wanted him to let the Government educate his children so they could better meet and compete with the white people. He promptly and emphatically said they "did not want to hear any Washington talk"; that their wants were all supplied and they needed no education or other outside help. I suggested that plows, hoes, axes, etc., might be acceptable. He said no, they wanted to be let alone. I told him of the conference at Fort Myers and invited him to be there, but he declined, saying he was too old and his pony was lame. I suggested that he had better send a delegate with us and that I would supply food. But he said no, none of them cared to go. They all parried my attempts to find out their numbers, but by various means during our stay and through the acquaintance the interpreter had with the community, we found that there were only about twenty-six Indians, of whom six were men.

Tom asked the interpreter, "Good whisky, Bartow?" The interpreter replied, "No! Good whisky Fort Mead." These were the only English words I heard them use, although I was told that all the men could speak some English.

The men and women were strong and well built and the children active and jolly. Tom was a model of manly strength and activity. They had only Kentucky rifles and bows and arrows, and the interpreter said they did not care for breech-loading guns. He told us there were some breech-loading guns among the Indians farther south. My self-acting Colts revolver excited most curiosity. Fearing an accident, before letting them handle it, I fired all the loads rapidly, whereat there was much interest and a desire to see the operation of loading, firing, and removal of shells.

We returned to Fort Mead, and I determined to go to Fort Myers by land via the west side of Lake Okeechobee, which the interpreter said was practicable and would take us by Tuscanugga's community. We proceeded through the open country, which for a long distance was flat and sandy, with sparse pine trees and only here and there more productive soil. Settlers were few, with limited improvements, living in log houses, many of them unchinked and undaubed. Many skins nailed on the outside and only small farm improvements told that the head of the family spent more time in hunting than in agriculture. Large families were the rule. Dogs always gave signal of our approach, and the family lined up in front of the house, usually the largest child next to the mother and tapering off to the smallest, the mother often having a child in arms. We were the passing show. Lieutenant Brown kept record of the number of children in each family for a considerable distance and announced that nine was the average.

We came to a notable spring where a large volume of purest water poured into and flowed from a little lakelet. There was a vacant, well-built frame house and picket-fenced garden with richer soil. We were surprised and asked the interpreter why that good place was not occupied. He said that the young couple that built the house had twins first, then another pair of twins, and then triplets, which led them to move away. Another couple moved in and they soon had twins and also moved away, and since then nobody had lived there. When asked what caused the overproduction, he said the people thought it was the water. May not Ponce de León, the discoverer and explorer of Florida in his four-centuries-ago search for an alleged marvelous spring promoting eternal youth, have been misinformed through mistranslation from Indian to Spanish, and the fact have been that the monstrosity was an equally marvelous spring whose waters multiplied the production of youth?

Before we reached the Lake Okeechobee region, we came to quite a stream where the water was rapid and dark. On one side was a large Indian mound, which we measured, took the dimensions of the trees which grew on it, and mapped the location as near as we could. Just below the ford across the stream was an island with trees, and a very large sapling at the upper end had been undermined by the water and nearly fallen down pointing upstream. It had been cut off just below where the water crossed, leaving a long stump projecting a little above the height of the wagon bed. We had a covered wagon, and as we drove across the stream just above and near this stump, the sand had been washed out, deepening the lower side of the crossing so much that our wagon nearly tipped over, and this stump went between the bows and broke one of them before the team was stopped. The water came into the lower side of the wagon bed, wetting our goods. The driver held the team, the guide held on to the stump to keep the wagon from going entirely over, while Lieutenant Brown, Tichkematse, and I got out and carried our stuff to the farther bank. The water was above our hips. While we were doing this, a tall lank native with an old-fashioned squirrel rifle and a big yellow dog came and sat on the bank and silently watched us. We finally got the wagon unloaded and by our united lift freed the top so it passed the stump and was pulled ashore, our horses in the meantime standing in water up to their sides. When we were loading up, we asked this native where all the water came from. He said from a big lake a short distance above. We asked him what made the water so dark. He said it was the decaying vegetation over a large district and that the lake was the home of big alligators. He further told us that a short time before one of his cows in crossing right there was seized by a "big gater" which caught her by the throat and took her off downstream, and that was the last he saw of her, and he had been expecting to see something like that happen to us.

We failed to find Tuscanugga's village, but had many miles of travel through shallow water and saw big alligators before we reached the Calousa-hatchee River. We sent our team back and boated down to Fort Myers, where we arrived July 6. Captain Hendry told us of the antipathy of his Indian friends for the United States Government because of the long war we had waged to compel them to remove to west of the Mississippi. He said the Indians frequented Fort Myers to trade their curios, pelts, and a mushy food preparation they made of some root that was popular with the Indians and also with the white people. They always came in considerable parties, and as soon as camp was established one was appointed to take care of the camp and remain sober; the rest bought whisky, and both men and women got helplessly drunk. After their spree, they sobered up, did their trading, and went home.

The messengers to the Indians had performed their duties and reported that the villages would send in their best men. A party of four arrived on the 7th and others on the 9th and 11th, only seven of whom were men. Six of the seven men shook hands with me when they first arrived, and answered questions, but in a haughty manner. The seventh, old Jumper, refused to shake hands or to say anything.

I had read Franklin's autobiography in which he told of his being one of a commission to treat with the Indians at Carlisle, Pennsylvania, in the early days, and as those Indians had the same whisky habit, Franklin concluded that he would prevent their getting whisky until they ended their business. Before they arrived, he told the dealers not to let the Indians have whisky without his order. The Indians were not pleased with his embargo, but when he told them that he had noticed that drunken people were not fit to transact business, and thought it best they attend to business first, the Indians consented and the agreement was concluded. The embargo was then removed and whisky allowed. They were encamped on the Carlisle Barracks ground. Late at night there was a big fire out there and the commissioners heard the Indians whooping and yelling, and walked out to see what was going on. They found a great bonfire, the Indians all drunk, whooping and chasing each other about the ground with fire brands in a way that seemed dangerous. Franklin on returning to town renewed his embargo against whisky. The Indians exhausted their supply and came to get more. The dealers refused to sell without Franklin's order. The chiefs then waited on Franklin and told him that the Great Spirit had made everything for some purpose, that he had made whisky for the Indians to get drunk on, and therefore it was all right and they wanted more whisky.

Franklin's story led me to do the same with the Seminoles. When they came to me I told them I was there as an agent of the Government to transact important government business with them, that drunk people were unfit for business, and that we had better attend to business first and after that I would take the embargo off. After a little consultation among themselves, Jumper very emphatically and with a good deal of force said they wanted nothing whatever to do with Washington, that they had no information to give, and that they would be pleased to have the Washington agent go away and let them alone.

I waited until the 11th, when having no word from the Okeechobee party I desired those who had arrived to meet with me and confer about the object of my visit. They sent word they had nothing to say and would not hear any Washington talk. Their good friend, Captain Hendry, with the interpreter, went and reasoned with them, but it was of no avail. Three of these men were quite old and considered among the most important of the Florida Indians. Their names were Doctor, Motloe, and Jumper, all of them survivors of the Florida war.

The whole party refused to accept the food and tobacco I had arranged to supply, saying they could buy what they wanted themselves. A message from the Okeechobee village said their chief, Tuscanugga, had been bitten by a rattlesnake and none of them would come in.

At this point, being satisfied that any further attempt to deal with them by visiting their villages or otherwise would be futile, and only give opportunity for them to further show their animosity toward the Government, I returned north and made my report to the Commissioner. In this report I told of the damper on my mission by newspaper dispatches to the Florida papers which preceded me from Washington.

Denying fraternity, driving Indians away from their ancestral homes, and forwarding depravity and death among them through whisky are the main reasons why they have cost the people of our Government many hundreds of millions of dollars and are now in their shameful condition, unsaved to American citizenship.

20. The Founding of the Carlisle Indian School

Three months after reaching Hampton with the Missouri River party, I wrote the Secretary of War saying the young Indians were now "accustomed to their new mode of life and interested in educational pursuits"; that, inasmuch as there was an excellent officer who had had Indian experience already detailed at Hampton under the law authorizing an army officer at each agricultural college receiving government allowance, I was no longer necessary to Hampton and thought I might be ordered to my regiment. Mr. Mc-Crary replied by personal note that he had my letter and would give it consideration and inform me later.

During this time General Armstrong and I had many talks, principally at night, when we walked the Hampton grounds sometimes until the midnight hour. I told the General my dissatisfaction with systems to educate the Negro and Indian in exclusively race schools and especially with educating the two races together. Participation in the best things of our civilization through being environed by them was the essential factor for transforming the Indian. The small number of Indians in the United States, then given as 260,000, rendered their problem a very short one. It was surely only neces-

sary to prove that Indians were like other people and could be as easily educated and developed industrially to secure the general adoption of my views.
All immigrants were accepted and naturalized into our citizenship by that
route and thus had a full fair chance to become assimilated with our people
and our industries. Why not the Indian? The Negro was under great prejudice by his change in the South from slavery to freedom under circumstances
destructive to the resources and wealth of the Southern people. He numbered
thirty times as many as the Indian and was now a citizen. The fitness he had
for that high place he had gained by the training he was given during slavery,
which made him individual, English speaking, and capable industrially. This
was a lesson which in some way should be applied to the Indian. The thing
to be overcome in the Indian's case was a fictitious prejudice on both sides.
The method we had adopted of driving the Indians away from our communities and from contact with our people and holding them as prisoners on
reservations inevitably aroused a great deal of bitterness on their part. That
condition was to be overcome and the Indian, as well as the white man,
taught that neither was as bad as the other thought. This lesson could never
be learned by the Indian or our people through the indurated system of segregating and reservating the Indians and denying them all chances to see and
thus to learn and to prove their qualities through competition. Both the
white man and the red man must learn the possibilities of the usefulness
the Indian could gain through seeing it demonstrated.

General Armstrong was tenacious of racial education. He secured a contingent gift to Hampton of a plantation of 400 acres in the back bay region
four miles from Hampton for the purpose of establishing an Indian school
to be a branch of Hampton and proposed to place me in charge of it. I went
with him and looked the farm over, but without sympathy for the General's
purposes. I pointed out that the woods were full of degraded Negros, left
there by the army after the war, that the remoteness from the observation of
our best people was a fatal drawback, and would still be using Indian education to further the segregating and reservating process, and I could not undertake it. I said: "You have a good army officer and do not need me in
connection with any Indian contingent you may undertake at Hampton.
Therefore I must insist that I return to my regiment. I have been absent a
long time and there is some army discontent about it and it is proper that I
should go back and overcome that."

The General took me on several expeditions to New York and New England to raise money for Hampton. On these trips he would take an Indian
or two and a colored student or two, as samples and to speak. They aroused
new interest in Hampton and the Indians. Hampton was largely sustained
by charity. The American Missionary Association, as I remember, gave

$10,000 a year, and the state of Virginia allowed $10,000 from the United States Government appropriation on account of agricultural schools, and for the balance needed for its large enrollment General Armstrong had to depend upon appeals to the northern public, which had been most responsive to the great needs of the former slaves, but that interest was waning.

The papers told that the army appropriation bill carried a clause providing for "the detail of an Army officer not above the rank of Captain with reference to Indian Education." It was introduced by the member of Congress representing the Hampton district. In the short discussion my name was mentioned. This seemed intended to fix by law my stay at Hampton. I plainly told the General that I could not bring myself to become satisfied with such a detail, and he allowed me to go to Washington and talk with the Secretary of the Interior and the Secretary of War about it.

I went first to Mr. Schurz, then Secretary of the Interior, and asked for a private conference.[1] He took me into his little side office and I told him briefly what I was passing through. I said: "You yourself, sir, are one of the very best examples of what we ought to do for the Indians. You immigrated to America as an individual to escape oppression in your own country. You came into fullest freedom in our country. You associated with our people, the best of them, and through these chances you became an American general during the Civil War, then a United States senator, and are now in the President's cabinet, one of the highest offices in the land. It would have been impossible for you to have accomplished your elevation if, when you came to this country, you had been reserved in any of the solid German communities we have permitted to grow up in some sections of America. The Indians need the chances of participation you have had and they will just as easily become useful citizens. They can only reach this prosperous condition through living among our people. If you insist on my remaining in the Indian school work, give me 300 young Indians and a place in one of our best communities and let me prove it is easy to give Indian youth the English

1. Carl Schurz (1829–1906), refugee from the German revolutionary movement of 1848–49, was for half a century the idol of the German population of the United States and, to countless immigrants, an example of the opportunities afforded by the United States. For services in mobilizing the foreign vote for the Republicans in the election of 1860, Lincoln appointed him minister to Spain in 1861, but he returned in 1862 to fight for the Union, rising ultimately to major general. After a time in the newspaper business, he won a seat from Missouri in the United States Senate in 1869 and retained it until 1875. President Hayes appointed Schurz Secretary of the Interior in 1877. In this office he did much to reduce corruption and incompetence in the Indian Bureau and to launch the Indian reform program that matured in later years. After leaving the cabinet, Schurz returned to journalism for the rest of his life. *The Reminiscences of Carl Schurz* was published in three volumes in 1907–08. There are also Schurz Papers in the Library of Congress and a six-volume edition of his papers edited by Frederick Bancroft published in 1913. All contain data on the Indian question. *Dictionary of American Biography, 16,* 466–70.

language, education, and industries that it is imperative they have in preparation for citizenship. Carlisle Barracks in Pennsylvania has been abandoned for a number of years. It is in a fine agricultural country and the inhabitants are kindly disposed and long free from the universal border prejudice against the Indians."

He listened until I was through and said, "Have you talked to the Indian Commissioner [Ezra A. Hayt]. I said, "No sir, I came directly to you." He said, "Bring the Commissioner here." I went and told the Commissioner the Secretary wanted him. We walked in silence to the Secretary's office. The Secretary said, "Have you told Mr. Hayt about it?" I said, "No sir." He said, "Tell him what you told me." I repeated to Mr. Hayt. The Secretary then said, "Mr. Commissioner, what do you think of it?" Mr. Hayt said, "We might find money for 100 or 125 students, but we could not find money for 300." The Secretary then said, "Go over to the War Department and tell Secretary McCrary about it, and if he will give Carlisle Barracks for an Indian school, we will establish one immediately and put you in charge."

I went to the War Department. It was then noon. The Secretary had gone to lunch. I went to Adjutant General [E. D.] Townsend. The General and I had had a number of talks about the Indian prisoners being sent to Florida, and he was gratified that he had selected St. Augustine and Fort Marion as the place for their incarceration and defeated the urgency that they be sent to the Dry Tortugas. I told the General my mission from the Secretary of the Interior and he said, "I suggest that you go to Mr. McCrary's house. Here there will be members of Congress and others waiting to see him and you will get a very brief audience." I went to Mr. McCrary's house. The butler showed me into the parlor and said the family was at the luncheon table. I gave my card and said, "Tell the Secretary I am in no hurry." Mr. McCrary came from the dining room with his napkin in his hand and asked, "What is it, Captain?" I said, "I can wait, Mr. Secretary." He said, "I would rather hear you now." I briefly told him of my interview with Mr. Schurz and Mr. Hayt. He at once said: "When I get back to the office I will look it up and if we can turn over Carlisle Barracks for an Indian school, we will do it immediately. If there are legal objections we will ask Congress to remove them. Come around to the Department about two o'clock."

At the time appointed, I was with the Secretary. He informed me that he had submitted the case to the Judge Advocate General, who reported that government property which had been appropriated for and held in one department had never been transferred to another department without a special act of Congress and that it was his judgment that Carlisle Barracks could not be transferred to the Interior Department without a special act.

Mr. McCrary then sent for one of his men and told him he wanted an act drawn to submit to Congress transferring Carlisle Barracks to the Interior Department for an Indian school, and that I would tell him all about it. We went to his room and he soon wrote the proposed law. The Secretary made some alterations and told the clerk to make two copies. I waited in the Secretary's office and in a little while the copies were brought in. The Secretary then said, "Do you know anybody in the House or Senate?" I said: "I do not. I have barely met Senator Pendleton of Ohio. Mrs. Pendleton visited in Florida while I was there and was greatly interested in the Indians, and we became well acquainted." He said: "That is it. We must have this introduced in both the House and Senate; but first you take it to Mr. Schurz and see if he would like to make changes." He kept one of the copies and gave me the other, which I carried to Mr. Schurz. Mr. Schurz was pleased with it, but suggested slight changes. The law had been drawn for Carlisle Barracks only. Mr. Schurz thought it well to insert "Carlisle Barracks or any other vacant military posts or barracks." As drawn, the law proposed "one Army officer to superintend." He thought it should read "one or more Army officers to superintend." With these alterations, I hurried back to the War Department. Secretary McCrary approved of Secretary Schurz' suggestions, called his assistant, and had him make out three copies, one to be retained in the War Department and two to be used in the House and Senate.

In the meantime, he had written a personal note to the Hon. Thad C. Pound, who was a member of the House Indian Committee and had been lieutenant governor of Wisconsin, asking him to introduce the measure in the House. I took the two copies and hurried over to the Capitol and sent in my card to Governor Pound. He came out and I handed him the Secretary's note and the copy of the proposed bill. He said the House was about to adjourn, but he would get it in the next morning. I then hurried over to the Senate and found that the Senate had just adjourned, at which time the Senate floor is open to others than members of the Senate. I went in and was fortunate enough to meet Mr. Pendleton on the floor just as he was about to leave. He gladly listened to what I said, took the proposed law, and said he would introduce it in the Senate in the morning.

I counted this one of the most eventful days of my life. Being ignorant of the methods and ways of legislating in Washington, I was elated to find that things could be so easily and quickly attended to if you only had best help and directions.

Mr. McCrary had asked me to come to see him in the morning. I did so and he said: "There are two things to be attended to. You had better go to Carlisle, look the barracks over, and make me a report of their adaptability and the changes and repairs needed. I will give an order which will pay your expenses, and will ask General Hancock, in whose department Carlisle Barracks is located, and General Sherman, who commands the Army, whether the barracks can be spared. They may have plans that need consideration." He gave the order and I went to Carlisle, found the barracks neglected and much out of repair, hunted up a builder, and we itemized the condition of all the buildings and estimated the cost of temporary repairs, and I returned to Washington and made my report.

Secretary McCrary showed me that General Hancock had approved, saying, "I know of no better place to undertake such an experiment," and General Sherman had "Approved, provided both boys and girls are educated in said school," in his own handwriting.

The Secretary then said: "You had better stop here in Washington and help us lobby the bill through. It is getting towards the end of the session, the bill will be well down on the list, and we will have to push hard if we succeed in getting it before Congress this session. You come and see me daily and I will give you notes to members of the House whom I think will take an interest, and see Mr. Schurz and he will tell you how to work on Senate members." The bill had been introduced in both branches as promised. I then began a daily system of explaining the scheme to members of Congress to secure their interest. This was a novel experience. The notes from Mr. McCrary and Mr. Schurz always obtained a prompt conference. These were generally arranged by sending in my card and meeting senators and House members at the Capitol and sometimes making an evening appointment. Some of the members were cordial and interested, and others bluff, even expressing opposition. In a few days Mr. Pound said the bill had been printed, referred back to the Committee for a report, and asked me to write it. He gave me some instructions as to how to word it and I accordingly drew up a report which he submitted to his Committee. It was accepted by the Committee, and the bill with the report went back to the House, and the report was ordered to be printed. The bill was then before the House but was so far down on the list that it seemed unlikely it would be reached that session. Under the directions of the two Secretaries, I continued to see senators and members of the House, and we got some favorable newspaper notices, but somehow the bill could not be brought before the House for its action.

In 1872 Carlisle Barracks had been abandoned as the Army School of Instruction for Cavalry Recruits because of a petition by the religious people of the town to have Sunday dress parades stopped. These were in the afternoon and crowds came to witness. When the petition reached General Sherman, he recommended that the school be transferred to the army barracks at St. Louis, because all the cavalry was on the western frontier and recruits going there would be on their way to their final destination, whereas at Carlisle many recruits enlisted in the West had to be sent east first and then, after training, sent west to their regiments.

While lobbying one day, Secretary McCrary said: "General Sherman tells me the people of Carlisle are likely to criticize and petition against the Indian school as they did against the Army. What do you say to that?" I said, "A good way to meet that would be to get them to petition for an Indian school." This pleased the Secretary and he said, "Good! You go to Carlisle and get such a petition." I went and on boarding the waiting Cumberland Valley train at Harrisburg found General Biddle, then treasurer of that road, and told him my mission. I had met him on my previous visit and found him friendly to the intended school. He said, "You go back to your work in Washington, and in a few days I will send the Secretary a petition for the school signed by every man and woman in Carlisle." I got off the Carlisle train and returned to Washington and in a few days the Secretary received an ample petition, which pleased him and satisfied General Sherman.

Congress was about to close when, seeing Secretary McCrary one morning, he seemed especially good natured and said: "Captain, I have discovered a way to handle our case. The bill is before both houses of Congress and has a favorable report in the House. I have talked with the Judge Advocate General about it and since the barracks are not in use, and we have the approval of both the General of the Army and General Hancock commanding the department, I have concluded to turn the barracks over to the Interior Department for an Indian school pending the action of Congress on the bill. Your detail for Indian educational duty is already authorized by an act of Congress."

A War Department order was accordingly issued, and Mrs. Pratt and I made our goodbye calls on Secretary McCrary, General Sherman, and Secretary Schurz. When our cards went in to General Sherman at his office in the War Department he met us at the door, took Mrs. Pratt's hand in both of his, and reminded her of his visit to us in our log house at Fort Sill in 1869, and of the exciting day when Satank, Satanta, and Big Tree were arrested, and said he hoped she was prepared for the hardships at Carlisle. Mrs. Pratt said that Arbuckle and Fort Sill had fully prepared her. Then turning to me and taking my hand, he looked me over and said, "I declare, Pratt, you remind me more of Stonewall Jackson than any man I ever met," and I said, "General, that is the biggest compliment I ever had and I shall remember it as long as I live." Jackson and Sherman were intimates at West Point, where they became lifelong friends.

I reported to the Secretary of the Interior and was directed to proceed to Rosebud and Pine Ridge Agencies and get thirty-six pupils from each of them and then secure the remainder to complete a total of 120 from the Indian Territory tribes. I protested that I had never met these discontented branches of the Sioux Indians; that they were then in a hostile attitude toward the Government, as their willfully leaving their agency on the Missouri River and going to Rosebud and Pine Ridge proved; that they had not yet taken up the school idea; and that I ought to be permitted to go to the Indians whom I knew and who knew me—that is, the Cheyennes, Arapahoes, Kiowas, Comanches, and other Indians of the Indian Territory who had had schools for two years. But Mr. Hayt, the Commissioner, was insistent that I must go to Spotted Tail and Red Cloud, because the children would be hostages for the good behavior of their people, but if I failed there I might bring the whole party from the Indians I knew.

I took Mrs. Pratt and our children to Carlisle, established them at the barracks, and started a contractor and builder at the repairs and changes needed.

Miss Mather, then sixty-three years of age, who had helped so loyally in the education of the prisoners in Florida, had urgently desired to accompany me to the Indian country if I again went after children. I could have no better assistant to help and take care of the girls, and I telegraphed her at St. Augustine, Florida, on September 8 that I was leaving for Dakota on the 10th and asked her to join me at Carlisle and go as assistant to look after the girls. She came and we proceeded to the Rosebud Landing on the Missouri River, going to Yankton by cars and from there by river boat. A telegram from Carlisle to the new agent at Rosebud brought the agency two-seated spring wagon. The driver was an Indian and had four blankets for his own use. No other bedding was available. From the landing to the agency was 100 miles.

I determined to make the trip in two days, so sat with the driver, used the "black snake" whip, and kept the mules at the necessary speed. When half way we stopped for the night. We made Miss Mather an army bed in the bottom of the wagon, taking out the seats, using a cushion for a pillow, and giving her two of the blankets which, by folding, we made into a camp bag bed with two thicknesses above and two below. The Indian and I slept under the wagon using the other two blankets, one to sleep on and one over us. We all slept in our clothing. It was a frosty night and we suffered from the cold. There being no other way, we had to hitch the mules to the wagon. Wolves came near and howled, and once I got up with my revolver to drive them away, but they were too far off to shoot. Sleep was practically impossible for me.

The cold led us to start long before daylight. During the afternoon Miss Mather became wretchedly seasick and we had to stop several times. We reached the agency before dark and the very capable agency physician soon restored her equilibrium.

Before our arrival, the new agent had received the order to turn over thirty-six boys and girls for Carlisle, and, acting under the advice of local opinion, he had called Spotted Tail and the leading Indians together in the council house and placed the matter before them.² The agent's unfamiliarity with the pros and cons of the movement and the objections of the white employees at the agency against sending children so far away prompted the chiefs to decide that they would send no children. I insisted on talking with them myself, and the agent summoned them to a conference with me in the council house, where only the agency interpreter and Miss Mather were present to help. About forty came, among them their foremost chiefs, Spotted Tail, White Thunder, Milk, and Two Strike.³ When we went in, they were sitting in a circle on the ground smoking their ceremonial pipe, passing it around the circle, each taking a whiff, and talking in an undertone. As they were not ready, we waited. The interpreter said he could not understand them when they were talking like that. Finally Spotted Tail sat up and looked at me, and indicated that they were ready to listen to what I had to say.

I stood up and, assuming all the dignity I could, said that the Government was about to adopt a new policy with the Indians; that it believed the Indian youth capable of acquiring the same education and industries our white youth had and this would make them the equals of our youth. The Government now realized that by keeping them separate from us and on reservations remote from any material chances to learn our ways, the acquirement of our qualities was a very slow operation; that the Government believed that if they were brought among our people, placed in good schools, and taught our language and our industries by going out among our people, in a little while their children could be made just as competent as the white children. The purpose in establishing a school so far east was to bring them near Washington, where all the people could see the improvement and where members of Congress and the administrative officials of the Government could visit and witness their progress and their ability to learn. They must surely see that being divided into so many languages, and living in small tribal groups away from these opportunities, was a great disadvantage to them; that eventually

2. The new agent at Rosebud was Cicero Newell, who served from the spring of 1879 to the spring of 1880 and whose administration was characterized by weakness and incompetence. His antagonist, Spotted Tail, was one of the truly great leaders of Indian history. Born in 1833, he had earned a bright reputation as a warrior and diplomat and had emerged as the leading chief of the Brulé Sioux in the years after the Civil War. His influence kept most of the Brulés at peace during the Sioux wars of 1866–68 and 1876–80. An excellent biography is Hyde, *Spotted Tail's Folk.*

3. A Brulé band chief, Two Strike had been Spotted Tail's lieutenant and close associate since the 1840s and 1850s, when as young warriors they had fought the Pawnees. He later played a conspicuous role in the Ghost Dance uprising of 1890–91 and died in 1914 at the age of about 93.

in some way the Indians must become a very part of the people of the country and that each Indian must become capable of living among our people and taking care of himself and his own affairs, and so relieve the Government of the expense of special tribal supervision. They could see by all the evidences coming to them that more and more the white man was occupying the whole country; his railroads and towns and farms would go everywhere and that there was nothing left for them but to become a very part of it all.

They listened in silence as the very efficient interpreter gave them sentence by sentence what I said. Then I sat down and they talked a little while among themselves, again passing around the pipe. Then Spotted Tail got up. He was a massive man with strong, purposeful features. He began by saying: "The white people are all thieves and liars. We do not want our children to learn such things. The white man is very smart. He knew there was gold in the Black Hills and he made us agree to give up all that country and now a great many white people are there getting out the gold."[4] He said that the Government had given them a reservation which took in certain points, and he named them, and that their people had gone out to live in places near what they believed the edge of their reservation and had made improvements, and then the Government sent its surveyors and they were now running the lines of the reservation and these lines were a long way inside of where they had agreed with the Government they should be, and these people had to move inside, and that they did not like that. "We are not going to give any children to learn such ways," he concluded.

Spotted Tail was graphic and his various points were applauded by the Indians saying "How! How! How!" When he sat down I remained sitting near him and made my talk directly to him. I said: "Spotted Tail, you are a remarkable man. Your name has gone all over the United States. It has even gone across the great water. You are such an able man that you are the principal chief of these thousands of your people. But Spotted Tail, you cannot read or write. You cannot speak the language of this country. You have no education. You claim that the Government has tricked your people and placed the lines of your reservation a long way inside of where it was agreed they should be. You put your cross-mark signature on the treaty which fixed the lines of your reservation. That treaty says you agreed that the lines of your reservation should be just where these young men now out surveying are putting posts and markers. You signed that paper, knowing only what the interpreter told you it said. If anything happened when the paper was being

4. The Custer expedition of 1874 discovered gold in the Black Hills—part of the Great Sioux Reservation set aside by the Treaty of 1868—and touched off a stampede of miners. In 1876, while a large share of the Sioux were in Montana fighting Crook, Gibbon, and Custer, government commissioners assembled the agency Indians and, by persuasion and intimidation, induced them to sign an agreement selling the part of the reservation that contained the Black Hills.

made up that changed its order, if you had been educated and could read and write, you could have known about it and refused to put your name to it. The young men running lines are getting $150 to $200 a month because they are educated and capable of doing that work. If you and these men had been educated you might have known how to run those lines and might be doing it now and getting the salaries those men get. You complain because the Government, by treaty, took over the Black Hills, which was the home where you delighted to camp in the valleys by the streams of good water at certain seasons of the year. Spotted Tail, cannot you see that if you and these with you here today had been educated as the white man is educated that you might right now have all your people out there in the Black Hills digging out the gold for your own uses? Because you were not educated, these mountains, valleys, and streams have passed from you. Your ignorance against the white man's education will more and more hinder and restrain you and take from you, in spite of everything that can be done by yourselves, as long as you are so ignorant and unable to attend to your own affairs. Under the laws of my government, one white man with education and intelligence can own all the Black Hills and hold them as his own against everybody. If you, yourself, had had education you might be owning the Black Hills and be able to hold them. No army is required among us to do a thing like that. The law does it. If you had been educated, Spotted Tail, you might be helping to make the laws that take care of us in these United States. What you have always needed is the same education, the same industry, and the same opportunity the white man has. Spotted Tail, do you intend to let your children remain in the same condition of ignorance in which you have lived, which will compel them always to meet the white man at a great disadvantage through an interpreter, as you have to do? Cannot you see it is far, far better for you to have your children educated and trained as our children are so that they can speak the English language, write letters, and do the things which bring to the white man such prosperity, and each of them be able to stand for their rights as the white man stands for his? Cannot you see that they will be of great value to you if after a few years they come back from school with the ability to read and write letters for you, interpret for you, and help look after your business affairs in Washington? I am your friend, Spotted Tail. I shall be near Washington. Whether you send children with me or not I shall still be your friend. You may want something done in Washington and I might be able to help you. You want to write me about it, but you must get this interpreter or the missionary to write your letter. When I get the letter I shall know it was written by someone else and will not feel sure that it tells me exactly what you meant it to tell me. Yet I will do the best I can, and try to help you, and write to you about it. Then this or some other interpreter has to tell you what

I say. You cannot be entirely sure he tells you exactly what I say. Cannot you see, Spotted Tail, what a disadvantage you and your people are under? The Secretary of the Interior told me to come to you first, that he wanted you and Red Cloud to have the first chance to send children to this new school. I wanted him to let me go to the Kiowas, Comanches, Arapahoes, and other Indians in the Indian Territory whom I know and who know me, because I felt I would be more successful there. But he said no. He wanted you and Red Cloud to have the first chance. He said that if you refused to send children, I could then go to the Indian Territory and get the full number from those Indians. As your friend, Spotted Tail, I urge you to send your children with me to this Carlisle school and I will do everything I can to advance them in intelligence and industry in order that they may come back and help you. Spotted Tail, I hear you have a dozen children. Give me four or five and let me take them to Carlisle and show you what the right kind of education will do for them."

I asked the interpreter in an undertone, "Who else has children?" He said, "Two Strike has two fine boys." I said, "Two Strike, give me your two boys to take to Carlisle and I will make useful men out of them." I again asked the interpreter, and he said, "Milk has a boy and a girl." I said, "Milk, give me your boy and girl for Carlisle and let me show you what I can do with them." I again asked, "Who else?" He said, "White Thunder has a fine boy and girl." I said: "White Thunder, let me have your boy and girl and take them to Carlisle. I will be a father to them and all the children while they are with me."

I then said: "This good lady came with me to look after the girls. She will talk to you and then we will go with the interpreter to the agent's house, sit on the porch and wait for your answer. Talk it over. Be sure of your ground, and then come and let me know."

After Miss Mather had emphasized my talk, we went and sat on the porch for nearly an hour. Then the Indians came out and stood around talking for a little while and looking toward us. Then Spotted Tail, Two Strike, Milk, and White Thunder came slowly to where we were. They sat down on the porch and kept talking in an undertone to each other, each of them intensely looking at me, and I realized I was being sized up. Spotted Tail finally got up and came toward me, holding out his hand. I stood up and took his hand and he said, "How Cola." I knew nothing of the Sioux language, but the interpreter said, "He calls you his friend"; so I said, "How Cola." He then said: "It is all right. We are going to give you all the children you want. I will give you five, Two Strike will give you his two boys, Milk will give you his boy and girl, and White Thunder will give you his boy and girl. The others are going to make up the party." I was elated and told them so, and then told them that while they were selecting their party I would go to Pine Ridge and get a party from there, then come back and make up theirs. The candidates must be examined by the doctor to see that they were well and strong, and I would have to take down their names, ages, their parents' names, and all the information necessary to make the school record complete and would be glad if they would have everything settled so that there would be no delay when I returned.

I then said: "I want to be at Pine Ridge tomorrow night. Have you an Indian with a light wagon and two ponies who can take me there, and after a few days bring me back, for which I will pay $25.00." They talked it over and selected one of the men in the council named Cook who had the able ponies and would like the $25.00. They sent him to me and we arranged to start at early dawn. Cook was prompt, took a bee line a little north of west, soon got his pace, and I realized he understood just how to make his ponies do the hundred miles in one day. It was a treeless and roadless route over rolling prairie with scant water. At noon we let the ponies rest an hour, fed them and lunched ourselves, then drove on and on. It was a talkless drive, for Cook could not speak my language, nor I his. Toward the end of the day we took another rest and some food, and then sped on, seeing no habitations, persons, or animals between the two agencies. The moon was late, and when dark came I fixed on a star, kept track of the direction by that, and saw that the Indian was doing the same thing. Near ten o'clock we saw far away a small light. The Indian drove directly for it and we found the agency clerk in his office struggling to keep up with his work. The agent had gone to Rosebud Landing, so the clerk had Red Cloud bring his chiefs and leading men together for a conference the next morning.[5]

I went over the same detail with Red Cloud and his men, told them what had happened at Rosebud, and the Indian driver was there to sustain me. I found that a local missionary influence was not friendly to the effort and that I would not meet with any considerable success. Red Cloud was an old man and had no children of his own of school age, but led the way by sending a

5. Although lacking the forceful personality and agile mind of Spotted Tail, Red Cloud was to the Oglala Sioux what Spotted Tail was to the Brulés. His reputation rested largely on the successful war he waged in 1866–68 against the military occupation of the Bozeman Trail to the Montana gold fields—a war that ended with the Treaty of 1868. Thereafter Red Cloud, though consistently resisting the reform program, remained close to his agency. His agent, absent when Pratt visited Pine Ridge, was the mercurial Valentine T. McGillycuddy, who served from 1879 to 1886. The clash of wills between these two strong-minded men rocked Pine Ridge for seven years and forms one of the most interesting chapters in the history of the Sioux. Red Cloud died at Pine Ridge in 1909 at the age of eighty-seven. See Hyde, *Red Cloud's Folk* and *A Sioux Chronicle;* and Julia B. McGillycuddy, *McGillycuddy, Agent* (Stanford, 1941).

grandson. American Horse, one of the principal chiefs, took a livelier interest and gave two sons and a daughter.[6] Then others were brought, but the best I could do was to enroll a party of sixteen, mostly boys. Girls were property. When they reached marriageable age, parents expected to realize an increase in their herd of ponies by letting their daughter marry. Marriageable value was determined by qualities and beauty.

I spent two days in this effort, had my driver arrange with an Indian with two good ponies to take my Rosebud driver's wagon and harness and for $5.00 drive me half way back on the third day, and that my driver, after one day's rest, should ride his ponies to that point and be ready to take me on to Rosebud. When the party of sixteen was completed, I hired the parents to take them the 200 miles to the Rosebud Landing. They were to start on the fifth day after my reaching Pine Ridge. The new Indian driver drove me safely to the meeting point and we there spent the night together. I paid that driver his fee and he returned, while my staunch Rosebud driver took me back to Rosebud the fifth day after our start from there.

Spotted Tail and the whole body of Rosebud Indians had grown enthusiastic about sending their children. I ruled out a large enrolling form, similar to army enlistment lists, so as to get all the data about each pupil in one place. Dr. Grinnell, the capable agency physician, and his wife made a careful physical examination. The authority was for only thirty-six from each agency, but upwards of ninety were presented at Rosebud. The pressure was so strong that I accepted fifty-six from Rosebud in order to complete the quota of seventy-two authorized from the two agencies.

While the examinations were going on and we were getting ready for the trip to the river, the Indians had a ceremonial expression of their satisfaction in what they were undertaking. Nearly the whole body of Indians connected with the reservation gathered at the agency and those who were sending children gave away horses, calicoes, muslin, and other goods and food they purchased of the trader. Some had the horses present and gave them direct; others presented sticks which meant a horse. The giver mounted on his horse, stood before the multitude, and announced that he was sending a son or daughter, or both, to the Great Father's school near Washington, and he felt happy about it and wanted to show that by giving horses. If he had brought the horse he led it out and asked some old man or woman who had no horse to come and get it, or if he had brought no horse, to come and get a stick which he gave, which was to be taken to his home and a horse would be given.

6. The son or nephew of the chief of the same name killed at the Battle of Slim Buttes in 1876, American Horse emerged as an Oglala chief of great influence in the early reservation years of the 1880s. Although hardly a tool of the agents, he was usually the spokesman and leader of the "progressive" faction at Pine Ridge and advocated cooperation in the reform programs.

It was intensely interesting and inspiring. The goods purchased from the store were given away in the same manner. Horses and goods went to the poor and needy. Spotted Tail was master of ceremonies, sitting on a magnificent horse, his whole appearance that of the strong and forceful man and chief that he was.

During the proceedings Miss Mather and I were near. Spotted Tail and the interpreter were near us. We told Spotted Tail how greatly we appreciated the good feeling the parents were exhibiting. A fine-looking Indian rode forward leading a beautiful pony, almost gazelle in its trim form. Miss Mather said: "That is the pony I want. I am an old woman and have no horse and if I can get it I will take it home to Florida." I had the interpreter tell Spotted Tail what she said and Spotted Tail advised that if the man asked for an old woman, she should go forward. We waited and the man made quite a speech about it. He wound up by saying he was giving this pony because his heart was happy and that he was going to turn it loose and whoever caught it could have it. Instantly young Indians began to mount their ponies. He slipped the lariat rope from the pony's head and turned it loose, when it bounded away for its home dodging the people and when outside the crowd flew over the ground like a deer, a dozen Indians in pursuit. Before the ceremonies were over the chasers came back, one of them leading the pony and beaming happily.

The Indians were so enthusiastic that repeatedly parents who had not tried to get their children into the party came forward and asked to have their children go, and I could have had several times as many as my authority allowed.

The best policy, based on my experience with Indian scouts and also with the prisoners in Florida, had shown that to mix the tribes and not take an excessive number from any one tribe or agency could be made a valuable energizer through tribal rivalry, but I finally concluded that the hostage idea of the Indian Bureau administration warranted increase to sixty-six from Rosebud. The medical examinations were completed, and I arranged to pay the Rosebud parents for taking their children to the landing. There was a long train of wagons and mounted Indians. The Pine Ridge agent was at the landing and was much disappointed because he had not been at his agency and secured a delegation as large as that from Rosebud. His people, with their small party, had arrived in good time. Rosebud Indians, disappointed in getting their children into the party, brought them to the landing. When the boat came, I had some difficulty from the loving goodbyes in getting my party separated and aboard.

I needed an interpreter. Not one of the Indians could speak our language. Spotted Tail's oldest daughter wanted to join the party. She had recently married a young mixed blood who spoke both English and Sioux well, and by employing him as interpreter I was enabled to include her as a pupil.[7]

After they were lined up on the deck and the roll called, two unenrolled boys were found who had sneaked aboard, determined to go anyway. I was about to put them ashore when the Pine Ridge agent urged that I take them. These aggregated the party to eighty-four instead of the seventy-two the Bureau had authorized.

The trip to Carlisle was even more spectacular than the Missouri River party to Hampton because the recent difficulties the Government had had with the Red Cloud and Spotted Tail Sioux had made the country familiar with that situation, and when it was published by the dispatches that the children were from these people it attracted wider attention.

On the way down the river, as the water was low, there was almost constantly a man on the front part of the boat with a long pole sounding the depth. He was on the lower deck near the water and the pilot on the upper deck. His drawled sing-song depth announcements to the pilot were a feature of the trip. All the boys and girls were greatly entertained by this and soon began to imitate the announcements until they had them quite perfectly, and even when the boat was going along without any soundings they would cry out the depth. This amused the captain and the crew. On the cars all the way to Carlisle and for some time after we had repetitions of the river soundings. Prior to forty years ago, the long light sternwheel steamboats for freight and passenger service over the 2,000 miles between St. Louis and Fort Benton, Montana, were able, when not loaded, to run in two feet of water, and were marvels of light and flexible construction. They had to be, for probably the world does not contain another river as long and shifting and shallow of bottom as the Missouri.

Nearly all the boys were soon smoking store cigarettes. Suspecting where they came from, I went to the trader on the boat and asked if he had cigarettes. He said he had. "How many have you?" I asked. He looked over his stock and said about 4,000. "What will you take for the lot?" He told me and I bought them all. I called the interpreter, had him assemble all the boys on the upper deck, and told them that I saw they were as fond of smoking as I was, and that I happened to know that when we reached Carlisle there would be a rule in the school against the use of tobacco, and then it would be necessary for all of us to say goodbye to tobacco. "Between here and Carlisle, as we will be traveling on the boat and as on the cars the boys will be in a separate car from the girls, we can all have a goodbye smoke all the way to Carlisle, but when we reach Carlisle we will all quit." I had been smoking

7. Charles Tackett, formerly an army interpreter and more recently a trader at Rosebud, had married Spotted Tail's eighteen-year-old daughter Red Road. Hyde, *Spotted Tail's Folk*, p. 278.

for about twelve years. My resolution was made on the moment, knowing the good and economical influence it would have. I gave the interpreter all the cigarettes except a small box reserved for myself and told him to issue them to the boys as they needed, keeping the supply under his care, which he did, and there was much tobacco smoked by us between that and Carlisle.

En route the crowds of people assembled at the railroad stations were even greater than on the former occasion. I telegraphed Mrs. Pratt that we would reach Carlisle about midnight on the 6th of October, and stop at the junction on the edge of town near the barracks. Our children were all in their Indian dress. As we got out of the cars at that late hour there were hundreds of people from Carlisle waiting to greet us and they walked up the lane with us, past the old guard house, and into the grounds. Mrs. Pratt had made some provisions of food for us. The matron who was to take charge of the girls was on hand to camp them in the unfurnished north tier of officers quarters, while the boys went into the north barracks under Interpreter Tackett's care, aided by sergeants from among themselves whom I had selected and given some training en route.

21. The First Year at Carlisle

Before going to Dakota for the Sioux party, I borrowed Etahdleuh from General Armstrong and Okahaton from Mrs. Burnham and sent them to their people for children, and I wrote Agent Miles at Cheyenne and Agent Haworth[1] at Fort Sill, asking them to aid the mission of these two former prisoners. Letters on my return from Dakota told that they had succeeded.

Mr. Alfred Standing, an English Quaker, had been in charge of the new agency school at Fort Sill while I had the prisoners in Florida; previous to that he was an employee of the agency, and I knew him during our troubles with the Indians. At different times he had lived for short periods in the Indian camps when the Indians were permitted to go far from the agency after buffalo for food and robes. His duty then was to influence their young men against raiding into Texas and to report to the agent if parties started on such raids. He had shown courage and ability in the discharge of these diffi-

1. J. N. Haworth had relinquished the Kiowa-Comanche Agency to P. B. Hunt in April 1878.

cult duties and as a teacher was as successful as could be expected where the possibilities were so limited. He had left the Indian Service and was farming in Kansas, but as he knew the Indians so well because of these experiences I asked him to go after Pawnee pupils and come to Carlisle and help. This was before the adoption of the monopoly system of finding all government employees through a commission called Civil Service, and when officials of the Government responsible for the performance of difficult duties still had some control in the selection of their help. Mr. Standing became my assistant superintendent and served for twenty years.

Before starting for Dakota, I had asked the Indian Bureau to have food, clothing, and school supplies at Carlisle on my return with the children, giving estimates of what I needed. Nothing had been received, and I telegraphed the Commissioner and was authorized to go into the market and buy the necessary food, pending the arrival of the Department's purchases. Making these temporary arrangements, I left the young Sioux Indians in their Indian garb under the care of Mrs. Pratt, aided by several good helpers I had engaged. Taking Miss Mather again as assistant, I went to Wichita, Kansas, and met the parties from the Cheyenne, Kiowa, and Pawnee Agencies. The Cheyenne party had to travel by wagon 160 miles to the railroad and the Kiowas 220 miles.

Through their agent's help, Etahdleuh and Okahaton had good delegations, as did Mr. Standing from the Pawnees, and I returned to Carlisle with 52 more pupils, making a total of 136, which was 16 more than was authorized in the order establishing the school. As in the case of the Sioux, the parents had brought these pupils to the railroad.

When I reached Carlisle, there were still no supplies from the Bureau, and I commenced a lively correspondence about the delay. Among the school furniture and books I had requested was a small organ to help in assembly singing. This article, the least necessary of all the supplies, arrived several days before anything else.

Finding suitable teachers and employees was a part of the anxieties. While in Florida with the prisoners, the superintendent of schools of the town of St. Augustine was a Miss Semple, a most efficient New England woman. I had had some correspondence with her, and at my request she came to Carlisle to take charge of the schoolroom work. I found on the grounds the widow of an army officer and her daughter living in one of the vacant buildings. The daughter was capable and became one of our teachers. Lt. George LeRoy Brown, whom I had met at the Cheyenne River Agency on my trip after the first party for Hampton, was on a leave of absence, and we corresponded. He expressed a desire to help, if there was an opportunity. I needed just his kind of ability to take care of the boys and he was kind enough to give the balance of his leave; he came to Carlisle and was an invaluable help in charge of the equipping and managing of the 100 boys.

Soon after my return with the second party, a Miss Burgess appeared with commendatory letters from leading members of her Society of Friends, who had supervision of the Friends' Indian work under President Grant's Peace Policy. She had taught school four years at the Pawnee Indian Agency, when her father was the agent. She had had a fellow teacher, a Miss Ely, in the same school, also a Friend, both of them then out of service, and I employed them. Both became most faithful and valuable helpers throughout all my twenty-five years as superintendent and remained with my successor.

Just before starting for the Indian Territory party, I employed a couple of barbers to cut the hair of the boys. This work was scarcely begun when I had to leave and the barbers were to finish the work under Mrs. Pratt's oversight. Upon my return Mrs. Pratt gave me this experience: The interpreter came to her saying all the boys had their hair cut except two of the older ones who refused to part with their long braids. She went at once to the room where the hair cutting was being done and asked these big boys why they refused to carry out the Captain's order. "Well," said one, "we were told we would have new clothes like the white men. We have none so we keep our long hair." "All right," said Mrs. Pratt, "the clothes will come later, and if you do not want to have your hair cut now, I must send away these barbers and then you must wait until the Captain returns." The spokesman relented and said that if she would stand by, he would let the man cut his hair, which she willingly did. The other, however, stubbornly held to his decision. Late that night she was aroused by a very discordant wailing, which grew in volume. Mrs. Pratt sent a boy for the interpreter. When the interpreter came, he gave the explanation that the young man who had refused to have his hair cut afterwards relented and did the job himself with a knife. He then said his people always wailed after cutting their hair, as it was an evidence of mourning, and he had come out on the parade ground to show his grief. His voice had awakened the girls, who joined with their shrill voices, then other boys joined and hence the commotion. Mrs. Pratt told the interpreter he must make the boys understand that the noise must cease at once, as they could be heard by the people in town, who likely would come out in force to see what was taking place, and added, "Something dreadful might happen." Soon all was quiet again. The next morning they held a council with the older pupils and impressed them with the fact that during the Captain's absence the ladies were working hard to make them comfortable, and they must have their sleep or they would be ill and could do nothing for them. This reasoning appealed to their intelligence and thereafter the nights were quiet.

A Mrs. Platt, who had been forty years in the Indian Service as a mission-ary-teacher among the Pawnees, voluntarily came and offered her services free to do anything she could. She was placed in charge of the dining room and kitchen, where she soon proved her worth and was employed under pay, and notwithstanding her age was most useful for nearly five years. She was exceptionally intelligent, motherly to the individual students, and most use-ful in all the assemblages of the school where Christian talks and inspiration were needed.

The north barracks became the boys' quarters. It was a building 250 feet long, two stories high, 24 feet wide, and divided into five large barrack rooms on each floor. A porch for each floor fronted the parade ground. The girls had the north officers' quarters, which were two stories divided into six sep-arate family quarters with brick walls between the sets. These buildings were inconvenient in arrangements, but had to serve for several years.

There was a very considerable delay in the arrival of clothing, and when it finally came it was delivered under a Bureau contract with one of our great American merchants. It was the shoddiest of shoddy clothing. As the price was insignificant, the worth was the same, but it illustrated the ill-considered system of buying the cheapest materials. Agent Miles stopped off on his way to Washington. I made a bundle of a cloth cap, through which I could push my finger, a coat out at the elbows and ripped, and trousers torn and worn out at the knees and seat, all in use less than a month. Addressing the package to Secretary Schurz, I wrote him a letter, stating that this was the sort of clothing sent for my pupils and that unless something better could be done immediately I would have to resort to extraordinary means in order to secure proper apparel. I told Agent Miles to personally deliver both the pack-age and the letter to Mr. Schurz, which he did, and I immediately received a telegram that money was placed to my credit with the United States Treas-urer and I could draw upon it and purchase suitable clothing.

We were scarcely under way when I received a letter from the Commis-sioner of Indian Affairs, enclosing a printed table of the per capita allowance of food for Indian schools. Experience in army service showed that children living on that ration would be hungry all the time. However, I put the school upon the allowance for two days and then telegraphed the Commissioner that the school allowance was wholly inadequate and it would be impossible for me to conduct a school of hungry children with any hope of success, and requested that I be authorized to use the army ration table. Authority came by telegraph to do this, and for the whole twenty-five years I was superin-tendent that was the allowance at Carlisle in contradistinction to the vary-ing tables used in other Indian schools.

The next time I visited Washington, the Commissioner, Mr. Hayt, laughingly told me that he wanted me to see how that table came to be adopted by the Bureau and sent for the chief of the division in the Indian Office having the matter in charge. When he came in, the Commissioner said, "I want you to tell Captain Pratt how you came to make up that school food supply table." The man said: "We had a ration allowance considerably more liberal than that for several years, and as nobody complained about it I thought there could be a reduction. I accordingly made up that table and have been waiting for complaints." I said: "You did that, without investigating allowances at boarding schools for young people or making inquiries of people who know about such things, and pushed it on the Indians as the conclusion of this Bureau?" "Well," he said, "I knew no other way. No one had complained and I thought it right to economize."

The school supplies were very much delayed. The boys were drilled daily by Lieutenant Brown. Simple bathing arrangements were established, and cleanliness and order soon prevailed. I went to Philadelphia and bought proper clothing for immediate delivery for both boys and girls, and gradually the routine of supply and demand was worked out. Desks and books came, and the south barracks, which contained five large rooms below and five above, became the school building. All rooms were heated with the large egg-shaped coal stoves left by the army. We were therefore dependent, in large measure, upon the students, who, under direction, kept fires going and the buildings warm. Winter was coming and the days getting colder.

The Indians were a great curiosity and only a low rail fence surrounded the twenty-seven acres of government land on which the barracks stood. This enabled free access from every side, and the numbers and quality of visitors interfered with the work. I made an estimate of the cost of a substantial seven-foot picket fence to enclose the whole twenty-seven acres. General Armstrong had loaned me eleven of the Florida prisoners and they and the newcomers directed by the carpenter could do the work. I asked the Commissioner to allow me the expenditure "in order to keep the Indians in and the whites out except they passed through the gate at the guardhouse." The authority came, and, directed by the carpenter, the Indian boys dug the holes, set up the post, nailed on the rails and slats, and we soon had a substantial barrier which remained a satisfactory protection during my superintendency.

The old guardhouse was historic. It had been built during the Revolutionary War by Hessians captured at Trenton and held prisoners at Carlisle. The walls were three feet thick. It had four cells on two sides of a narrow hallway with massive doors, one general room for confinement of prisoners, and a guardroom for the guard. The other original barrack building had all been burned during the Civil War.

When Lee was moving his army to Gettysburg for the great battle there, he sent one of his commanders up the valley to Carlisle with an army corps, and with this corps was Fitzhugh Lee, his nephew, commanding a cavalry division. When a young lieutenant of cavalry just out of West Point, "Fitz" Lee was stationed at the barracks. "Fitz" Lee went through Carlisle and on to Harrisburg, and the infantry and artillery turned south to Gettysburg. Lee came back and found that Carlisle had been occupied by a small force of Federal infantry during his absence. He called on them to surrender, but they refused. He then fired into the town with his artillery, drove the Federals out, burned the barracks, and marched away to Gettysburg. The barracks were rebuilt in 1865, using the old brick walls still intact.

The buildings needed repairs throughout, as they had been vacant for seven years, except as occupied by a sergeant and small guard of a dozen soldiers under a lieutenant. A carpenter was employed to instruct the boys and use them in making repairs. While waiting for supplies to arrive, the same boys were kept at this work, which soon made them efficient. In a few months they and the carpenter erected a permanent hospital building, which filled the needs for ten years, when the growth of the school required an addition. Remodeling the old buildings to make them more adaptable was a perpetual job.

From the beginning the program was to be practical in all training and make every industry productive. Doing that which had to be done to make things better was the inspiration.

Not many days after the arrival of the second party there appeared at the school Miss Susan Longstreth, an elderly Quaker lady from Philadelphia. She and her sister for a period of fifty years had carried on a famous young ladies' school in the great city of brotherly love. Then on account of age both of them had retired. She brought with her one of her pupils, a Miss Brown. They wanted to see the school and to know all about it. One of the teachers showed them around, then they came to the office and asked many questions, and Miss Longstreth said: "Captain, thee is undertaking a great work here. Thee will need many things. Thee must remember if thee would receive thee must ask. Will thee take thy pencil and put down some of the things thee needs very much just now and the cost?" I accordingly wrote: "This is to be an industrial school to teach young Indians how to earn a living among civilized people by practicing mechanical and agricultural pursuits and the usual industries of civilized life. I have nothing with which to begin mechanical training. I shall want to teach carpentry and will need . . ." then listed, with probable cost, carpenter's tools and materials; blacksmith's tools and materials, including forge, anvil, etc.; tailor's equipment, including sewing machines; harness-making tools, painter's tools, shoemaker's tools, a printing press with type, etc.; tinner's and coppersmith's tools. "The last trade I can myself teach, having served an apprenticeship of over four years before the Civil War." The estimated total cost was a little above $1,200. Future experience, however, proved I was far too modest.

They were waiting and talking at one side, and when I handed Miss Longstreth the paper they went to a window, and I heard them saying, "I will take that," "I will take that," "I will take that," and then Miss Longstreth handed back the list and said, "Buy all and send us the amount of each bill, and we will send checks to pay."

My recollection of that little scene now, more than forty-two years ago, is so vivid I feel in relating it the same rush of blood to my brain and heart that I did then. From that time forward these ladies until their death were among my most invaluable aids and helpers in promoting the prosperity of the school.

On a Sunday morning early, very soon after we started, I discovered the Commissioner of Indian Affairs, Mr. Hayt, walking across the grounds, looking right and left at the buildings and property. I invited him to my house, but he said he was in a hurry and wanted to look things over quickly and take the next train back to Washington. I took him about the grounds, showed him the buildings from the outside, and told him the intended use of each, answered his many questions, and he seemed satisfied with the outlook. During our walk and talk he asked: "Who have you for teachers and helpers? Where did they come from?" I gave their names, the different places they filled, where they came from, what experience they had had, and when I spoke of one of the Quaker ladies he said: "What! You haven't got that little red-headed thing here! We have tried her in the agency service and had to discharge her. She is not a suitable teacher. You had better discharge her at once." "Well, sir," I said, "she is recommended by the leading members of her Friends Society, who have been helping the Government in its Indian work for years. She is not red-headed and is not little, and she has had four years' experience. Among the many qualities I need here is experience, and persons who know Indians and understand what they will have to do are the ones who can advise and help me best. She has come here from Nebraska. It would not be fair to discharge her without trial. If after trial she proves inadequate, I will then recommend her discharge." There the matter dropped. She remained at the school for more than twenty-five years and was among its ablest and most devoted helpers.

In 1880 the Administration brought thirty-one Sioux chiefs and their principal men to Washington to confer about their tribal affairs. Red Cloud and Spotted Tail were the leaders. They came to Carlisle and we gave them the best entertainment we could, showed them every feature of the school, and gave them full liberty out of school hours to see and talk with their children. Spotted Tail asked to have the Sioux children brought together so that he and the other chiefs could talk to me and the children could hear what was said. We assembled in the chapel. The Episcopal bishop of central Pennsylvania and his wife and a small party were visiting the school, and as the Spotted Tail [Rosebud] Agency had sent our largest delegation of students and was in the care of the Episcopal Church, under General Grant's Peace Policy, I asked him and his party to be present. The chiefs had talked things over among themselves, and Spotted Tail was the principal speaker. He found fault with the school because we were using soldier uniforms for the boys. He said he did not like to have their boys drilled, because they did not want them to become soldiers. He also found fault with the sleeping accommodations and the food. He then had a personal complaint to make, saying that his youngest boy had been in the guardhouse for a week.

After he finished, as it seemed best to first get out all the virus there might be in the party, I asked if there were others who would like to speak, and two of the Rosebud chiefs ventured to briefly uphold Spotted Tail's complaints. Then they said they had nothing more to say. Red Cloud and the Pine Ridge delegates said nothing.

I then replied to Spotted Tail in regard to clothing, explaining that the means were limited and that I had to get on with such a small allowance that I was compelled to buy the best-wearing clothes for the least money. Finding I could buy army clothing from the supplies left over from the Civil War, I had purchased the army sky blue trousers and the dark navy blue coats. I explained the benefit to health in the drilling and answered his other criticisms. When I came to his youngest son's being put in the guardhouse, I asked his oldest son to explain how it had come about so they could all understand. I had difficulty in getting the older son to talk, but he finally told that his brother had quarreled with a schoolmate and with his jackknife stabbed his comrade in the leg. A court martial of the student officers had tried him; he himself as an officer was a member of the court, and the court's sentence was confinement in the guardhouse for a week. The sentence was not severe under our laws.

Then the Bishop asked to speak. His wife had a picture of their son which she carried in her satchel, showing him in uniform and having a gun, and Carlisle did not have guns. He explained that his son was going to a military school because it was a good place to teach him how to stand up straight and to walk with his head up, and that the drills made him healthy and strong. Spotted Tail's complaints were fully met and before the conference ended the delegation was on our side, and during the rest of their visit the other chiefs, including Red Cloud, said they were glad to have their children at the school.

The evening of that day, when all the school and the visitors were together in the chapel and the pupils had finished monthly declamation exercises, Red Cloud, with much feeling and dignity, arose and said the following, as afterwards told by Tackett to the editor of the school paper: "Great Spirit, look at me and listen. My Great Father, this land is ours. My friends, the paco-faces, have a land across the ocean. The man stands before us who has our children all in charge. Shake hands with him, Great Father, that they may live long and prosper in the future. Our Great President Father has told me that the land on this side of the ocean is the red man's land. We want to all shake hands with a good heart that in the future we may live in peace. That is the reason I say these few words. I want all the present and the generations to come to find the good road of our Maker and follow His words."

Spotted Tail asked to take his son-in-law, Tackett, with him to Washington as his interpreter, and also to go with the delegation to see the Hampton School. The pupils had gained enough English to enable our doing without an interpreter, and I told Spotted Tail that when he returned he might take his son-in-law home with him.

The party went to Washington, visited Hampton, and finally returned to Carlisle. Spotted Tail then told me that he had talked with the Secretary of the Interior and that the Secretary had said that his son-in-law should remain at Carlisle as interpreter with more salary. I told Spotted Tail we wanted to push the English speaking of the students, and as all could now speak a little English they could learn faster if forced to use it all the time. We wanted Carlisle to become an English-speaking school as quickly as possible. Therefore it was best he take his son-in-law with him; that I had no order from the Secretary to continue his son-in-law as an employee and doubted if the Secretary would order it without consulting me. Spotted Tail then said that I would have to keep his son-in-law or he would take all the Sioux children away. I said: "The children came here for three years and must remain until the period expires. You have a right to speak your wishes only about your own children. Other chiefs and fathers of children here have told me that they are satisfied and do not agree with you. The Government cannot afford to pay the expense of bringing children here for three years' schooling and in a few months send them back. Besides, they have not learned enough to be useful to you." He then said he would take his own children anyway even if he had to pay for it himself. I said: "Very well, if that is the way you feel about it, I will recommend to the Secretary that you be allowed to take them but it must be at your own cost."

A newspaper woman was visiting the school at the time and I asked her to send out a brief dispatch of the affair to the New York and Philadelphia papers and to the Washington *Post,* which the Secretary read before he went to his office each morning. She detailed the situation and I sent a full telegram to the Secretary, which he would receive when he reached the office in the morning, stating Spotted Tail's determination to take his children and that I was willing he be allowed to take them provided he paid their traveling expenses. I told the Secretary of my desire to get on without an interpreter and the reasons. An immediate reply came directing that if Spotted Tail persisted and would pay the traveling expenses of his children, he be allowed to take them. He also sent a full telegram to Spotted Tail, remonstrating against his course and urging him to allow his children to remain. Spotted Tail remained obdurate, and having a wealthy friend in Carlisle who had for years been a beef contractor for the Sioux, he went to him and borrowed the money to take his children home. All the Sioux children went to the train to see their parents and the chiefs start home.

All of Spotted Tail's children desired to remain and the two youngest cried, so that Spotted Tail had to exert authority and even force, especially with his oldest son, who was very determined. The delegation was practically a unit against Spotted Tail's course and made it so unpleasant for him that, as I was informed later by the agent in charge, he took his children into another car and rode apart from his delegation all the way home. On their arrival at their agency the people assembled to hear the news from Washington, and when Spotted Tail rose to speak the people left the conference and would not listen to him.[2]

Crow Dog, one of the chiefs, and Spotted Tail had long been enemies, and Crow Dog preceded Spotted Tail on the way home, waited for him at a

2. As this account of the episode differs markedly from that of George Hyde in *A Sioux Chronicle,* pp. 54–56, this portion of the manuscript was submitted for comment to Harry H. Anderson, Director of the Milwaukee County Historical Society, who investigated official documents concerning the affair in the National Archives and on whose notes Hyde's account was largely based. According to Anderson, Pratt's account in his memoirs follows closely his contemporary account in a report at the time to the Indian Office. Two important discrepancies are noteworthy: (1) "Pratt says the Sioux chiefs other than Spotted Tail did not address the students. His report of 1880 makes no mention of such a gathering during the first visit of the delegation to Carlisle (while en route to Washington); but it does describe such an assembly on the return leg. The children were gathered in the chapel, and Red Dog, Two Strike, Red Cloud, Spotted Tail, and American Horse all made speeches. 'All of them,' reported Pratt, 'were offensive and prejudicial to the discipline of the school.'" (2) "Pratt's account also conflicts with the 1880 report on the matter of the children being taken back by the chiefs. According to the latter, Red Dog tried to take one of his relatives, but offered no resistance when the child was removed from the train by school officials. White Thunder's son and another girl sneaked aboard the train, but were discovered and sent back from Harrisburg. Spotted Tail's son, Max, was the one who did not want to leave the school, crying and hanging back until just prior to the train's departure."

place away from the crowd, and shot and killed him. Crow Dog was tried by civil court and sentenced to be hanged, but the sentence was finally remitted. Sometime after his release Crow Dog was killed by Spotted Tail's eldest son.[3]

Just before Lieutenant Brown's leave ended, I made application for his detail at Carlisle, notwithstanding there had been no law passed as yet that would authorize it. General Sherman wrote me a personal letter about it, in which he said: "If Army officers will persist in getting away from their legitimate duties in this way, I will make it my business to see that the sergeants and corporals who have to perform their duties in their absence shall get their pay." When next in Washington I went to see General Sherman personally. He said it was ineptitude for army officers to undertake the subordinate duties of the Indian service and be controlled in their actions by politically appointed superiors, ignorant of Indians and what was best for them. Most of our dangerous duty on the frontier in suppressing Indians was forced upon us by the maladministration of these incompetents, and he said, "With all your enthusiasm, Pratt, these fellows will down you and eventually get your scalp." I said, "General, I am responsible for Carlisle because of my suggesting it and the Secretary of War and the Secretary of the Interior and the President are with me in it, and I can see no way but to go ahead and do the best I can."

Lieutenant Brown had to return to his army duties. My expression in regard thereto is contained in a paragraph from our school paper, the *Eadle Ketah Toh,* as follows:

> The detail of Lt. Brown, 11th Infantry, as an assistant at this school, has been denied by the War Department on the ground that it is not a military duty and there is no law of Congress authorizing it. Lt. Brown came to our help on the 11th of November, when we were pressed for just such services as he knows so well how to render. He organized the 120 boys into companies, drilled them, established a routine of duty, police, etc., built a gymnasium, and in many ways labored incessantly, early and late, for four months to help establish the work. These four months were part of a six months leave of absence, from a long service of eight years on the frontier. The loss of Lt. Brown's services is a source of deep regret. He has the satisfaction of knowing that his labor here

3. Crow Dog murdered Spotted Tail at Rosebud Agency on Aug. 5, 1881. The deed had its origins in the bitter political factionalism that reservation policies and programs produced among the Sioux leadership. Spotted Tail's action at Carlisle occurred more than a year earlier and had no direct bearing on the murder. Tried by jury and sentenced to hang, Crow Dog was released by the U.S. Supreme Court, which ruled that Federal courts had no jurisdiction on reservations secured to the Indians by treaty. Two years later Young Spotted Tail, motivated like Crow Dog by a desire for the Brulé chieftainship, murdered Chief White Thunder, not Crow Dog as stated by Pratt; Crow Dog lived to figure prominently in the Ghost Dance uprising of 1890–91. The story is told in Hyde, *Spotted Tail's Folk,* pp. 300–06; and Hyde, *Sioux Chronicle,* pp. 64–66.

honored both his head and his heart, and that his name is identified with
the origin of this school and will remain as a part of its history.[4]

.   .   .   .

The president and all the professors of Dickinson College were at once
friends of the school. A Sunday intervened while I was absent in the Territory, and Mrs. Pratt and the ladies thought it best to have a minister and religious services. The ladies suggested different pastors, but Mrs. Pratt said:
"The president of the college is a minister and I will ask him." She therefore
wrote a note to Dr. McCauly, who accepted and through the interpreter gave
a very pleasing and acceptable talk—to the students especially but also to the
few helpers—and from that time forward Dr. McCauly became an adviser
and most valued friend to the school.

Dr. Charles F. Hines, who stood next to Dr. McCauly in the college, offered
his services and suggested that the students might be interested in the forces
of electricity, which was a part of the college curriculum under his direction.
In the spring of 1880 he invited me to send a large delegation into the college,
where the apparatus was convenient, and gave the party an illuminating talk.
Our *Eadle Ketah Toh* paragrapher, Miss Burgess, went along and gave the
following account:

> About forty of the older boys and girls are again made to wonder at
> the power of the white man's "medicine," by a lecture on "Lightning,"
> from their good friend Prof. Chas. F. Hines, of Dickinson College. The
> stroke of lightning that knocked the miniature house to pieces was so
> real that all were startled, and the girls gave the usual little civilized
> screech. The most amusing thing was when the spark of electricity
> passed from Roman Nose's nose to High Forehead's knuckle, and while
> they two were badly shocked, the remainder of the party were convulsed
> with laughter. Prof. Hines seemed to have enough lightning to go
> around, for when Mr. "Talks with Bears" and Mr. "Kills without
> Wounding" and Mr. "White Whirlwind," and Mr. "Short Leg," and
> Mr. "Runs after the Moon," and Mr. "Wants to be Chief," and Mr.
> "Makes Trouble in Front," and Miss "Wooden Ear Rings," and Miss
> "White Cow," and Miss "Red Road," and Miss "Stands Looking," and
> Miss "Brave Killer," and a dozen others took hold of hands to test the
> strength of Prof. Hines' electric medicine, most of them found it
> stronger than they could stand, but a few of the boys held on to the last,
> although they did get badly jerked.

The following letter from my old friend, the Quaker agent John Miles,
is in common sense and in exposé of the facts worthy of a place here:

4. Omitted here is Lieutenant Brown's farewell printed in the school paper—a long essay on
culture change from ancient to modern times.

Darlington, I. T., Feb. 12th, 1880.

Capt. Pratt:

I see no reason why the balance of the Florida boys should not be permitted to come home, provided you are willing, and smaller youth be taken in their places. You can now get all of this class of youth that you may desire. We have now in school at this Agency 170 Arapahoe children and 162 Cheyennes. We ought to have 500 more children receiving the same advantages. The children *must* be taken *from* the camps if we expect them to advance from savage life, and I count it money wasted to continue the large annual appropriations to feed and clothe these children *in camp* and under camp influence.

Congress may go ahead from year to year and appropriate means to supply the youth *in camp* and they will still be the same dirty, ignorant, camp Indians; while if it would increase the appropriation just sufficient to clothe and support them *in school* (Industrial schools) and make it available while in attendance at school, either on their reservations or at "Training Schools" similar to the Carlisle School, then we might expect a decided forward movement from our present Indian status. There are so many points gained in placing Indian children in school that I cannot forebear speaking of them briefly, for I know you are anxious to get all the points to be gained in the management of Indians looking towards their improvement.

1st. The child being in school the parents are much easier managed; are loyal to the Government, to the Agent, and take an interest in the affairs of the Agency, and never dare, or desire, to commit a serious wrong. I am yet to know of the first individual Indian on this reservation who has joined in a raid, that has had his child in school; and I know the "Dull Knife" raid [see p. 199, note 7] would never have occurred had the children of this band been placed in school. Had there been sufficient accommodation on this reservation for schools at the proper time the "Dull Knife" band were here, I could have secured the attendance of at least a majority of their children of school age. This may look to you like *compulsory* education. Well, if it is, is there any serious objection to such a course? Was not the taking of thirty-three Cheyenne braves and chiefs from this reservation *in chains* in the spring of 1875 compulsory in the superlative degree? Who is there today that would question the charity and justness of that measure? If there is one, let him come to this Agency and take a seat in the assembly room of our own schools and listen to the discourse of some of these same men pleading with their more *unfortunate* (in a sense) people to come out from their heathen degradation and step up into a higher and more enjoyable scale of existence.

2nd. The Agency schools are made the principal feature of attraction for the Indians, as by having their children in school the parent becomes personally interested in the progress of his child and the prosperity of the school. This induces a desire to locate in the vicinity of the agency, and his habits are consequently localized. This effect is still more apparent in the case of those who have children away—at Carlisle and other points in the States. The parents of these children are as completely committed to the general welfare of the whole people of the United States as any other loyal citizen, and by this mixing and blending of common interests they will the sooner be prepared to enter into and take upon themselves the duties and responsibilities of a common citizenship.

3rd. In the management of the school upon the reservation the service of the police is called into requisition—looking up truants, absentees, etc., and in this way the Indian police force becomes interested in the school and its progress.

Trusting that your efforts in the future may be crowned with success as in the past, I am

Your sincere friend,
JNO. D. MILES[5]

.　　　.　　　.　　　.　　　.　　　.

Clarence Three Stars, a Sioux, had exceptional mental ability. His mastery of arithmetic was remarkable. But he was at first disposed to bother his teacher. All his classmates at this time were Sioux and adult primaries. The superintendent received a note from his teacher stating that Clarence was giving trouble and asking him to come to the schoolroom with the interpreter to help straighten out the situation. When the superintendent had the teacher's statement, he said, "Clarence, stand up." Clarence stood up. "Hold up your head." He complied. "Put your hands down by your side, palms to the front." He obeyed. "Put your heels together." It was done. "Push your shoulders back," and he became chesty. All these directions were given through an interpreter, and the superintendent executed each movement himself as he gave the order. Standing at attention as a soldier, and Clarence in the same attitude, the superintendent then said, "What is the matter?" Clarence at once began to talk rapidly in his own language, but his voice quavered, and Robert, the son of American Horse, said something in Sioux at which all the others laughed. The superintendent asked the interpreter what Robert had said. The answer was: "Robert says to him, 'If you are so brave, what makes your voice shake so?'" The superintendent then

---

5. Omitted here is Pratt's first annual report, for which see Commissioner of Indian Affairs, *Annual Report* (1880), pp. 178–82.

said to the teacher, "He seems to obey promptly. I guess things will go all right now." The teacher agreed, and that ended the matter. After his brief three-year term at Carlisle, Clarence was returned to his agency and became an efficient helper in the agency and in the business affairs of his tribe and has often been selected to go to Washington as a representative of his people in their contentions for their tribal rights. Forty years have passed, and Clarence is still a sturdy, highly respected and useful man among his people.

This teacher also had in her room at the same time one of the very largest of the Sioux pupils who had on several occasions bothered her by not reciting. She wrote a note to the superintendent asking that he come with the interpreter and help her over a difficulty. It was about three o'clock in the afternoon. The teacher met the superintendent outside the room and told him that Amos had refused to recite his lesson in the forenoon and that she had told him that he could not leave the room until he recited his lesson, and she had remained with him during the noon hour. Amos was put through the same performance of standing up and taking the position of a soldier at attention. The superintendent then asked, "What is the trouble?" Amos at once replied, "She has tried to whip me out and I have whipped her out," meaning that he had not called for reinforcements, but she had. The superintendent said to him, "Amos, you will remain after school and recite your lesson as the teacher requires, and she will come by the office and report. I will then determine what I ought to do about your refusing this morning." The teacher reported after school that "Amos never recited his lesson better. I do not want anything more done about it." On account of Amos' size, the superintendent was very glad to heed this request.

Another of Amos' self-determinations overtook him when he was detailed one forenoon to dig at a trench in which was to be placed a sewer pipe. The trench was being dug by details of two Indians at a time and was going forward so slowly that the superintendent said to the disciplinarian, "One student alone ought to do it quicker. Try only one this morning." Early in the morning the disciplinarian reported that Amos refused to dig and stood stubbornly inactive by the side of the trench. The superintendent went with the disciplinarian and, surmising that Amos thought the work beneath his dignity, took the pick, jumped into the trench, loosened a lot of earth, shoveled it out, and repeated the operation several times, then said, "Amos, go to work." Amos quickly took up his job and the superintendent and disciplinarian went about their work, and when his detail ended at noon Amos had dug more in the same time than any two boys previously.

Twenty years after leaving Carlisle, Amos was doing as well as seemed possible under the limitations of our segregating reservating Indian policy.

22. Transformation

The second year of the school at Carlisle was filled with more hope, more anticipation of great results, and then greater disappointment and sorrow than its superintendent experienced at any other period in his quarter century of control.

During the Civil War I had met the man who, in 1880, was the candidate of the Republican Party for the Presidency, General James A. Garfield. I had also met his cousin, General William B. Hazen, whose acquaintance I renewed at Fort Sill in 1869. After General Garfield's election to the Presidency, I wrote the following letter to General Hazen:

Indian School, Carlisle, Pa.,
Nov. 16th, 1880.

Dear General Hazen:

Last night's Army & Navy Journal indicates that you may be in Washington a few days yet, and it occurs to me that your long acquaintance with Genl. Garfield may give you his ear on topics of interest to his coming administration. I have watched carefully every utterance of his during the campaign, and have not seen that he said "Indian" once, but all he has said about education, the interests of all classes and the Negro, has been broad and grand, and I am sure the aborigines will be lifted into a better state during his control. Your long service in the Army on the frontier before and since the war, and your duties at one time in charge of the Indian Territory tribes, will, I am sure, endorse the state-

ment that education and training for the young is our only sure way to
relief from Indian complications and burdens. You will remember that
in all the great treaties of 1868, with the Sioux, Cheyennes, Arapahoes,
Kiowas, Comanches, Navajos, Shoshones, Bannocks, Pawnees, and
other tribes, composing all our nomadic Indians east of the mountains,
a special educational clause was inserted, promising educational advantages to every child between 6 and 16 years of age. Now I believe in regard to that, that if in the hereafter of our country we are burdened with
Indian pensioners, vagabonds and criminals, very much of it will come
upon us because we failed to carry out in good faith that part of our
self-assumed obligation.

The present [Hayes] administration has done more than any previous
one to improve the Indian status, but it has only begun to open the way.
There is no doubt in my mind but that during General Garfield's administration a lifting up of the Indians can be accomplished, that would,
of itself, leave its mark on the history of this country so bright that all
the future would not erase it. We have at the outside 50,000 Indian
children who are of proper age to attend school. This is less than half
the number in the schools of Philadelphia alone. Now it seems to me a
small matter for this great country of ours to reach out and gather all
these children into educational and training influences for self-support
and manly living of some kind. If we had made no promises it would be
economy and statesmanlike. How far more binding upon us is it since
that is our promise. It will require vigorous and intelligent management, with possibly some pressure of force, but I am sure less of the latter than we bring to bear on our own children in some of our states.
Success depends on completeness. We have agreed to give to all, we can
give to all, and we ought to give to every Indian boy and girl of suitable
age the privileges of schools and training in civilized ways. To do less
than the whole invites proportionate failure. The obligation of the Indians to send their children to school is clearly undertaken by them, in
their treaties, and the right to enforce attendance is clearly defined as
resting with us through our agents.

My plan would be to create an educational department for the Indian
service and to place at its head a great and earnest educational man
like General S. C. Armstrong of Hampton Institute, for instance, and to
provide him with all the means necessary for the work. We must feed
and clothe the children, and it should be done so liberally that disease
will be driven away instead of enticed, as I am sorry to say my observance
shows to have been the case in the past. Properly fed, clothed, and well

taught, and as much industrially as possible, would in four years send the children into a new life and destroy savagery in this country.

The Bill, twice reported favorably from the House Committee on Indian Affairs, to use vacant military posts and barracks would be a large means for beginning. And if the system of congregating our Army into large commands at a few important points, which has been urged for several years past, should prevail, many additional places for schools would be created, in very many of which all the needs of sheltering and for agricultural training are already provided.

I write this to you because you are in the way to say something to General Garfield on the subject with less suspicion of selfishness than anyone I know.

I am, dear General,

With greatest respect,
Your obedient servant,
R. H. PRATT,
Lieut.

Soon after the inauguration of President Garfield, I went to Washington and called on him at the White House. I was admitted to see him in his private office, and he was kind enough to get up from his desk and come and take my hand and with his great big eyes looking me in the face say appreciative words. He told me that one of his plans was to come to Carlisle just as soon as the Senate adjourned and see the school, and he said, "I am going to make the Indians a distinct feature of my administration." I told him of my great pleasure in hearing that. He asked how he could best get to Carlisle. I said: "You can leave Washington at eight o'clock in the morning, be at Carlisle at twelve o'clock by way of Baltimore on the Pennsylvania road, stay with us three or four hours, and return down the valley via Chambersburg, at Hagerstown take the B. & O., stop off at Antietam if you want to, and be back in Washington at eight o'clock in the evening. If you desire I can arrange the details of your trip." He said, "Good! Do that and send me the schedule. Go and see Lincoln [Robert Lincoln, Secretary of War] and see Governor [Samuel J.] Kirkwood [Secretary of the Interior] and say to them for me that I am going to Carlisle as soon as I can get away and I want them to go along." I received a fine reception and acceptance from both Secretaries and returned to Carlisle.

I went immediately to Chambersburg, saw President Kennedy of the Cumberland Valley Railroad, always our good friend, and told him the situation. He called his office boy and said, "Tell General Boyd to come here." General

Boyd was superintendent of the railroad. He told the General my mission and said, "I want you to make up a schedule that meets Captain Pratt's promise to the President and send a copy of it to Captain Pratt, and he will send it to the President, and when he gets ready we will see that the arrangement is carried out."

Conditions lingered in Washington. President Garfield had some difficulties with members of the Senate in regard to appointments. Before he could get away, the fatal shot was fired in the railroad station which ended a life that promised so much in many directions and, as I believed, most of all indicated vast strides in Indian civilization.[1]

The influences and conclusions moving me are best told in other letters I previously and subsequently wrote, and the following copies from my letter book are made a part of this record. They are a continuation of the lobby work Secretary Schurz, Secretary McCrary, and even President Hayes had pushed me into doing.

Indian School, Carlisle Barracks, Pa.,
January 14, 1880.

Hon. T. C. Pound,
   U. S. House of Representatives,
      Washington, D.C.

Dear Sir:

I send you today a few photographs of the Indian youth here. You will note that they came mostly as blanket Indians. A very large proportion of them had never been inside of a school room. I am gratified to report that they have yielded gracefully to discipline and that our school rooms, in good order, eagerness to learn, actual progress, etc., are, to our minds, quite up to the average of those of our own race. Isolated as these Indian youth are from the savage surroundings at their homes, they lose their tenacity to savage life, which is so much of an obstacle to Agency efforts, and give themselves up to learning all they can in the time they expect to remain here.

Now that the schoolroom work is well started, we are turning attention to the Agricultural and Mechanical features proposed. One of the two large stables, 200 by 40 feet, will make us an excellent workshop where we may carry on instruction in carpentry, wagon and harness making, blacksmithing, boot and shoe making and repairing, etc. And this, too, without very great expense. I have proposed to the Department and am encouraged to make wagons, harness, tin-ware, etc., for issue to

1. President Garfield was shot by a disappointed office seeker in the Washington railway depot on July 2, 1881, four months after taking office. He died on September 19 from the effects of the wound.

the Agencies. This getting rid of what we make without, by its sale here, imposing on the local trade will be a great relief, and will not only enable us to teach Indian boys the trades, but will be a saving to the Department.

The location is healthy, buildings commodious for four hundred pupils and there is a strong current in favor of this kind of work among the Indians. I believe I told you I was asked to take 500 more boys and girls, from Rosebud. Since my return from Washington I have a letter from the Navajoes asking to send some of the children of their chiefs and headmen here, and I have asked the Department to allow 50. The last annual report of the Commissioner of Indian Affairs shows that out of 4000 children this tribe has not one in school. (See Com. Report 1878, page 180.) Both the Spotted Tail and Red Cloud Indians have heretofore antagonized education. Now I could fill several institutions as large as this could be made (say 500 each) from those Agencies alone. I am sure of it. They see in this a fair chance for their children to become capable like the whites, and this is the supreme idea with the Indians of the plains. Your bill proposes a number of vacant military posts which the Adjutant General informed the Committee would be available. General Sherman named others to me. I know a number of Army officers who would render valuable service to this complicated Indian question, in this connection. I should be glad to appear before your Committee and also be glad to have a delegation from it visit the school.

With great respect,
Your obedient servant,
R. H. PRATT.

Indian School,
Carlisle Barracks, Pa.,
January 28, 1880.

To His Excellency, R. B. Hayes,
President of the U. S.
Sir:

A few days since I ventured to send you views of the buildings and groups of the Sioux youth here.

I hope your interest in this feature of your administration will increase as it ought. It has grown up under your encouragement and will not fail in itself to demonstrate your wisdom. I believe it is destined to expand and urge forward all Indian educational work to meet the needs of the Indians.

If the means can be found and all our manual labor schools will undertake delegations of Indian youth, and all suitable vacant military posts or barracks not otherwise needed can be utilized for Indian Industrial Schools, and then every Agency effort pushed, a very short time will show that the number of Indian youth not at school can be represented by as small a number as is now required to represent the number actually in school. When that happens there will be fewer Indian troubles.

I am glad to report that we have the greatest encouragement to go ahead. Our students meet our highest hopes. The influence has reached to other tribes than those represented here; tribes like the Navajoes and Utes who have taken no interest in education heretofore.

As these tribes have educational treaty claims, they ought to be fully met in all advances of this kind. I propose to continue to seek authority and means from the executive and legislative branches of the government until I am allowed to increase this school, to double its present number, and preferably from the tribes mentioned.

With great respect,
Your most obedient servant,
R. H. PRATT,
Lieut. 10th Cav'y.

Indian School,
Carlisle Barracks, Pa.,
March 9th, 1880.

(Confidential)
To His Excellency, R. B. Hayes,
    President of the U. S.
Sir:

I enclose to you a copy of a letter received by me on Saturday last.

Govr. Bagley's letter in favor of Lieut. Brown reached me after I personally and at the instance of the Honorable Secretary of War, approached General Sherman on the subject of Lieut. Brown's detail. Finding General Sherman hostile to the detail of Lt. Brown, I did not formally submit to him nor the War Department the application of the Indian and Interior Departments, made at my request, and which I had been allowed to carry to the War Department. I rather determined to make another application to have Lt. Brown go after the Ute and Navajoe children which the Interior Department intends sending here, hoping that on his return the bill which is favorably reported from the Indian Committee of the House, covering the detail of army officers in this connection, might by that time have become a law. This application I have made.

When Govr. Bagley's letter came I did not feel free to withhold it and so endorsed it forward to Genl. Sherman to whom it was addressed.

Answering General Sherman's criticism, I feel free to say to the President, that I know I am at this time "fighting" a greater number of "the enemies of civilization" than the whole of my regiment put together, and I know further that I am fighting them with a thousand times more hopes of success.

.   .   .   .   .   .

I see that about sixty officers are detailed as staff and instructors at West Point, where there are scarcely more students than I shall have here, when those arrive whom the Department contemplates soon adding from the Utes and Navajoes. There a Major General has charge with all this immense staff and corps of instructors to help. The objective there is mostly like that at Carlisle, *the Indian.* Here a Lieutenant struggles to evolve order out of a chaos of fourteen different Indian languages! Civilization out of savagery! Cleanliness out of filth! and is forced to educate the courage of his own instructors to the work, and see that all the interests of his government and the Indian as well are properly protected and served.

Mr. President, I need Lt. Brown to help me at this school, and I believe it is right I should have him.

He can be detailed by your order to go after the Ute and Navajoe youth, and on his return to remain and assist in this work. He will do the country a hundred times more service here than he will with his regiment. If I could advise in this matter, I would urge the immediate establishment of fifty more schools like this, and the detail of a hundred officers to manage them. The evidence of greatest good resulting from this system multiplies daily. It is lamentable that so small an atom of the needs of such work finds encouragement. General Sherman himself, four years ago, in a personal letter which is now before me, endorsed my course at St. Augustine. This and that are one, only this has grown bigger. Knowing as I do that I am supremely right, it would be wicked to falter, even though pressure to that end came in threats from the General of the Army.

With greatest respect,
Your obedient servant,
R. H. PRATT,
Lt. 10th Cav'y.

P.S. That you may know the ground fully I enclose a copy of my former application to the Indian Office for Lt. Brown.

Indian School,
Carlisle Barracks, Pa.,
April 7, 1880.

Hon. H. L. Dawes,[2]
U. S. Senate.

Dear Sir:

If a majority of the Senate and House concur in the views you expressed upon the Ute Bill day before yesterday, in reference to the education of Indian youth, and will legislate accordingly, the "beginning of the end" of Indian troubles is reached. Education and industrial training for Indian youth, *for all Indian youth,* will, in a very short period, end Indian wars and, in a not very long period, end appropriations to feed and clothe them. I don't believe anything else will.

With great respect,
R. H. PRATT,
Lt. in charge.

Indian School,
Carlisle Barracks, Pa.,
April 8, 1880.

Hon. Carl Schurz,
Sec'y of the Interior.

Sir:

I am most anxious to make a telling break on the Navajoes, and goad on the Presbyterians.[3] The Navajoes furnish the most promising field for educational and industrial training of any Indians we have, and are only second to the Sioux in population. The Presbyterians who have had ten years to move upon this tribe are only now waking up to their responsibility. This is a Presbyterian Valley [i.e. the Cumberland Valley], and fifty Navajoe youth at this school will incite the whole church to work. I place the matter before you, with my opinion, that

2. Henry Laurens Dawes (1816–1903) of Massachusetts was probably the most influential worker in the cause of Indian reform during the 1880s. His outstanding probity, character, and intelligence, combined with congressional experience dating from 1857, gave him a commanding influence in the Congress, and as chairman of the Senate Committee on Indian Affairs he was largely responsible for marshaling the essential congressional support of the Indian education program. He is best known as sponsor of the Dawes Act of 1887, which provided for allotment of land in severalty to the Indians. "While he held the reins," said Everett Edward Hale, "nobody talked of dishonor in our dealings with the Indians." Dawes served in the House of Representatives from 1857 to 1875 and in the Senate from 1875 to 1892. *Dictionary of American Biography,* 5, 149–50.

3. The Presbyterians were the leading missionary group on the Navajo Reservation of New Mexico and Arizona.

the 15 youth you have allowed from the Navajoes are too few; really weakness both ways, i. e. for success with the Indians and the Presbyterians.

If Agent Thomas of the Puebloes has not returned to his station I would like him to visit us on his way home.

If we have failed in getting Lt. Brown, we have developed the enemy. One experience in this matter I reserve to tell when I can see you.

The mechanical and industrial work is coming forward in a manner I am sure will gratify you. I shall have harness and tin-ware for shipment to Agencies. The blacksmith and his boys have made our agricultural implements. What I shall do for something to keep that branch going puzzles me just now. It is too important to fall behind.

I have informed the Commissioner that I can go after the Utes and Navajoes. The importance of securing proper subjects must not be overlooked. We who have the work to do feel that most.

With great respect,

Your obedient servant,

R. H. PRATT,

Lt. in Charge.

Indian Industrial School,

Carlisle Barracks, Pa.,

April 24, 1880.

Hon. Carl Schurz,

Secretary of the Interior.

Sir:

I send you photographs of most of our apprentices at work, and in the same package a set for the President.

Unless the Department will recognize my statements on this point and allow the direction of our manufactures to the Agencies in the matter of harness and tin ware, in particular, we shall be struggling against too many obstacles, and in great danger of failure. I wrote the Indian Office on March 8th and asked for sample sets of harness and such articles of tin ware as would be acceptable for issue to Agencies if made by us to correspond in quality. My letter is unnoticed. I then asked Mr. Karr, who has charge of the New York warehouse [of the Indian Bureau], to send me samples and I would either pay for them or return as soon as I knew their quality, sizes, etc., but Mr. Karr has twice put me off, on a quibble, and when I conform to his views and request him to send on the articles, I hear nothing more of it.

If the last Indian Office report shows the needs of the Department each year, I can say that we will make about all the handmade tin-ware here the Department may need for issue and the same may be said for the harness. This would give us a practical means for teaching the Indian boys these trades. In shoe making, carpentry, and blacksmithing, we have much of our own to do; of the two former, quite enough for some time to come.

I should like very much to see you and the Commissioner just now, and it would be better if I could see you here.

With great respect,

Your obedient servant,

R. H. PRATT,

Lieut.

Carlisle Barracks, Pa.,

May 25, 1880.

To His Excellency,

The President.

Sir:

It would probably be premature to have anything like a general exhibition and invite the multitude at this early date in our work here, but I do consider it proper and most desirable that you should know and see just what we are doing, because this work has grown up under your administration, and will remain after your administration closes, as one of the best evidences of its wisdom and humanity.

Several times Secretary Schurz has spoken of his desire to bring yourself and Mrs. Hayes here, and that has always been before us as one of the incentives in our work, and I have endeavored to keep you somewhat informed of our progress by photographs and other methods. Wishing to bring the work up to something near what I believe would be a demonstration of the administration's idea, before pressing for a visit from you, I have delayed that consumation of what we have so much anticipated until now. It will be gratifying to us if you can visit us at an early day. We should be disappointed if Mrs. Hayes and your son Webb and others of your family are not of the party.

I am just informed that the Sioux Visiting Committee, consisting of the parents and chiefs of many of the children here, and of which the Secretary of the Interior spoke in his last annual report to you, will reach here on Thursday next, the 27th inst., and we have fixed upon Friday, the 28th, as a day to exhibit to them by special exercises, the progress we have so far made with their children.[4] I mention this incidentally, thinking it might be convenient and interesting to you to make that the occasion of your visit. The season is delightful here now and the grounds have on their best appearance and I am sure that the brief time you might be able to give to us would be a grateful relief from the cares of your office.

With great respect,
Your obedient and humble servant,
R. H. Pratt,
1st Lt., 10th Cav'y., In Charge.[5]

.   .   .   .

Carlisle Barracks, Pa.,
September 28, 1880.

Hon. Carl Schurz,
Secretary of the Interior.
Sir:

Knowing that the donation of so large a sum would please you, I have written my Quaker friend in Philadelphia that you, as the real head of the school, should know all about it, and asked to send forward her letter, here inclosed, for your information. With your allowance of $800.00, I now have steam heat in the boys' quarters. (Note: The lady had sent $1000.00.)

I have asked the Indian Office for the Hospital. I have only this to say, that I consider it extremely important, and that if you do not feel able to give me the whole sum asked, but will give two-thirds, putting it on the basis of a want of funds, I can go to New York, Hartford and Boston friends and raise the other third, so that we may have a suitable building and too, in that way, interest our people in our work.

I have talked freely with Dr. McCauley about the Board of Visitors, composed of eminent educators. He shares my views of its value, and appreciates the delicacy of the situation. He apprehends no difficulty in securing the presence of the persons named, as most of them are deeply interested. Miss Mather is in correspondence with some of the parties named and knows of their desire to forward your efforts in this direction. Dr. McCauley has blocked out the enclosed letter which can be

4. This was the delegation that included Spotted Tail, who collided with Pratt as previously narrated and withdrew his children from school. See above, pp. 236–40.

5. Omitted here is a lengthy memorial to Congress and the Executive by a committee of the General Assembly of the Presbyterian Church pressing for an Indian policy featuring allotment of land in severalty, extension of law to Indian reservations, and an expansion of the Indian education program.

modified to suit your views, and he will gladly undertake any correspondence you may desire. He suggests the names of Dr. McCosh of Princeton, and Pres. Gilman of Johns Hopkins University, Baltimore, as additional members whom he knows to be interested.

It would suit us best to have them here early in November.

With great respect,
Your obedient servant,
R. H. Pratt,
Lt.

Indian Industrial School,
Carlisle Barracks, Pa.,
November 9, 1880.

(Informal)
Hon. Carl Schurz,
    Secretary of the Interior.
Dear Sir:

I have received several letters from unknown parties in the Indian Territory asking the privileges of the school here for the children of Seminoles and Creeks. Considering that these applications should come properly from the authorities of the Department on duty among these Indians, I have generally responded advising them to that effect. You will remember you sent me to Florida last year to look after the Seminoles in the southern part of that State and that at the time my visit seemed to produce no favorable results. Since then I have been in correspondence with parties I became acquainted with at that time, who probably come more in contact with these Indians than any others, and I find that there is a growing interest which will soon develop into an opportunity to get hold of these people through the education of the children. A letter received from Captain Hendry, Fort Myer, Florida, within two or three days informs me of his success undertaking to educate one of the Seminole boys. There was a connection in their minds between their own interests and that part of the tribe who emigrated to the Territory and a desire to know about the welfare of those who had emigrated. I have kept parties there posted and have sent photographs of our school to them which have aroused quick interest.

It seems to me if we could have a few of the Indian Territory Seminoles and Creeks it would furnish a connecting link and a better opportunity for us to work up the welfare of these in Florida. There will be no trouble in securing children from these tribes. I write this, anticipating that those from the Territory who have written me will make application through their Agent as I have advised, and that the matter will come before you properly as it ought.

While writing to you I desire to speak of some matters connected with my recent visit to Wisconsin and Dakota. The whole system of Agency schools seems to languish and I judge that the schools at the Green Bay, La Pointe and Sisseton Agencies are as fair samples of Agency schools as we have. One of the most annoying difficulties at the Agency schools I find is the clothing. That purchased by the Department is miserably shoddy, very soon ragged and worn out. The boys with their trousers out at the knees and clothing held on by strings certainly cannot feel much of a tendency upward and I know from talking with the teachers that many of them are worn out and discouraged from this one difficulty. I have found Indians more sensitive to the pride of dress than many civilized people and it seems to me that true economy would favor the adoption of some more respectable and durable goods for clothing, especially for the boys.

At the Sisseton Agency I had more time and saw more of the workings of the system than at the other Agencies. I found that a very considerable number of the children were prevented from attending school by scrofulous and consumptive complaints, and that numbers died. One very intelligent Indian talking to me about his own children who were loathsomely affected by scrofula said that it seemed to him as though some great punishment were resting upon his people. Numbers of children who wanted to come here and [whose] parents wanted to send them, I could not accept because of scrofula.

I was shown through the school and present at meals and found that the only meat provided for the children was pork and bacon. I found also that that was the meat provided by the government for issue to the Indians at that Agency generally. I was then reminded of the statement made by one of our best army surgeons that if we wanted to kill the Indians off the best way was to feed them on pork and bacon. Certainly from all I saw at the Sisseton Agency the killing process is going on and I believe that it is in a great measure through these means.

It may be presumptuous in me to bring these matters before you, but they bear so heavily upon my mind that I feel I ought to. Something can and should be done to give new life and better health to the work at Agency schools.

With great respect,
Your obedient servant,
R. H. PRATT,
Lt. in Charge.

Indian Industrial School,
Carlisle Barracks,
January 13, 1881.

Hon. Thaddeus C. Pound,
    U. S. House of Representatives,
        Washington, D.C.

Dear Governor:

I wish you could get a delegation of the Indian Committees of Congress to come up and see our school before the session closes.

It seems to me that the educational question with the Indians just now is the vital point. Whether the Bill you proposed in the House and which has been so favorably reported upon twice by the Indian Committee, is best or not of course is for you to determine. It seems to me there can be no wiser use of the abandoned military posts and barracks than this and if the movement, which has been urged by the War Department for several years past to concentrate the army into posts of large command for purposes of economy, should be brought about, many more posts would be available for this purpose, in very many of which all needs for shelter and school purposes are satisfactory, without material additional expense and many of them have an abundance of arable land where agriculture can be taught. The use of these posts for a few years longer, before being sold, as is customary, would be no detriment to the government because the lands and property would be increased in value all the time.

There is no doubt but that a well directed effort for the education and training of all Indian youth of suitable age can be made successful and certainly nothing will tend more to save us from a large pauper and vagabond population. I know that Indian children of nomadic parents, properly trained, can be made self-supporting men and women. They can learn to speak the English language, they can take on a fair education, and be trained industrially in civilized pursuits, they can be made self-supporting and industrious, and I think these facts will be apparent to the members of Congress who may come to look at our work here.

The weakness of this effort and all other efforts to help the Indian up, is the leaving of such a large "pull down" element unhelped. By the treaties we have now in force with the Sioux, Cheyennes, Arapahoes, Kiowas, Comanches, Pawnees, Navajoes, Utes, Shoshones, Bannocks and some other tribes, they have a full and complete claim upon the government for educational privileges for *all* their children. If in the future we find our country burdened and troubled with these people it will be in a great measure due to our failure in carrying out our treaty stipulations with them in this regard. We have promised to give to all the children school privileges and they are now ready to receive them. Delays dishearten and discourage them. It is pressed upon me here continually that it would not be a difficult task to gather into school training all the children of these tribes. Partial effort invites partial failure. All educational work for the Indians is good; I believe that the system of removing them from their tribes and placing them under continuous training in the midst of civilization is far better than any other method. In an Indian school at an Agency the civilizing influences are limited to the instructors with perhaps a few examples of agency employees, with a tremendous pull against what they may do in the persons of the fathers and mothers and all the members of the tribe. In fact, such an effort might properly be called theoretical, while here, or removed from their tribes and placed in the midst of civilization, the teaching is all practical, all the surroundings help. The industrious farmer and mechanic is in sight daily. The evidence that man must obtain his living by the sweat of his brow is constantly before the children and it becomes an easy matter for them to join with the sentiment of the community in that direction. We had difficulty at first to get our boys and girls to work but now I am frequently asked by the students to be permitted to work more than our school regulations require. Boys esteemed too young to be put at trades frequent the shops, witness the productions of the older ones in harness making, tin ware, boots and shoes, clothing, blacksmith and wagon making, and they ask to be permitted to learn a trade. The few put out on farms during vacation are anxious to go back. One boy, who for the sake of health, I permitted to remain with a farmer over his time, has formed such a liking for farm work that he begs to be allowed to remain through the winter. The farmer finds him particularly useful in caring for the stock and doing the chores with his own boys, so that he is glad to have him remain. He goes to school with the farmer's children and thus being isolated he learns English rapidly. His health has improved very much. A girl that I had allowed to remain with a farmer for some time formed such an attachment for the place that she calls it home and cries to go back to learn to milk cows and bake pies and cakes. My purpose is during the coming summer vacation to plant out with the good farmers of this valley all the boys and girls whom we cannot use in the shops and upon our farm. I am sure that if we could bring to bear such training as this upon all our Indian children for only three years, that savagery among the Indians in this country would be at an end. This bringing their children east among the whites is to many of them now, and would be to all in time, an open door by which they can migrate into civilization. I can see by their correspondence and by what the parents say to me when visiting here that they appreciate most highly this privilege and desire to make use of it. The Cheyenne and Arapahoe chiefs when here, after understanding what I intended to do in the way of putting children out, all asked that their children be put out in this way. They want their children to see just how the white man lives. White Eagle, the Ponca chief who was here a few days ago, speaking for all the chiefs who were with him, approved in the strongest terms all that he saw. He said among other things that for a very long time it seemed as though the Great Spirit had forgotten all about the Indians but just now when he saw what privileges their children had, how fast they were learning in the school and how well they worked in the shops, he believed the Great Spirit was remembering the Indians and was now going to help them. Having all the affection of the most loving father for his boy, both of them crying and embracing each other warmly at parting, he as well as the other chiefs cheerfully left their children here and said they would send more if I would take them.

This effort is to these far-seeing leaders among the Indians evidence that they are to be permitted to become like the whites, that their declarations that they "want to travel upon the white man's road" are at last accepted. That in fact there is a hope that they may become citizens of this country and as such have the rights, privileges and protection granted to other citizens and that before this grave responsibility is thrust upon them they are to be in some measure provided and prepared for it by education and training in just exactly the same way that the white man is prepared for the same status; that is, by education and training their, and our youth together.

I invite your attention to the report of the Honorable Commissioner of Indian Affairs for 1880, pages VII and VIII where our work is mentioned by the Commissioner and to what is said upon education by the several Agents on pages 26, 45, 48, 59, 69, 75, 84, 117 and 134. These testimonies from the Agents of the tribes whose children are represented here ought to have great weight.

This system, which is so very new and necessarily imperfect, can be made to exert an influence upon the civilization of the Indians greater, to my mind, than it is possible to effect with the same expenditure in any other direction.

By every means that I have been able to bring to bear I have invited inspection and criticism and if you concur with me in the wisdom of a Congressional visit I would specially desire that those in Congress who are prejudiced and unbelievers should be of the party. I believe that a visit might be arranged so that by leaving Washington early you could spend four or five hours with us and return the same night. Could this be brought about?

Very respectfully yours,
R. H. PRATT,
Lieut.

Twenty-five years after this letter I met a number of pupils of this period at their homes and asked, "What feature of the Carlisle School helped you most," and all said, "The Outing."

Governor Pound asked to use the foregoing letter, and I wrote the following letter in reply:

Indian Industrial School,
Carlisle Barracks, Pa.,
January 21, 1881.

Dear Governor:

Do what you think best with my letters. If they will help push the work in any way I shall be glad. There is a well-developed public press sentiment in favor of education for the Indian and I am sure we have spurred on the Presbyterian memorialists and others. Old Dr. Riggs came here on his way to Washington to meet the Commissioner and then returned and spent Sunday with us.[6] He was an enemy. Said we were "too far away," "too far south," etc., for the Sioux. Was sensitive about removal from Agencies. He was thoroughly captured before he left. I gave him a big meeting in town, where he came out grandly, acknowledged his previous prejudice, and said he was cured. I invited him to come and be our Chaplain here for the few months he is required to be east to oversee publications. He said he would. Now, if Congress will only push matters a little, things will grow rapidly. I have felt that we are a healthy criticism upon the years of religious failure [i. e. of the missionaries]. May be we can wake them up.

I wrote President Taylor of Wooster, Ohio, University for his experience in Indian work to use and today received the enclosed reply. [See below.]

6. With his wife Mary, Stephen Return Riggs (1812–83) went among the Sioux of the upper Mississippi in 1837 and dedicated the rest of his life to missionary work among them. His assignment by the American Board of Commissioners for Foreign Missions had been based largely on his aptitude for linguistics, and throughout the years he produced a notable series of publications in and on the Sioux language. The labors on which he was engaged when Pratt became acquainted with him were not finally published until after his death—"Dakota-English Dictionary" in *Contributions to North American Ethnology*, 7 (1890), and "Dakota Grammar Texts and Ethnography" ibid., 9 (1893). An autobiography, *Mary and I: Forty Years with the Sioux*, appeared in 1880. *Dictionary of American Biography*, 15, 605–06.

If General Garfield's administration does not end our Indian troubles almost entirely, it will omit a chance to make good, that will never come to but this one administration. The present administration has only prepared the way. Inside of two years from this date nearly every Indian child of school age can be put under educational training, and training in industry can be given to very many through agriculture. The whole fifty thousand children in school is a leverage to settle the Indian question that is worth all the other schemes put together. Then will come the "know how" for "citizenship" and "law" and "lands in severalty." Before education is given, these other schemes are "pearls before swine."

Yours respectfully and faithfully,
R. H. PRATT.

Hon. Thad. C. Pound,
   House of Representatives.

(Enclosure)

The following letter from the President of Wooster University, replying to our inquiries as to progress and capacity of the Creek Indian students at that institution, is conclusive testimony in favor of the broadest opportunities for Indian youth.

Wooster University, January 19th, 1881.

My dear Sir:

We have had four or five Indian students from the Creek Nation with us for the last five years, three having left meanwhile with others taking their places. They were all from schools in the Nation where they have been trained some years before coming here. With but one exception they have been quite as bright as the average white students who have had no more opportunities than they have enjoyed. Some of them are very bright and able to think deeply. They are quiet and very studious, giving us never the least trouble. One or two of them have had great taste for mathematics, while one took the latin prize in the 3rd preparatory year, in a class of over 60 who were entering Freshmen. We see no difference and make no distinction between them and others. So far as we have had experience we have every confidence in their ability to acquire an education as well as any other human beings. In my judgment their education and that alone, will solve the problem of the future preservation of the tribes from obliteration and the elevation of their people to the position of useful members of society. To make them educated, Christianized citizens, will solve the Indian problem, and I cannot see what else would do the same.

Yours truly,
A. A. E. TAYLOR.

Indian Industrial School,
Carlisle Barracks, Pa.,
March 24, 1881.

Hon. H. L. Dawes,
    Chairman, Committee on Indian Affairs,
        U. S. Senate,
            Washington, D.C.

Dear Sir:

There is so much pressure through applications to take more children here from the different Indian Agencies that it seems to me extremely necessary to enlarge this kind of work by the establishment of more schools. Certainly the tide has now set in the direction of education so far as the Indians are concerned and it seems criminal not to fully meet it. The applications for us to take children here cover thousands and this leverage for good on the uncivilized tribes who make these applications is to my mind greater than any other means. As this is purely a governmental work under the direction of the Department and in the interests of a people having treaty promises from the government for help in education, it seems consistent for me to say that it should meet your consideration upon its merits as such.

I am here under the authority and by the act of Congress and have committed to my charge two hundred and eighty-six children from twenty-three different tribes. As having a bearing on what might be done for all Indian children I am sure it will be esteemed worthy the attention of Senators to witness the mechanical and other industrial skill of our pupils, as well as the progress Indian children can make in education and the use of English when placed under favorable circumstances.

I do wish the subject could be looked into and thoroughly understood by your committee, not in the interests of anything we need at this school, but in the interests of the whole Indian work. Would it not be possible for you to visit us with the members of the Indian Committee and such others as you like and to give this matter your attention from the standpoint of a personal inspection?

Very respectfully,
Your obedient servant,
R. H. PRATT,
Lieut. in Charge.

United States Senate Chamber,
Washington, 31st March, 1881.

Lieut. R. H. Pratt,
My dear Sir:

I thank you for your very interesting letter of the 24th. I take great interest in the success of your undertaking and have watched it from the beginning at Hampton. I wish for it all the success which your endeavor deserves and certainly I could not wish you more. I hope the Indian Committee of the Senate will take interest enough in the work to visit your institution during the regular session of Congress, and I think they will; but at this session we can do nothing but executive business, and it is impossible to awaken interest in other matters.

I have had some doubts about which I would like to know your views, I do not wish to limit the operation of your school or that at Hampton, but desire to extend them to the utmost limit of permanent usefulness. This is my trouble. We cannot take all the Indian children away from the tribes to educate them in such schools as yours. Why would it not be better to attempt their general education among the tribes themselves on the ground where they are to live, and employ such as you educate for that work, opening schools of practical industry in every tribe and employing the educated of that tribe as teachers. I want to see every Indian child taught at least this much—first to work; next, to know that what he earns is his. That nobody can take it away from him, and that he has a permanent abiding place because he has earned it and not because somebody promises him that he shall have it. After that I would push the education of the young Indians as far as I could; but I am impatient that every young Indian of the present generation should have implanted in him so much that makes up a man as I have indicated.

Now I wish you could write to me and tell me what you think of these notions.

Truly yours,
H. L. DAWES.

Indian Industrial School,
Carlisle Barracks, Pa.,
April 4, 1881.

Hon. H. L. Dawes,
    U. S. Senate,
Dear Sir:

Allow me to express my gratitude for your interest in these school matters for they will solve the question and nothing else will. Would it not be possible for you yourself to visit us before or just after the close of the special session, as it seems impossible to get the Committee. From your interest in the work and the probability that during the recess of Congress you will think upon and discuss the subject more or less, it seems to me very desirable that you should know and consider us from personal observation.

You say "we cannot take all the Indian children away from the tribes to educate them in such schools as yours. Why would it not be better to attempt their general education among the tribes themselves on the ground where they are to live and employ such as you educate for that work, opening schools of practical industry and employing the educated of that tribe as teachers?"

I agree with you that it is not practicable to take all Indian children away from the tribes to educate them nor would it be wise to do so, for not all Indian children have sufficient capacity to justify the outlay. There should be now on the reservations together with those off, a large enough number of industrial boarding schools to provide for *all* Indian children. From the Agency schools judicious teachers will readily determine what children are worthy of increased advantages away. There is to my mind not the slightest fear that the work will be overdone. Though you should establish schools like Carlisle sufficient to accommodate three or four or even five thousand children this would be so small a proportion of the whole number of Indian children that Agency schools would still find themselves loaded with the responsibility of educating the great mass. Day schools on the reserves are generally impracticable and a positive injury, because they beget expectations of quick and large development that cannot be realized. But there could be a system of industrial boarding schools on the reservations from which the most competent should be taken for final training in the schools in the midst of civilization. This would enable the whole work to go forward harmoniously and to the greatest advantage and the hope of going away to school furnish a healthy incentive to pupils of the Agency schools. The problem to me seems not how it is done but to get it done at all. Whenever those in whom is vested the power to accomplish it determine that the work shall be done and shall apply the necessary means and forces to do it, the best plan of doing it will develop itself very quickly in the light of experience, if the best plan is not then considered to be already developed.

The question of using graduates from this school and Hampton for the industrial and literary work of the Agency schools is one for the future to decide. It takes years of training under the best facilities and opportunities to make a good mechanic, farmer or teacher of a bright white boy or girl, and it will be even more necessary to give to Indian boys and girls the same environment and opportunities and long and thorough training if we wish them to become competent to instruct in these different spheres.

I suppose the end to be gained, however far away it may be, is the complete civilization of the Indian and his absorption into our national life, with all the rights and privileges guaranteed to every other individual, the Indian to lose his identity as such, to give up his tribal relations and to be made to feel that he is an American citizen. If I am correct in this supposition, then the sooner all tribal relations are broken up; the sooner the Indian loses all his Indian ways, even his language, the better it will be for him and for the government and the greater will be the economy to both.

Now, I do not believe that amongst his people an Indian can be made to feel all the advantages of a civilized life, nor the manhood of supporting himself and of standing out alone and battling for life as an American citizen. To accomplish that, his removal and personal isolation is necessary. One year in the midst of a civilized community where, whichever way he may turn he can see the industrious farmer plowing his fields or reaping his grain, and the industrious mechanic building houses or engaged in other manufactures, with all the realities of wealth and happiness which these efforts bring to the farmer and mechanic is worth more as a means of implanting such aspirations as these you desire for him in his mind than ten years, nay, than a whole lifetime of camp surroundings with the best Agency school work that can be done. If this year is spent in taking hold with the farmer and with the mechanic and by actual daily experience the effects of industrious civilized life grow in, so much the better. If the proper system of education is adopted and it is made general, lands in severalty and citizenship will be a natural result, and the Indians themselves demanding it, and just this spirit which you propose and which can be implanted in Indian children is a necessary part of that education. It will take plenty of good patient workers to do that.

I think you are wrong to place the education after that as you seem to by saying "after that I would push their education as far as I could." Both should go forward together. To end our Indian troubles the Indian must have intelligence enough to manage himself and his own affairs, and be able to do that in competition with his white neighbor. It would be kindness to him to give him education and industrial training and let him begin without lands. This, I believe, you intimate when you say, "first to work, next to know that what he earns is his."

I hope I may have the privilege of meeting you soon and understanding what your Committee in Congress may be disposed to do in these matters.

It is encouraging to us to know that we are working in the line approved by you, and certainly all that we do should be but carrying out the wishes of Congress, who ought to dictate the whole plan.

As you are at the head of the Indian Committee, I take the liberty of sending you a set of our school photographs.

> With great respect,
> Your obedient servant,
> R. H. PRATT,
> Lieut. in charge.

23. Self-evident Truths

If enforced, the Declaration of Independence and the Constitution of the United States, as they read, amply provide the complete and economical cure for our every Indian trouble. I therefore at once took them to be the guides. To successfully accomplish the Americanization of the millions of immigrants we invite to membership in our national family, we give them individual welcome to citizenship and through compelling participation in our affairs absorb them. Our 300,000 Indians, because native, should always have had a preferred welcome as subjects for this common-sense method. It is self-evident that the greatest glory to government and highest beneficence to the Indian was to be achieved in at once transforming him into a capable, co-ordinated citizen, able as such to live and thrive among us without special control over him and his property. When the Declaration announced, "We hold these truths to be self-evident, that all men are created equal; that they are endowed by their Creator with certain inalienable rights; that among these are life, liberty and the pursuit of happiness," it meant nothing unless it included the native Indian even more than the foreign immigrant. Inasmuch as all the Indian's former vast game resources had been destroyed by our people, and his free roving life ended through our wresting from him his immense regions, his place and needs were preeminently a righteous burden on us, in which the integrity of enforcing our national principles was being tested.

Looking into the future, it was inevitable that the Indian, in order to hold on to "life, liberty and the pursuit of happiness," must adopt all the abundant resources the white man found and had developed within his ancient habitations. To do this successfully, the Indian, no less than foreigners, must be unified with and adopted into the nation. It was useless to even hope that, through the wicked devices of imprisoning on reservations, his tribal organizations could be successfully promoted and the resources for a new way of independent tribal living be engrafted on his small groups. Contiguity compels competition. The Indians could only come to compete and prosper as "self-determining" peoples through equality of intelligence, and this, if tribal autonomy were to be preserved, demanded the creation of vernacular systems of education for each of their more than 100 different languages, which was impracticable. By a long and wide experience I knew that the Indian himself saw the inevitable and desired the change from aboriginal to civilized life. His often-expressed desire in his councils, to "get on the white man's road," showed that he knew, if we did not, that he had all the possibilities of other men. He saw, though we did not, that this was the only way to tranquilize our differences.

Going forward from the Declaration to the Constitution, I read, "Article XIV, Section 1. All persons born or naturalized in the United States and subject to the jurisdiction thereof are citizens of the United States and of the State wherein they reside. No State shall make or enforce any law which shall abridge the privileges or immunities of the citizens of the United States; nor shall any State deprive any person of life, liberty or property without due process of law, nor deny to any person within its jurisdiction equal protection of the laws." I presumed that this also meant just what it said, and that because it was a part of the Constitution it was the highest law of the land. All our Indians were "born in the United States," and the facts showed that, most imperiously, the Indian, both in his person and property, was under "United States jurisdiction," which through shrewd manipulation had become a degrading surveillance. It was equally plain that denying the Indian all citizen rights to quickly develop his powers under the high influences and examples of American environment is the great aim of our self-perpetuating Indian system.[1]

1. The framers of the Constitution clearly regarded the Indian tribes as a special class of persons with whom the Federal Government would continue to deal, as had the colonial powers be-

Both our Indian administration and our religious forces, by their every word and act in control, have always said to the Indians: stay on your reservations, stick together as tribes, and we will bring to you all we think best for you.

I was in Washington getting acquainted with the subordinate Bureau people who wrote the authorizations doling the money the Government gave for Carlisle. In talking with the chief of this division and pressing my views of the principles which should govern in order to promote useful independent citizenship for Indians, the division chief said: "I have been in this Bureau thirty-four years. If you succeed my occupation is gone." I replied: "You are mistaken. If you will get out of your Bureau reservation into the same lines of work you have here your fine ability will command a much larger salary than you now receive." His reply was, "I have been here so long I am handicapped for anything else." So he remained and passed from the Indian Bureau to his final reward.

One of the most noted missionaries to one of our largest tribes, whose parents were missionaries and he therefore born to the idea of holding the Indians together as tribes, wrote a four-column article for our leading educational journal opposing the Carlisle aim of giving the Indians citizenship ability through citizen environment, opportunities, and rights.

To the segregating methods of these Bureau-perpetuating and church-enlarging people the country is indebted for the long-drawn-out and dependent conditions of the Indians. They are therefore morally responsible for the forced delay in accomplishing the useful citizenship of the Indians and for the vast expenditure and needless waste of government and charity money that their misdirection has brought about.

If we had adopted the segregating Indian system for each language group of immigrants and held them in racial communities on reservations remote

---

fore the Revolution, as independent nations. The contradictions inherent in defining and regulating relations through the vehicle of treaties between the Federal Government and the tribes constantly intruded itself on executive, legislative, and judicial authorities. Despite John Marshall's apt definition in 1831 of the tribes as "domestic dependent nations," the Supreme Court a year later reaffirmed the independent status of the tribes. (Cherokee Nation vs. Georgia, 5 Pet. 1, 8 L. Ed. 25 [1831] and Worcester vs. Georgia, 6 Pet. 515, 8 L. Ed. 483 [1832].) Even after the House of Representatives forced the abolition of the Indian treaty system in 1871 (Revised Statutes, Sec. 2079), the fiction of independence was partly maintained through the early reservation decades by means of "agreements" that were treaties in all but name. Taking up the question of individual Indian citizenship in 1884, the Supreme Court pointed out that, although Indians might and had in fact become citizens by complying with the provisions of certain treaties and acts of Congress, the Constitution did not confer citizenship on every Indian; and in this case the Court decided, moreover, that the Fourteenth Amendment did not confer such blanket citizenship either. (Elk vs. Wilkins, 112 U. S. 94, 5 S. Ct. 41, 28 L. Ed. 643 [1884].) Finally in 1924 Congress resolved the issue by enacting "that all non-citizen Indians born within the territorial limits of the United States be, and they are hereby, declared to be citizens of the United States."

from the environment of our American life, it would have just as effectually prevented their Americanization.

We have unlimited proof that Americanization is easily accomplished for hundreds of thousands of diverse-language immigrants yearly, and also ample evidence that it can just as readily be accomplished for our few Indians, but the evidence also proves that it can only come through giving the competitive opportunities of participating in the environment of America. The recipients must prove through apprenticeship and productivity in our great Americanizing workshop that they can fit in and become valuable as a very part of the general population. In no other way can they secure these benefits; in no other way can we be released from the expense their inefficiency entails.

The unfortunate words of the Constitution, "excluding Indians not taxed," so successfully used to withhold all Indians and their property from taxation, makes them the one exceptional class and is a perpetual bribe to them to remain tribal. It has been insidiously utilized as a propaganda among them and a persuader against citizenship throughout all our management, increasing in power as their property values grew. The companion invention of segregating on tribal reservations just as supremely and logically both bribes and forces them to remain tribal and eliminates individual initiative.

The great powers of schools, especially when located among the Indians and administratively utilized to that end, have easily become potential racial and tribal promoters of cohesion. The supreme Bureau control through advising and commanding government appropriations has further established itself by issuing unearned food and alleged helps of many sorts. After the destruction of the buffalo, the Bureau schemes inaugurated for giving the tribes herds of high-bred cattle and flocks of sheep; for the gratuitous issue of cattle and sheep to individual Indians; for the gift to them of high-bred males to improve their horses and other stock; for giving agricultural implements; for the distribution of reimbursable loan of millions of dollars of Bureau-solicited and Congress-appropriated government money among influential Indians bearing no interest, much of the principal never to be returned; for the promoting of tribal irrigation and alleged conservation schemes; for the selection and appointment of Bureau-paid lawyers for Indians in legal emergencies; for the selection and appointment of percentage-paid white guardians over the incomes and properties of not only minors but of grown and advanced-in-years Indian men and women—all these have insidiously destroyed, instead of builded aspiration among the Indians for citizenship. These contrivances were as plainly and as completely bribing the Indians to remain segregated tribally and racially under Bureau control as any bribery ever resorted to in the history of the world. The same course would just as effectively have undermined the manhood of the people of our own or any other race.

The management of the vast affairs of the Indians, their properties and schools, and of the employee forces in control of the Indians, has long been a political plum. Each change of administration brought reward for political service by change in the head of the Bureau, but made little change in the thousands of Bureau subordinates. As these subordinates *are* the Bureau and are on the job continuously, entrenched by Civil Service laws and the skill of experience at the headquarters of the government, and as the new heads are almost universally purposeless because weak in experience and knowledge of their job, it is easy for the perpetual Bureau to lobby new Congresses and new administrations into continuing the Bureau system. The permanent Bureau personnel only needs to kow-tow just a little to each new administration to easily carry forward from one administration to another and thus deeper indurate its system.

Fuller facts about the other cooperating and equally segregating influence bearing upon the destiny of the Indians from the very earliest days of Anglo-Saxon occupancy in America should be told. In some of the settlements there was a plain intention to recognize that the Indians belonged to the brotherhood of mankind.

In 1633 Massachusetts enacted: "For settling the Indian title to lands in this jurisdiction it is declared and ordered by this Court and authority thereof, that all the lands any of the Indians in this jurisdiction have improved by subduing the same, they have a just right unto, according to that in Gen. I, 28, and Chapter IX, I, and Psalms CXV and 16, and for the civilizing and helping them forward to Christianity, if any of the Indians shall be brought to civility and shall come among the English and shall inhabit their plantations and shall there live civilly and orderly, that such Indians shall have allotments among the English, according to the custom of the English in like cases." (Laws of Massachusetts, Edition of 1672, p. 74.)

This indicated the seed of the Declaration of Independence and the American Constitution and plainly invited the absorption of the Indians. The main opposition to this program was the church. At the same time and in the same community a noted missionary to the Indians encouraged and provided for the Indians to live separate from the colonists under his overlording. He spent many years in translating the Bible into one of the several and entirely separate languages within his jurisdiction, was supported by the church at large, and zealously and even abstemiously gave himself up to his purposes. He never seemed to comprehend that his Bible would be of no use to the Indians unless a system was arranged and the Indians had the accompanying education in their own vernacular which would enable them to read it. The creation of his Bible was clearly wasted time, energy, and money. It was never effective. He seems to have never realized that education in the language he spoke opened to them not only the Bible but the archives of the world's knowledge. Contrary to the teaching and example of his Master, he used his opportunities to build alienation instead of brotherhood between the races. Using religion as a racial separating wall became perpetual purposes in missionary enterprises and a leading influence in establishing the segregating, reservating government system.

To overcome these conditions and conduct the Indian into civilized environment and open a way to his rightful place as a co-equal man and fellow citizen, Carlisle labored from the very start. The location of the school, where there were fullest opportunities for Indian youth to see the best activities of our American life and participate in them, and where the broadest observation by our own people was easily had to convince both the white man and the red that neither was as bad as the other thought, was Carlisle's great aim. Every facility to help its students to see and participate, and thus come to fully know, accept, and enjoy our civilization was utilized. Every report, speech, and publication Carlisle was able to put out was made to present these facts to administrative and legislative heads and to the public.

Many distinguished people visited the school from the beginning, and the retained files of correspondence contain many letters from foremost officials and citizens showing warmest interest. A most distinguished party came five months after the school began, on the 21st of February, 1880, led by the Hon. Carl Schurz, Secretary of the Interior. It included other government officials, among them the chairman of the House Indian Committee and most of his committee, one of whom was our special friend Governor Pound. Some of these gentlemen were accompanied by their wives, and the party contained a number of well-known newspaper reporters. After the party had inspected all the departments of the school, the children were assembled in the chapel, where they were addressed by Secretary Schurz and others, giving most encouraging expressions of interest and appreciation.[2]

. . . .

2. Omitted here is Pratt's second annual report, for which see Commissioner of Indian Affairs, *Annual Report* (1881), pp. 184–94.

24. *Progress in the School and in Public Sentiment*

The industrial work at the school was under the supervision of the assistant superintendent, Mr. Standing. One of the boys, about fourteen years old, had offended, and Mr. Standing put him at work for an indefinite period feeding the pigs morning and evening. A large barrel containing the slop had been hung on hooks between the wheels of a push cart. The pig pens were several hundred yards away from the kitchen back of the old cavalry stables. Pushing the swill barrel cart from kitchen to hog pen, emptying the contents into the troughs, and returning the barrel to the kitchen was his job. After a couple of weeks at this service, I received the following note:

> Captain Pratt:
>   I want another trade. I have learned the pig trade.
>
> (signed) _____.

The human nature of the Indian was abundantly apparent daily. Miss Mary R. Hyde, the matron in charge of the girls, was a woman of great poise, and at the beginning, in addition to her large duties, she played the piano and led the singing for the school assemblies. Maggie Stands Looking, a daughter of American Horse, a chief of the Red Cloud Sioux, had neglected her room and Miss Hyde took her up, showed her what was wrong, and told her that she must attend to it and do that every morning. Maggie, who was mature and exceptionally large and strong, stood looking at her for a moment, Miss Hyde looking at Maggie. Then Maggie deliberately slapped Miss Hyde in the face. Miss Hyde made no effort to resist, but just continued to look at Maggie for a moment, and then said, "Why, Maggie!" Maggie, evidently anticipating a return slap and a chance to show her physical qualities, looked at Miss Hyde for a little while, without saying anything, and then threw her arms around Miss Hyde's neck, laid her head on her shoulders, and cried bitterly. Miss Hyde quietly let her have her cry out, and then said, "Maggie, you will keep your room in better order, won't you?" From that time forward Maggie was one of the model girls of the school.

Maggie went out to one of our good country homes during the year 1881, and two weeks later she wrote the following:

Dear Captain Pratt:
What shall I do? I have been here two weeks and I have not bathe. These folks have no bathe place.
Your school daughter,
MAGGIE STANDS LOOKING

This was my reply:

Dear Maggie:
When I was a boy on my grandfather's farm there was no "bathe place." It was a log house and two of us boys slept in the attic, to which we had to climb by a ladder through an opening left for that purpose. We washed out the wash tub, then carried it and several buckets of water up the ladder and had fine baths.
Many times in my travels I have been in frontier hotels having no bath tubs, and by filling the large wash bowl with water and taking one of the towels for a wash cloth and rubbing my body well, have had a bath that made me feel as good as jumping into a river.
Your friend and school father,
R. H. PRATT.

After her three years at Carlisle away from camp life, with no knowledge of English to begin with, Maggie returned to her people and was, under the Bureau program, made teacher and head of a reservation day school. She became the wife of the chief of the Indian police. Part of her husband's duty was to see that the pupils were prompt and regular in attendance. There were other of the returned students placed in charge of day schools. It came to me that Maggie's school was distinctive in the regularity and promptness of attendance, in its discipline, and the cleanliness of the pupils.

The progress of the school and the appreciation of the public went hand in hand. There were many illustrations of the growth of public sentiment. Among the strongest was the persistent action of the great Presbyterian Church, whose first memorial we gave in a former chapter. After presenting that memorial to the administrative and legislative heads of the Government, the next General Assembly concluded to emphasize its purpose and present another the following year. The committee to formulate and present the second memorial was increased from seven to eleven, and I became one of the additional members. The duty of writing the memorial for the committee was entrusted to Dr. Stephen R. Riggs, the devoted life-long missionary to the Sioux Indians; Dr. Sheldon Jackson, then in charge of Presbyterian missions among the Indians in the central West, and afterwards for many years the United States Commissioner of Education for Alaska; Dr. Byron Sunderland, a distinguished pastor of Washington, D.C.; and myself.

Dr. Riggs was then revising his dictionary of the Dakota (Sioux) language, which was to be reissued by one of the government departments, and he desired to be in or near Washington to oversee its publication. I received the verbal consent of the Secretary of the Interior, and upon my solicitation, during his service with the dictionary, the doctor became the chaplain of the school. Mrs. Pratt and I invited him with his wife and daughter to be our guests in order that we might be more together for interchange of ideas. Dr. Jackson had brought students from New Mexico and other parts of his territory to Carlisle. He was the brother of Mrs. Norcross, wife of the pastor of the Second Presbyterian Church at Carlisle. Dr. Jackson was strongly in sympathy with the Carlisle movement, realizing by observation and experience the vast benefits it would be to the Indian peoples if carried out on a sufficiently large scale. Dr. Sunderland, being in Washington and observing things from that standpoint, had ideas which were best expressed by his statement that he would build a wall as high as the sky around every Indian reservation to keep from the Indian and his affairs all other supervision and allow only the missionaries full opportunity to transform the Indian from his aboriginal life and habits into civilization.

After discussion and correspondence, we concluded the memorial, and it was accepted by the general committee, which then went in a body, read it, and by speeches from different members presented it to the President, the Secretary of the Interior, the Commissioner of Indian Affairs, and to the

Committees on Indian Affairs of the Senate and the House of Representatives. The memorial committee found Governor Wright in Washington and invited him to help in the speaking. He was one of the ablest speakers. Governor Wright was a Choctaw Indian, a university graduate, and long a power in the five civilized tribes.[1]

. . . .

This further appeal for change in the purposes and methods of Indian management did not have the salutary influence we anticipated simply because the indurated Bureau system, through its many avenues and Washington advantages, was continually on its job and influenced contrary to our urgings daily, while the committee and its large backing in the church was scattered all over the country and had to rest its efforts entirely on what the memorial committee had done.

After President Garfield's death, Mr. Arthur, the Vice President, became President. A change was made in the office of Secretary of the Interior from Governor Kirkwood of Iowa, who was thoroughly in sympathy with our purposes, because influenced by President Garfield, and having accepted the conclusions of his predecessor, Secretary Schurz, who was the large influence in establishing the Carlisle School. Senator Henry M. Teller of Colorado became the Secretary.[2] Being from the West, I was apprehensive, especially because the feeling against the Indians in the state of Colorado had been exceptionally antagonistic. After several visits to Washington and interviews with President Arthur and Secretary Teller, I soon felt that they were both on our side. Mr. Teller, with his wife, visited Carlisle, staying long enough to look things over and to talk freely, and when I visited Washington he in-

1. Miss Muriel Wright, editor of *The Chronicles of Oklahoma*, supplies the following sketch of her illustrious Choctaw grandfather Allen Wright: "He was born in 1826 in Mississippi and died in 1885 at Boggy Depot, Choctaw Nation—now southeastern Oklahoma. Left an orphan shortly after the Indian Removal from Mississippi, the lad attended the mission schools and Spencer Academy for Choctaw boys. Selected in 1848 to attend an eastern college, he was graduated from Union College at Schenectady, N.Y., in 1852 and completed study for the ministry at Union Theological Seminary in New York City in 1855. Returning to his people in Indian Territory, he held many positions of trust and served as principal chief of the Choctaw Nation from 1866 to 1870. He was a dedicated missionary to his people, minister of the gospel, translator and writer, and preeminently the scholar of the Choctaws until his death."

The memorial described by Pratt, here omitted, was dated Jan. 12, 1882. Like its predecessor (p. 255, note 5), it called upon the Government to foster land allotment, extension of law to Indians, and expansion of the educational programs. In this document, however, the memorialists placed greater emphasis on the need for education.

2. Henry Moore Teller (1830–1914) was a leader in Colorado political affairs and a prominent corporation lawyer before his election to the United States Senate when Colorado became a state in 1876. He served as President Arthur's Secretary of the Interior from 1882 to 1885, then re-entered the Senate for four more terms, the third as an Independent Silver Republican and the fourth as a Democrat. *Dictionary of American Biography, 18*, 362–63.

vited me to become a guest in his home; Mrs. Pratt and I went down at one time and spent a week in Washington as their guests. Having been a Senator, he was in a position to carry large weight with Congress, and throughout his whole administration of the affairs of the Interior Department he showed broad intentions to uplift the Indian peoples, so that the adverse Bureau influences were temporarily more or less ineffective. I could always present any case with utmost freedom to Mr. Teller.

During one of the several visits of Mr. Teller to Carlisle he was present at our Sunday evening meeting. The children were encouraged to speak, and to give passages of scripture they had learned. One of the Indian boys got up to say something, and stood a little while, evidently being confused and forgetting what he intended to say. He finally said, "If a man won't work, he shan't eat," and sat down. This pleased Mr. Teller. I was sitting by him and he said, "The quotation is incorrect, but the gist of it is all there." He then gave the school a talk based on that text, assuring the students that wherever they were, whatever they had to do in life, if they followed that text they would be sure to reach success.

Mr. Teller, following Mr. Schurz' example, was interested in having the leading chiefs and Indians who visited Washington about their tribal affairs stop at Carlisle too, either going or returning. This had a wonderful effect on them and the pupils as well. The school records contain many expressions from the chiefs in the talks we always urged them to give to their own and the children from the other tribes. They always spoke through the interpreter. The following, from one delegation as reported in our school paper, illustrates many such speeches:

Kushiway (Sac and Fox)

My Brothers and Sisters:

I am glad that we have met together tonight. Your parents have done something that is wonderful to send you here to be educated. Now we look back; our old parents did not know anything; that time is all passed away. I am a man, but I begin to see something that is better than the old men used to see. We know it is good for you children to be here among the white people. There is only one tribe that knows much; that are like the white people—that is the Cherokees. They have men today equal to the Great Father; they are educated, they are wise. We other Indians belonging to the different tribes are blind. Today we just come back from the headquarters, and here we are tonight. While we were there at the headquarters we could not do anything; we were like blind men; we could not help ourselves, because we were not educated. Now, my young friends, that is the reason why I feel pleasure in seeing you receive these benefits. So when you become men you can go ahead and talk to the Great Father just as you think is best. We who are grown will soon die off and leave you young people, but you will know something—know how to work for yourselves.

I have a son here—not my son, but step-son. He got up here and made his little speech. I am glad; I am more than glad to hear that young man make his speech. We do not know anything at all. We came to Washington; we went all over the ground trying to do something, but we did not know how to do much. We want you children to get education, then you can do something. I see you all learning here and I feel like sending some more children, but the rest are too small. I wish they were big enough so I could send them. Children, you must try to do the best you can for yourselves in every way. We have the Great Spirit above looking down on us and we must try to do right.

Kihega (Sac and Fox)

All the children from the different tribes: It was the Great Spirit made us meet today. What you know today you do not know yourselves; the Great Spirit gave you that. A while back our people were not this way. We used to fight one another, and kill one another off. Here are the old people sitting right here that used to follow that. Now they have turned their arms away. There are a good many different tribes here, and you all shake hands though you are different. Here are people, too, trying to teach you. You must try to learn and when you come back your people will be glad to see you, for what you learn will be a benefit to them.

Moless (Sac and Fox)

Young Men and My Sisters:

You all look at me! I am old. I was myself sent to school once, but I only went to school two years. Young men, it is a good idea for your parents to place you here, so you may grow to be men. I never bloodied my hands from my white brothers. My tribe is the Missouri Sacs. I am thankful to shake hands with the white man at any time. That is one reason why I put my son here; but it is the will of the Great Spirit, and I do not feel grieved about it. The reason I sent my son to school I thought I would make a man of him.

During this year, three years after it was first introduced into Congress, Governor Pound's bill passed both the House and Senate, showing that Congress itself had finally come to consider nonreservation schools worthy of its support.[3]

.   .   .   .

During the school year 1882, Philadelphia had its great bicentennial exposition for which there was organized one of the most wonderful parades in all history. This parade covered miles and gave illustrations of the progress of the country. The Carlisle School was invited to participate with floats and marching by its cadet corps, headed by its band, and preceded by a mounted party of twenty painted and war-bonneted Indians brought in from western tribes. The managers of the parade gave me command of the educational division and placed Carlisle at the head of that division. The authorities of the Pennsylvania Railroad gave the school transportation from Carlisle to Philadelphia and return, but our seven floats, illustrating Penn's treaty and our mechanical and school work, had to travel the 120 miles by horse teams. It was a proud day when we marched and countermarched for hours through Broad Street in the presence of two million onlookers.[4]

.   .   .   .

The school paper contains a number of sentiments from different students in regard to their experiences and observations at the bicentennial. The following is an extract from the letter to his home of one of our Creek boys: "While we were away we saw many wonderful things, large buildings. When I saw them I couldn't help but to say to myself, 'Shall the Indians some day be able to build such buildings? Can they learn?' Then I said, 'Yes, they can learn, but as long as they are together all the time on reservations they never will be able but if they go out among the white people and work with them and learn there may be some hope.' "

We returned quite a number of students to reservations where they were used in the agency service. In the same paper I find this from one of our largest Sioux:

> Amos, one of our Dakota boys, who became quite skilled in wagon-making during his three years' stay at the school, writes from Pine Ridge to a friend here: "I have work to do all days and so now I fixed many wagons, and every day Indian men come to see me and say, 'Amos my wagon you fix for me will you please if you can.' Every day Indian man

3. At this point in his narrative Pratt introduces the text of Representative Pound's bill as enacted into law, together with lengthy extracts from the speeches of congressmen in behalf of the legislation. This is omitted here. The act authorized the Secretary of War to turn over unoccupied military installations to the Secretary of the Interior for use as Indian schools and to detail one or more army officers for duty at such schools.

4. Omitted at this point is a long account from the Carlisle School paper giving the details of the students' participation in the festivities at Philadelphia.

said to me. So I make quick and well done, another one I take and fix all the time his wagon. I will do it every day, and did not get tired and very well it is my arms have work to do.

"Three things I am glad to tell you, Roger is cooking one month, Paul is making stove pipe joints 1550, Baldwin is cut hay four weeks and Guy worked two months."

And the following from one of the girls:

One of our girls who has gone home and is employed in a mission school writes, "I got very nice present from one of the school boys it is a silk handkerchief and a pocket knife. I like it very much. He gave me them because I iron his shirt and collars last Saturday. He said, 'O my! I didn't expected iron that good.' I laughed and said, 'Didn't you knew I am one of the Carlisle girls?' "

25. Propaganda

It required no special gumption on my part to see failure in the enforcement of the doctrine that three years of school was enough education for Indian youth, any more than it would require gumption to show that a limit of three years of school meant failure in the education of the youth of any people. Notwithstanding this, it seemed impossible to get my superiors to include that idea in their consideration of what was necessary for the Indians in order to reach competitive ability for civilized life.

It takes eight years for the child of civilized parents to pass through our system of education to the end of the grammar grade. But by the administrative purposes, Indian children beginning without any knowledge of English were to receive but three-eighths of what the white child must receive to reach the beginning of the high school grade, and this was then only about one-half of what the white child was expected to have in order to fit himself for any high duties of civilized life. Indian children, equipped with only three-eighths of the white child's primary education, were to be returned to their reservations under the delusive theory that they would then be able to civilize their parents and people. The folly of such expectation needs no comment. I argued with my superiors against this and urged that the Indian youth had the same rights to the same fullest opportunities to come into and remain in the same American environment which we so freely open to immigrants from other lands.

The slogan early adopted at Carlisle was: "To civilize the Indian, get him into civilization. To keep him civilized, let him stay."

I was able to prove at this early date in the school's history that three years in properly conducted non-reservation Indian schools was sufficient to make Indian youth acceptable in our public schools, and the way would then be open for them, and they be able to pay for their further education by their labor out of school hours, even to include college and university equipment. Carlisle School demonstrated this fact continuously and kept it before the public through hundreds of experiences, by forwarding its pupils into the public schools and higher educational institutions.

The intelligent reader will ask what has hindered? My answer is that the government-salaried denizens in the Indian and Ethnological bureaus saw their occupations vanish with every development of the Indian into the ability of citizens. Their headquarters in Washington and administrative opportunities gave them daily access to legislators and administrators, and "self-preservation is the first law of nature." If these insidious influences had had to fight their battle for official life outside Washington, their methods would have ended long ago. Very early in the campaign I advocated placing the Bureau of Indian Affairs on the Sioux or Navajo Reservation, in direct contact with its responsibilities. I would do that now and demand that it Moses its charges into the promised land of our American citizenship. If anybody has a better plan to prove the impotence of the Bureau to conclude its job, I will withdraw mine.

To enlighten the public, Carlisle from its charity funds hired the Academy of Music in Philadelphia and took a large company of its students to the city and gave a practical demonstration of their gains in education. Both Secretary Teller and Commissioner Price were present and spoke. The general conference of the Methodist Church was being held in the city at the time, and on our invitation it was present in a body as part of the audience which filled the Academy to overflowing. Mr. Teller in his address outlined his plan. In my talk I ventured to use Mr. Teller as my illustration, saying that what he and all of us needed were props. He had a college education but lived in civilized surroundings, where all the influences propped him up to perform the high duties that came to him. Indians needed just the same props of environment in order to make their civilization a success. Therefore it was irrational to keep them reservated in their aboriginal environment, away from and outside our civilization, and expect success in promoting their Americanization.

Mr. John Wanamaker, the great merchant, was presiding. One of my teachers, as a diversion, had one of our pupils coached to give a speech which she had arranged for him. This was Amos Lone Hill, heretofore spoken of, a big Sioux of twenty or more years, who was beginning to speak the English language effectively, notwithstanding his late and meager schooling. His features were the rare kind that illustrators put forward as racially "typical"—that is, his cheek bones were high. His subject was directed at some features of our civilization. Among other things, he said: "A lady gives twenty dollars for a hat—that is foolishness. A merchant buys something for ten cents and sells it for one dollar—that is business." Mr. Wanamaker spoke up sententiously at once, saying, "That is not the way we do at Grand Depot," which greatly helped out the intended amusement.

About that time the same teacher with the same Indian in a considerable class of her "adult primaries" appeared before the state's annual convention of educators at Williamsport, Pennsylvania. I had listened to the prepared program at Carlisle and it seemed all right. When, however, this particular class came before the large audience, the teacher began with the same Indian: "Amos, which would you rather have—the third of a watermelon or the half of a watermelon?" He at once said, "The third of a watermelon." The great audience of teachers, and also the officials on the platform where I sat, were amused and I felt somewhat annoyed. When the audience became quiet the teacher said: "Why would you rather have the third of a watermelon than the half of a watermelon?" Amos spoke up loudly and said: "Because I do not like watermelon." This produced another applause and ended my annoyance. After the convention was over and we were on the way back to the hotel, I said to the teacher, "When did you put that watermelon problem into Amos' head?" And she replied, "On the way from the hotel to the hall."

During this time, on invitation, we held an Indian meeting in Rev. Dr. Cuyler's great church in Brooklyn, presenting students in the same manner. The Commissioner of Indian Affairs, Mr. Price, and Rev. Henry Ward Beecher were the principal speakers.

We first gave illustrations of the intelligence, qualities, and gains of the students in class recitation, in addresses, and in music by singing and the school band. In introductory remarks, I said: "The Government can send young Indians who have never been in school and who cannot speak English to a school like Carlisle, and in two or three years give them enough of the English language, intelligence, industry, and discipline to enable them to find a welcome in our American schools and families and thus enable them to earn their own way by labor out of school hours and during vacation. They can then acquire a better education and ability for civilized life than can be given in any purely Indian school. The further they go in these lines the more anxious they become to succeed, provided they are properly advised and encouraged."

Mr. Beecher began his talk by saying very emphatically: "Well! If, as Captain Pratt says, we can take young Indians and in two or three years give them enough of the English language and of our industries to enable them to pass out into our public schools and then go on and take care of themselves, *that is the end of it.*" The last words he spoke with greatest emphasis. Soon afterward, there went the rounds of the papers a pronouncement from Mr. Beecher which seemed based on that experience. This was: "The common schools are the stomachs of the country, in which all people that come to us are assimilated within a generation. When a lion eats an ox, the lion does not become an ox, but the ox becomes lion."

The influences against Carlisle's purpose—"to civilize the Indians, get them into civilization; to keep them civilized, let them stay"—flowing from the two government bureaus of Indian Affairs and Ethnology were most insidious as they came to me from time to time from indubitable sources. Law makers and law enforcers fell under their influence, and even the White House was invaded by their sinuous approaches. Because secreted in administration alcoves, these enemy activities were difficult to reach, and in one instance almost led to calamity both to me personally and to my cause.

I received a telegram from the Commissioner of Indian Affairs asking me to come to Washington and help secure more appropriation for the Pacific Coast industrial school at Forest Grove, Oregon, by going before the subcommittee compiling the Indian Appropriations Bill for the Senate Indian Committee. When I reached Washington, the Commissioner said that Mrs. Wilkinson, the wife of Captain [Melville C.] Wilkinson, U. S. A., the Forest Grove superintendent, had come east to try to secure $10,000 for an additional building. The school was small, the pressure to take more children great, and the limited quarters not at all adequate for what they already had. After a conference, the Commissioner thought I had better present the case to Senator Dawes, chairman of the subcommittee. I went to Senator Dawes and urged the appropriation, and he said that he and Senator [Wilkinson] Call of Florida were both in favor of the addition, but that the third member was against it and would oppose it in the Senate, and he was the man to work on.[1]

Senator Call and his wife had visited St. Augustine several times during

1. This was Senator Preston B. Plumb of Kansas. Wherever in the following pages Pratt has left a name blank, Senator Plumb is the official referred to.

the three years I held the Indian prisoners in Fort Marion and were much interested then, and when he became a senator he said I could rely on him to aid what I was undertaking. My conference with Senator Dawes was in his Senate committee room late in the afternoon just before the adjournment of the Senate. He suggested that I send my card in to the opposing senator and arrange a conference between him and Mrs. Wilkinson. I hurried to the Senate and found that it had just adjourned. Immediately after adjournment, outsiders were permitted to go in on the floor. I looked in and saw the senator who was against us. As I had never met him, I asked my senator, General [Benjamin] Harrison of Indiana, to introduce me. The senator invited me to bring Mrs. Wilkinson to his house at seven o'clock that evening.

We went. The senator, who was a heavily built man, had taken off his coat and shoes and was walking the floor in his stockings. We were not invited to sit down. What occurred is told in the following letter I wrote to Senator Dawes from Carlisle two days later:

March 18, 1882.

Hon. H. L. Dawes,
   U. S. Senate, Washington, D.C.
Dear Sir:

   As you advised me to see Senator _____ and take Mrs. Wilkinson with me, in reference to the additional appropriation of ten thousand dollars for the Forest Grove School, recommended by the Indian Department, I feel, after having thought the matter over two days, that it is best I should make to you a record statement of that interview.

   After seeing you, I was introduced to Senator _____ in the Senate Chamber by Senator Harrison just after adjournment on the 14th. As I knew from the Congressional Record his recent words about the Memorial you presented, I used General Hazen's name, for which I had authority, in asking an interview. Senator _____ invited me to his house at seven o'clock that evening. I went and took Mrs. Wilkinson that she might state her own case as you suggested. The Senator had not yet returned from the Capitol and we went to Mr. Haskell's near.[2] Mr. Haskell encouraged our visit to Senator _____ and we returned there, when I was subjected to a violent and unprovoked assault, such as I had not supposed possible from one occupying such a position. Thinking it would be better to have another's statement of what occurred, I asked Mrs. Wilkinson the next day to write briefly what she could remember, and I here copy her account, which agrees with my recollection but does not cover all I recall. There is enough, however, in her statement to show you the reception we met.

2. Rep. Dudley C. Haskell of Kansas, chairman of the House Committee on Indian Affairs.

"Capt. Pratt began the conversation regretting to intrude, knowing his many calls and cares, and began to speak of the Forest Grove School, when Mr. _____, without waiting to hear him through, launched out into the most violent attack upon Capt. Pratt and all officers who were carrying on Indian education. He said they were all frauds and they knew it; that they did it to shirk military duty, and get soft places, and that Capt. Pratt was a swindler and he knew it—that his school at Carlisle was a farce and that the post was secured by fraud and was held illegally, and that the extra allowance of $1,000.00 per annum was illegal, that he voted against it, and should again, and that he should break up the school if he could. Capt. Pratt was the worst enemy the Indians could have; his posturing before the country was ridiculous, and only done to make for himself notoriety, and gain credit for doing great things, that the articles in the papers commendatory of this work were silly twaddle and made him sick. He repeated over and over again the epithets of swindler and fraud, disputing in the most offensive manner every word that was said—would not admit of explanation, but insisted he knew all about the Indian question, and the Captain nothing at all, and if he said that he did, he was either a fool or a fraud. The conversation was very one-sided, for Captain Pratt could say very little—lasted about half an hour, when Mr. _____ threw open the parlor door with a bang that was an invitation to leave."

Mrs. Wilkinson was entirely ignored and not permitted to utter a word in behalf of her cause. I would not trouble you with this unpleasant account were it not that it may aid in showing the animus of the opposition to Indian education which seems to head in Senator_____, who is evidently governed by impulse without knowledge. If he has any data it might be well to get it. So far, I have seen nothing in his utterances, that proposes anything except destruction to what others do. Milton's "of whom to be dispraised were no small praise" is ample healing for me in this case, directing that I go ahead until Congress by whose authority I am here says stop; never neglecting nor forgetting to claim that in the education and training of the masses of Indian children and in demanding for them such treatment, contact and liberty as will grow in them a love for the white race, and a desire for home among them, in the land, is to be found the complete consummation of their civilization and citizenship.

I write this letter for just such use, confidential or otherwise, as your judgment cares to make of it, and am, Sir,

With great respect,
R. H. PRATT.

To this letter Senator Dawes sent the following reply:

United States Senate Chamber,
Washington, March 23, 1882.

Capt. R. H. Pratt,

My dear Sir:

Yours in reference to the interview with Senator _____ was duly received and it very much astonished me. I do think the treatment was hardly creditable, and must think he was sick with dyspepsia, or something else worse. He and I have had the Indian Bill in charge as a sub-committee for the last week. You can judge how unpromising the outlook would be; yet I hope that something has been accomplished for the education of the Indians. We have gotten $30,000 for Forest Grove, with some minor limitations upon it, which I hope will not very much embarrass it. We have some other provisions which, as soon as the Bill is printed, I would like you to read and give me your opinion about. I have had pretty hard work to get what has been obtained.

I reported the Bill this afternoon, and it will come up the beginning of the week.

Truly yours,

H. L. DAWES.

After this conference I conducted Mrs. Wilkinson to her boarding house and returned to the Ebbitt House, where I was stopping. There I met a colonel of General Sherman's staff. We had met a number of times beginning during General Sherman's trips to the West when he visited Fort Sill, and then afterwards at army headquarters. I thought I would like to have his views and took him aside and detailed to him what had occurred at Senator _____'s house, and said, "I think never in my life was I as near striking a man in the face as I was to hitting the senator. But my position in the army was at stake, and I refrained." He said: "Pratt, I think you made a mistake. You should have given him the best black eye you possibly could, and he would afterwards have respected you for it." "Well," I said, "it would have been an ugly thing, particularly if made public, and I am glad I didn't do it. Besides, he was in fighting trim, and I might have been hurt myself."

On my next visit to Washington, in talking with Senator Dawes, he told me that when the committee came together the next day Senator _____ at once introduced an amendment to the bill giving Forest Grove the additional $10,000 we had asked.

Senator _____ was for several years a persistent opponent of Carlisle and it was plain his opposition was prompted. During the passage of the Indian bill each year he said ugly things. At one time the Commissioner wrote that Senator _____ was going to make an attack on Carlisle and move its abandonment, and said I had better come to Washington and go before the sub-committee. The Commissioner, Mr. Price, took me to the committee room and explained to the committee different portions of the bill and the needs of the Bureau, omitting Carlisle. When he finished he told the committee he had asked me to come down and explain the needs of the school, and then he went out.

Immediately when my opportunity came, Senator _____ said he was going to move the abolishment of the Carlisle School. He was going to do it because of two letters he had received and intended to read in the Senate, one from an Indian agent telling that one of my students who had returned home some time before had two wives, and the other from the colonel commanding the military post at the same agency which stated that a certain Indian and his wife had brought their daughter, a former Carlisle student, to the precincts of the post at pay day and prostituted her to make money. I said to the committee: "I submit that I am entitled to know the names of the agent and the commanding officer of the military post, and all they say, before I answer." The chairman, Senator Dawes, submitted the question to the committee and Senators Call and Dawes voted that I was entitled to have the information. Senator _____ then gave the names of the colonel and the Indian agent and the names of the students and the father of the girl.

I then said: "I submit to your committee this view. The Indian agent is in full charge of all the Indians at his agency. He has a police force to enable him to execute the government regulations, and any he may himself make. He represents the great United States Government and has all authority and power to execute its purposes for the Indians at his agency. And when he writes to a senator of the United States that an Indian young man who has been returned to his care from a distant school has taken two wives, he confesses that he permits the act of which he complains and therefore he himself becomes a condoner of the offense. The same would be true if he permitted any Indian, old or young, who had never been to school to have two wives. It is not in accord with the laws of the United States and he is there to execute those laws and prevent the very thing of which he complains. So far as the commanding officer of the nearby military post is concerned, his authority and power to control matters within his bailiwick and keep them respectable and in accord with the laws of the United States is even greater than that of the Indian agent. He has a large force of soldiers to enforce all regulations, and when he permits the act which he describes to the senator to happen within his jurisdiction, he impeaches his own qualities and shows himself to be an unfit official of the government. The young man and young woman were by government decree returned to their homes, where those habits are permitted, if not encouraged."

I then explained the needs of the school and went out of the committee.

As the iron horse carried me back to Carlisle I grew more and more indignant over what Senator _____ had said, revealing as it did the base quality and sinuous sources of opposition, and tried to find a way to get the case so adjudicated as to stop that sort of chicanery. I thought at first of alleging charges against both the Indian agent and the post commander for incompetency in discharge of their official duties. When Carlisle was reached, I had concluded what I would do, and I went immediately to my office and wrote a letter to Senator Dawes, chairman of the committee, stating that I desired to make what had transpired before his subcommittee a matter of official record and therefore was writing this letter. I then detailed what had occurred before the committee and closed the letter by saying: "I request that a copy of this letter be sent to the commanding officer of the military post and to the United States Indian agent who wrote the letters Senator_____ alleged he was going to read to the Senate." I also sent a copy to the Commissioner of Indian Affairs. Senator Dawes told me afterward that copies were forwarded to the Indian agent and to the commanding officer of the military post.

The Indian agent was not long in service after that. Years afterward I saw the colonel at a function in Washington and found that my shot had been effective.

Senator _____ did not read the letters to the Senate, nor did he further oppose the Carlisle appropriations; from that time he was friendly, and when we met he gave me views he thought valuable to the administration of my duties.

About that time Senator _____ put into the Indian bill one of the very best clauses ever advanced and which was calculated to promote civilization of the Indians and which has continued for all the years since. It could easily have been made to grow into vast and best results. It has never been used with any set purpose of the Indian administration to carry out the intention of the senator. This clause provided a sum of money year after year for the Indian Bureau to use in transporting young Indians to and from their homes to localities where they could be placed out in good families with the best civilized environment and have the benefits afforded by living in such families and working in summer for wages and in winter working mornings and evenings for their board and keep while attending the public schools. Although the Outing at Carlisle grew until one year it reached over 900 during vacation and 360 attending public schools during the winter, Carlisle never under my superintendency used a dollar of this money. At first it was required that the patrons pay transportation, but soon afterward it was arranged that the expense should come from the pay of the student, which expense was small because the railroads gave us half rates.

As soon as the Outing was well established and had grown to high favor, we were able to fix the pay that students should receive according to their size, intelligence, and ability, and that method of compensation was satisfactory to both the students and the people who employed them. Our habit was to consult the student and the patron and have the pay accord with their views.

The school had good friends in the Indian committees of both the House and the Senate, and I now and then had from them confidential information covering the individual efforts of Bureau oligarchists opposing Carlisle and its purposes. Bureau-salaried people secretly lobbied against Indians being taken from their tribes for education. Whenever I had their emanations, I was enabled to meet them, but this secret approach to legislators was most detrimental and was continued throughout my quarter-century as superintendent. As the Bureau people are permanently entrenched at the Washington headquarters, they hold inequitable and commanding ascendancy over the field forces who bear the brunt of the work and should be responsible for its success or failure.

On one occasion I talked these matters over with a chief clerk of the Indian Bureau, who was a man with strong common sense. In one of his personal letters soon afterward, he said, "The Indian Bureau is a bull in a china store," which was about as complete an exposé of an important truth as could well be made.

In the early summer of 1899, the Commissioner of Indian Affairs, Mr. [William A.] Jones, invited me, while in Washington over night, to be a guest in his home in order that we might better talk over matters. On the way down to the office next morning he said: "I notice you have not attended our annual school conventions lately. Why is that?" I said: "I am tired of contending with my brother superintendents of the agency and the other non-reservation schools near the Indians. They have opposing views and purposes in part begotten of their environment and which I think are encouraged from your office, and they are largely banded against Carlisle. There are so many of them and so few of me that they carry the day." He said: "I want our people to think as you do. I wish you would go to the National Educational Convention at Los Angeles this year, where our annual Indian school convention is to be held, and stand for your views and endeavor to make our people accept them." I said: "If that is your wish, I shall go with greatest pleasure."

I went to this convention, which was one of the largest ever held by the Indian school administration. Dr. [Merrill E.] Gates, a member of the Board of Indian Commissioners,[3] and several of the nonreservation school superin-

3. Organized in June 1869 as a feature of President Grant's Peace Policy, the Board of Indian Commissioners consisted of ten philanthropic citizens serving without pay. The Board was charged with supervising the purchase of supplies and annuity goods by the Indian Bureau, with inspecting the field agencies and reporting any derelictions of duty or needed changes, and gen-

tendents stood by me in trying to carry out the wishes of the Commissioner. I wrote three resolutions. Dr. Gates offered the first one. It was:

"RESOLVED, that the true object of the Indian schools and of Indian management is to accomplish the release of the Indian from the slavery of tribal life and to establish him in the self-supporting freedom of citizenship to take his place in the life of the nation, and that whatever in our present system hinders the attainment of this object should be changed."

The second, upon my request, was presented by Miss Rose Bourassa of the Phoenix school. She was a graduate of and had been a teacher in the Carlisle Indian School before going to Phoenix. This resolution was:

"RESOLVED, that the public schools of the United States are fundamentally and supremely the Americanizers of all people within our limits and our duty to the Indian requires that all Indian school effort should be directed toward getting the Indian youth into these schools."

The third I offered myself, as follows:

"WHEREAS, local prejudice on the part of the whites against the Indians in the vicinity of every tribe and reservation is such as to make attendance of Indian youth in the public schools there impracticable, and WHEREAS there is no prejudice preventing the attendance of Indian youth in public schools from such nonreservation schools as are remote from the tribes or reservations, therefore BE IT RESOLVED that it is the duty of the government to establish industrial schools in our well-populated districts as remote from the tribes as possible, and it is hereby suggested that ten more such schools be tentatively established at once, each with a capacity for carrying 300 at the school, with a distinct understanding that each such school shall carry 300 additional pupils placed out in public schools living in white families where the children shall give service in the home to pay for their keep."

These resolutions were warmly discussed and all carried, and when I returned east I went at once to Washington, elated that I had been able to meet the Commissioner's wishes. I carried with me and gave to him copies of the resolutions and gave him the incidents connected with securing their passage. He was greatly pleased and said, "I wish you would take these and see Mr. [James S.] Sherman, chairman of the House Indian Committee [and Vice President of the United States, 1909–13], and get him to help us carry them out." I went immediately to see Mr. Sherman, gave him copies of the resolutions, and told him the Commissioner's wishes. Mr. Sherman cordially endorsed the plan and said, "I will have one in Utica," which was his home town.

I reported to the Commissioner my success with Mr. Sherman and returned

---

erally with advising the Bureau and keeping the public informed on the conduct of Indian affairs. See Priest, *Uncle Sam's Stepchildren,* pp. 42–56.

to Carlisle. These resolutions may be found on page 450 of the Annual Report of the Commissioner of Indian Affairs for the year 1899.

That I held up my head and walked with steadier pace for some time thereafter was not to be wondered at, for it had been a long fight. A few weeks later, when the same annual report of the Commissioner came out, I found on page 9, in his part of the report and over his own signature, the following: "The present number of nonreservation schools is sufficient to meet all the requirements of the service. But they should be enlarged in some cases and better equipped in others."

The import of this was at once apparent, and when I went to Washington and asked the Commissioner about it, he doubted that anything of the kind was in his report. I showed it to him, and when he read it he seemed indignant and said: "That was written by Mr. _____ [chief of a division]. I did not know it was there." It was plain that we could not go ahead and ask Congress for the increased number of nonreservation schools, for his own report would be quoted against it and kill the attempt, so the matter was dropped. This incident well illustrates how the permanent double-headed Bureau oligarchy has for all the years assiduously manipulated to keep the Indians from the opportunities and environment of civilized life, which would long ago have transformed them into useful citizens. This would have compelled the ending of both the Bureaus of Indian Affairs and of Ethnology, and any need for the cooperating services of the two committees of Congress. Their fight to keep the Indians intact as tribes means preeminently Bureau perpetuation which can only be successfully maintained through keeping the Indians carefully laid away in the dark drawers of their tribal reservations.

In all my intercourse with the students I encouraged their utmost freedom in coming to me at any time with any of their personal matters. Many of the students reached the school having a given English name added to their Indian name. Others who came without any English name were given one. To one of these we gave the name of Conrad, which led to the following:

> Dear Captain Pratt:
>
> I am going to tell you something about my name. Captain Pratt, I would like to have a new name because some of the girls call me Cornbread and some call me Cornrat, so I do not like that name, so I want you to give me a new name. Now this is all I want to say.
>
> Conrad.

26. The World's Columbian Exposition

During the year 1891 there was wide national interest in the plan for a world exposition at Chicago commemorating the 400th anniversary of the discovery of America. It was to be called The Columbian Quadri-Centennial. The immensity of the project compelled the postponement of the opening until 1893, but 1892 was commemorated in various ways throughout the country. The two largest events were parades in New York and Chicago, both in October. Carlisle was invited to take part in these. The parade in New York was on October 10 and that in Chicago on the 20th.

Carlisle's contribution to the parade in New York was 270 boys and 52 girls. A large and most elaborate silk banner was provided on which was emblazoned in large letters, "United States Indian Industrial School, Carlisle, Pennsylvania," and conspicuously under that, "Into Civilization and Citizenship." It was carried by one of our stalwart boys, assisted by small boys who marched on each side far enough separated from the carrier to help, by cords from the banner to each, to hold it steady for best display.

I cannot better present the appreciation of this Carlisle expedition than by quoting from some of the many encomiums in the great newspapers. The New York *Recorder* of October 11, 1892, said in part:

And then followed what was unquestionably the most interesting feature of the whole pageant—the battalion of youths and maidens from the United States Indian Industrial School at Carlisle, Pa. The young braves, divided into four companies of twenty-five files front, were clad in a neat uniform of dark blue, with fatigue caps of the regular army pattern, each bearing an American flag and wearing the national colors pinned on the left breast. . . . But for their straight black hair and swarthy coloring, they might easily have passed for a battalion of West Pointers. . . . They were headed by a fine band of thirty pieces, led by the band-master and musical instructor, Dennison Wheelock, an Oneida Indian. The company of comely maidens, clad in a neat uniform of blue serge with felt sailor hats, each one bearing a tiny flag, fell in in the rear. . . . The banner of the battalion was borne by a gigantic young brave, and bearing the inscription "Into Civilization and Citizenship."[1]

.   .   .   .

As we were part of the great attraction which brought together millions of people for observation, arrangements for railroad transportation were made at low rates, paid by friends of the school, and therefore without cost to the Government.

To the opening ceremonies parade in Chicago we took only boys. The same banner was carried at the head of the battalion, but the students were divided into ten platoons, each representing a characteristic of the school, through which we expected them to attain civilization qualities and citizenship. The first platoon carried school books and slates. The second represented printing; the front rank students carried sticks, galleys, cases, etc., and the rear rank papers and pamphlets which they had printed. The third represented agriculture, the front rank carrying agricultural implements, the rear rank the products of agriculture from our school farms. The fourth platoon represented our baking department, the front rank carrying paddles, ovenpeels, etc., the rear rank bread. The fifth represented carpentry, the front rank bearing tools, the rear specimens of their skill in woodwork. The sixth represented blacksmithing, the front rank bearing tools, the rear rank horseshoes, chains, etc. The seventh represented shoemaking, the front rank carrying knives, lasts, hammers, etc., the rear rank shoes. The eighth represented harness making, the front rank bearing tools, the rear rank parts of harness, etc. The ninth represented tinsmithing, the front rank carrying shears, mallets, and other tools, the rear rank buckets, coffee pots, etc. The tenth and last platoon represented tailoring, the front rank carrying lapboards, shears, tailor's goose, etc., the rear rank madeup clothing. The tools

1. Omitted here are additional press descriptions of the parade from the New York newspapers.

and articles were each on little platforms on top of short poles, carried as a soldier carries his gun.[2]

.   .   .   .

The Secretary of the Interior [John W. Noble] and one of his principal assistants were among the official observers on the platform. The assistant, knowing our struggles to get Carlisle and its purposes before the country without government aid, and the denial of government funds and the opposition plans of both the Indian and Ethnological Bureaus, told me that the ovation that came from the reviewing stand greatly pleased the Secretary, who slapped him on the back and said, "The Interior Department comes out on top every time."

The Carlisle battalion was quartered in the largest building on the exposition grounds with the units of the regular army. Our quarters were on the gallery or second floor. The military display was to be the feature of the following day. We were to form a part of the civic parade and to be the head of the division immediately behind the fair and government officials and the governors of the several states and their staffs. General Nelson A. Miles commanded the whole parade. When we had formed for marching out, I said to the boys: "Heads up, shoulders back, eyes front, lines straight, perfect step. I belong to these regulars and I want them to see that you can execute our military movements and are as good material for our army as any other people. We must do all we can to make them think well of us. Execute every movement carefully." As we started from our place on the long march around the gallery, down the great stairs, and through the building to the door, led by the band, the march, even down the stairs by fours, was executed in perfect step and alignment while the thousands of men and officers of the regulars, making a wide way for us, were massed on both sides as we formed platoons. Our equipment of the implements and products of industry, in place of guns, both amused and was highly appreciated by the army officers, as they expressed themselves after our return.

It was six or seven miles down through the city to our place in the line of march, which, together with the other miles of the main parade, carrying their novel equipment under the eyes of millions of observers from every possible vantage point along the line, was a supreme test of their endurance and qualities. Not one faltered, and they stood up to the work wonderfully. As we were halted in front of the grandstand, which contained all the officials, we had time to execute several movements, and we used the opportunity. After leaving the grandstand some distance, we came to General Miles sitting on his horse with his staff in line behind him at the point of dismissal. He

2. Press reports from Chicago papers describing the Carlisle contingent in the parade appear at this point in the manuscript.

motioned me to come to him, and he complimented our appearance, class-ing it as a foremost feature. We then marched back to our place on the ex-position grounds. I had marched at their head throughout, and was greatly fatigued. Just outside the exposition grounds, I brought them into close or-der in their platoon formation and said to them: "Boys, I don't remember that I was ever more tired in my life than I am now. My feet are sore and it is very difficult to keep my legs going, but I am not going to let a single one of those regulars in there see that I am a bit tired." I then gave the command to move forward in proper order, and so we marched back into the grounds in the best alignment, step, and heads up, led by our same exhilarating mu-sic. There was no fatigue apparent in appearance or in the promptness with which they executed various formations as directed, breaking by fours, form-ing platoons, wheeling to the right and left, etc. They again kept up the good step marching up the stairway and along the long gallery, back to their temporary quarters, with the same multitude of regulars looking on.

The next day we saw the regulars form and march away by regiments to join with the militia. They were in fine shape—their precision, units, bands, flags, uniforms, steps, and movements in one great body were a fine sight. Our boys were greatly interested. We had our day of rest.

When we returned to Carlisle, the spirit of the school was greatly energized by these experiences. It was a memorable thing for the boys and girls to have marched through the streets of our greatest city, New York, in the same line with the many thousands of school children of the city, and those who had participated became anxious to see more of the outside world. One of the Apache boys, soon afterward, in his monthly declamation to the school, gave his view of the vastness of the city and the immensity of the population by saying, "The United States can whip any nation in the world because it has New York to back it."

Some of the newspaper notices about our participation in the two parades were printed in our two school papers—the *Red Man,* which was especially designed for informing the general public as well as the administrative, leg-islative, and agency authorities; and the *Indian Helper,* which we printed weekly for the special edification of the pupils both past and present and for circulation among their parents and people in their remote homes. The pupils became more thoroughly alive to their opportunities and there was a general longing to see the great exposition itself. That became so ardent that finally in the early part of 1893 I told the students that those of them who could earn and save enough money by the close of their summer's Out-ing should have the opportunity to go to Chicago and spend a week seeing the exposition. The railroad had given us such extraordinarily low rates for the 1892 parades that I felt safe in fixing the amount that each would have to pay for railway fare, their hotel, and food for a week, with five dollars each for spending money, at twenty dollars, and I so announced it.

There was then a struggle on the part of everyone large enough to get the opportunity to earn the money. After the Outing was well established, all the pupils were eager to go out to work on farms each year during vacation, and farmers were anxious to have them; thus places were available every year for all we could spare from the building and repairs of the school. That year, however, the number to remain and help at the school was trimmed down to the lowest notch. The monthly reports from the outing students showed that we would have about 500 who would have the savings to pay for the trip.

As soon as this was sufficiently established, I began to arrange the details. I wrote the situation to my good friend the general passenger agent for the Pennsylvania Railroad, and I asked him to name me the lowest possible rate at which he would transport 550 of us from Carlisle to Chicago and back, anticipating that he would say seven dollars each, as he did for the opening ceremonies parade. The rate he named was $16.50, the regular one-way rate. I then went down to see him personally and told him I could not meet it, but found him inexorable. That was as low as the officials of the road would make for any parties. I then went to see one of the vice presidents who had shown exceptional interest in the school and told him the situation. I said, if they were crowded for cars, that during the Civil War I had had a number of experiences of long transportation of troops in freight cars; if he could furnish me a train of freight cars, I could in the course of a day or two, with the train on our Carlisle siding, fix it up with chairs, etc., by using the mechanics at the school, and we could go in freight cars. He immediately said: "Captain, the war is over, and neither of us can afford to undertake the expedition in that way. If anything happened, it would be disastrous for us and for you. We will have a meeting of the administrative officers of the company this afternoon. If you come around about three o'clock I think perhaps I can help you out." So I returned at three and he told me that they had knocked off $6.50 from the rate, making it ten dollars. This was still three dollars above the 1892 rate to the opening parade. I thanked him and told him that I was afraid that it would be impossible for me to compass it at that rate.

As I left his office, remembering that I had gone over the head of the general passenger agent, it seemed best to drop in to his office and make some apology. When I went in he at once said, "You have jumped on me a little, Captain, and have accomplished your purpose without my help." I said: "I am sorry to say that I have not accomplished my purpose. I cannot afford to pay the amount that the administration has fixed for us, and I see I will have

to mount my boys and girls on their bicycles and go through in that way."
He laughed at that idea and said, "What can you afford to pay?" To this direct query, I said: "I want to take 550 of my students and employees. I shall
need a train of ten passenger coaches and two baggage cars and a sleeping car
for the employees. I would like to leave Carlisle at midnight on Sunday night,
taking your train which leaves Harrisburg soon after that hour, and returning from Chicago leave there just before midnight the following Saturday
night and reach Carlisle Sunday at midnight. For that train I can give
$3,500." He at once replied: "All right Captain, we will give you the train.
Let me know your date of departure."

That part of it accomplished, most satisfactorily, I turned to the expenses
at Chicago. It so happened that the director general of the fair had been a
member of Congress whom I had met in Washington.[3] I went to Chicago and
stated my case. "Can't you get us in to the exposition each day without
cost? We are an exceptional body; there will probably be no request from
any other Indian school for a like service. The Indians are a part of the obligation of the whole country. We want them to see and understand the best
and greatest things in our civilization. The Government is helping the fair
with large money and it will be no more than right for us to be admitted
free." He said: "Those matters are all in the hands of three men who meet
every day and determine such questions. I have only to execute. I will give
you a letter to the chairman of this body." He dictated a letter and told me
where to go. They were all strangers and so far as I knew not familiar with
Carlisle or its purposes. The chairman read the letter to the other two gentlemen and at once said that they had made an iron-clad rule that there should
be no deviation from the regular admission of fifty cents for every person.
Not even schools of any sort would be given lower rates. They had fixed the
rate as low as they felt was at all compatible with the expenses and were enforcing it everywhere. They had had many applications.

I said: "Well, gentlemen, I submit this proposition to you. Our boys will
be a battalion of 300; they are under a military system of training, in companies, having captains, lieutenants, sergeants, and corporals of themselves,
and are very well drilled; they can execute army movements to include the
school of the battalion in a way that will interest all our people very greatly,
I am sure. I can give you a parade and drill at such point as you may indicate
every day for an hour that will, I believe, attract thousands of people to come
specially to witness. I have a band that Mr. Sousa says is exceptionally good.
They are all Indians, even the leader, and they play the best of band music;
they have won high approval everywhere they have gone. The band can play
at such stands as you may indicate for an hour or two every day, and if these

3. George R. Davis, Republican congressman from Illinois, 1879–85.

performances are advertised in your daily bulletin I am sure that they will attract a considerably larger daily attendance. I also have some orators and considerable vocal and instrumental musical ability among the students. We can give daily in your choral hall illustrations which can be advertised as another attraction. I am very sure, gentlemen, that with these three services, instead of losing money, you will, by using us, be making money."

The chairman of the committee again said: "We made this rule in the very beginning, and we cannot set it aside. It opens too wide a door. We must not have any free admissions." One of the other gentlemen was very tall and slender, and the other a rather short, stout man. The tall gentleman spoke up and said: "I believe that Captain Pratt is right about it—that he is not asking us for free admission. He is offering to pay us more than we are charging. I believe, as he does, that by daily advertising we will bring increased attendance and more than cover what we would lose by admitting his party without cost. The short gentleman spoke up and said: "Mr. Chairman, I agree to that view. We can rope off a parade ground here between this building and the railroad terminal and it will be a fine sight." The chairman then said: "The vote is against me and we accept the captain's proposition." He then told the Secretary to write a letter to the director general advising him of the conditions under which the Carlisle School would come in free and I would name the gate at which we would enter daily. I told them also that the whole body of boys and girls would be formed in marching order at the gate on entering, move through the grounds as a military command to the particular place where I wanted them to begin their day's observations, and that if advertised in the day's events that would also help to attract visitors.

I went back to the director general with the letter, and so it was arranged that we would pay our entrance into the World's Fair by our daily drills, the band, and the choral hall gatherings, and he would arrange the times and places for the drills and the band later.

Several hotels had been built a mile or more beyond the exposition grounds in the outskirts of the city, near the shore of the lake, and being away from the city they had little patronage. One of these, commodious and well equipped, had never been opened and was in the hands of a receiver. It was a mile and a half away from the exposition close to a street car line which crossed the Pennsylvania Railroad tracks at a suburban station several miles away and ended at a gate of the exposition. There were extra large beds and running water in each room, and by a little crowding it would accommodate our whole party. I negotiated with the receiver and secured the use of it for $200 a day, guaranteeing the cleanliness of our pupils and the perfect care their property would receive, and that no help would be necessary because our students were well instructed in the care of their rooms.

I then found nearby a large restaurant with little patronage, able to accommodate us by having two sittings, and after a full explanation the proprietor agreed to give us breakfast, a lunch to carry with us, and a dinner at fifty cents per day each. I showed him that the food supplied at the school cost only thirteen cents and a fraction per day each and that by buying as I knew he could, and by giving us the same food, he would make at least twenty-five cents on each person per day, which would profit him above $125.00 per day. We were to be on hand so early each morning and back so late each evening that we would be out of the way of his other patronage. We were to take our noon lunch with us. He agreed to it, but after it seemed to be all settled he said: "Why, I can't do it. I will have to pay too much for waiters." I said: "You will not need waiters; I shall bring fine waiters with me. My girls are all trained in waiting on the tables and washing the dishes at the school. In fact, I have good cooks among them and could take care of that, too." That settled the bargain, and he made more money than I promised. I then went to the street car company and arranged for a train that would carry 550 from the second street in front of the hotel directly to the least-used entrance of the exposition, paying a per-trip sum for the train. The trains were to be in front of the hotel at a fixed minute each morning and the boys and girls scattered along the track so as to be on the cars inside of two minutes and go without stop to the exposition gate. Then we were to be out of the exposition and along a siding track, where our trolley train would be waiting in the evening at a certain fixed minute, and be transported back in the same way. The trolley was also to meet us on arrival at the suburban station and on departing take us back to the railroad.

Returning to Carlisle, paper boxes which would hold three meals and a cup for each student were purchased, to serve on the going and return trips. We also purchased several thousand cheap folding paper lunch boxes, each having a string handle, for the noon lunches. The tinners made the cups and large cans with spouts, one for each car, from which coffee could be distributed through the cars, and by correspondence it was arranged that we have the number of gallons required at each of several stations en route.

I then notified the general passenger agent of the Pennsylvania Railroad that we would be ready at midnight on Sunday October 1, and at the time appointed our train was on our school siding. It so happened that we were the fourth section of the train and were over an hour late in reaching the suburban station where we were to get off. The trolley company had had some difficulty holding the cars there after the time appointed, but we were all soon aboard, after a famous railroad ride, taken by as jolly a lot of youth as could be found anywhere, and we reached our hotel in time to get several hours sleep.

The Pennsylvania Railroad had issued a very complete map of the exposition grounds and gave us 600 copies. By dividing the map into portions for each day's observation, beginning with where we entered and carrying it around the grounds until the last day, we covered the whole exposition in the days we were there. The divisions were made on the map at the printing office, and a printed slip attached to each map gave fullest instructions for each day's observations. Each boy and girl had a map with a memorandum book and pencil attached. The printed instructions required that they make notes of each day's observations. These were to be submitted to the teachers for criticism on their return to enable deductions as to the keenness of their observations and then be retained by the pupil as a memento.

Finding that I had money enough, I hired a steamboat one night to take us out on the lake in front of the exposition grounds to witness the wonderful fireworks. There was a wharf not far from our hotel, where the steamer received and returned us. That was a great treat.

I went to the mammoth ferris wheel and endeavored to negotiate for the whole school to be taken, in sections, and have a ride up into the air for a bird's eye view of the exposition and the city. But the superintendent of the ferris wheel was obdurate. The price had been fixed for him and he could not change it. Fifty cents each meant $275.00; I had no service to offer as compensation. Expressing my disappointment, he said, "Well, Captain, you need not feel bad about it, for I think all of your Indian boys and girls have taken the ride already." A trip on the aerial railway gave us an overlooking view of the exposition.

Only one mishap occurred during the whole period of our stay at the exposition. One of the Apache boys from the prisoners then in Florida persuaded one of the girls to take a ride on the lake in an Indian canoe he hired from the Indian camp. Neither of them had ever had such an experience. When some distance from shore the canoe upset, and they were rescued with some difficulty—the girl was so far gone that it required a good deal of first-aid treatment to bring her back.

The military demonstration attracted many thousands of spectators daily. The roped-off place between the administration building and the main entrance to the exposition grounds was the most popular place at our drill hour. The boys were commanded by the school's disciplinarian. While standing in the crowd watching the boys go through their movements on the last day, a gentleman behind me put his hand on my shoulder and said, "Captain, did you come through all right on the way out?" It was the vice president of the Pennsylvania Railroad to whom I had applied for freight-car transportation. I told him that we had a fine trip except that we were the fourth section and an hour behind time, which complicated the street railway arrangement. He said, "I will fix that; you will go back as the first section," and we did.

I suppose no young people from any school ever had more to talk about for weeks after that than those 500 Indian boys and girls at Carlisle. Transit to and from, the housing and feeding, and the going around through the exposition was carried out as we had planned. The teachers and employees in the party were among the students daily as they went about in the sections fixed for their observation and aided them greatly to take in the evidences of the white man's best accomplishments. Not many features of the fair escaped notice in their memorandum books, and those books were preserved and treasured for years afterward. No doubt some have them to this day. The total cost to each student including five dollars spending money was $19.50.

By far the most important illustration of Carlisle's "into civilization and citizenship" purpose was its permanent exhibit placed by the side of the many exhibits from schools all over America and from other nations. The making of this special exhibit of Carlisle's activities was forced upon the Carlisle administration by the Indian and Ethnological Bureaus because of their opposite and inimical purposes. Carlisle aimed and showed how to make acceptable productive citizens out of Indians and so end the need and expense of Bureau control through its system of exalting Indianisms.

Carlisle's exhibit showed how the Indian could learn to march in line with America as a very part of it, head up, eyes front, where he could see his glorious future of manly competition in citizenship and be on an equality as an individual. The exhibit contrived by the two government bureaus was calculated to keep the nation's attention and the Indian's energies fixed upon his valueless past, through the spectacular aboriginal housing, dressing, and curio employments it instituted. The illustrative Indian boarding school in their exposition camps said to the Indians: "You may have some of our education, but not enough to enable you to become one of us. You are to remain a separate and peculiar people, and continue under our Bureau supervision."

Nearly thirty years have since passed, and the two bureaus have had their way about it, and now the annual cost to the country in overseeing our Indians is double what it then was, and the course pursued has promoted rather than ended Indian dependence on the Bureau.

As soon as it was settled that the Bureau was to have a liberal appropriation for an exhibit at Chicago, I urged the Commissioner of Indian Affairs to eliminate anything like an aboriginal and wild west feature. My argument to him was that Buffalo Bill would be on hand and present his spectacular exaggeration of the aborigine. Mr. Cody had already secured a commanding front place, and it was plain to me that administrative duty only required that we illustrate what could be done in the way of advancing Indian civilization and merging them into citizenship. My views were not accepted. I therefore began to plan a special exhibit of Carlisle and its purposes. Through influential and official friends in the exposition management, ample space was secured for a Carlisle exhibit in the industrial education section, and the forces of the school were set to work to create as complete a showing as was practicable.

In the early fall of 1891 occurred the first convention of officials and employees of Indian schools at Lawrence, Kansas. I was notified by the Commissioner [Thomas J. Morgan] of his plan for this convention and that my part, in addition to the discussions, would be to make an address before a public meeting which was to be held in the city opera house. I therefore began to arrange an address. While engaged upon it, I had a telegram from the Commissioner that he was coming to Carlisle to see me on his way to Chicago and Lawrence for the opening of the convention. I met him at the station conveyance; he had a small trunk which we brought out to the school, and he said that he would stay that night to talk it all over. As soon as he reached his room, he began to tell his plan for the bureau presentation at Chicago [i. e. at the World's Fair.] He had secured an acreage on the border of a lakelet in the exposition grounds and proposed a wide illustration of Indian camp life, bringing delegations from various far separated tribes and keeping them in tribal units and garb, living in their tepee, hogan, and wickiup homes. Then on one side of these encampments a boarding school was being built to which he would bring for a month at a time model delegations from the several largest reservation and nonreservation schools, giving to Carlisle one of the periods. The Indians in their camps were to be provided with material and manufacture the various petty articles which have become curios our people buy. This would give visitors a chance to carry home souvenirs of the Indians. Indian blankets of various tribes, Navajo women weaving blankets, and Navajo men engaged in metal work, using their primitive blowpipes, seated on the ground before a little fire, were to be among the inducements. The Government was to bring the delegations to Chicago, provide material, and help them to build their habitations. The articles they made and sold were to be a revenue to them to encourage interracial traffic. Then they were to give exhibitions of their various tribal characteristics, including those that were spectacular, which white people look upon with such wonder. They were all to live before the public in their aboriginal ways. Indians from the north country would have their birch-bark canoes, and their articles made of birch bark, and they would give canoe races, etc.

After elaborating his plan fully, he said, "Captain, I wish you to take charge of the boarding school throughout the exposition." As agency schools, both boarding and day, were becoming one of the chief methods of the Bureau to promote tribal cohesion, I was unfavorable to the service at once, but asked, "Who is to take charge of the general exhibit?" He named a noted ethnologist living in Washington who, he said, "will be my representative."[4] As the ethnologists were the most insidious and active enemies of Carlisle's purposes, and this subordinated Carlisle to them, I said: "Mr. Commissioner, you must excuse me from taking part in your proposed exhibit. Carlisle will be there, whether it gets government aid or not, with an exhibit that, as I think, will be a helpful illustration of the Indian's progress in civilization and far more creditable to the government of the United States than what you propose."

He at once said, "When does the next train leave?" I said, "There will be one in twenty minutes." He said, "Can I reach that train?" "I think so," I replied. "I want to take that train to Chicago," he said. I sent word to my man to bring the carriage quickly. He and I carried his trunk out into the lane, and when the carriage came we drove quickly to the station in silence. As we were standing a few minutes waiting for the train to come, I said, "Mr. Commissioner, you had better excuse me from attending the educational convention at Lawrence." He said sharply, "I cannot do that. You are advertised to speak at the one important public meeting. I notified you and you accepted. I shall expect you to be there." I said, "Very well, sir." Without saying goodby, when the train came in, he climbed aboard and was off for Chicago. I then hastened the preparation for the best exhibit of Carlisle's work we could make. All the industrial and schoolroom people worked zealously to perfect each branch. We included a fine spring wagon made by the boys in the wagon and blacksmith shop. Large glass-enclosed cases were made, in which our smaller exhibits could be displayed. A space like that allowed us at the exposition was laid off in the gymnasium and the exhibit arranged thereon in the best order and as the months passed we became satisfied that we had as good a portrayal as we could make.

I went to Lawrence to the convention and immediately discovered that I was *persona non grata* with the head of the Indian Office and some of his leading assistants. But among the school people from the other nonreservation schools and from some of the reservation schools I had the warm grasp of friendship, and my views had some help.

4. Under the close supervision of Director John Wesley Powell, Dr. William H. Holmes had charge of the Bureau of American Ethnology exhibit at Chicago. Whether he represented Commissioner of Indian Affairs Mogan, too, is not apparent. BAE, *14th Annual Report, 1892–93* (Washington, 1896), p. xxxvi.

Before the public meeting occurred, I was informed that I was excused from speaking, that the Commissioner himself would make the principal address, and that the general superintendent of Indian schools [Daniel Dorchester], a former Methodist presiding elder, would also speak. J. B. Lippincott, an old friend then living in Topeka, near Lawrence, who had been for quite a number of years chancellor of the University of Kansas, was attending the meetings because he was greatly interested in what I was doing. Before he became chancellor, he had been a professor in Dickinson College at Carlisle and was a valued helper and adviser to me for a number of years. He and his wife accompanied me to the public meeting, which packed the opera house, and we had seats in the back central part of the audience. A former governor of Kansas presided. The Commissioner read a long and labored address, bringing statistics and statements of the Bureau and its administration, calculated to lead the public to believe that the Bureau was doing about all that could be done for the Indians, and that it was on right lines in maintaining the tribal relations and the reservation methods, and that the great need was more tribal schools, both day and boarding. The superintendent of schools followed, expatiating along the same lines.

The meeting was about to close when Dr. Lippincott got up and began to talk. I was at once aware of his purpose and tried to get him to stop, but he stepped away from me and continued. He had the attention of the audience because he was a noted man in the community. He said many of the people had come to the meeting for the special purpose of hearing a person who had been advertised to speak but had been excluded from taking part, and that he thought it right that the people should know that the gentleman was present and ready as had been arranged. He then sat down. I sat still and nothing was said from the platform where the Commissioner and the presiding officer were seated. The audience began to call my name and kept it up until, standing in my place, I thanked them for their appreciation and sat down.

Then the audience began to call, "Speech, speech!" and "Go to the platform!" The presiding officer stood up and said, "Captain, I guess you must come up here and say something." I then went to the platform and occupied four or five minutes in controverting the Commissioner and Superintendent of Schools, showing wherein I believed they were not right. I pushed my views on the need of giving the Indians, and especially their youth, opportunities to acquire our civilization in the environment of civilization, and that our duty was to advise them to do those things that would enable them to quit being tribesmen and take upon themselves the obligations and advantages of American citizenship. I gave my experience that this was not a difficult thing to do and then returned to my seat. What I said was warmly received by the audience and endorsed by the presiding officer.

Very early in the year 1893 our exhibit was moved to its place in the exposition, and two of my people were present a month at a time to explain our display and give information. One of our foremost pupils, Chauncey Yellow Robe, who came in the first party of students, a fine specimen of gentlemanly young manhood, was part of the exhibit as a sample and to assist in giving information. We had no interest from the Bureau chief. During the exposition the Commissioner was on the grounds, and my agent in charge invited him to come and see our display. This he declined to do, saying he was not interested.

Buffalo Bill with his Wild West, from a vantage point near one of the main entrances, coined money throughout the exposition. He was taking Indians away from their reservations, but only to exhibit their aboriginal and combative methods.

During this time, at one of my meetings with the Commissioner, I told him that, inasmuch as we were not at one in educational and civilization purposes for the Indians, I felt it was better that I be relieved and returned to duty in my regiment. He was unwilling to do this, saying that there was room for both purposes, but the emphasis of his acts and writings were upon the home school. One of his public pronouncements on the question contained these words:

> It should also be borne in mind that the money expended at these Indian schools is put at once into circulation in their immediate vicinity and the employees are mostly white people, men and women carefully chosen. That the money they receive for this work enters largely into the financial growth in their respective communities and becomes a part of the general prosperity of the country.
>
> A great burden rests upon the western states and territories, which embrace Indian reservations, for Indian lands are not taxed and the Indians not only do not contribute to the advancement of these growing communities but the progress of the states or territories is often and sometimes necessarily hindered to a greater or lesser extent by their presence.
>
> It would, therefore, seem only a matter of equity that the burden of these western states and territories should be lightened by the distribution among them of such money as may be necessary for the education of the Indians.

This was a frank exposé of the Bureau's purposes and clearly made progress toward citizenship subordinate to the white man's greed.

A considerable part of Carlisle's exhibit at Chicago, including the wagon, was purchased by an English educator and shipped to his Zulu school in

South Africa as an object lesson to encourage the natives and strengthen the English authorities in promoting industrial schools for them.[5]

.   .   .   .

As students came to feel at home in the East, used the railroads, and had experiences among our people, there was a growing independence and occasionally, though not often, there were runaways from among the boys. The telephone had come into use, and by using the telephone and telegraph in a lively way I could usually get on their trail, intercept them, and get them back to the school.

Two boys from a far western tribe left the school together. They were well advanced, approaching graduation. Both of them had been satisfactory students, and I was surprised that they should go away. Information came from chiefs of police in different towns, and they were making their way across Ohio. I telegraphed to the chief of police of a city they would pass through, asking him to have them arrested and send one of his men with them back to Carlisle. The boys were brought to my office, the policeman standing by, and I said to one, "James, what made you run away?" His lip quivered as he said, "I didn't get enough to eat." I said, "Did you ever tell me or the assistant superintendent or the dining-room matron that you did not get enough to eat?" He replied, "No, sir." I said, "As I am the father of the place, don't you think you should have told me?" "Yes, sir." "Then, don't you think it was your own fault if you did not get enough?" "Well, maybe it was, sir." "Well, now, James, this is your school as well as the Government's. It belongs to all of us and we are all trying to make it do the work the Government intends. It may be that there are other students who do not get enough to eat. Did you ever hear any of them say so?" "Yes, sir, sometimes." "Can't you see how wrong it was not to let us know about it?" "Yes, sir, I guess I was wrong." "James, I am giving you what the Government gives me to issue to you, but I am very sure that if there is need, and if I try, I can get more. You boys and girls must not go hungry. Don't you now think it is your duty as well as mine to help make things go right at the school?" "Yes, sir." "Well, hereafter if you see anything going on you think is not right, come to me and I will be glad to hear you and try to make it right."

While talking I noticed that his comrade was eyeing me sharply, and when I turned to him and said, "John, what made you run away?" he replied promptly, "I just wanted to let you know I wasn't stuck on your durned old school!" To that I said: "I am not greatly stuck on it myself. I have been here much longer than you and am perhaps more tired of it than you are, but the Government says I must stay and makes it my duty to keep you here

5. Omitted here is the text of a citation awarded to Carlisle School by the Exposition authorities.

until you know enough to be of some use. I shall have to stick to it and hold onto you until you graduate. Both of you report to the disciplinarian. Clean up and begin where you left off." Both graduated, and my last information was that they were prosperous cattle raisers in their native state.

Another runaway incident is worth relating. One of the large boys working for a farmer in Bucks County, Pennsylvania, was reported by the farmer to be persistently violating a regulation of the Outing, notwithstanding the admonitions of the farmer. I accordingly sent the employee who had charge of the boys' Outing to bring him back to the school. He found the farmer and the boy at work in a field, told the farmer that he had come to take the boy back to the school, and that if he desired, another would be sent in his place. They adjourned to the house for the boy to pack his trunk, and the farmer and the employee waited out on the lawn where they could look out over the farm. The farmer discovered the Indian far across the farm running toward a wood and said to the employee, "If you are going to take that boy to Carlisle, you will have to be quick." The boy had such a good start the employee was unable to overtake him. We could not hear of that student notwithstanding most diligent inquiries. He did not return to his home, and his relatives were also greatly worried. After months of inquiry and effort, we finally concluded that something serious had happened.

Four years passed. The Carlisle football team was to play with Yale in New York. My daughter and I, on invitation from Mr. and Mrs. Russell Sage,[6] went over as their guests, and they went with us to the game. Just before the time for the team to start for the field, I went to the hotel on Fourth Avenue where the team was stopping to give the boys more incentive. While I was talking to them, my runaway Indian came in. He had grown and was well dressed and came up to me very frankly and said, "How do you do, Captain." I said: "Great Scott! Where have you been all this time? We thought you were dead."

He said: "Well, Captain, when I ran away from Bucks County, I knew if I stayed anywhere around this part of the country you would find me, make me come back to the school, and maybe punish me, so I came over here to New York and went down along the dock until I found one of the biggest ocean steamers and asked one of the officers if he wanted to hire a man. He looked at me and said, 'I'll see.' He told me to wait there and went on the ship. In a little while he came back and said, 'We can give you work down in the engine room, shoveling coal, if that will suit you.' I said, 'All right.' So I went down and began to help shovel coal into the fires under the boilers. I kept out of sight in New York, but when we got out on the ocean I could go

6. Prominent Wall Street capitalist, railway executive, and former member of Congress. Mrs. Sage later became eminent as a philanthropist.

up and see it. We went over to Liverpool and there I felt safe, had permission to go ashore, and saw something of the city. I have been on that steamer ever since. I got acquainted with some of the men and officers, and after a while they asked me if I would work up in the cabin to help keep things clean, etc. I took that job, and they gave me better pay. I did things for the passengers and got tips. I have been saving my money and I have over $400 in the bank." I said "Hurrah! I wish they would all run away and do something like that." He returned to his place as part of our great transatlantic ocean service, and so far as I know he is still a good serviceable Indian and not dead!

27. The Carlisle Outing

The outing feature of the Carlisle School was its right arm and deserves a more detailed account than it has so far received. It enforced participation, the supreme Americanizer. Preventing participation stops Americanization. The native Americans have been, without exception, most harshly and by many devious demoralizing devices excluded from participation in our American family.

I was in the Army during the Civil War. This enabled me to see slavery in its home and to help "Father Abraham" carry out his early-formed purpose to end it, if he "ever had the chance." As a Civil War cavalryman, I marched over vast stretches of slavery's domain, serving the four years in a war which led to broader Americanization, through participation in the duties of American citizenship, for the recent primitive Africans. Again as a cavalry-man I served twice four years and through two Indian wars in a district of our country reservated for the special purpose of compelling the exclusion of our native Indian aborigines from all participation in the responsibilities of our American life. In one case my government used me in war to end a system which had forcibly transformed millions of primitive black people by transferring them from their torrid zone homes and life across a great ocean and compelling them to live with, and make themselves individually useful in, our temperate national family and by abandoning their own meager languages and adopting the supremely prolific language, life, and purpose of America. In the other case, in obedience to the same behest, I was used in wars to enforce my country's exactly opposite scheme of a supremacy worse than slavery over the 300,000 native aborigines, which compelled them in their own native land to live apart from the American family, amenable to a tyranous un-American system which forces them to become dependents on a remote Bureau control, potentially engaged in perpetuating and enlarging itself by restraining them from participation in our American civilization and life.

These experiences plainly showed that, through forcing Negroes to live among us and become producers, slavery became a more humane and real civilizer, Americanizer, and promoter of usefulness for the Negro than was our Indian system through its policy of tribally segregating them on reservations and denying this participation. It is impossible that any man entering any national family can become acceptable therein unless made useful to it.

The Outing was instituted to gain this essential quality for the Indian. Both the American citizen and the noncitizen Indian must learn that Indians quickly gain this quality when permitted participating experiences. That the lesson is easily and quickly learned by both, and the resultant proof ample and entirely acceptable to both, was from the very beginning successfully established.

I was never able during my twenty-five years as superintendent of Carlisle to get more than one of the dozen Commissioners of Indian Affairs to come and see the Outing in operation. When he did come, although previously somewhat eminent as an educator, professedly friendly to Carlisle's purposes, it was plain that he could not function against the system's behest.

Each patron in charge of a pupil was required to send in a monthly report and at the close of the outing a final brief of the student's worth and conduct. The following selections were given for that year:

> The two Indian boys, Davis and Darlington, left under my charge by you from the 18th of June to the second of September, 1881, have given perfect satisfaction in every particular, and their conduct deserves the highest regards and the kindest praise.
>
> HENRY KRATZ.

> In returning William Snake to your care and to school, I wish to say to you respecting his conduct while with me that I have found him in all respects equal to white lads of his age and in some points quite above them. He is a quiet, orderly, respectful lad, quick to learn, not meddlesome, attentive to what is assigned him to do, *and can be trusted*. He has become a member of our family, we are attached to him and are

sorry to part with him, but for his sake gladly return him to school and wish him success.

F. DYE.

John Shields has given entire satisfaction. I would rather have him than half the white men around here to work for me, and I am sorry to part with him.

ARTHUR B. SMITH.

This is Samuel's day for departure from us for school. We regret his going very much as we have become very much attached to him. He has been faithful, obedient, industrious, and a very good boy. I would be pleased to have him come back next vacation.

SIMON H. ENGLE.

The Indian boy John D. Miles you sent me from Carlisle Indian Training School on the 27th of last May I have found to be honest and willing to do more work than any boy of his size and age I have ever had in an experience of 25 years farming. He has never given us trouble in any way.

STEPHEN BETZ, JR.

In returning the Indian girl, Leah Roadtraveller, to you, it affords me considerable pleasure that I can say she has been obedient, cheerful and apt in learning of household duties.

MARY ANN DAVIS.

Cora's visit has been very satisfactory and pleasant to us. She has been a good worker and always did her work well. She had two or three spells of being cross and disobedient but they soon passed over and the last few weeks we have passed very pleasantly together. We got to understand each other better.

M. E. LONGSHORE.

I will now send Cyrus home, but hate to part with him as he is the best boy we had among thirteen boys and I thought as much of him and more than any boy we had. I paid him the same wages as I paid the rest.

G. W. MILLER.

Hayes has always been a good boy to work. He soon learns and he does his work well. Very seldom any cause to find fault about that. I think but very few white boys of his age and experience would do as well. I have often had to admire with what precision he accomplished the different jobs, some of which I suppose he had no knowledge of before.

ABRAM R. VAIL.

Sam Scott's conduct and character during his stay with us was unexceptionable, and in appreciation of his service will say that if he wishes to spend another vacation with us, we would be pleased to have him do so.

J. E. WILEY.[1]

Anything I might write about Carlisle and its friends and especially its Outing would be incomplete did I not tell of the strong friendship and large aid and sympathy I received from various distinguished members of the Society of Friends. A number of them I cannot mention without reverence. Among the foremost, both in help and in wise advice, was Dr. James E. Rhodes, first president of Bryn Mawr College, whose many letters of kindly interest and advice were most forceful. For years he was the head of the Orthodox Friends committee to control and direct their efforts in behalf of the Indians.

Mr. and Mrs. Wister Morris of Overbrook, Philadelphia, were two others, who not only many times gave large aid but who insisted on making their home my stopping place whenever I spent a night in Philadelphia. Mr. Morris was for many years one of the controlling officials of the Pennsylvania Railroad. His wisdom and interest in public affairs was unusual. In talking over the principles I advocated, he endorsed most heartily the position I held in regard to the Americanizing of races. He saw and condemned the segregation of foreigners in particular localities in his great city of Philadelphia and contended that the Negroes should not be so segregated.

Mrs. Morris was greatly interested through all the years in Indian girls. She at one time desired to establish, at her own cost, a school for Indian girls in a large building she would rent near her home, where she could give personal oversight. The matter was discussed for a considerable time and I carried it to the Commissioner and the Secretary of the Interior, who finally concluded against the plan because it might establish a precedent and lead to a multitude of applications to undertake such private enterprises, which could not well be brought under the dominating system's oversight, deemed so essential.

Mrs. Morris took warm interest in using Indian girls to help in her own home, that they might learn American family life, and for a considerable period she used Indian girls almost exclusively in her housekeeping. The letter below is from one of four who did most of the household work. She employed and kept in her home a most excellent special teacher, her cousin, Miss Eliza M. Thomas, who gave the girls collectively and individually daily

---

1. In this chapter of his manuscript memoirs, Pratt reproduces many excerpts from his annual reports concerning the Outing, but they have been omitted here as repetitive and excessively long. They may be consulted in the published annual reports of the Commissioner of Indian Affairs.

instruction which enabled them to make greater progress than their school-mates at Carlisle because of the refined environment and the personal touch which always gives the best results.

Though Mrs. Morris is past eighty-six years of age, I have within a few weeks of this writing had a letter from her enclosing one from one of the girls for whom she has held a motherly interest and correspondence for more than thirty years. The letter is a model of fine penmanship and frank expression. It is conspicuous as evidence of what may be accomplished for a tepee-born child of primitive Indian parentage through such means. Carlisle was her only school.

Martin, S.D., Dec. 28, 1921.

Mrs. Morris,
Overbrook, Phila., Pa.
Dear Mrs. Morris:

I received your letter not long ago and was very glad to hear from and that you remember us. It has been a long time since I heard from you.

The rest of my family are all well, and are at home.

I am happy to say that my husband and I have been faithful as well as workers for our church. I am sort of a captain under Rev. Joyner, who is in charge of one of the two districts of our reservation. In the year of 1917, the annual convocation (Episcopal) of the Sioux Indians, covering nine reservations of South Dakota and one in Nebraska, was held in our reservation.

At this convocation I was elected chairman of the committee which cared for the hundreds of delegations from various parts of the state. I am telling you about these, that you may see the results of yours and Gen. Pratt's teachings over thirty years ago.

A large box of Christmas presents was sent to me last week for our home church by the St. Lukes Church of Utica, N.Y. I am glad that we, the Indians, are not without friends.

Mrs. Martha Whirlwind Horse nee Bordeau, who was in your home with me, is now living in Rosebud Agency, So. Dak. I very seldom see her but I know that she is a church worker. And Winnie Kinneg who was also there at the same time, died about 1895.

I shall be very glad to have a photo of yourself and your home. It has been many years since I came away but I remember everything there so well. I often remember you. And may further ask you where Gen. Pratt is living at present.

With love,
Victoria Conroy.

28. Compelling Respect: Football, Baseball, and Music

More and more, as the experiences enlarged, we realized that the Indian was a man with the same capabilities as the white man, needing only the same development through education, training, and environment to reach the same competitive qualities.

The sports at the school in the beginning were divided between those of the Indian and those of the Anglo-Saxon. Those students who came directly from camps, never having attended any school—and these at the first were the most numerous—brought their native games and practiced them. Others, who came from western schools, brought something of the games of our own youth, taught them by the reservation teaching force. The people gathered to help carry on the work at the school soon introduced the intensive games of our public schools and colleges. We had the advantage of contacting and contending with our distinguished neighbor, Dickinson College, with its more than a century of success in developing strong and eminent men to fill the highest places in our national life. Gradually these rivalries were widened to include the aggregations of the schools and colleges of the neighboring towns and then far afield to include champions of the whole country.

Football and baseball early became a great motive force in the school life. A gymnasium established in one of the old cavalry stables enabled intensive indoor physical training for all pupils, both boys and girls. Grounds for football and baseball were graded, and students were encouraged to form class or shop teams where all had a chance and where the best personnel for the strong school team was developed. The trips away from the school for the boys, and for all students attending the games at home or in the town, especially with Dickinson College, stimulated their efforts, and it soon developed that we had exceptional pitchers, catchers, basemen, and outfielders in baseball, and fullbacks, halfbacks, quarterbacks, endmen, and captains in football. Young Indians, seeing their chance for physical development, were quite as ambitious to seize their opportunities as our own youth.

Not having had experience with football and finding here and there a victim of accidental or intended violence, I was not especially pleased to encourage it. One day Stacy Matlock, a Pawnee, one of our largest and finest young men, a foremost player, while playing with Dickinson on their field, had his leg broken below the knee and was brought in great agony to the school in a carriage. I had not gone to the game but went down to the hospital, helped lift him from the carriage to the operating table, and stood by to aid in setting the bone. This produced such a revulsion against the game that I said, "This ends outside football for us," and had outside football dropped from the school's repertoire. The broken leg was healed, and though the athletic activities of the victim were renewed without hesitation, I maintained my position.

The next year I was waited upon in the office by about forty of the foremost athletes, headed by the champion orator of the school. While they stood around my desk, their black eyes intensely watching me, the orator gave practically all the arguments in favor of our contending in outside football that it seemed possible to bring and ended by requesting the removal of the embargo. The orator was a descendant of the family that produced the great chief Logan, who said, "I appeal to any white man to say that ever he entered Logan's cabin hungry and he gave him no meat, came cold and naked and he clothed him not, etc." As he went on with his speech, the genius of his argument almost compelled me to relax the judicial mien and release my pent-up laughter. When he had finished, I waited a little and then said: "Boys, I begin to realize that I must surrender and give you the opportunities you so earnestly desire. I will let you take up outside football again, under two conditions.

"First, that you will never, under any circumstances, slug. That you will play fair straight through, and if the other fellows slug you will in no case return it. Can't you see that if you slug, people who are looking on will say,

'There, that's the Indian of it. Just see them. They are savages and you can't get it out of them.' Our white fellows may do a lot of slugging and it causes little or no remark, but you have to make a record for your race. If the other fellows slug and you do not return it, very soon you will be the most famous football team in the country. If you can set an example of that kind for the white race, you will do a work in the highest interests of your people." They all with one voice said, "All right, Captain, we agree to that."

"My other condition is this. That, in the course of two, three, or four years you will develop your strength and ability to such a degree that you will whip the biggest football team in the country. What do you say to that?" They stood silent and then the speaker said, "Well, Captain, we will try." I said: "I don't want you to promise to try. I want you to say that you will do it. The man who only thinks of trying to do a thing admits to himself that he may fail, while the sure winner is the man who will not admit failure. You must get your determination up to that point." They thought that over seriously and then said, "Yes sir, we will agree to that." I said: "Very well, now I know that you cannot win unless you have as good or better instruction than your opponents, and I will write to Walter Camp, the great football authority, and ask him to name me the best coach in the United States, and if possible to get him he will be your instructor." That greatly pleased them. I immediately wrote to Mr. Camp and he named "Pop" Warner, a graduate of Cornell and then its coach. I engaged him at what seemed for us an almost impossible figure. He came, and soon the football forces of the country began to respect the Indian for his prowess on the football field.

Prior to his coming, we had voluntary help and advice from noted football stars. Among the first of these was Mr. Vance McCormick of Harrisburg, in his day one of the champions of the Yale University aggregation. He was on the field one day taking part in instructing the boys how to fall on the ball when chasing it down the field. The ground was moist from recent rain, but he disregarded that and was giving them most enthusiastic incentive. The boys failed to execute the movement properly as he explained, and to show them how, without removing his hat or coat he rushed after and fell on the ball, as the game required. When he got up, his hat and clothing were some admonition against too sudden enthusiasm.

The boys gave themselves up to the severest practice, with such energy they soon met all conditions. They reached a climax in a game with Yale in New York, spoken of in another chapter. During the progress of the game, one of our strong players carried the ball behind the goal for a touchdown. The umpire was a former Yale champion. He disallowed the touchdown. Our team was so indignant they started to leave the field. Forty thousand people were looking on and yelling "Carlisle!" Dr. [M. W.] Stryker, the president of Hamilton College, with my daughter and I, were guests of Mr. and Mrs. Russell Sage, and we all went to the game as guests of the team. Dr. Stryker with a wonderful ringing voice kept yelling "Carlisle!" with all his force, and this led the vast audience to do the same. Notwithstanding this, the boys continued to move away.

I saw the disaster impending, ran across the field, and stopped them. I told them it would not do. "You must fight the battle out; if you leave you will be called quitters and probably lose us future opportunities." I said: "Listen, can't you hear that the crowd is with you? Now go back and play the game out and don't quit for any reason whatever." They all started back except the player who had made the touchdown. He was very indignant, saying, "Captain, that was as fair a touchdown as was ever made, and it belongs to us." I said: "Jakey, it is ours. The umpire's decision will not take it from us. Go back and do your best and wait for tomorrow morning's papers, and you will find that you are a bigger man because the touchdown was denied than you would be if it had been allowed. Now go and help the boys keep Carlisle at the top." He said, "All right, Captain," and went back and the game was renewed, much to the delight of the vast audience. That decision was all that gave Yale the game, but the papers were for us.

If the touchdown had been allowed at the Yale game, Carlisle would have overcome the then strongest football aggregation in the country. During the years it did win from Harvard, Pennsylvania, Cornell, and other of the strong aggregations, and it did win a reputation as a non-slugger.

Twenty-five years after that, I was on Jakey's reservation making inquiries about my old students, and I found that he had established on his own property in western New York a baseball and football park, where he trained Indians in both branches of sport and sent teams to travel the country thereabouts to make money. Two of his big lusty sons were on the teams, and I had a happy meeting with him and his players.

There are many incidents worth relating. During the years our football contentions reached from Boston to San Francisco and from Georgia to Minnesota. It was our habit after each season to let the boys have a banquet in the gymnasium, where they were the hosts and invited their own guests. At the close of one year, the team had been captained to highest victories by Bemus Pierce, one of the largest and most commanding football players in our history. During his progress through the school he had never taken part in public speaking, although his teachers had often urged him to enter the monthly declamation field, and the several debating societies had tried to merge him into their activities. At the banquet each player invited his girl. Several of the team and their girls planned to force a speech from the captain by persistently calling for him as the first speaker and keeping at it until he got on his feet. The captain sat stoically shaking his head. Finally he began to waver and then got up and stood in silence for a time. He then said: "I have a confession to make. When we played with Wisconsin in Chicago, I noticed a big fellow on their team slugging our boys and, watching my chance, tackled him, and as we went down I let my elbow go into his ribs, a little hard, you know"—emphasizing his words by showing just how he did it. "The fellow said, 'What do you mean?' I said, 'I just tackled you, that's all!', but I watched him after that and he did not slug anymore." This brought great applause from the banqueters.

In a game with a visiting institution on our own field, one of our fleet athletes, "Little Roberts," performed a feat worth relating. In the gymnasium his champion stunt was a double somersault starting from a low springboard and landing on his feet on the mats. He had seen the circus athletes do that, going over two or three elephants. During the progress of this game, he got the ball and was making a good run for a touchdown when one of the opposing team rushed at him from one side of the field and plunged to grab his legs, but his legs were not there, for he turned a somersault over the tackler and, landing on his feet, ran on and made the touchdown.

Our baseball aggregation soon won its way to high results in contentions with the best of the nearby educational and YMCA teams. A number of its products after leaving school went into professional baseball and gained large pay and national reputation, Bender among the foremost.

In world athletics, Carlisle products like Thorpe and Tewanima reached highest international honors.

In football a number of the star players of Carlisle had distinguished careers as captains of their teams in college and university football while gaining higher education.

Within my knowledge several who became regular coaches for colleges and universities have received larger salaries for coaching during the football season than is paid a brigadier general in the United States Army for a full year.

Exendine, who graduated from Carlisle and then from Dickinson College School of Law in Carlisle, had been practicing his legal profession for quite a number of years in association with another Carlisle Indian lawyer, engaged largely in the affairs of the Indian people and their legal difficulties. During the football season he coaches. For the last eight years he has coached and led to victory the team of Georgetown University in the city of Washington. Georgetown in a hard-fought battle with one of its most prominent opponents closed this 1922 season with a victory which led his university boys to show their estimate by carrying him around the field on their shoulders after the game.

Welch, another Carlisle Indian football star, has been the successful coach of the college of Washington State for several years. He was overseas and rose to the rank of captain in the National Army. It would not be difficult for a real author to write quite a book about Carlisle footballers and their athletic successes and other professional and industrial successes in civilized pursuits accruing to them by going away from their tribes.

Bemus Pierce has been a professional coach for more than twenty years, coaching a number of well-known educational institution teams. He was called across the continent in 1921 to coach the team of the Indian school at Riverside. His success led to his engagement for 1922, and his continued success and qualities have led to his appointment as physical director of the school.

A chapter of incidents having an important bearing on the physical culture and athletics at the school grew out of the pressure for more and better dormitory accommodations for our boys. The school grew in numbers so that the girls' building first needed attention. I failed in securing from Congress the means to enlarge the six separate sets of officers' quarters under one roof in which the girls were quartered. Having the consent of the Secretary of the Interior, I appealed to friends of the school for the means to do that. The need was to make openings through the different walls between the sets of quarters on the first and second floors so the building would be a unit, add a third story and a fifty-foot addition to one end, then sixty-foot projections to the rear from each end, and also large bathing facilities. We estimated that this could be done for ten to eleven thousand dollars using our own forces with some contract help.

Letting our friends know what was needed, we soon had evidence that the money would be forthcoming and so made the many changes and additions called for. This was a good summer and fall's work for us, and we all felt happy—except the boys. The boys urged that their dormitories should also be improved. They were then quartered in a two-story building 250 by 24 feet in ten rooms 50 by 24 feet each, with porches for each floor fronting the parade. I made several visits to Washington but failed to secure the money. There was an undercurrent of opposition to Carlisle that seemed impossible to overcome.

When I returned from Washington with information that I had been defeated, a number of the boys waited on me to argue their case. They complained that living together in large dormitories gave no privacy, and they said, "You found money for the girls' good quarters without going to Congress; why can't you do the same for us?" I said: "Boys, you have earned and saved $6,000 which is to your credit in the bank. If you will get together and give me $1,000 of that, I will go ahead with the building immediately. I will first hire a brick maker and have you help him, and we will make all the additional bricks we need. Then I will go to our friends for the money to do the rest."

They got together that evening in the chapel and after discussion sent for me. I explained that it would be a three-story building, 300 feet long and 36 feet wide with a hall from end to end and rooms on each side for only three in a room, but that these three would be from different tribes, for we must break down the walls of language and tribal clanishness. It would help them to learn English quicker, and then we could all work together better.

I suggested that the boy who gave the largest sum would have the first choice to select his room, and the one who gave the next largest have the second choice, and so on—always, however, carrying out the principle of having no two from the same tribe in one room. They accepted and immediately one of the boys said, "I want a room high up on the third floor, so I am going to give $30.00." That started the ball rolling, and they made up a sum of over $1,800 in less than an hour, and we immediately established a brick yard. We were to take down the old buildings entirely and use the material in the new building, and it was necessary to raise a sum much larger than we had required for the girls' quarters.

An expedition to Philadelphia, New York, and Brooklyn, taking 142 students, teachers, and helpers, was arranged to show the public what the school was doing in all its branches. Having the dimensions of the platform of each of the academies of music in the three cities, we laid out the different industries in sections, presenting as a first scene the girls at their various work, showing a girl making a bed, a busy dozen girls making and mending garments, the small girls darning stockings, several girls setting a table and washing dishes, the laundry with its wash tub and ironing, etc.

While rehearsing the girls' industrial scene, a Cheyenne girl named Caroline, big and stout, who was to manage the wash tub, refused to act her part, and I was asked to come and help get her in motion. She simply stood by the wash tub in silence and refused to begin. Realizing her feelings, I said: "Caroline, don't you know that 'cleanliness is next to Godliness?' You have one of the most interesting places in this whole exhibit. A woman's duty is to keep her home and family clean." She said not a word, but whirled around and cheerfully commenced operations and after that was activity personified.

The presentation of the boys' industries was in the same manner. With curtain down, in three minutes, having trained at the school, we removed the girls' illustrations and had the boys' benches, tools, etc., placed. All the trades were represented, the blacksmith with forge and red hot iron hammering it on the anvil and making the sparks fly, a printer setting type, another making up a form, another running a printing press, with harness makers, shoemakers, carpenters, painters, and wagonmakers all actively engaged in their several pursuits.

Various classes showed the schoolroom activities. A class in American Government standing on the platform had as teacher one of the girls of the class who came in from the rear, stood in the central part of the audience, and asked different members of the class questions in regard to our governmental system and its administration. The band filled the interludes and there were several student orators.

An admission fee was charged to cover expenses. We had a special train at a low rate over the Pennsylvania road. The Philadelphia, New York, and Brooklyn academies of music cost in the aggregate $550. We had to put up at hotels in Philadelphia and New York. Leaving Carlisle in the morning, we gave the first presentation in Philadelphia that evening, went to New York and gave the presentation there the next evening, were in Brooklyn the next afternoon, and returned home that night. In each place the audience was told of our need for the large boys' building and the cost. When I summed up expenses and receipts we were $1,200 below the cost of our expedition.

In a few days, however, checks began to come in from all these points, and friends in the several cities worked for us. Before the flow of funds had ceased, we had $9,000 more money than we had estimated was necessary for the building. We then concluded to erect a gymnasium and burned another kiln of brick for thick walls for a building 150 feet long and 70 feet wide. Skilled builders were employed to help put up these buildings, using large forces of our students as brick and hod carriers, carpenters, and helpers, and we carried the two buildings up together. We then realized that our Ben Franklin school motto, "God helps those who help themselves," was not fiction.

I have told how the band came into the school and something of its value as a feature. Within the first four years, we had a trained choir of both boys and girls, and the girls were instructed in instrumental music. There was no material difference in the quality of accomplishment between the Indians and the white race. Our students responded as fully and promptly to their opportunities as white youth. This was the judgment of all our instructors and everyone who witnessed the results of our efforts. Gradually voices were developed that attracted special attention, and we always had a number of soloists whose parts in our school entertainments were highly appreciated. Some of them, as they went out from the school into larger fields, continued to aid the musical forces wherever they were located. William Paul, one of our Alaska boys, became leader of the choir of the most prominent Presbyterian Church in Portland, Oregon, and took part in the local musical efforts of the city.

At one time, Dr. [Thomas D.] English, the author of the old familiar song "Ben Bolt," came to Carlisle commencement as part of the House committee of Congress having charge of Indian legislation. Knowing that he was coming, I had our vocal instructor teach one of the best voices among the girls to sing "Ben Bolt" as a solo. He had written the song forty years before. It was a surprise to him, and as a reward we got from him the story of how he came to write it and who had set it to music and how it had gone throughout America and over to the continent of Europe. In giving an illustration of the Carlisle School before an audience in Washington, where we had invited members of the House and Senate to be present, we had the same girl sing "Ben Bolt" again for that audience, and he again gave the story of its popularity. Within a few years it has come to me that the girl who sang "Ben Bolt" has made a successful living by using her voice commercially and traveling with musical organizations.

Development in music aroused the same ambition for the girls and boys who found in themselves excellence in these qualities that football and baseball had for the boys, and this won for their race the same public appreciation.

Our perpetual friend Miss Susan Longstreth, although a Friend [Quaker] with their peculiar views about music, was so charmed with their voices that she at one time insisted on giving the hymnals, of which we needed 500, and later when in her last illness I visited her, not long before she passed away, she asked if the Moody and Sankey hymnals were not worn out. I admitted that they were in a dilapidated condition, and she gave her check for $300 to replace them.

29. The Great Heart of America

There appears incidentally throughout this book the glad response of the heart of America to the needs and plain rights of our Indians. The multitude of written messages enclosing large material help to every emergency of the school and the undeviating interest through many years from staunchest citizens were indubitable proof that our great generous American heart is open and ready to receive the Indians into participating citizenship.

Had the immediate controlling administration over them been as ready to utilize this help and been actuated by the same Americanizing lofty purposes, we should long ago have been free from the shame which now blotches our national character, because the Indians would now all be a developed, useful, and welcome part of our otherwise prosperous country. Not only that, but there would be many more of them because their improving physical condition would have kept pace with their progress in civilization.

I have given some samples of these pulsations, but it is due the purposes of this book that I emphasize this quality of our national character.

One day in the early winter of 1877 there appeared in the old fort at St. Augustine a trim, solid, broad-shouldered, big-faced, large-headed, quick-stepping gentleman who seemed by his movements to want to look at things from his own standpoint, and I left him to pursue his own way. The schools were in session—five or six classes—each having most earnest and competent teachers. He looked in upon each class and then looked in to the bakery and the cooking and dining-room casemates. He then looked at the ancient cannon and stacks of cannon balls in the open court and went up on the terreplein and through the large room where the Indians slept. When he came out, he walked around the terreplein, looked east over the ocean, south at the town, then west and north, and came back to my casemate office.

I invited him in but he declined, said he would like to ask a few questions, and wanted me to walk with him. We walked about and then toward the door. Just before we reached it, he took out of his pocket a twenty-dollar gold piece and said that we certainly needed help, and he wanted to have a part in what he had seen. I declined taking money, saying that we had plenty of food and clothing and that our facilities, crude as they were, educationally and otherwise, were sufficient. The generous services of the teachers were ample for the situation, and we had money enough to buy the books and other helps needed. He was urgent and I said, "If you want to, you can give it to the teachers and let them determine its expenditure." He went and gave it to a teacher and with kindly expressions left the fort. I did not know who he was and did not see him again until several years later, but he wrote me from New York and proved to be one of America's greatest eye and ear specialists, Dr. Cornelius R. Agnew, in his day among our best known and most public spirited citizens. He had been a member of the Christian Commission, that noble Samaritan of our Civil War.

From then on, he was an unfailing friend of what I was trying to do for the Indians. After Carlisle was established, I visited him when on a trip to New York and was urged to make his home my stopping place whenever in the city. He brought me in contact with some of its greatest and best citizens. His efforts to help only ended with his death, which alas was all too soon.

He was not only a personal friend, but a benefactor to my family. Mrs. Pratt was not well, and the cause of her illness was obscure. In my correspondence I mentioned the fact. He came to Carlisle immediately, examined Mrs. Pratt, and asked my very excellent school physician about her. He then came to me and said: "I am going to take Mrs. Pratt to New York on the evening train. There is a through sleeper and I have arranged with the railroad. She will go to my house and I will see what we can do for her." He took her away, called in Dr. Thomas, an eminent surgeon, and I was informed that she would go into Dr. Thomas' hospital and be operated upon. She was there for weeks. The operation was of such a nature that I was told that 60 per cent of those on whom it was necessary to use it in order to save life passed away. It was successful, and she went back to Dr. Agnew's home for convalescence and in time returned home, restored to health. I was not allowed to pay. When I asked Dr. Thomas for his bill, he wrote, "Dr. Agnew is my professional father and there is no charge for his patients."

Dr. Agnew took young Indians with difficult eye trouble to his Manhattan Eye and Ear Hospital near the Grand Central Station and restored or greatly benefited them. President Arthur and he were warm personal friends. President Arthur asked him to become a member of the Board of Indian Commissioners. The doctor wrote and told me of it and said that before accepting he wanted to see something of the Indians in their homes so as to get an idea of what it would be possible for him to do if he accepted the appointment. I arranged a trip, and we went first to the Osage Agency. He wanted to stop at each place long enough to see the Indians in their homes and to learn what each agency was doing for its charges. Naturally he was most interested in the health conditions of the Indians. He had a long conversation with the agency physician. When we left and were on our way to the Mescalero Apaches in southeastern New Mexico, talking of his visit to the physician at Osage, he said, "I wrote President Arthur that he was unfit for his position and ought to be replaced at once."

We reached El Paso from which we had to travel by wagon to the Mescalero Agency. After registering at the hotel, we started out to see the town. The doctor wore a low-crowned natty plug hat of gray color. As we walked along the main street, three noisy drunken cowboys, flourishing pistols, came riding by. One of them yelled, "Shoot that hat." I said, "Pay no attention to it, walk along." They went by and we quickly returned to the hotel. The doctor asked if I thought they really might shoot. I said, "There is no telling what these eminent products of our frontier activities will do." He had a soft felt hat rolled up in his valise, and he put his plug hat away and wore it no more until we were on the cars for home. That evening El Paso had a night-long cowboy carousal, with some shooting.

When we reached the Mescalero Agency[1] we were guests of the agent. We slept in a big room with two double beds. During the night I was awakened by the doctor, who had lit his lamp and turned the covers of his bed back and was sprinkling a white powder all around the outside edge of the sheet. He then got over the powder line inside the circle with his pillow and pulled the covers over him. I asked what it all meant, and he said that he had brought ammunition along and was repelling an invasion of *cimex lectularius* [bed bugs].

At Mescalero the doctor found the same medical infirmities. We then went

1. Located in the Sierra Blanca about twenty-five miles northeast of present Alamogordo, New Mexico.

to Laguna, New Mexico. At that time the twenty Pueblo agencies in New Mexico had only one doctor, and he radiated among them from agency headquarters in Santa Fe. Just before we arrived at Laguna, scarlet fever had broken out at Acoma, a Pueblo village some eight or nine miles from the railroad and about twenty miles from Laguna.[2] The people at Laguna told us that the Acoma people had sent for the doctor and that the doctor had telegraphed that he would reach the railroad station on a certain train. The Acomas sent to the station a burro for the doctor to ride on; this was the only transportation they had. When the doctor saw his diminutive transportation, he refused to go and returned to Santa Fe. Dr. Agnew established these facts and wrote President Arthur recommending his dismissal. He also informed the President that it would be utterly impossible for him to serve on the Board of Indian Commissioners, because the work to be done was too great and the conditions against accomplishing good results too impossible.

Throughout the years I retained in my personal files many of the letters he wrote me and in my letter books copies of those I wrote to him. These are a valued part of the history of my quarter-century service at Carlisle.

Whenever Dr. Agnew visited the school, as he did quite a number of times, he always went to see the worst cases with the school physician and fully advised their treatment. He did not stop there. One winter we had quite a siege of pneumonia among the students. In my correspondence I told the doctor about it; he came from New York, went to the hospital, called in the doctor and the nurse, and went over all the cases. We had, as we thought, comfortable accommodations in the hospital for them. There had been a death, and there were five or six under treatment, some critical. The doctor told us of a siege of pneumonia in the army before Washington during the Civil War and of the vast hospital and how he had gone to Washington and insisted that the patients should at once be placed in hospital tents so as to be in the open air. He asked if we had a hospital tent. Fortunately we had. He himself directed the pitching and arrangement of it by the side of the hospital and had all the cases moved into the tent. He gave our doctor and nurse the most minute directions how to handle each case, and no further deaths occurred.

When Dr. Agnew died, it had happened that Dr. L. Webster Fox and Mrs. Fox had been among our visitors from Philadelphia at recent commencement exercises. Knowing my dependence on Dr. Agnew, he wrote and offered his

2. Laguna Pueblo is located on U. S. Highway 66 about fifty miles west of Albuquerque, New Mexico. Acoma Pueblo, the "sky city," lies on a great rock rising 357 feet above the plain southeast of Laguna. Believed to be the oldest continuously inhabited settlement in the United States, dating from about A.D. 1200, Acoma was the scene of a bitter engagement between its residents and Spanish soldiers in 1598.

free services and the service of his hospital in Philadelphia. These I gladly accepted. Philadelphia was only about half as far away as New York. Dr. Fox for more than twenty years gave attention to the severe eye cases of Carlisle from time to time, taking numbers of our worst cases into his hospital and giving them his personal attention. There was no cost for professional service, but when we put students into the hospital we were expected to meet a small charge of one dollar a day to cover the other expenses. The Indians and the country as well are indebted to Dr. Fox for these invaluable services. On one occasion, having received a large number of new pupils from the agencies, my school physician reported that there were twenty-three who ought to go to Dr. Fox for special treatment. Carlisle sent Dr. Carlos Montezuma, a full-blood Apache Indian then the school physician,[3] in charge of these to Philadelphia, and Dr. Fox gave each of them his personal attention and also instructions to the school physician how to proceed with those returned to school, keeping seven of them in his hospital for special treatment.

In 1881 and 1882 we were concerned to develop larger accommodations for mechanical instruction. The old cavalry stables were 200 feet long and 40 feet wide; the two buildings were parallel with each other and 80 feet apart, connected at the rear by a building of the same width. We had used one-half of the front section of one of the stables for a gymnasium and wanted to develop our industries in the remaining sections. To floor this large space, knock out the little windows in each stall and put in large ones, build divisions between the shops, and arrange a heating system, we needed $1,500. I urged the Department and Congress to let us have this amount, but Congress had not yet been willing to appropriate for Carlisle, and the independent fund on which Carlisle was being operated was running low and there would be no increase except by appropriation by Congress. This fund had originally been quite a number of hundreds of thousands of dollars in the Treasury from the sale of lands coming to the Government by treaty with the Osages. The treaty had provided that the money was to be used for any general purposes of Indian civilization. Failing in getting the money from the Government, I approached our friends.

A Rev. Mr. Miller, a Presbyterian minister at Bryn Mawr, Pennsylvania, had turned many hundreds of dollars our way for the girls' quarters and I wrote him about it. I also wrote to Dr. Agnew. He urged me to come to New York and stop at his house and he would give me notes to people he thought

3. Captured by Pima Indians in his youth and by them sold to a white man, Carlos Montezuma was educated in Chicago and Galesburg public schools and received a B.S. degree from the University of Illinois in 1884 at the age of seventeen. Graduating a medical doctor from Chicago Medical College in 1889, he pursued a distinguished career as a physician and writer on Indian matters. His life was a dramatic expression of the views Pratt advocated. He died in 1923. *Who Was Who in America, 1897–1942*, p. 855.

would help, then I could canvass and raise the money that way. It was my first venture in direct personal solicitation. I spent a week with Dr. Agnew, giving every day to a number of visits, and soon became convinced that my talents in that direction were not of very high order. The responsibility for the school was bearing heavily and I felt that my place was there and not in begging activities. I had secured about $500 and told the doctor my misgivings—that I was going back to Carlisle and that if the good Lord intended me to have the money, he would send it some way. If not, I would do the best I could with what came to me.

When I reached Carlisle and got off the cars, I met my Presbyterian friend from Bryn Mawr. I had not sent word that I was returning, but the school carriage was waiting for him. On the way out to the school he told me that he had made up his mind to visit the West and see something of the Indians and that he had come to Carlisle to get letters of introduction to different agents so that he might have a good opportunity to see the Indians in their homes. I told him of my week's work in New York and of my discovery of my disabilities in the begging line. When we reached the school, Mrs. Pratt had the guest room ready, for the minister had sent word of his coming. When I took his hand baggage into his room, he gathered me in his arms and kissed me and called down a benediction upon me. He then said he was going out to hunt up two Indian boys in whom he was personally interested and whom he had had at his parsonage for a week's visit sometime before. Mrs. Pratt was watching us, and after he left she said: "I knew by your face you did not know anything about it. Read this letter." The letter was from the Presbyterian preacher and enclosed a check for $2,000.

I still have the letter. It began: "When father died he left my share of his estate in Tennessee State bonds. When Tennessee seceded the bonds became worthless. Tennessee has recently concluded to pay 50¢ on the dollar and I have received a part of my inheritance. I want to reinvest it immediately where it will bring me returns of 1,000 per cent. I, therefore, enclose you check for $2,000 to turn the old cavalry stables into shops for our Indian boys." When he came back to the house, we had another hugging time.

Until his death he was a towering strength to my efforts. I asked him if he would come to Carlisle and be chaplain for the school. He came up to look it over and concluded that, if it were perfectly acceptable to the administration, he would come and help me. I carried the matter personally to the Secretary of Interior, who called in the Commissioner of Indian Affairs. After consultation I was informed that the school, being a government institution, could not be carried on under any particular sect, and it was thought best that I have no chaplain but make such use as I could of the different ministers of the town.

The Congress of the United States was unwilling to give $1,500 to enable us to develop our facilities for mechanical instruction, but a Presbyterian minister in a small town on a meager salary gladly gave $2,000 to enable us to accomplish that purpose.

One day in 1883 there came to the school two elderly Quaker ladies, one of whom was 90 years old and the other, her daughter, 70. The mother was active and full of interest, and she insisted on seeing the whole establishment. We were interested in her refusing to sit in a rocking chair and to see that, instead of using the back of the chair, she uniformly sat bolt upright without leaning against the back. She asked many questions. One was about the returned students. Did they really go back to the blanket as was so constantly asserted? I told her our short experience was not sufficient to determine that question fully, but that the evidence coming to me was that most of them did not relapse even though they were remanded by the Government back to associate with blanket conditions; that there were few lapses and these were mostly those who had spent a very short time with us. The old lady said: "Is it any wonder that some of them do fail? We don't know how much they overcame before forced to yield. I am surprised that any succeed." The two ladies returned to their home, and soon afterward the elderly lady sent $3,000 for our emergencies.

We started with very meager facilities for our printing office. Needed were larger presses, more type, and greater variety of equipment of all sorts. I wrote to Miss Longstreth, mentioned in an earlier chapter, and soon received a check from a neighbor of hers, a Friend and a widow, for $1,000 to improve the printing office.

Mary Anna Longstreth, the elder sister, died. Happening in Philadelphia a few days later, I called to express sympathy, and Susan, Carlisle's special friend, said: "Just before Mary Anna died she told me to give thee $500 for the girls' building. If thee will wait a few minutes I will go and write thee a check and not wait for the settlement of the estate." When she came back she handed me a check, saying "that is for sister," and then said, "I thought while I was writing one for sister I would write one for myself to help thee in rebuilding the girls' quarters," and handed me a second check. When I left the house and got around the corner, I looked at the other check and it was for $1,000.

We had been limited for agricultural opportunity. I heard of a suitable farm, and having enough to make first payment and finding it heavily mortgaged and the mortgagees anxious to let the money remain on it, I concluded to buy it for the school at $20,000. I was gradually paying off the mortgages when one day I received notice from a lawyer in New York that one of his clients, a Quaker lady, wanted him to advise me that she had put $5,000 in her will for the Carlisle school. I wrote my friend Dr. Agnew and told him the glad news, adding that it would be a great relief if we could have it at once to help pay the debt on the farm. He called upon the lawyer, stated the case, and the lawyer informed his client and the $5,000 was soon sent.

A wealthy merchant in Philadelphia, then past eighty but still directing his large business, wrote me that he had as a young man been a teacher for a short time among the Indians under the missionary auspices of his Presbyterian church. He was early dissatisfied with the outlook, returned east, and went into business. He had prospered and wanted to help in what I was undertaking and so enclosed $1,000. Thereafter, when visiting Philadelphia, I occasionally dropped in to see him and report progress.

The duties at Carlisle which bore upon me daily and nightly occasionally wore heavily, and for relaxation, when in Philadelphia, I would slip in to hear Carnacross and Dixie's nightly minstrel performances, and the hearty laugh drove the cobwebs away. Passing the place of business of Carlisle's aged benefactor, I dropped in to see him. He was exceedingly cordial and at once demanded that I spend the night with him because he had as a guest a distinguished Presbyterian preacher from Ireland, and they were holding a revival meeting in his church near his home. Determined in my purpose, I tried to beg off, but he was very insistent. I finally said that I had promised myself a little treat and was sorry not to tell him what it was, but it was essential to my happiness just then. If he would permit me to have the evening to myself, I would dine with him and then excuse myself for the evening. He could give me a key so I could come in late. He agreed to that. His family was away and the servants taking care of the house. We had an early evening together, very pleasantly and profitably, and dined, and when the time arrived I said that if he would let me have the night key I would go. He was an elder in his church. He went with me into the hall, and before giving me the key he said, "Now, Captain, won't you please tell me where you are going tonight." "Well," I said, "I am tired of my load and have promised myself a good laugh this evening, and I am going to Carnacross and Dixie's minstrels." He at once said, "Wait a few minutes and I will send the preacher off to church, then I will go with you." When we reached the little theater on Eleventh Street, he jumped in ahead of me and asked the ticket seller for the plan of the house and where he could have two good seats toward the front. The ticket seller showed him; he bought the tickets and we both enjoyed the evening to the full.

Early in the history of the school, the voluntary contributions flowing in became so material that I told Mr. Teller, the Secretary of the Interior, that I had better have help in the responsibility for the money and its use. A farm could not be bought with the meager government funds available, and I had bought one and was paying the $20,000 that it cost from these donations. Secretary Teller was visiting the school and advised that by a deed of trust we create a board of trustees to hold the farm and in addition to oversee and audit all expenditures made from these contributions, calling them the "Charity Fund." He suggested that one member be a lawyer from Carlisle who would draw up the proper legal document and that it be recorded in the county records. I accordingly asked the following to serve as trustees:

Dr. C. R. Agnew, distinguished eye specialist, New York City; A. S. Larocque, lawyer and distinguished citizen; Hon. Joseph C. McCammon, Assistant Attorney General of the United States; Susan Longstreth, Philadelphia, Pa.; Hon. Daniel M. Fox, former mayor of Philadelphia; Dr. James E. Rhodes, President of Bryn Mawr College, Pa.; Hon. William McMichael, Philadelphia; Albert K. Smiley, Board of Indian Commissioners, Lake Mohonk, N.Y.; Mrs. Mary C. Thaw, Pittsburgh, Pa.; Wister Morris, Overbrook, Philadelphia; Dr. J. A. McCauley, President of Dickinson College in Carlisle. As death invaded our ranks, Mrs. Agnew succeeded her husband, Rev. Dr. Norcross of Carlisle succeeded President McCauley, and President Merrill E. Gates succeeded Mr. McMichael.

All consented. Then Judge Henderson consulted with Secretary Teller and drew up the legal document, which the Secretary approved, and it was made part of the county records. This brought me at once into intimate relations with Judge Henderson, our nearest neighbor, whose property and home adjoined Carlisle Barracks. From that time forward he was the premier counselor and friend of the school and its superintendent. Never was there a material interest at stake that he was not consulted, and he gave for my remaining twenty-two years as superintendent his invaluable counsel, legal and other advice, without stint.

There were scores and even hundreds of like experiences which showed that the real heart of our America is warm toward our native people and only needs the chance to welcome and help them to become useful fellow citizens.

30. End of Service at Carlisle

Conditions were approaching a crisis in my relations with our Government's Indian system. Twenty stories, pure inventions, were widely published during a brief period defaming alleged Carlisle "returned students." I wrote to a number of the papers publishing these stories but received no evidence that they recognized my contradictions. In all these cases but two, not only the acts but the names were ficitious. One of these two covered the alleged atrocities committed by an Arizona Apache outlaw named Kid. It was stated that Kid had been well educated at the "Carlisle Indian University." The facts were that Kid was an outlaw years before Carlisle was established and never attended any school. Before beginning his outlawry he had served as a scout for our army posts in Arizona.[1]

In the other case a Cheyenne named White Buffalo, who had been one of

1. An Apache scout with the army on the San Carlos Agency, Arizona, the Kid in 1887 murdered another Indian in a revenge slaying and deserted the military service. His subsequent life of crime, lasting more than a decade, was one of the most notable in Arizona history and has today assumed legendary qualities. The Apache Kid was never apprehended, and his final fate is not known. Joseph Miller, *The Arizona Story* (New York, 1952), pp. 78–88.

Carlisle's students, was wrongfully alleged to have committed three murders at his agency and had confessed and was in jail at El Reno, Oklahoma. I asked the Commissioner of Indian Affairs to use his high office to publish the facts in these two cases, but he declined.

The transfer of the school to the West was published as part of the system's intentions, alleging that it was better and more economical to educate Indian children at their homes.

It was plain that race cohesion and prolonging the ostracism of the Indians from American opportunity formed the system's program and that doctrines and influences favoring their escape from tribalism into citizenship were to be quelled. It seemed best to force the issue and compel action that would change the system or end my relations with it.

In 1883, on invitation of the authorities of the Baptist Church, I presented Carlisle before the World Convention on the fiftieth anniversary of the foreign missionary interests of that church in New York, using a number of students to show their qualities. Dr. Moorehouse, the secretary of the mission work of the church, who had invited me, introduced me to the vast audience, saying, "Captain Pratt is not a Baptist, but in Indian matters he is a good enough Baptist for us to listen to." I began by saying: "In Indian civilization I am a Baptist, because I believe in immersing the Indians in our civilization and when we get them under holding them there until they are throughly soaked."

Twenty-one years later a friend to my cause who had been president of a university was living in retirement in New York. He was a member of the Baptist preachers' weekly meeting of New York and Brooklyn. He wrote and asked if I would give a forty-minute paper before one of their meetings in the same Madison Avenue church. This seemed just the occasion I needed to help force the issues. I accordingly gave the paper, exposing facts, views, and principles, and showing counter influences. This was the climax. Parts of this paper were printed in a number of our greatest eastern dailies, and I printed it in full in the school paper. There were no statements in it I was not then, and am not now, ready to meet, and its very utterance courted opportunity to do that. Two days after the speech I received the following letter:

Secretary's Office
DEPARTMENT OF THE INTERIOR
Washington, D.C.

Col. R. H. Pratt,   May 11, 1904
Superintendent Indian School,
Carlisle, Pa.

Sir: I enclose with this a clipping from the New York Daily Tribune of yesterday, in which appears a statement reported to have been made by you in an address at the Baptist Ministers' Conference, and will thank you to advise me as to the correctness of said statement.

Yours respectfully,
E. A. Hitchcock,
Secretary.

Enclosure
It Harms the Indian

Colonel R. H. Pratt, U. S. A., superintendent of the Indian School at Carlisle, Penn., addressed the Baptist Ministers' Conference yesterday on work among the Indians. He said in part:

"I believe nothing better could happen to the Indians than the complete destruction of the Bureau which keeps them so carefully laid away in the dark of its numerous drawers, together with its varied influences, which only serve to maintain tribal conditions.

"Better, far better, for the Indians, had there never been a Bureau. Then self-preservation would have led the individual Indian to find his true place, and his real emancipation would have come speedily. The early death of the Freedmen's Bureau, with its 'forty acres and a mule,' was an infinite blessing to the Negro himself, and the country as well.

"To leave or build any race or class as special or alien, hinders growth, multiplies expense and fosters anxiety and violence.

"Indian schools on the reservations are weak and inefficient, because lacking in the essential elements of practical experience, association and competition, and are calculated to educate the Indian to shrink from the competition necessary to enable him to reach his place as an independent man and citizen."

This was my reply:

Indian Industrial School,
Carlisle, Pa., May 12, 1904.

Hon. E. A. Hitchcock,
Secretary of the Interior,
Washington, D.C.

Sir:

Replying to yours of the 11th inst., with clipping from the New York Tribune, I have to respectfully enclose to you a full copy of my address at the Preachers Conference referred to, with paragraphs marked, as quoted.

Very respectfully,

R. H. Pratt,

Col. & Supt.

A month later I received the following:

War Department,

Washington, D.C., June 11, 1904.

Special Orders, No. 137

    Extract.

15. Brigadier General Richard H. Pratt, U. S. Army, Retired, who while serving as 1st Lieutenant, 10th Cavalry, was detailed, under the provision of section 7 of the act of Congress 1879, for special duty with reference to Indian Education, is relieved from the further operation of Paragraph 7, Special Orders, No. 194, August 23, 1879, Headquarters of the Army, and from all duty under the Interior Department, to take effect June 30, 1904.[2]

By order of the Secretary of War:

ADNA R. CHAFFEE,

Lieutenant General, Chief of Staff.

Official:

    F. C. Ainsworth,

    The Military Secretary.

2. Pratt retired a colonel on Feb. 17, 1903, and by operation of a law enacted in 1904 conferring promotion on retired officers who had served creditably in the Civil War was advanced to the grade of brigadier general. He continued his superintendency of Carlisle as a War Department official detailed to the Interior Department, and his formal relief therefore had to come from the War Department.

Pratt reached the discretionary army retirement age of sixty-two in 1903 and, even though two years remained to him before attaining the mandatory age, he was summarily retired by President Theodore Roosevelt. Pratt's biographer (Eastman, p. 260) ascribes this to a feud over Civil Service reform dating back to the years when Roosevelt headed the Civil Service Commission, but it is possible, too, that a wish to clear a path of regimental promotion blocked by an officer long on detached service may have been an additional factor.

1. In 1867 Pratt was commissioned in the regular Army Tenth Cavalry, a Negro regiment with white officers. In his eight years of duty with colored soldiers and Indian scouts, he formed a deep sympathy for minority peoples that guided his philosophy for the rest of his life. Here Frederic Remington depicts a trooper of Pratt's regiment in field gear.

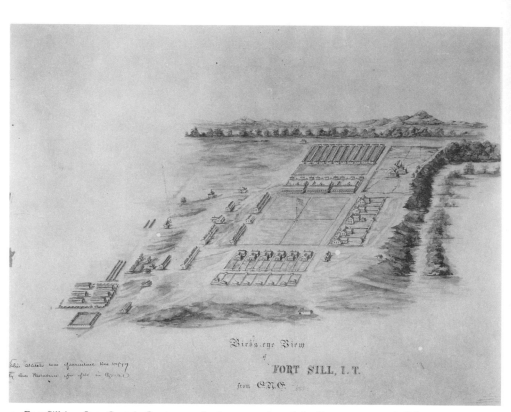

Bird's-eye View
of
FORT SILL, I. T.
from E.N.E.

2. Fort Sill in 1877. Captain Pratt supervised construction of the first permanent buildings, still standing, in 1870. Five years later he assembled the Indian prisoners from the Red River War here for the journey to St. Augustine, Florida. From a water color by Col. S. B. Holabird, original in the Fort Sill Museum. Courtesy U. S. Army Artillery and Missile Center Museum, Fort Sill, Oklahoma.

3. Squadrons of the Fifth and Seventh Cavalry on the Fort Sill parade ground in 1890. Officers' quarters in background. Courtesy U. S. Army Artillery and Missile Center Museum, Fort Sill, Oklahoma.

4–6. Leaders of the Kiowa war faction, Satanta, Satank, and Big Tree were arrested at Fort Sill in 1871 after a dramatic confrontation with General Sherman. Satank was shot and killed while trying to escape, but Satanta and Big Tree served time in the Texas penitentiary. Released, they resumed old habits and, after the Red River War of 1874–75, were again sent to prison. All three were photographed at Fort Sill in 1870 by William S. Soule.

7. One of the most active of the Kiowa raiders on the Texas frontier, White Horse was imprisoned at Fort Marion with a long list of atrocities charged against him. Photograph by William S. Soule about 1870.

8. Kicking Bear headed the Kiowa peace faction and kept many of his people quiet during the Red River War. He died shortly after its close in 1875. William S. Soule made this photograph at Fort Dodge, Kansas, in 1868.

9. Lone Wolf emerged as leader of the Kiowa war faction after the imprisonment of Satanta in 1871. Confined in Florida at the close of the Red River War, he died in 1879, a year after his return to the reservation. Photograph by Alexander Gardner in Washington, 1872.

10. To Kiowas and Comanches, captives as well as plunder were the fruits of raids deep into Mexico. Quaker agent Lawrie Tatum is shown here at Fort Sill about 1872 with a group of Mexican children freed from bondage.

11. Castillo de San Marcos National Monument, Florida. As the United States Army post of Fort Marion, the old Spanish fortification at St. Augustine served as a prison for Captain Pratt's exiled Indians from 1875 to 1878. Courtesy, National Park Service.

12. Some of Pratt's Indian prisoners shortly after arrival at Fort Marion in the spring of 1875.

13. Group of prisoners at Fort Marion in 1875. Seated in center are the Comanche Black Horse with his wife and child. Castillo de San Marcos National Monument.

14. Captain Pratt with four of the prisoners and the interpreter at Fort Marion in 1875. Castillo de San Marcos National Monument.

15. Dressing the prisoners at Fort Marion in old army uniforms, Pratt managed them as a military unit. Castillo de San Marcos National Monument.

16. Pratt dispensed with the army guard and made the prisoners at Fort Marion responsible for guarding themselves. They proved more reliable than the regular soldiers. At left is the Cheyenne chief Heap-of-Birds. Castillo de San Marcos National Monument.

17. Minimic, or Eagle's Head, was a prominant war chief of the Southern Cheyennes during the wars of 1868–75. He was later imprisoned in Florida, where J. Wells Champney painted this portrait. Yale University Library.

18. Minimic's picture letter. See pp. 182–83.

19. Sioux boys who formed part of the first student body as they appeared on October 5, 1879, immediately after their arrival at Carlisle. U. S. Army photograph, courtesy Army War College, Carlisle, Pa.

20. Sioux girls from Rosebud and Pine Ridge reservations immediately after their arrival at Carlisle, October 6, 1879. Left to right: Miss S. A. Mather, Emma Black Crow, Horace Black Crow, Maggie American Horse, Rebecca Big Star, Ida Kills Plenty, Ruth Big Head, Dora Brave Bull, Zonie McKenzie, Nellie Black Twin, Hattie Long Wolf, Rose Long Face, Nancy Shooting Cat, Agnes White Cow, Julia Good Voice, Lulu Bridgman, Lizzie Glode, Alice Lone Bear, Mary Iron-on-the-Head, Hope Blue Teeth, Winnie Pawnee, Stella Chasing Hawk, Maud Swift Bear, Pollock Spotted Tail, Lucy Day, Sarah Tackett, Charles Tackett (interpreter).

21. Sioux youth at Carlisle in June 1880 are (standing, left to right) David Blue Tooth, Nathan Standing Cloud, and Pollock Spotted Tail, and (sitting, left to right) Marshall Bad Milk and Hugh Whirlwind Soldier. The last was Spotted Tail's grandson. National Archives.

22. Spotted Tail, able chief of the Brulé Sioux, visited Carlisle in 1880 and in a stormy scene withdrew his children from Captain Pratt's new school. From a painting by H. Ulke, 1877. Smithsonian Institution, Bureau of American Ethnology.

23. Captain Pratt in January 1886.

24. Chiricahua Apache Indians on arrival at Carlisle Barracks in 1887. Pratt stands on the porch, center, behind the students. These children were part of Geronimo's band confined at Fort Marion, Florida, since 1886. U. S. Army Photograph, courtesy Army War College, Carlisle Barracks, Pa.

25. Chiricahua Apache students four months after entering Carlisle in 1887. Yale University Library.

26. The first graduating class at Carlisle, 1889. Standing left to right: Frank Dorian (Iowa), Joel Tyndall (Omaha), William F. Campbell (Chippewa), Edwin Schanandore (Oneida), Thomas Wistar (Ottawa), Joseph B. Harris (Gros Ventres). Seated left to right: Kish Hawkins (Cheyenne), Clara Faber (Wyandotte), Eva Johnson (Wyandotte), Esther Miller (Miami), Lilly Cornelius (Oneida), Katie Grinrod (Wyandotte), Julia Powlas (Oneida), Cecilia Londrosh (Winnebago). Yale University Library.

27. The Carlisle student body on the campus, about the turn of the century. U. S. Army photograph, courtesy Army War College, Carlisle Barracks, Pa.

28. The Carlisle Band in the 1890s. U. S. Army Photograph, courtesy Army War College, Carlisle Barracks, Pa.

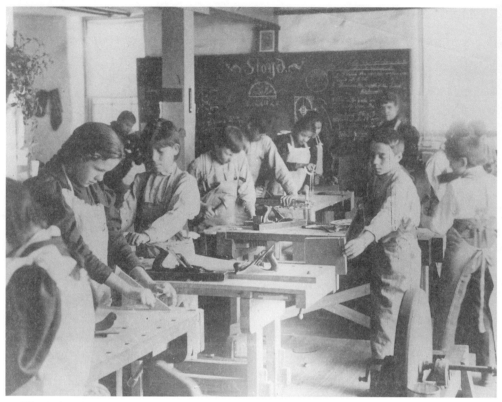
29. The Carlisle Woodworking Shop. Yale University Library.

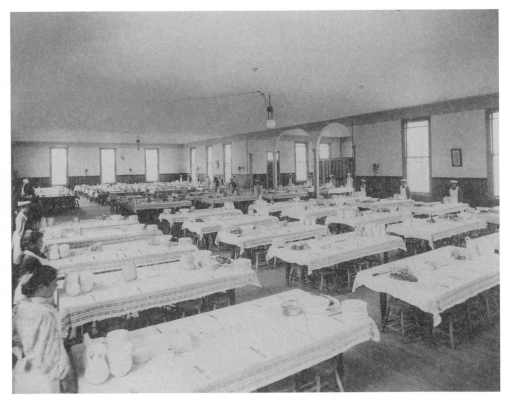

30. The Dining Hall at Carlisle Indian School. U. S. Army Photograph, courtesy Army War College, Carlisle Barracks, Pa.

31. Sewing room.

32. The Blacksmith and Wagon Making Shop at the Carlisle Indian School. U. S. Army Photograph, courtesy Army War College, Carlisle Barracks, Pa.

33. Major Pratt in 1898. Yale University Library.

Index